THE OXFORD ILLUSTRATED HISTORY OF

ITALY

THE OXFORD
ILLUSTRATED HISTORY OF
ITALY

Edited by
GEORGE HOLMES

OXFORD
UNIVERSITY PRESS

OXFORD
UNIVERSITY PRESS

Great Clarendon Street, Oxford OX2 6DP

Oxford University Press is a department of the University of Oxford.
It furthers the University's objective of excellence in research, scholarship,
and education by publishing worldwide in

Oxford New York

Athens Auckland Bangkok Bogotá Buenos Aires Calcutta
Cape Town Chennai Dar es Salaam Delhi Florence Hong Kong Istanbul
Karachi Kuala Lumpur Madrid Melbourne Mexico City Mumbai
Nairobi Paris São Paulo Shanghai Singapore Taipei Tokyo Toronto Warsaw

with associated companies in Berlin Ibadan

Published in the United States
by Oxford University Press Inc., New York

First published 1997
First published as an Oxford University Press paperback 2001

British Library Cataloguing in Publication Data

Data available

Library of Congress Cataloging in Publication Data

Data applied for

ISBN 0–19–820527–9 (cased)
ISBN 0–19–285444–5 (paperback)

3 5 7 9 10 8 6 4 2

Printed in Italy

EDITOR'S FOREWORD

From the fifth century to the nineteenth Italy did not exist as a political unit. It was broken up into shifting, larger and smaller fragments, generally jealous of their independence and frequently at war with each other. This state of affairs was not unique—Germany was arguably a similar case—but in Italy it went on for a very long time and had more interesting cultural effects than anywhere else in Europe.

The political fragmentation was paradoxically accompanied by striking universalist connections. Italy was at the same time the home of the Papacy, which was the heart of the Christian Church, then, from the eleventh century, of the western Church. The Church employed many Italians in multifarious positions abroad as bishops—like Anselm of Aosta, archbishop of Canterbury in the late eleventh century—as legates and nuncios, as collectors of taxes. The Holy Roman Empire was not actually centred in Italy, but the obligation to secure coronation at Rome and the hope of conquering territory elsewhere in Italy made the emperors' visits frequent and involved many links and conflicts with Italians.

There was a contrast between Italy south of Rome, which was unified as the monarchy of Naples or Sicily, and Italy north of Rome, which was richer but much more divided politically. The fragmentation in Tuscany, Romagna, and Lombardy was due essentially to the fact that the German kings and emperors who claimed sovereignty ruled only intermittently and feebly. The result was that cities asserted their power to run their own affairs and then their right to do so. Because they were breaking out of a weak monarchy, and because the social importance of the city was so much greater in Italy than in northern Europe, as the natural place for families to assemble for self-defence, the extent of fragmentation was extreme. In the twelfth and thirteenth centuries places which we would think of as not much more than villages, Colle Val d'Elsa or San Miniato, felt they had to behave as sovereign states, carrying on elaborate diplomatic relations with their neighbours.

Eventually states grew by absorbing the lesser towns nearby. By the sixteenth century Italy was in effect divided between Milan, Venice, Florence, Rome, and Naples, though important lesser units like Mantua and Lucca survived for a long time. The development of the political geography was greatly affected by monarchical invasion from abroad and by the evolution of principalities internally. Italy was of course for more than a millennium invaded, plundered, and subdued. One after another came the Ostrogoths, the Lombards, the Franks, the Arabs, the Germans, and the Spaniards. In the early modern period large tracts of Italy were in effect absorbed into the empire of the Habsburgs, who ruled at Milan and in Sicily. The domination of foreign monarchs did not necessarily quell the native temperament but it did tend to engender a kind of political passivity of the sort that Stendhal described as existing at Milan under the Habsburgs and Napoleon.

Italian cities were also, however, the builders of the first European commercial empires since the ancient world. Venice's connections with Byzantium led from a very early period to the establishment of a seaborne empire, both commercial and territorial, in the eastern Mediterranean, and to the sack of Constantinople in 1204, succeeded by the bringing of treasures to St Mark's. Pisa followed Venice in the Mediterranean. Genoa was for a long time Venice's rival there, but was eventually forced by Ottoman expansion to turn its attention to Iberia and thence to the new American world, where Genoese money was important in the sixteenth century. Florence was not a landed empire-builder beyond the sea, but its merchants bridged Europe and Asia by their trading activities and long dominated the world of international finance. Italians thus had both a central position and a broadly diffused importance in the medieval and early-modern worlds, which to some extent distinguished them from other nationalities. Marco Polo and Christopher Columbus, whose activities spanned the world outside Europe, were typical Italians, easily the most adventurous explorers before that role was taken over by northerners. In its most formative and explosive period, from the twelfth century to the seventeenth, Italian society presented the paradox of extreme disunity and frequent invasion combined with worldwide influence.

Some of our instinctive assumptions about Italian society, arising perhaps from the prominence of Machiavelli, who had a stronger influence on European political ideas than any other Italian, are bound up with the idea of the republican city. But the local despot has been a commoner feature of the Italian scene. Communal republicanism was important and Venice remained a republic until its extinction as a separate state in 1806. But the more normal type of regime was a despotic one. Burckhardt's *Civilisation of the Renaissance in Italy* began with a chapter on 'The State as a Work of Art', the point of which was the capacity of individuals to seize power and shape states in accord with their will. A directing force was exercised not only by the foreign invaders but also by the native rulers of towns, who commanded armies and employed diplomatists. The part played in Italian history by the Visconti of Milan, the Medici of Florence, the Gonzaga of Mantua, the Malatesta of Rimini, and the Montefeltro of Urbino was fundamental. Visitors to Italy are struck by the numerous great palaces—provincial cities in other countries do not often contain such extensive complexes as that of the Gonzaga at Mantua—which are a result of the political fragmentation of the country.

Political fragmentation has also had more important results than this. Of all European countries Italy has been the one with the richest and most varied cultural life, the result of the fact that there have been so many separate centres of art and thought, independent enough to preserve their own individuality. There are, of course, other reasons for the particular importance of Italy in the cultural history of Europe: the long ancient history of civilized life from the Etruscans and the Greek settlers onwards, the legacy of Rome to the medieval world. It is impossible to imagine Italy without the backing of layer upon layer of ancient culture, which makes it quite different from other parts of Western Europe and gave Italian society an extra sophistication. Throughout the Middle Ages and Renaissance the Italians were drawing heavily on the resources of the past, either in the form of crumbling architectural ruins or of literary works hidden in parchment manuscripts in cathedral libraries.

The modern flowering of Italian civilization, however, was also the result of the fact that Florence, Venice, Rome, and Milan, not to mention Naples, Mantua, Ferrara, and Urbino, each created its own art and thought. The Italian experience is, from one point of view, the supreme argument for decentralization, allowing each town to manage its own destiny. In this case it produced an unparalleled richness. The contrast between Florence, with its patrician aestheticism struggling to accommodate Christianity; Venice, jealously guarding its secularity and bursting into the richest exploration of painting; and Rome, the capital of the Western Church, produced a diversity of cultural creation unparalleled in other countries. It was precisely the separate existence of such centres and the interchange between them which was responsible for the painting of the Sistine Chapel and the villas of Palladio.

When Petrarch addressed *Italia mia* in poetry and deplored the desecration by her barbarian invaders he was in one sense expressing a quite theoretical idea reinforced by classical allusion. Many other Italians did the same. Petrarch's language was Tuscan, which many other Italians would have found difficult to follow. In the end Tuscan won general acceptance and the Risorgimento made Italy into a nation-state with many similarities to other European countries. This is only the last phase of the Italian story, still just a century and a quarter old. To understand the Italian world and its achievements it is essential to look back over the past two millennia, from the Roman unity, through the barbarian invasions and the medieval and early-modern diversity. The writers of this book aim to give readers an introduction to the whole story: the empires, the city-states, and their art and literature. The plan of the book is governed by the idea that narrative is essential but that history should also show the interrelationship between society, politics, and culture. In this case we are dealing with a cultural history of exceptional brilliance and a political story which is exceptionally complicated and difficult to recount in outline. We hope that we shall have been successful in conveying to readers the way in which contemporary historians see Italy, past and present.

GEORGE HOLMES

CONTENTS

LIST OF COLOUR PLATES

MAPS

CONTRIBUTORS

Simon Swain
University of Warwick and All Souls College, Oxford

Bryan Ward-Perkins
Trinity College, Oxford

Michael Mallett
University of Warwick

George Holmes
All Souls College, Oxford

Stuart Woolf
University of Essex and European University Institute, Florence

Robert Oresko
Institute of Historical Research, University of London

John Davis
University of Connecticut

Jonathan Keates
City of London School

Adrian Lyttelton
University of Pisa

Paul Corner
University of Siena

David Forgacs
Gonville and Caius College, Cambridge

David Hine
Christ Church, Oxford

FROM AUGUSTUS TO THEODOSIUS: INVENTION AND DECLINE

SIMON SWAIN

The political history of Italy in the four centuries from Augustus to Theodosius is dominated by Rome and the Roman Empire. At the same time, historical and archaeological investigations are telling us more and more about life in the towns and countryside of imperial Italy. This, together with what we know of art, architecture, and literature, makes it possible to get a good idea of cultural, social, and economic matters away from the distorted environment of Rome itself. The present chapter deliberately avoids Rome and Empire and focuses on this real Italy, from its invention to its decline.

Tota Italia

The idea of Italy as a unified political structure centred on Rome owes much to the first Roman Emperor, Gaius Julius Caesar Octavianus, who is known to history by the name he adopted in 27 BC, Caesar Augustus. As a geographical term, Italy in its modern sense is also Roman. The name occurs first in early Greek sources of the sixth and fifth centuries BC, where it denotes the area settled by Greek colonies in the south of the peninsula. The modern meaning is found first in the Roman playwright Plautus, writing at the turn of the third and second centuries BC. The intervening shift stems from Rome's desire to promote herself as the national champion of all the Italian peoples against foreign invaders like Pyrrhus of Epirus and the Carthaginians, who had sought to check her growing power in the previous century. By the time of Augustus Rome's identification with Italy was complete after a long period of problems and strife between herself and her Italian neighbours and allies.

   The problems between Rome and the allies (*socii*) in the period before Augustus turned on the allies' demands for political rights and a share in the prosperity their levies had helped to create. Rome's refusal to grant them full

THE SOCIAL WAR (91–87 BC) was fought by Rome's Italian allies (*socii*) because of Rome's refusal to share power with them. 'Italy' was believed to mean '(land of) bull-calves' (cf. Latin *vitulus*, 'bull-calf') and the symbol of a bull crushing the she-wolf of Rome was a natural choice for the short-lived allied coinage.

ITALY IN THE ROMAN EMPIRE

citizenship led to the so-called Social War (91–87 BC), in which the allies turned the idea of Italian unity against Rome. The war was ended by Rome's concession of citizenship to all Italians south of the Po. Communities north of the Po, such as Brixia (Brescia) and Mediolanum (Milano / Milan), still belonged to the province of Gallia Cisalpina. They were first given citizenship in 49 BC and incorporated into *Italia* shortly after. Geographically and politically Italy had now assumed its familiar form.

The main practical result of unification was the conversion of Italy's towns into *municipia*; that is, towns with an identical political-municipal structure dictated by Rome. The process of integrating the Italians themselves into Roman life was begun by the man who made Augustus his heir, Julius Caesar. Part of Caesar's power base was drawn from the recently enfranchised Italian élites, who were given entry to Rome's Senate. Augustus completed this process. The major incentive was his quarrel with Mark Antony (Marcus Antonius) during the final bout of the Roman civil wars leading to the Battle of Actium in 31 BC. The local Italian nobility had long looked to noble Roman families for patronage (without which nothing could be done in Roman society), and Roman families had been happy to use their support. Oaths and vows had been given by Italy to the tribune Livius Drusus in the 90s. Now in 32 BC 'all Italy [*tota Italia*] swore an oath of allegiance to me without prompting and demanded I serve as its leader in the war I won at Actium'. This is how Augustus liked to remember Italy's support in the autobiographical document he wrote at the end of his life, the *Res Gestae*. The invention of Italy was an imperial fact.

Tota Italia gave Octavianus (as he was then still called) more than just an air of 'national' justification for his dynast's war. It is certainly true that he knew how to manipulate opinion (the patriotism of the Augustan poets is only one well-known part of a sophisticated programme of image-building), and what we see now is seen through the winning side. But much suggests that the Italian aristocracies did indeed identify with the party of the new Caesar. Augustus proved his Italian credentials by again incorporating men from the 400 or so cities of Italy into his government. There were now senators with funny-sounding Italic names like Mamius Murrius Umber and Sextus Sotidius Strabo Libuscidius. There was the Etruscan plutocrat Gaius Maecenas, patron of Horace and Vergil, and perhaps also the emperor's chief ally Marcus Agrippa (whose precise origin is unknown). Above all

AFTER HIS VICTORY OVER MARK ANTONY in the civil wars C. Julius Caesar Octavianus took the title 'Augustus' ('Reverend') in 27 BC. This representation of spiritual calm and military energy was a favourite image (some 170 versions are known) and neatly blends Greek ideal types of victorious athletes with Augustus' Roman majesty and leadership.

3

there was a wave of pro-Augustan feeling in the *municipia*. For the power of Augustan Rome lay, as Vergil's Juno put it, in 'the power of Italian manhood'.

A Numinous Land

Symptomatic of Rome's new alliance with Italy is Augustus' reorganization of the peninsula into eleven administrative *regiones*. Gallia Cisalpina had been dismembered to form Aemilia, Liguria, Venetia–Istria, and Gallia Transpadana (regions VIII–XI). To these were added Latium–Campania, Apulia–Calabria, Lucania–Bruttium (Bruttium corresponding to the modern Calabria), Samnium, Picenum, Umbria, and Etruria (regions I–VII). The sense of these units is shown by the fact that many of them endured in some form till the Lombard invasion and beyond. Populations were also affected by the new emperor. One of the vehicles of Romanization under the Republic had been the establishment of colonies of Romans and the closely allied Latin peoples in Italian territories. The civil wars of the first century BC produced a large number of veterans who looked to their generals for land. Thus Augustus says his reorganization of Italy included 'twenty-eight colonies founded by my authority, which were thriving and densely populated during my lifetime'. It is difficult to identify all of these (which were additions to existing towns) or determine their prosperity; but the claim is as significant as the reality.

Romanization is an ambiguous term. It refers not only to the adoption of Roman material, political, and linguistic culture, but also to its imposition. It is often misleading to distinguish these processes, as the sphere of religion shows. Romans were good at using religion to impose and foster their power. All colonies brought with them *Capitolia*, or temples of the Roman 'State' triad of Jupiter, Juno, and Minerva. These spread throughout Italy and elsewhere. But it is more important to realize that Rome and Italy shared key religious practices. Indeed, religious life was important both for Italian community (a part it plays in Vergil's *Aeneid*) and for Augustus' organization of power around himself.

Apart from gods like Jupiter, Mars, and Ceres, who were worshipped throughout Italy and were duly identified with the gods of Greek mythology, there was also a native Italian religion, which is represented by the network of sacred groves and shrines that stretched over a numinous land. The bronze tablet from Agnone in Samnium, dating to about 200 BC, lists eighteen statues and seventeen altars to different deities, including one to the grove where it hung. Similar sites flourished in the imperial period. Lucus Feroniae ('Grove of Feronia') to the north of Rome became an Augustan colony and an extensive religious complex in the first and second centuries AD. Diana of the Grove (Diana Nemorensis) at modern Nemi south of Rome with its strange ritual of the Grove King was a source of commentary and fame even in ancient times.

Facing: THE CULT OF THE EMPERORS developed rapidly after its institution by Augustus. Deification of dead imperials was a natural part of it. The ascension of Hadrian's wife, Sabina, is the first such depiction of an empress.

Pliny the Younger's charming description of the shrines dotted around the source of the Clitumnus in Umbria shows the togaed river-god presiding over a local oracle.

It was not until the second half of the fourth century that this world came under terminal threat from Christianity. Its nature and meaning are not easy for us to comprehend. The pagan Italians certainly believed in their gods, but without any conception of doctrine or requirement to worship one god alone. Rather, on a personal level religion was a matter of offering sacrifices or vows to the gods in return for safety or prosperity, though ties to a particular god are certainly known. Occasional attacks on the mainstream divinities and their stories by intellectuals do not necessarily imply a crisis of belief, nor do the introduction and undoubted popularity of salvationist gods like Mithras and Isis disclose a hankering for a Christian heaven.

For the Roman state propitiation of the gods was also a serious business. There was a close relationship at Rome between holding a priesthood and exercising political power. It was Augustus, following Julius Caesar, who set the pattern for the Empire by making the title *pontifex maximus* part of his imperial office. He also cemented his personal power as sole ruler by allowing provincials to worship him, a new development. The imperial cult, as it is called, had earlier Greek antecedents, though it never became as routine then as it did in the Roman Empire (where it even survived under the first Christian emperors). Like his successors Augustus was careful to avoid cult at Rome itself. But in other parts of Italy temples to the emperors were common, such as the surviving temples of Roma and Augustus at Ostia, built under Tiberius, or to the Fortune of Augustus built at Pompeii in 3 BC. Frequently the cult was joined with that of a traditional god. The ministrants in Italy and the western provinces were almost always freedmen (*liberti*) operating as *seviri* (i.e. a board of six) *Augustales*, and the cult was clearly conceived early on as a means of integrating this economically powerful group, which was excluded from regular municipal politics, and of focusing its loyalty on the emperor. But the municipal élites themselves often sought permission to house such temples in their towns as a way of furthering contact with the centre.

From Rome to the Regions

There were also important factors limiting the extent of Rome's influence on Italy. The geography of the land precluded easy access to all the regions. This helped to preserve an ancient diversity. It seems likely, for example, that the languages of central and southern Italy, Oscan (the language of the Agnone tablet), Umbrian, and the minor related dialects known as Sabellian, were still being spoken into the imperial period, when they were extinguished by their Latin cousin. Oscan, at any rate, was a living tongue at Pompeii, where grafitti were being written in it in the period between the great earthquake of 62 AD and the eruption of Vesuvius in 79. Greek too hung on, despite the geographer Strabo's lament about the 'barbarization' of Greek Italy except for Taras (Latin Tarentum, Taranto), Rhegion (Latin Regium, Reggio di Calabria), and Neapolis (Napoli/Naples). In the case of Naples the apparent absence of Latin in public inscriptions before the reign of Constantine in the early fourth century AD points to the influence of the heritage industry (and Romans' fascination with things Greek). In general the picture of life in the small towns of Italy that Cicero draws in his speeches for Roscius of Ameria (Amelia) in Umbria and Cluentius of Larinum (Larino in Molise) must have remained true throughout imperial times. The same political jostling, leading to violence or judicial intrigue; the care to preserve the circulation of wealth among the few; the investment in local office to advertise status; the mystique of ancestry in forging dynastic links—these doings of Italy's 'market-town monsters' (as they are described about 100 AD by the historian Florus) would have been recognizable throughout the imperial age and owed little to Rome.

That said, imperial Rome did exert a great deal of influence over the *municipia*. Road and water provision would have been welcome benefits. The road network began in the Republic. But Augustus' renovations and extensions set the tone for the following centuries. 'When I was consul for the seventh time,' he says, 'I restored the Via Flaminia from the City to Rimini, including all the bridges except the Mulvian and the Minucian.' Augustus persuaded those of his generals who had earned triumphs to rebuild all the other Italian roads. The results of his repairs are well illustrated by the partially surviving but still impressive bridge which carried the Via Flaminia over the Valley of the Nar at Narnia (Narni) in Umbria. A hundred years after Augustus the Emperor Trajan embarked on an equally ambitious programme in Italy, which the great Galen deigned to compare with his own progress in building the road of medicine: 'he paved wet and muddy parts or carried the roads on high causeways, cutting through scrub and heathland and throwing bridges over uncrossable rivers; where the way was unreasonably long, he cut another short one, and where it was difficult due to the height of some hill, he diverted it through easier terrain; if the route was exposed to wild animals or isolated, he departed from it and joined with main highways, improving those which were rough.' This is the view from Rome in the 190s and may be compared with Horace's description in the *Satires* of his leisurely trip down one of the earliest roads, the Via Appia, to Brundisium (Brindisi), with its comic history of 'evil innkeepers', small-town officials, failed assignations, and tasty local fare. In Horace's time travellers along this road faced a stiff climb up to Anxur (Tarracina, modern Terracina) and its famous temple of Jupiter on its 'shining white cliffs': it was Trajan's engineers who made the cutting that enables the road to pass underneath the headland.

Aqueducts and water supply are another good example of benefits linking centre and country. Wells and cisterns must always have been the most important source of water for ordinary purposes. The prestige building of aqueducts (a term which includes piped supplies) allowed towns to provide public fountains and bath-houses, and we find many examples of these constructions in the first two centuries, beginning, of course, with Augustus. The improved health and environmental appeal of the towns of Campania is noted by the historian Velleius Paterculus in a reference to the great Serino system, whose 60 miles of piping served among others Naples, Puteoli (Pozzuoli), Pompeii, Nola, and Cumae (Cuma). Imperial benefaction of this sort was concentrated on Rome, where Claudius' enormous 59-mile Aqua Anio Novus is the queen of them all (it survives where it was incorporated with its sister Aqua Claudia into the Porta Maggiore). But it was only natural that Italy benefited too.

Probably more important than aid from the emperors was the regular spending of local magnates. A key part of the ideology of the ancient élites was public munificence. Displaying wealth by spending money improving one's community was as important as political preferment. Many inscriptions attest the interest taken by local bigwigs in their home towns. For example, Seius Strabo, who rose to the prefecture of Egypt in the early first century, typically found time to equip his home town of Volsinii in Etruria (Bolsena) with handsome new baths, an act he naturally recorded on stone. A man who was as happy in Rome as in his own small town of Comum (Como) was the younger Pliny (Gaius Plinius Caecilius Secundus), and it is worth considering his municipal doings in detail.

Honest Poverty

Pliny was no 'market-town monster'; rather, he was among the super-rich of his age and achieved various political promotions, including a 'suffect' consulship in 100 AD (i.e. he was not one of the two consuls who gave their names to the year) and a special governorship in the province of Bithynia and Pontus (the north-western part of Turkey) from about 110 till his death in 113. All our information about his career and finances comes from his famous ten books of *Letters*. It has been estimated that his fortune was several times greater than the 8 million sesterces which contemporaries thought of as the capital needed to sustain a senator in what Tacitus calls 'honest poverty'. To put this figure into an intelligible modern context is notoriously hard; but we can compare, for example, the second-century wage of the Roman legionary, which was 1,200 sesterces per annum (of which perhaps a fifth would have gone on food), or note at the other extreme that 16 million is the figure casually provided by the enormously rich Athenian tycoon Claudius Atticus for the Emperor Hadrian to complete an aqueduct at Roman Troy. Besides property at Com-

um, Pliny owned a large estate in Umbria at
Tifernum Tiberinum (Città di Castello) and a
seaside retreat 17 miles from Rome at Vicus Lau-
rentium. As he says, he was 'almost completely in
land'.

One of Pliny's largest gifts to Comum was the sum of
perhaps a million sesterces for the building of a public
library. In a letter written to Pompeius Saturninus, he assures us
that he was not seeking celebrity through this gift, but was simply
trying to set an example. He had, however, made a speech before the decurions (the local councillors, probably numbering 100), in which he was
'obliged to speak both of my own munificence and of that of my ancestors'.
In another letter he pledges to give Comum 400,000 sesterces which had been
left to it in a technically invalid will made by a friend. Why, he asks, should he
grudge the town this much, when he has already 'contributed 16 hundred
[thousand] sesterces'? Tifernum Tiberinum also received Pliny's benefaction.
Here he built a temple, which was to contain the statues he owned of various
emperors, including Trajan, whose permission he was careful to solicit. The
temple was nominally built because the Tifernians had 'with more enthusiasm than judgement made me their *patronus* while I was still a boy'. Its dedication was marked by a public feast, a chance for Pliny to display himself to the
locals.

The people of Comum benefited too. An inscription lists three testamentary benefactions: the sum for the upkeep of the library (100,000 sesterces); a
large bequest of 1,866,666 sesterces to maintain one hundred of his freedmen,
which was to be used after their deaths to provide a 'feast for the people of the
city'; and thirdly a sum of ?1,000,000 sesterces to construct a baths together
with two further sums of 300,000 sesterces to pay for fitting it out and 200,000
to cover its upkeep and repair. Much the most interesting gift was made during Pliny's lifetime. In a letter to his fellow-townsman Caninius Rufus, he
advises him how to secure a sum he wishes to donate to the *municipes* for an
annual feast: 'I can think of nothing more suitable than what I have done
myself.' Pliny's solution was part of his plan for setting up a system of social
aid for the children of the town. Such schemes, known as alimentary schemes,
are widely attested in Italy at the beginning of the second century. Governmental assistance is plainly the most important type; but private initiative can
be seen too. Pliny gave land to Comum's municipal agent, and then leased it
back at 30,000 sesterces (6 per cent) a year. Private money would go on paying
for the scheme, because the rental was far less than the land was worth to a
producer and there would be no difficulty finding a *dominus*.

It has been argued that Pliny's foundation supported about 175 children in
all. This compares well with the two substantial pieces of evidence we have for

THE SO-CALLED
'HARANGUER': the
small-town aristocrat
Aulus Metellus of Peru-
gia, dressed in the
Roman toga of the late
Republic, gestures his
fellow-citizens to atten-
tion as he prepares to
speak.

government schemes. These come from two very small Italian towns and give details of landholdings and distributions in the early years of Trajan's reign. The bronze tablet from Ligures Baebiani, a town in south central Italy, describes an alimentary foundation in operation in the year 101 AD. Under this the government provided landowners with a loan of 401,800 sesterces, which produced an annual income at 5 per cent of some 20,000 sesterces. This sum supported about 110 children.

Far more important is the almost complete bronze table from Veleia (Velleia), a town in northern Italy situated some 18 miles to the south of Placentia (Piacenza). The 674 lines of this text give exact details of the value of estates associated with two schemes established between 98 and 113 AD with a target of 300 beneficiaries (of whom 12 per cent were girls) and a total loan cost of approximately 1,200,000 sesterces. Pliny's rationale in setting up his own scheme was, he boasts, public-spiritedness. This may be a reason why others invested in alimentary schemes, for although some have argued that Trajan was primarily interested in promoting Italian agriculture through

THE ROMAN RULING CLASS had been worrying about the decline of the Italian population for more than two centuries before Trajan started his 'alimentary' schemes about AD 100. Whatever the truth of the problem, this image of the emperor feeding the children of Italy as her cities look on is a brilliant advertisement of imperial care.

cheap credit, there is no good evidence for this. Rather, we have an early form of family allowance for children with needy parents, as the low rates of the handouts show (16 sesterces per month for boys, 12 for girls at Veleia, hence the very low take-up for the latter).

Need was not, however, the focus of imperial attention. Pliny's speech celebrating Trajan at the beginning of his reign presents the *alimenta* as a means of making it more attractive to raise children for the army. This shows a concern about the number of available legionaries that is familiar from the second century BC onwards, when the turbulent Tiberius Gracchus lamented the absence of freeholders in Etruria. Augustus' family legislation responded to similar anxieties. By the time of Trajan the fear was in some ways an unreal one, for during the first century AD there was a rapid reduction in recruitment from Italy, and by the beginning of the second century we have good evidence to show that not more than 1 per cent of legionary soldiers were Italians. (The fact that five new legions could be raised by Marcus Aurelius and Septimius Severus in the later second century shows the possibility of recruiting Italians,

if need be.) Nevertheless, alimentary schemes are known from forty-nine towns (10 per cent or more of the total), and while regions I (Latium–Campania), IV (Samnium), and VI (Umbria) show the greatest distribution on surviving evidence (regions I and VI also contain the greatest density of towns), it is clear that the idea was promoted throughout Italy. Nor did it lapse with Trajan. The schemes continued during the century after his death in 117. Significantly, they are virtually unknown outside the peninsula. This once again demonstrates the vitality of the Italian ideology.

The alimentary foundations reveal the existence of a healthy rural landowning class at the beginning of the period of the Antonine emperors (96–192), which Gibbon famously called the 'most happy and prosperous' known to man. Over a quarter of those taking loans in the Ligures Baebiani tablet were worth under 50,000 sesterces, with the smallest estate valued at 14,000. In many towns the latter figure would have ruled out membership of the body of decurions. Thus in Comum Pliny tells his friend Romatius Firmus that 'your membership of the decurions is proof that your *census* is 100,000' (and promptly offers him a further 300,000 to top his fortune up to the level needed to belong to the equestrian order, the élite social stratum below the *ordo senatorius*). At Veleia the smallest estate is put at 50,000. But, given the tendency of the loans to be secured against larger holdings (for obvious reasons), even the Veleian information points to a considerable number of smaller farmers in the vicinity of the town.

The Rural Economy

According to Pliny's uncle, Pliny the Elder, who was writing his *Natural History* in the 70s, 'if we tell the truth, we must admit that large-scale estates [*latifundia*] have ruined Italy, and indeed lately the provinces too'. Branded criminals and slaves were performing agricultural work, and 'we should not be surprised that slave gangs do not bring in the profits that the generals [of yore] used to!'. These comments have been extremely influential in modern times, and discussions of the health of Italian agriculture often begin with them rather than evidence of the sort we have been looking at. The truth is difficult to ascertain. Undoubtedly some aristocrats had extremely large estates; the point at issue is whether these were held at the expense of the small free landowner or tenant farmer. The term *latifundia* first occurs in Pliny's time. What he says about their spread appears dramatic and fanciful. His idealization of the generals of yore is a clue. For here we have a combination of the familiar moralist's evocation of past simplicity with that specially Roman concept of the peasant patriarch, a type of national leader who existed in the early days of Rome, when he was liable to be called to the front or to the Senate while tilling his little (but profitable) plot.

In the Elder Cato's treatise on agriculture (which was written about 160 BC) a mixed slave and freeman labour-market is envisaged, with small-scale production of produce (with vines and olives as well as, more importantly, staple cereals such as wheat and barley, and also some livestock) considered the norm. That is not how everyone saw things in the second century BC. According to Plutarch, 'Gaius Gracchus has written in a certain pamphlet that as his brother Tiberius was travelling through Etruria on his journey to Numantia [in 133 BC], he was able to see that the countryside was deserted and that those who were working its soil or tending its flocks were barbarian slaves imported from abroad.' It is now known that the Gracchi were making political capital out of what we might call a moral panic about human resources. The evidence which undermines their allegations comes from the branch of archaeology known as field survey.

The technique of collecting surface remains and identifying habitation on the basis of datable pottery types has come into its own since the Second World War. The most important work in Italy has been in southern Etruria around Veii (Veio), where the survey has been sufficiently large and detailed to allay most doubts about the validity of its results. Impressive work has also been carried out in and around Rome's early third-century BC foundation of Cosa, also in Etruria about 100 miles north of Rome on the Via Aurelia. The most important finding of the southern Etruria survey is the large number of smallholdings existing both in the late republican period, when Gracchus made his journey, and also in the first and second centuries AD. A good example for us is the small dwelling and barn at modern Crocicchie a little north of Rome on the Via Clodia: constructed in early imperial times, the estate was sufficiently prosperous in the third century AD for the then owner to add on a bath-house complete with a black and white dolphin mosaic (though habitation apparently ceased soon after). Recent work on the site of Tuscana (Tuscania) confirms a continuing pattern of settlement around the Via Clodia from Republic to high Empire. The significance of this is increased, if we remember that the buildings peasant farmers would have lived in are likely to leave relatively few traces. What attracts attention easily are the villa sites, those 'pieces of cities broken off', as Ramsay MacMullen has described them. Survey archaeology brings these back into contact with the land's less wealthy inhabitants.

A good example of the villa's relation with surrounding settlement is the complex at Settefinestre in the immediate vicinity of Cosa. This fine example of a terraced 'platform' villa going back to the early first century BC was not only a residence. It also had good wine-producing facilities and ample storage areas, including room for animals. It must have used slave labour, but how much cannot be known. The Settefinestre villa underwent extensive renovation towards the end of the late first century AD, but both it and the several other large villas in the Ager Cosanus went into decline in the second century and were apparently deserted by the 170s. This confirms suspicions of a more general decline thereafter. It is true that other survey zones paint a varied picture. An exploration of the corridor south-east of Horace's birthplace of Venusia (Venosa) as far as modern Gravina (?ancient Silvium) in Apulia revealed eleven sites in occupation under Augustus and a similar level of habitation through into the third century. Again, recent work in the Lower Liris (Liri) Valley to the east of Interamna (Pignataro Interamna) has concluded that there was a marked increase in settlement in the second and third centuries. Nevertheless, there is a consensus that a decline of population should be assumed from the second century onwards. As to actual numbers, for the late first century BC the best estimates range between 3.5 and 4.5 million for the free population with 2 to 3 million slaves, followed by a peak in the mid-first century AD of between 7 and 9 million in total, then a gradual fall to a low of 2.25 million by 650.

We can point to changing trading patterns in Italy between the first century BC and the second century AD as a comparable phenomenon. One fashionable method of assessing Italian trade is the investigation of ship wrecks. From the typology of the containers used to carry goods, especially wine, it is clear that the majority of these wrecks are datable to the first century BC. A large proportion of known wrecks are from boats sailing between Italy and Gaul, with high numbers from the coasts of Campania, Latium, and southern Etruria (the great wine-growing areas of Italy), northern Sardinia, and southern France. But one scholar has recently noted a correlation between the findspots of wrecks and 'the delights of summer beaches', and we must not generalize from what is a trade in one major commodity. If wine exports reached their height in the first century BC and were all over by 100 AD, this may help to explain the decline of villas in a wine-growing area such as the Ager Cosanus—but the limitations of maritime survey are obvious.

More relevant, perhaps, to general economic health are production-rates and types of pottery. Much of our evidence depends on the red glazed pottery known as *terra sigillata*, or Arretine ware, that began to be produced at Arretium (Arezzo) in the Upper Arno Valley in the mid-first century BC. This good quality product was immensely successful at home and abroad. However, it is clear that within a hundred years (export) production at Arretium and elsewhere in Italy had been totally eclipsed by centres in southern Gaul, as imports at Pompeii and elsewhere suggest. Rome itself is bound to have a distorting impact on the figures and should perhaps be left aside: a recent sorting of amphorae from the port of Ostia again suggests a decline of Italian agricultural products and a corresponding rise of imports from Africa and Spain (especially of the ever-popular fish relish, *garum*)—but much Italian produce would have entered Rome by other routes.

Another indication of relative prosperity is building work. The feeling that there was less construction after the second century is largely connected with a decline in inscriptional testimony. This is not just an Italian phenomenon. Throughout the Empire commemorations of bequests, foundations, honours, buildings, etc., tail off rapidly in the third century AD. In many regions this is interpreted as a sign of social, economic, and military crisis at a time when there was a rapid turnover of emperors and central government was without stability (at least till the accession of Diocletian in 284). It is now being felt that the idea of a blanket, Empire-wide crisis is too crude. For a start, except for an incursion into the Po Valley by the German Marcomanni, Italy itself saw no 'barbarian' invaders at this time (unlike much of the East); though the Aurelianic walls of Rome (c.270–80) are a reminder of the German threat. But it is true that public building work and the establishment of new funds, games, etc., virtually comes to a halt after 250. The first century is the heyday for new public building, while funds which were set up to distribute food or money peak around the middle of the next.

ARRETINE WARE (*terra sigillata*) was one of the most successful Italian industries in the centuries before and after Christ. The high-quality red glaze and attractive reliefs of the bowls and plates that were the dominant product found a ready market at home and abroad.

Nevertheless, building went on in some form, and can be demonstrated in distinctive techniques and styles or from brick stamps. The super-rich continued to build villas, such as the monumental one at Sette Bassi outside Rome (mid-second century), some of whose decorative touches, like the high lighting of the main buildings, anticipate trends found in the palaces of the later Empire. Public construction in country towns went on too. At Alba Fucens (near Avezzano in the central Apennines) the baths and market area were renovated in the third century. A recently found inscription from Cosa proudly asserts the overhaul of buildings in the civic centre under the Emperor Maximinus Thrax (235–8). What we may say, then, is that there probably was a decline in the Italian economy during the first three centuries and after. But we must not make undue generalizations or be tempted to dramatize. Each region has to be looked at on its own. In the absence of securely datable pottery fragments (owing to the use of indistinct local varieties) there lies a particular danger for those who depend on field survey. We have to assume continuity as well as breakdown, permanence as well as rupture.

Patronage and Politics

One of the ways in which this continuity can be demonstrated is to consider more directly the political life and institutions of the Italian town. In this period the great were tied to their towns by genuine local loyalties and networks of patronage and kinship. Honours and status from acts of public munificence have been mentioned. Important also in keeping the rich home-ward-looking was the system of *munera*, or 'duties', which Romans took over from the Greeks as a method of securing public service from the élite. The importance of these *munera* is shown by the word *municipium* itself (a com-pound of the word for 'duty' and a word here meaning 'perform'), for Roman citizenship was felt to entail particular duties and obligations. In a small town duties were anything from providing oil for the baths to leading deputations to high officials. There was always a tension in the system between local ser-vice and imperial service, to which the élite were naturally attracted. In the high Empire central authority was careful not to grant exemptions from local obligations too easily, but from the end of the third century it became accepted policy to excuse those with senior rank or status, and it is thought that this had a decidedly adverse affect on local finances. Even before this there were attempts at evasion on the part of potential payers and, equally, attempts to extend liability by municipal authorities. An obvious target group was per-manent residents from elsewhere. Thus an inscription of 105 AD from a statue base at Aquileia honours a local aristocrat whose high imperial career allowed him to request from Trajan that such *incolae* 'should perform duties in our town', a welcome gain.

Aquileia was big enough to have men of senatorial rank to intercede on its behalf. Many smaller towns had to take what opportunity they could in find-ing someone suitable to speak at Rome. A local man like Gaius Torasius Severus of Spoletium (Spoleto) was ideal. He commemorated his building of a baths and other benefactions to his home town and finally notes with pride that 'on account of his service to the Republic [i.e. of Spoletium] the order of the decurions adopted him as the patron of the municipality'. Likewise the small town of Matilica in Umbria (Matélica) turned to its distinguished son Gaius Arrius Clemens, a career soldier with numerous decorations from Tra-jan and Hadrian. His suitability for the job of patron is shown by the fact that the emperor appointed him *curator* of the town. Such *curatores* were active in the Roman Empire from the reign of Domitian, if not before, and had fairly wide powers over local finances. It is now thought that they do not represent a curtailment of local independence so much as a contact between local and central authority—for which a man like Clemens would have been perfect. Patrons themselves are attested until the end of the fourth century.

Canusium: Roman Status and Greek Roots

One of the most interesting documents relating to the political organization of the small town is the Album of Canusium (Canosa di Puglia). This bronze tablet lists all the decurions of Canusium serving in the year 223 AD, and also includes a list of its patrons. The date is already into the period which many modern scholars like to portray as the 'Third-Century Crisis'. In high imperial politics the last thirty years had certainly seen violent civil wars and murders following the assassination of the last Antonine emperor, Commodus, in 192. The new dynasty of Septimius Severus, which emerged from the turmoil, was of an altogether different character. Most important for Italy is the fact that Severus came from the African city of Lepcis Magna, a Carthaginian–Phoenician foundation undisturbed by Roman settlement. His (second) marriage to a member of a probably Arabic dynastic family from Emesa in Syria highlights the fact that he was the first emperor from outside Italy who was not of Italian stock.

It is not going too far to say that the traditional exclusivity of Italy and the idea that the Empire looked to Italy as its centre goes into a steep decline from this time. A little over a hundred years after Canusium catalogued its governing class, a Christian emperor who looked to a very different set of priorities and paradigms would build his 'New Rome' of Constantinople on the shores of the Bosporus. The beginning of this process is marked by the decision of Severus' son Marcus Aurelius Antoninus (a name asserting links with the good Antonine emperors), better known as Caracalla, to extend Roman citizenship to all free inhabitants of the Empire. The reasons for this move are still disputed. But one consequence was that a right which had been held by all Italians and only a portion of those in the rest of the Empire was henceforward a privilege in no sense at all. From now on imperial society divides even more sharply between rich and poor, divisions which are increasingly enshrined in law between those with *honor* (*honestiores*) and those with none (*humiliores*), and Roman citizenship—and Italian preeminence—ceased to matter.

It was in this political situation that two of the leading citizens of Canusium immortalized themselves and their colleagues. The text begins with a list of the thirty-one Roman senators who had agreed to serve as Canusium's patrons (one of these has been crossed out). Whether this represents an unusually high number, we cannot say: being on the main route to the important harbour city of Brundisium, the town had ample opportunity to attract the attention of the great. The next item on the tablet is a list of eight patrons from the equestrian order. These may have been local men, since four of them are serving in the *ordo* as *quinquennalicii*, i.e. men who had held the chief magistracy (the duovirate) in a census year. In normal years the *municipium* was

THE SEVERAN DYNASTY, founded by Septimius Severus (AD 193–211), broke the domination of the Roman world by Italian emperors and marks the beginning of Italy's decline as the centre of the Empire. The unclassical 'frontality' of the staring royal family looks forward to the striking portrait styles of later antiquity.

headed by duovirs, recalling the annual pair of consuls at Rome and the principle of collegiality which was a cornerstone of the old republican government. The Romans had also evolved a more senior magistracy, the censorship, which two men held for eighteen months every five years. The censors' main task was to oversee the list of citizens, to check property ratings (the *census*), and membership of the equestrian and senatorial orders. They also had wide powers to investigate public and private morality, an area Romans were always obsessed by. The role of the *duoviri quinquennales* at Canusium was presumably comparable.

The high status of the *quinquennalicii* is reflected in the next group in the album, four men *allecti inter quinquennalicios*, i.e. men 'adlected' to this rank without having to progress through the usual sequence of offices. These are followed by twenty-nine *duoviralicii*, nineteen *aedilicii* (with responsibility for buildings, entertainments, etc.), nine *quaestoricii* (financial magistrates), thirty-two *pedani* (decurions with no experience of office, i.e. adlected into the *ordo*), and twenty-five *praetextati*. This last group is particularly interesting, as it offers a clue to the formation of the *ordo*. The *praetextati* are young men wearing the *toga praetexta*, a toga with a purple hem discarded at the coming of age (varying between 15 and 18) and the assumption of the all-white toga of adulthood. The names of the *praetextati* indicate that they are the children of current decurions or other office-holding families. They had no vote on the council, but were waiting to take over vacant seats. They suggest, in other words, that membership of the council was hereditary. A legal text of this period speaks of a restriction of office to those who were already decurions. It is not known whether there were still formal elections at Canusium, as there were for example at Pompeii in the first century. But it seems clear that there was no possibility of entering the order by election. This is indeed the situation assumed in the Theodosian Code, which collects imperial legislation from 312 to 438.

At Canusium there was the usual number of one hundred decurions. Over sixty families are represented, but the *gens Abuccia* is outstanding (failing to appear only among the *pedani*). It is often said that office-holding was becoming increasingly unattractive by the end of the second century. One of the arguments in support of this contention is the appearance of men with names indicating they are descendants of freedmen. *Liberti* themselves were not allowed to become decurions, but there was no bar against their children doing so. Many of these would betray their ultimately servile origin by having a Greek-sounding name as the last of their usual three Roman names (the first two elements being borrowed from their former master). The obvious example of a small-town freedman made good in the business world is Petronius' oriental-sounding Trimalchio, whose famous neoplutic dinner in the *Satyricon* takes place in a *Graeca urbs* in Campania. At Canusium many Greek names

This LUXURY BOWL (*left*) from
Locarno-Muralto was found in a
tomb of Tiberian or Claudian date.
Its bird, vine, and ivy motif is not
untypical of the enamelled glass of
the early Roman Empire, which
may have come from a single
major workshop in northern Italy.

HADRIAN'S GREAT VILLA AT
TIVOLI brought a revival of poly-
chrome 'emlemata' or inset panels
in floor mosaics. 'The marvellous
dove drinking and casting a
shadow with its head on the water
while others sun themselves and
preen on the lip of the bowl' is
how Pliny the Elder describes the
original (*below*) by the famous
Pergamene mosaicist, Sosus
(second century BC).

THE MODEST VILLA
AT BOSCOREALE, a little
to the north-west of
Pompeii, yielded an
unexpectedly fine set of
silver. The workman-
ship of this wine-pourer
takes its inspiration
from earlier Greek
models, but its
triumphant symbolism
of a Victory sacrificing a
bull is no less a part of
the Augustan age when
it was made.

are found in the album. But Canusium was a special case. It was a Greek colony by foundation. In the first century BC Horace sneered at its bilingualism. In the mid-second century Herodes Atticus, the son of Claudius Atticus, gave it an aqueduct. Thus the evidence cannot be used to support a picture of unwilling decurions (which is certainly true for the later Empire). For some, respectability may have been felt to depend on a completely Roman or Italian name. One of the *praetextati*, Titus Aelius Nectareus, must be the son of one of the three T. Aelii higher up the *ordo*, all of whom have fully Roman names (which Nectareus is not). On the other hand, several names of Greek origin do appear among the higher magistrates and the Canusini were hardly ashamed of their ancestry.

Pompeii: Money and Votes

No inspection of municipal politics would be complete without a trip to Pompeii. The recent history of this town begins after the Social War, when Sulla punished it for siding with the allies by imposing on the original Oscan-speaking population several thousand of his own veterans. At the time of its destruction in 79 AD, the most likely estimate of the urban population is between eight and twelve thousand (it is difficult to guess at the size of the rural population because the extent of the town's territory is not known). Pompeii was clearly a prosperous place, and is a celebrated case among students of the Roman economy. Quite different conclusions are drawn about the nature of its wealth. Some recent work has challenged the traditional idea that the Pompeian landscape was heavily involved in producing cash crops, especially wine. Emphasis is laid instead on cereal production to feed the local population. Pompeian wines, which were not particularly famous for their quality, are also thought to have been mainly for the local market—though their cheapness may actually suggest large-scale selling (cf. again the wrecks of wine-carrying ships off the Campanian coast). It does at least seem plausible to see the town's manufacturing base, e.g. in textiles (including fulling, dyeing, felting, etc.), as serving local needs rather than those of other regions, and this hypothesis is supported by the number of different trades in the town (some eighty-five have been counted, suggesting a diversification of services needed by any local centre).

At Pompeii we have good illustrations of how politics and economics coexist in a *municipium*. One of the most interesting bodies of economic evidence is the archive of 153 charred wooden writing-tablets from the house of the

L. CAECILIUS JUCUNDUS, wart and all, is the best-known example of the local businessmen of Roman Italy, a man active in private and public finance. These coarse features graced the entrance hall (*atrium*) of his Pompeian home.

19

banker and money-collector (*argentarius coactor*) Lucius Caecilius Jucundus. One of Jucundus' activities was farming local taxes. Throughout the ancient world public services were routinely 'privatized', either (as we have seen) through the system of duties, or by means of letting out contracts, especially to collect revenue. Roman citizens had been free of direct taxes since Aemilius Paullus' conquest of Macedonia in the second quarter of the second century BC. Under the Empire Italy was free of direct taxes until the end of the third century, when Diocletian assessed the north of the peninsula, and the beginning of the fourth, when Galerius extended the census to the rest, including Rome (which, however, escaped for the duration). But indirect taxes were always important at local and national level. Jucundus apparently farmed a tax on municipal pasture and some sort of market-tax.

Jucundus' other transactions concern his auction business. We have 137 declarations by sellers (including six women) that Jucundus had paid them. These documents mostly belong to the years 54–8. Many of them tell us nothing of the objects sold, though the sums involved make it plain that Jucundus did not deal in trivial amounts (the mean has been calculated at 4,500 sesterces). It seems that occasional sales formed the bulk of the business, with objects like boxwood or slaves as the main items. This is the sort of commercial activity to be expected in a developed, but still pre-industrial, society.

As interesting as the financial information in the Jucundus archive is the data it provides on social matters. Up to ten witnesses sign their names against the sales tablets. It has been argued that there is a strict hierarchy in the order of signing, with members of the *ordo* coming first. This is as we should expect. Comparison of the relative status of people mentioned as witnesses backs up the impression gained from legal codes and well-attested individual examples about the complexity of Roman social relations and the possibility of mobility. Freedmen, like Petronius' figure of fun Trimalchio, were trapped within their legal status no matter how much wealth they possessed or how big their *domus* (house, household) was. In the main dynasty and kin counted for more than money.

Pompeii is famous amongst other things for the 2,500 or so election posters (*programmata*) painted in red on a white ground urging support for candidates in the municipal elections. These can give the impression of a lively, participatory democracy, where the citizens' votes really counted and persuasion really mattered. Indeed, many commentators have taken them this way. A number of facts about ancient society make this interpretation unlikely. The élite's main concern was always that of keeping urban populations quiet by feeding and entertaining them, for rioting, often due to shortage of staples, was a constant danger, and one which could easily turn political. The Pompeian riot of 59 AD, which started between the Pompeians and Nucerians at a show and was fomented, according to Tacitus, by illegal political 'clubs' at Pompeii, is a good

example. It is certainly true that communication between rulers and ruled was often more direct and open than it is today. The media did not exist, and public addresses and harangues to the masses were of vital importance. But there was never any dialogue as such. Elections offered no real auditing of politicians' performance in office, for election to a junior magistracy, such as the aedileship, secured membership of the *ordo* of the decurions for life. Nor would the Romans have tolerated any truly democratic system. Throughout Roman history it is no surprise to find them constantly intervening on the part of high status groups. This is not simply a familiar economic alignment. Patronage and clientship were a basic, institutionalized part of Roman society. Neither the lower nor the upper orders thought democratically—which did not exclude some democratic mechanisms, but only the use to which they were put.

RIVALRY BETWEEN NEIGHBOURING TOWNS was a serious problem in the ancient world. The fighting in the amphitheatre at Pompeii in AD 59 between Pompeians and Nucerians was evidently enjoyed by the Pompeian house-holder Actius Anicetus, for he took care to commemorate his fellow citizens' victory in his house.

21

Examples of Pompeian *programmata* are 'ALL THE GOLDSMITHS ASK FOR GAIUS CUSPIUS PANSA AS AEDILE!' or 'I ASK YOU TO ELECT AS AEDILE HOLCONIUS PRISCUS, A MAN OF THE GREATEST PROPRIETY AND MOST WORTHY OF THE REPUBLIC!'. In Greek and Latin the language of political evaluation often takes the form of moral concepts, and Pompeii is no exception. We know from the surviving charters of new *municipia* in Spain, also from the first century AD, that voting took place in wards (*curiae*). Winning an election was a matter of winning a major- ity of such wards: the presiding magistrate would go on declaring 'until there are as many magistrates as it is necessary to appoint', as the Charter of Malaga puts it. It is difficult to detect the precise channels of patronage within the wards which would lead to the election of the local bigwig. A recent study has focused attention on the local 'clubs', or *collegia*, which looked after cults in the *vici* (neighbourhoods), and which were often run by freedmen. (Whether these clubs were the same as those involved in the Pompeian riot of 59 is unknown.) It has also been observed that the spread of rich residences throughout the town points to a more familiar clientage system. Outside one's own district patronage from those already in the *ordo* must have been important in winning support.

For the lowest magistracy, the aedileship, control of elections at Pompeii is suggested by the fact that some candidates operate as pairs who are supported jointly in the *programmata*. It is believed that in no year were there more than two pairs contesting the two available posts. For the election to the duovirate competition seems also to have been restricted. It has been suggested that only two candidates are known per year for two posts in the final period. This partly reflects the progression from the aedileship. But the candidates for the duovirate still seem to stand as a pair, thereby emphasizing the importance of obligation between themselves and to their supporters. There is nothing democratic about this. Further, we should not forget that there must also have been a group of decurions who had never been elected. The annual entry of two aediles would not enable the *ordo* to retain the one hundred members which the evidence suggests was the normal size of the councils in large towns. A good proportion must have been given a place, as at Canusium.

Art and Culture

So much for politics. Pompeii also tells us much of what we know of Italian decorative art under the high Empire, and something should be said about this aspect of its life. The town was undergoing rebuilding at the time of its destruction. But it still looks rather old-fashioned compared with what we know was happening in the Rome of Nero and Vespasian. The first century AD marks in fact the start of a revolution in building that shapes the architecture of the next three centuries. Concrete was crucial here. It was not until the sec-

ond half of the century that architects first took advantage of its possibilities for transforming internal space by curvilinear, polygonal design of the sort we see in public and private buildings throughout the Empire. Brick-arching was another enduring Roman technique. Neither is seen much at Pompeii. Nor do we see too much evidence of the changing use of urban space that is so noticeable in the second century, whereby the large townhouse was yielding to the rural retreat, leading to the break-up of older urban dwellings and redesign on a more compact scale. Nor is there yet much sign of the most significant development of the second century and beyond, the brick and concrete *insulae* or apartment blocks. In fourth-century Rome there were no fewer than 46,000 *insulae* against 1,790 townhouses. Rome's port of Ostia has many good examples of such homes. But at Pompeii this process is only just beginning, and there are no purpose-built tenements.

In terms of internal decoration the end of Pompeii's life seems to present forms which are backward-looking. It is difficult to be sure that this impression is not a trick of the evidence. Nevertheless, there is nothing in the Italy of the second to fourth centuries that recalls the fast-developing styles of the first

ROMAN WALL PAINTING is a sign of wealth and status. In Pompeii at least there is an obsession with external architectural forms. Historians interpret this as a reflection of the dual public and private role of the great Roman house.

centuries BC and AD in the town. During the late Republic Pompeian wall-painting underwent dramatic changes, replacing the painted stuccowork of the so-called First Style with an imaginative use of shading and perspective to create the very illusionistic depiction of architectural forms known as the Second Style. In the first century AD two further styles are distinguished by the experts. The first introduces a mannered, ornamented effect into the architectural environment, whose structural realism is now abandoned. The second and final style marries this fantasy architecture with baroque elements and various new forms of decoration. Art historians detect in some of the very last work a sort of overloading of techniques and a failure of taste.

This is a modern view, of course. We actually know very little about the development of art in Italy after Pompeii, and certainly nothing about its reception. Generalizing about trends is virtually impossible. Second-century evidence from Ostia seems to show a move away from perspective and form. In the second and third century mythological panels seem to become rarer, with scenes from the hunt and the circus coming into prominence. Also at this time, at least in and around Rome, comes a liking for purely linear decoration, a strange—or striking—deployment of lines, dashes, angles, and lattice-work. Techniques of execution are certainly less resourceful than before; whether this allows us to diagnose a decline is another matter. Under the new Empire of Diocletian and Constantine, with its centralized, bureaucratized structure, and the extraordinarily god-like figure of the Emperor, it is no surprise to find a marked trend towards pictorial 'frontality', a sort of self-advertisement on the part of the very great that has a distinctly unclassical feel.

THE HAIRSTYLE OF THIS LEARNED POMPEIAN is typical of the fashions of the period leading up to the city's destruction. Comparable portraits suggest that the pen and tablets represent social status rather than a deep love of writing.

From art we may turn briefly to literature, for the most famous surviving Latin authors of the 'golden age' are almost entirely Italians (Livy, Cicero, Catullus, Propertius, Vergil, Ovid, Sallust, Horace). Thereafter Italians take their place with other provincials (virtually all of them working in and around Rome). The most striking event in Latin literature in the Empire is the great dearth of literary production in the second and third centuries. With the exception of Juvenal (from Aquinum/Aquino), there are no major Latin poets after the Flavian era, when Valerius Flaccus and Silius Italicus (?from Patavium) wrote their epics, until the fourth century. These rather baroque, stilted pieces are not to modern taste. A better Flavian poet is Papinius Statius from Naples. Statius at any rate displays a mastery of form in occasional verse, though his own epics are often excessively theatrical with a bizarre taste for variation and novelty. The most interesting thing about him from our point of view is his Neapolitan background. The son of a teacher of rhetoric, his five books of *Silvae* suggest a lively bilingual education and intellectual environment in that city during the mid-first century.

In prose too the middle Empire is rather bare. After Suetonius (?from Africa) and Tacitus (?from a north Italian background) in the Trajanic and Hadrianic periods, there is again a lacuna, which is hardly filled by the miscellanist Aulus Gellius, the letters of Fronto, or the bombastic 'novel' of Apuleius (*The Golden Ass*). None of these authors are from Italy (the last two were certainly African, as perhaps was Gellius), and we have to wait a long time to find one who was. The only decent Latin literature in the third century comes from the Christian authors Tertullian and Cyprian (again from Roman Africa). The fourth century sees a revival, but the closest we can get to a Roman or Italian author is the astrological writer-turned-Christian Firmicus Maternus, from Sicily. It is not until the second half of the century that a group of leading literary figures was again centred on Rome in the form of Quintus Aurelius Symmachus, his marriage-relation Virius Nicomachus Flavianus, and others. This circle tells us much about the late antique pagan aristocracy and the idea of Rome they still cherished, but little about Italy itself.

The World of the Fourth Century

To men like Symmachus Italy was the place where they held their vast tracts of lands. Some details of the world of the fourth-century aristocratic landowner can be glimpsed in fragments of a land-register from Volcei (Buccino) in Lucania, which dates to the year 323. This is a more concrete guide to priorities than literature. It is plain that the origin of the Volcei document lies in the tax demands the new Empire was making on Italy, which was now a province (or rather several mini-provinces) like everywhere else. At least seventy properties are involved. These are arranged in seven *pagi* (the rural districts of a country town). Curiously there is no indication of individual owners, such as we would expect in a census (and as we find, for example, in the second-century alimentary registers). The farms and dwellings take their names from a former owner, but, since these names are not found among contemporaries or preceding generations in this area, we must either diagnose a sharp break in landholding patterns or understand centuries of land acquisition by *one* family. The latter is the correct alternative. The landowner's name is in fact known, for he is the Turcius named in the preamble of the inscription. Turcius is to be identified with Lucius Turcius Apronianus, prefect of Rome in 339, a man known to be from an extremely rich family. The Volcei inscription, then, is tangible evidence of the intermarrying and accumulated property-holding that made the Italian aristocracy stable and successful throughout the imperial period, a pattern of life that was not disrupted until the barbarian

25

SYMMACHORVM

THE SCENE OF A PAGAN PRIESTESS sacrificing at a country altar is one half of an ivory diptych executed for the great families of the Nicomachi and Symmachi. That the same workshop produced equally fine Christian designs is no surprise in an age when pagans and Christians lived together in the same communities.

invasions of the fifth and sixth centuries and the Justinianic wars of reconquest, when Italy and its apostolic see again became ideologically valuable.

The history of these times lies with the next chapter. But one event which presages them and demonstrates the new dominance of Christianity at the end of the fourth century will be a convenient place to pause here.

The power of Christianity at this time is not to be measured by the number of Christians, for it seems clear that many people continued to worship the old gods well into the sixth century. Rather, the most important result of Constantine's conversion and promotion of the new religion as sole emperor (324–37) was the steady appropriation of secular power by the bishops and their organized flocks. One of the most eloquent testimonies to this fundamental change is the confrontation that occurred in 390 at Milan between the Emperor Theodosius I and the great Ambrose, bishop of that city. During the fourth century Milan and Aquileia (which was to be devastated in the invasions of the fifth and sixth centuries) became the most important cities in Italy owing to their strategic positions on the major road systems linking east and west. Theodosius was a very religious man. The cause of his climbdown before the bishop was Ambrose's refusal to allow him communion until he had undergone penance for authorizing a massacre at Thessalonica. Ambrose's sanction struck at the late Roman emperor's need to process from one place of majesty, the palace, to another, the cathedral. The result of Theodosius' reinforced devotion was a series of edicts forbidding any role for pagan religion in public life. He thereby effectively ended a social-political system that had been in existence for centuries, not only in Italy and Rome (to whose 'ancient rural vigour' he cunningly appealed at this time in support of a law against homosexuality), but throughout the Empire as a whole. It is well known that the great landowning families of the west like the Turcii and the Symmachi long resisted abandoning the pagan religion which had served them so well. In their literature they constantly looked back at the past to early Rome, her leadership of Italy, and acquisition of empire. They were hidebound by tradition. Ambrose and Theodosius on the other hand look forward to the future to the medieval age and its conflicts of kings and popes.

THE MEDIEVAL CENTURIES 400–1250: A POLITICAL OUTLINE

BRYAN WARD-PERKINS

Barbarian Conquest and Rule: From the Sack of Rome (410) to the Death of Theodoric (526)

On 24 August 410 an army of Goths led by Alaric entered Rome, and then looted the city for three days. The shock felt in the Roman world was considerable—nothing of the kind had happened in 800 years, since the Gauls captured the city in 390 BC, and even then the Capitol had been saved by its honking geese. Why, the Christians asked, had God abandoned the newly converted Empire? In the province of Africa, the learned bishop of the small provincial see of Hippo, Augustine, was prompted by the event to write *The City of God*, a thousand pages long in its English edition, and a masterly exposition of the workings of divine providence and of the relationship between human and godly power.

The year 410 might seem a good clear date with which to begin the Italian Middle Ages—an alien invader from the north devastates the peninsula and sets up a puppet emperor, and a cleric is prompted to write one of the great books of Christian learning. This is definitely not the world of Augustus explored in the previous chapter, with Roman legions triumphant throughout the Mediterranean and Roman imperial power celebrated in the great pagan epic of Vergil. However, it is obviously also true that single dates rarely mark abrupt and complete transitions. Rome's dominance had already been severely challenged during the third century, when barbarian invaders had failed to take the city but had been enough of a threat to prompt the building of a 19-kilometre-long defensive wall around it. Nor was the might of the Empire broken by the events of August 410. The Goths eventually moved out of Italy in 412 and were settled as allies of Rome in the south of Gaul in 418. Indeed politically and militarily the city mattered little anyway—the last emperor to live there was Maxentius, defeated and killed by Constantine in 312, and the real centre of power had moved north to the frontier capital of

LEAF from a pair of linked ivory tablets (a diptych), produced to commemorate a Roman aristocrat, probably of the early fifth century. He is watching the slaughter of wild animals, imported at his own expense, to mark the beginning of a term of office. More animals (elephants) also had to die to produce the commemorative diptychs.

Trier in modern Germany, and to the north Italian cities of Milan and Ravenna. Equally, Augustine who in his Christianity 'looks forward' to the Middle Ages, was not the only writer to respond to the crisis. In the early fifth century paganism (or polytheism, as it is currently fashionable to call it) was still very much a live force in Italy—while Augustine questioned the eternal and divinely sanctioned position of Rome, a pagan Rutilius Namatianus composed a much more traditional poem celebrating what he saw as the reviving greatness of the city following the Gothic sack.

Rutilius, however, was wrong, since Rome's greatness did not revive. During the fifth century, provinces were gradually lost: at first outlying and unimportant ones like Britain, but then (in 429) Africa, vital for the corn-supply of the city of Rome and for the tax-revenue necessary to support the imperial armies. By the end of the fifth century Italy was no longer the centre of a far-flung empire, and had become instead a 'victim' of aggression from outside (for instance, the Vandals periodically raided Sicily from their new North African home, and subjected Rome to a second, more systematic sack in 455). This role of victim is one which the peninsula has played more or less consistently ever since, sometimes with surprising relish—in the present day, for instance, many Italians have chosen to forget their recent enthusiasm for colonialism and Fascist aggression, but are happy to remember the brutality of the German occupation of 1943–5.

Inside Italy the end of imperial power in the fifth century meant the end of security and of a certain guaranteed wealth and status, but it did not change society overnight. The rich and highly cultured landlords continued to rule over their estates and even continued to hold immensely expensive games for the enjoyment of the people. Increasingly, the imperial army came to be led by men of barbarian blood, but these were very happy to find a niche in Roman society by adopting Roman ways. The barbarians after all entered the Empire, whether as its servants or as its invaders, to enjoy, rather than to destroy, the high levels of material wealth and culture that they had observed over the Rhine and Danube frontiers. As important within Italian society as the loss of empire, were slower changes, not attributable to barbarian invasion. In particular, the late fourth and the fifth centuries saw the definitive triumph of Christianity, so that the temples were gradually closed and allowed to rot, or were despoiled for their building materials, while new churches were built in the cities and over the graves of the martyrs. By the end of the fifth century the sacred and, increasingly, the monumental geography of an Italian town revolved no longer around a forum with its temple of the Capitoline gods, but around an intramural cathedral and a ring of extramural cemetery churches.

Even when the then barbarian commander of the imperial forces, Odoacer, deposed the last western Roman emperor, Romulus Augustulus, in 476, and seized enough land to convert himself and his Germanic troops into aristocrats, remarkably little changed on the surface. Odoacer was careful not to alienate the emperor in the East, and therefore ruled Italy as a mere king under nominal eastern overlordship: and he was equally careful to flatter the Italian aristocracy, by retaining for them all the traditional ranks of the civil service, and by granting them tiny, but symbolic, areas of power, such as the right to mint coins. Under Odoacer, copper coins were minted in Italy for the first time since the third century with the proud legend 'SC' (*Senatus Consulto*: by Decree of the Senate). Perhaps no one was really fooled by this façade of unchanging Roman and imperial power, but it suited everyone to maintain it: the Italian aristocracy were able to feel that they were cherished and ruled in a suitably Roman way, the barbarians could believe that they belonged in the heart of the Empire (where they evidently didn't), and the eastern emperors

IVORY DIPTYCH, probably of *c.*AD 400. The figures shown are not identified, but are probably the barbarian general in Roman service Stilicho, his Roman wife Serena, and their son Eucherius. All are shown in a classicizing style and Roman dress. Stilicho supports a shield bearing the busts of the reigning emperors, and Eucherius holds a tablet of office, probably to celebrate a recent honorific appointment.

29

could pretend that the western provinces were really in their hands, even if under barbarian stewardship. The shock for Italy of moving from centuries of unchallenged imperial power to subjection under barbarian rule had to be cushioned by an appearance of business as usual.

This situation continued into the early sixth century, despite the arrival of a new barbarian warlord Theodoric the Ostrogoth, who defeated and killed Odoacer in 493 and ruled Italy until his death in 526. The Goths in their propaganda presented themselves as the people prepared to take on the arduous job of governing and defending Italy, so that the peninsula's Roman inhabitants could enjoy peace and a suitably elevated lifestyle: 'The glory of the Goths is the defence of civilized life.' Theodoric certainly gave peace to Italy, and he even extended his power abroad, through a series of marriage-alliances and treaties with other barbarian kings, and through the annexation of Provence. Not only was Italy ruled by all the traditional array of prefects, governors, etc. that it had known under the Empire, but there was even again a prefect of the Gauls, resident (as he had been in the fifth century) at Arles.

With the benefit of hindsight and of abundant Ostrogothic propaganda, it is easy to see the reign of Theodoric as a golden age for Italy, a period of peace and tranquillity 'when everyone could carry out his business at any hour he wished, as if it were in daylight', and when, for the last time for some fourteen centuries, the peninsula was politically united. However, it is not clear that contemporaries, who were not to know of the disasters which were to follow, viewed things quite so cheerfully at the time. The Goths, despite their undoubted wish to rule within a Roman framework, could not suddenly cease to be barbarians, indeed they are likely to have remained proud of their own Germanic past and achievements (which included the defeat and death of a Roman emperor in 378 at the hands of fellow Goths, and even the sack of Rome in 410).

Theodoric ruled from a marble palace in Ravenna, built entirely in the Roman style, but this palace was peopled not only by Latin-speaking Italian courtiers, but also by moustached and Gothic-speaking barbarians who held on to their own heretical Christian faith. Within the capital at Ravenna, and within other towns with a substantial Gothic presence, there were rival churches and rival baptisteries, one celebrating the Catholic mass in Latin and the other the Arian mass in Gothic. Furthermore there was no doubting which of these groups, Latins and Goths, held military power, and therefore no doubting which held effective political power. Italy was certainly protected by the Goths, and some Italian aristocrats, like Cassiodorus, rose high and became rich in Gothic service; but, whatever the propaganda pretended, this was all a far cry from the days of the Republic and early Empire.

It is not therefore very surprising that some prominent and historically minded Italians seem to have dreamt of a return of empire, which by the sixth century, with no surviving native imperial dynasty in the West, would mean placing the then eastern (or Byzantine) emperor in control of Italy. When in the East Justinian, a man with both the drive and the ambition to 'reconquer' the western provinces, assumed power, first under his uncle Justin (518–27) and then in his own right (527–65), trouble inevitably followed in Italy. Even under the powerful rule of Theodoric, there were plots, or at least the suspicion of plots, and a bishop of Rome died in prison and two prominent senators suffered brutal execution—one of them, Boethius, writing the *Consolation of Philosophy* while languishing in a Gothic prison.

Boethius was one of the last of the long line of cultured Roman aristocrats, for whom knowledge of the classics was the highest mark of status, rather than the size of their war-horses or the strength of their right arms; and it is tempting to see his execution at the command of a Germanic king as symbolic of the stamping-out of classical culture at the hands of ignorant barbarians. However, this would scarcely be an accurate assessment, since it was in fact the Ostrogoths who, by their careful patronage of the Roman aristocracy, provided the conditions in which the cultured ease of men such as Boethius could flourish as late as the sixth century.

A Divided Peninsula: Byzantine and Lombard Italy, and the Emergence of the Papal State (535–774)

After Theodoric's death in 526 and following a successful and rapid reconquest of Africa, Justinian launched an invasion of Italy in 535. We are well informed about the war that followed, because amongst the staff of Belisarius, Justinian's principal general, was the great historian of the reign, Procopius. Unfortunately the Byzantine invasion of Italy, which like the Allied landings in 1943 began with a rapid take-over of Sicily and the south, similarly got bogged down around Naples, and then degenerated into a frustrating and slow war of attrition, fought principally through sieges. Only in 562, after a full twenty-seven years of war, did the last Gothic strongholds in the north surrender.

The main losers in the war were, of course, the Goths, who were deprived of all their power and privileges, much of their wealth, and many of their men in battle. However, the fighting also took a severe toll on the natives of Italy. Procopius summarized the consequences of the war with a story of three groups of ten pigs who were temporarily starved by a Gothic king in order to predict the outcome of Justinian's invasion: of the ten 'Gothic' pigs, all save two died, while of the 'Byzantine' pigs most survived. Of the 'Italian' pigs, however, only half survived, and these had lost all their bristles.

In theory, with the reconquest complete, Italy was back to normal—ruled by an orthodox Catholic Roman emperor. However, though it had not

·MAXIMIANVS·

MOSAIC of about 547, in San Vitale, Ravenna, showing the emperor Justinian, Archbishop Maximian of Ravenna, and male members of the court. The emperor is shown bearing a gift for San Vitale. Justinian never visited Italy, so the mosaic is symbolic, rather than a representation of a real event. It probably marked the dedication of the church, and the triumph of orthodox Catholicism in Italy (exemplified by archbishop and emperor standing shoulder-to-shoulder).

seemed so at the time, in comparison with Byzantine rule, the regime of Theodoric soon took on the appearance of a golden age. The new regime had no plans to move the capital of Empire back to Rome or Ravenna; and Italy, from being, if no longer the centre of Empire, at least a kingdom in its own right, now became a rather minor frontier province. The considerable taxes raised in Italy were now not spent in Ravenna and elsewhere in the peninsula, on lavish new buildings and the reward of Italian servants, but were sent to Constantinople, to be used principally in the defence of the Empire's eastern borders. Equally, the Byzantine emperors had no particular interest in courting the Italian aristocracy, whom they saw as their taxpaying subjects by right. Even the Church, which might have expected to benefit enormously from the reinstatement of orthodox rule, found it a mixed blessing. It is true that the Catholics gained from the confiscation of Arian churches and Arian church-lands; but, whereas the Ostrogoths had carefully left the Italian Catholic Church in peace in order to avoid stirring up any trouble, Byzantine rulers in Constantinople had no qualms about attempting to impose their particular interpretation of Orthodoxy on their new Italian subjects.

Nor was the new Byzantine regime able to give peace to Italy. In 568, only six years after the surrender of the last Gothic garrisons, the Lombards entered Italy from the north-east, and proceeded to conquer most of the Po Plain, and much of central and southern Italy as far as Benevento. The Byzantines, however, held on to much of the far south, including the rich island of Sicily, and to a strip of central and northern Italy between their capital Ravenna and Rome. Thus began a period of political fragmentation in the peninsula, which was to last until 1870.

The division of Italy into two main blocks of power created a situation of frequent warfare, and encouraged further political fragmentation: the Lombard kings of the north, ruling from their capital at Pavia, rarely had the strength to exercise effective political power in the central and southern Lombard duchies of Spoleto and Benevento; and, equally, the Byzantine exarch in Ravenna rarely had enough forces adequately to protect the far-flung outpost of Empire that Rome had become. Consequently the city was generally left to fend for itself.

The enforced self-sufficiency of Rome was extremely important for the development of the bishopric which we now call 'the Papacy'. Rome had to defend itself against frequent Lombard aggression through much of the sixth and seventh centuries, and the people of Rome and its duchy turned increasingly to their bishop to provide protection and sustenance. That it was the pope who emerged so early as leader of Rome and its territory is in fact surprising, because only a little earlier, in Ostrogothic times, there was definitely an alternative and much longer-established source of power in the city, the Senate, made up of rich Italian landowners and tracing its origins, of course, to the first days of the Republic. The Senate, however, apparently did not survive, as a political unit, the ravages and disruptions of the Gothic wars and the neglect of its privileges that followed the imposition of Byzantine rule: in 625–38 its seat, the Curia in the Forum, was transformed into a church. As we have seen, Alaric's sack of Rome in 410 was only the beginning of the end, but this conversion of the Curia must mark the definitive demise of classical antiquity in Italy. With the disappearance of the Senate, and in the absence of effective Byzantine control, like it or not, the bishop of Rome was the obvious person to look after both the spiritual and the temporal needs of his central Italian flock; and already in the time of Gregory the Great (590–604) the popes were feeding the city, negotiating peace-treaties, and paying troops in a manner familiar from later history.

It is not currently fashionable to defend papal temporal power, even in Catholic circles, but it is important to note that it did have its advantages, and that it was very important in the development of the Papacy as a European-wide institution. The bishop of Rome, of course, always had some very good cards in his hand: the name and traditions of the great city itself, and a superb array of local martyrs, including two of the best saints mentioned in Scripture,

Peter and Paul. Furthermore, in the case of Peter and in the tradition that he had been the first bishop of Rome, the popes also had Christ's powerful words in Matthew 16: 'thou art Peter, and upon this rock I will build my church . . . And I will give unto thee the keys of the kingdom of heaven'. Not for nothing is the first sentence of this grant written in huge mosaic letters around the inside of the Renaissance dome which crowns the present church of St Peter. However, in order to achieve its full stature, the Papacy also needed a degree of independence. If the pope had become a mere mouthpiece of Byzantine imperial policy, as the patriarch of Constantinople often was, or if he had become a bishop under Lombard royal control, it would have been much more difficult for him to exercise the wide spiritual authority that he did. On the one hand, the emergence of a central Italian papal principality involved future popes in much squalid politics, greatly to their detriment; but, on the other hand, it ensured the papal independence and autonomy which were vital to the stature of the institution. Sadly, one consequence did not come without the other.

At the same time as the papal principality was beginning to emerge, the popes were spreading their influence as wide as possible amongst the new barbarian peoples of Europe. In most of Europe at this date the pope counted for little: for instance, in all the records of the Church councils of sixth-century Gaul, there is only one very vague reference to papal primacy. But in one area, Britain, the popes achieved a notable success: the mission of Augustine, sent by Pope Gregory, which arrived in Kent in 597, was subsequently remembered by the English as the origin of their conversion from paganism; and this memory created a bond between the English Church and Rome which was to last until the Reformation.

The Lombard invasion of Italy is often seen as heralding a dark age for the peninsula, and it is certainly true that many scholars see the seventh century AD as something of a low point, with very little sign of wealth and very little sign of cultural achievement. However, to blame the Lombards specifically for this is probably wrong. There are reasons to believe that Italy had in fact been sliding slowly into greater poverty from as early as the second century AD, and there were probably other milestones along the route of this decline than the Lombard invasion, such as the loss of empire in the fifth century and the Byzantine war of reconquest in the sixth.

The Lombards were undoubtedly less bothered by the need to present themselves in a Roman manner than their Ostrogothic predecessors had been, and only occasionally did they dress their rule in an antique style. This makes them seem less civilized than the Ostrogoths; but the contrast is perhaps at least in part one of presentation rather than substance: by the end of the sixth century Italians had perhaps become accustomed to foreign domination, and even the Byzantines were abandoning some of the traditional

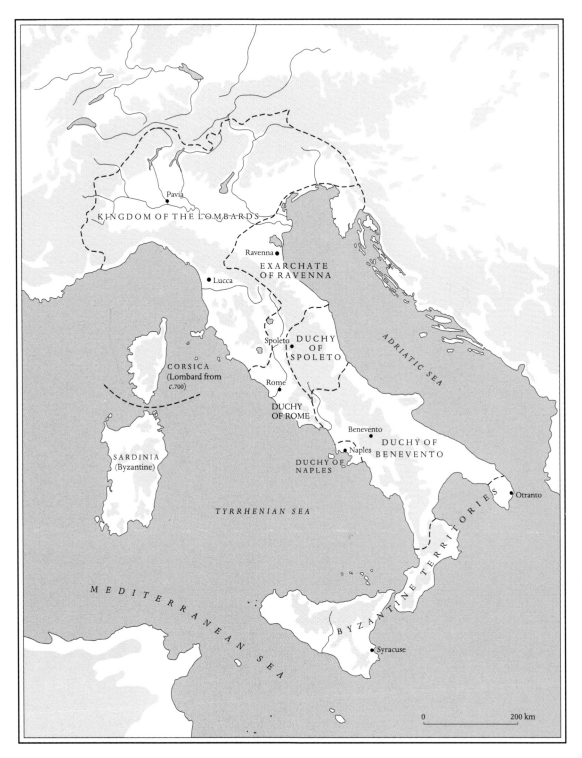

Pavia

KINGDOM OF THE LOMBARDS

Ravenna

EXARCHATE
OF RAVENNA

Lucca

CORSICA
(Lombard from
*c.*700)

Spoleto

DUCHY
OF
SPOLETO

ADRIATIC SEA

Rome

DUCHY
OF ROME

Benevento

SARDINIA
(Byzantine)

Naples

DUCHY OF
BENEVENTO

DUCHY OF
NAPLES

Otranto

TYRRHENIAN SEA

B Y Z A N T I N E   T E R R I T O R I E S

M E D I T E R R A N E A N   S E A

Syracuse

0   200 km

ITALY IN ABOUT AD 700

trappings of Roman rule. Making sure that one looked Roman possibly mattered less than it had before. If instead we take the use of written documents and the habit of living in towns as hallmarks of civilization, the Lombards were certainly much more civilized than their Germanic cousins north of the Alps: in eighth-century Lucca, for example, Lombard aristocrats were living in the town and endowing churches there, and making certain that these transactions were recorded for posterity in written charters, many of which they themselves signed.

It is also very important to note that it is not just in Italy that the seventh century represents something of a 'dark age': the same is true of most of northern Europe, and even true of Byzantium, where, in the face of Persian and then Arab attack, much that was characteristic of the high levels of civilization achieved in classical times disappeared for ever. Indeed, compared to other areas, Italy in the Lombard period may have been an exceptionally rich region, and may have seen unusual levels of continuity in some areas of life. For example, both the Lombards and the Byzantines in Italy never broke the tradition of government of the peninsula from its cities, which undoubtedly helped sustain town life. Though transformed and without any of the monumental trappings of classical urbanism, most towns in Italy never died. Parts of Byzantine Italy may indeed have been amongst the most prosperous and peaceful areas of the whole of Europe and the Mediterranean. In 663 the Emperor Constans II left Constantinople for Italy, and after visiting Rome and campaigning against the Lombards of Benevento, settled in Sicily at Syracuse. This experimental shift of capital did not survive Constans's murder in 668, and looks, with the benefit of hindsight, like an eccentric aberration by an emperor with poor judgement. But it was in fact sensible in the context of the seventh century; the entire Aegean region, including even Constantinople,

THE GILT-BRONZE EYE-PIECE of a helmet, known as the 'helmet of Agilulf'. Agilulf (590–616) was particularly keen amongst Lombard kings to present his power in a Roman style, rather in the manner of the earlier Ostrogoths. He is shown here seated on a throne, with the long hair and long beard from which the Lombards (*Langobardi*) derived their name, while Victories bearing standards usher in subjects with gifts. The scene is purely Roman in its iconography and Agilulf is given the Roman title 'D[ominus] N[oster] (Our Master)'.

was under threat from the Arabs, and southern Italy and Sicily were a small haven of prosperity and tranquillity.

The basic balance of power within Italy, between the Byzantine Empire and the Lombard kingdom and duchies, persisted into the eighth century, although the Lombards did make some significant territorial gains, taking Liguria in around 640 and Corsica in around 700. However, in 751 there was a spectacular change in the military and political shape of the peninsula, when the Lombard king Aistulf captured the capital of Byzantine Italy, Ravenna. Thereafter effective Byzantine control was restricted to Sicily and the south.

In this situation, with a powerful and growing Lombard kingdom to the north and no effective Byzantine force to act as a buffer or as an ally, the popes in Rome felt very exposed; there was every chance that the city and bishopric were finally going to disappear into the Lombard kingdom. Faced with this situation, the popes asked the dominant power north of the Alps, the Frankish Carolingians, to intervene in Italy on their behalf. In exchange for military help against the Lombards, the popes offered the Carolingian dynasty recognition and divine sanction for its coup against the previous Frankish royal

LUCCA, the Roman amphitheatre, adapted and built over by private houses to form an oval square (Piazza del Mercato). Much of the original structure survives under the modern plaster. Although many of the trappings of classical urbanism, such as entertainment buildings, were abandoned in the Middle Ages, life often continued in a new form as here.

house. In 754 Pope Stephen II travelled to Francia and anointed the Carolingian Pepin as king, and in the same year (and again in 756) Pepin campaigned in Italy, forcing the Lombards to renounce their gains in papal territories.

Conquests from North and South: The Frankish and Arab Invasions (774–962)

The 'Lombard question' was not, however, definitively solved until Pepin's successor Charlemagne intervened again in 773–4, this time capturing Pavia, deposing King Desiderius, and having himself crowned 'king of the Lombards'.

Charlemagne is, of course, a great uniting hero of European mythology, admired in France, Germany, Britain, and Italy alike, and in recent times his Empire has even been cast as an early version of the European Union (his capital and burial-place at Aachen is even conveniently close to Brussels). But from an Italian perspective, Frankish intervention was not necessarily a good thing, and it has certainly not always been seen as such. In the period of the Risorgimento, when papal alliances with great powers north of the Alps were again frustrating attempts to absorb Rome into an Italian kingdom, Charlemagne's alliance a thousand years earlier with the Papacy, and his consequent defeat of Lombard expansion into central Italy, could be portrayed as a clerical plot, forestalling an early attempt by Italy (under the Lombard Desiderius) to achieve its destined unity! Certainly, for the first time, but by no means for the last, the Po Plain and much of central Italy were conquered and absorbed into the empire of a great north European power. The military and political balance between the regions north and south of the Alps had definitively changed, away from the world of Caesar's legions imposing Rome's rule on the reluctant Gauls; and it was a change that persisted, being last manifested in the German occupation of northern Italy in 1943–5.

The events of 773–4 brought the northern half of the peninsula firmly into a north European political orbit. Further south, however, the Frankish invasion had much less effect. Byzantine control remained in Sicily and in Calabria and Apulia, and the eastern emperors also retained close links (if little effective power) in some duchies further to the north, centred on Naples, Gaeta, and, at the head of the Adriatic, the newly emergent town of Venice. The Lombards of Benevento too were unconquered by the Franks, and established in the late eighth and ninth centuries powerful principalities ruled from Benevento itself, from Salerno, and from Capua (which were not extinguished until the coming of the Normans in the eleventh century).

The elimination of Byzantine power in the north of Italy and the fact that the Franks never successfully extended their military and political control into the south were, in the long run, to prove very significant in the shaping of

Italy. Up until the mid-eighth century the political and cultural divisions criss-crossed both north and south: with Greek-speaking Byzantines in Ravenna, and in Sardinia, Apulia, Calabria, and Sicily, and Germanic Lombards spread along the peninsula from Benevento to Piedmont, including, from about 700, Corsica. But by the end of the eighth century new broad political zones had formed, which (as it happens) then had long histories, and therefore helped create distinct regional identities: a northern zone, at this date under Frankish control, and thereafter often affected by intervention from north of the Alps; a central block of papal territory and papal power; and a southern zone with close political and economic links to the East and to North Africa.

In destroying the Lombard kingdom, the Papacy had removed its traditional threat and its traditional enemy; but it had, of course, gained in the Franks an ally that was dangerously powerful. Successive popes attempted to clarify their relationship with their Frankish protectors in different ways—in particular by inventing, and asking the Franks to ratify, a famous medieval forgery, the 'Donation of Constantine', which was almost certainly concocted in the eighth century, but which claimed to be a massive grant of territory from the first Christian emperor, Constantine, to his contemporary, Pope Silvester. On Christmas Day 800 Pope Leo III tried to regularize the relationship of papal spiritual power and Frankish secular power by the revolutionary step of crowning Charlemagne in Rome as a new 'Roman emperor'. Leo's action was, at one level, a pragmatic and sensible expedient, recognizing the political realities of the end of the eighth century. But it was also to have long-term repercussions, since the rebirth of a western empire caught the imagination not only of contemporaries, but also of later generations, creating the idea that there might be a legitimate 'super-power' in Europe, and that the legitimation and destiny of that power were intimately linked to the Papacy. Subsequent armies from north of the Alps who sweated down to Rome in support of imperial claimants, only to die there of malaria, and generations of Italians who were to see their crops and livestock destroyed by these same troops, would not necessarily bless Leo for his bright idea.

In southern Italy, of far more importance than the imperial pretensions of some far-away northern king was the arrival of the Arabs. In the ninth century fleets and armies from North Africa gradually conquered from the Byzantines the whole of Sicily. It is easy from the viewpoint of the modern world to see Sicily as inevitably part of Christian Europe, with a vast political and cultural

MOSAIC set up in the dining-hall built by Leo III within the papal palace at Rome. It survives only in this eighteenth-century copy. The mosaic expressed Leo's vision of the correct ordering of the world: St Peter grants him a *pallium*, as a mark of spiritual authority, while giving victory and a lance to Charlemagne. Pope and emperor are as equal partners, with different roles to play, whereas later in the Middle Ages popes in their propaganda emphasized both their own temporal power and their superiority over emperors.

gap separating it from North Africa. That is how things turned out, and that is how the member states of the European Union currently wish them to remain. But geographically Sicily is close to the North African mainland, and in a Mediterranean world in which links by sea could be as strong as links by land (especially when the closest piece of the Italian mainland was the poor and mountainous region of Calabria), Sicily might easily have become permanently part of the Islamic world. In fact, two-and-a-half centuries later the Norman conquest absorbed it into a new and lasting south Italian Christian state; but not before many of its inhabitants had become Muslim and Arabic-speaking.

Arab raiders also brought substantial disruption in the ninth century to much of mainland southern Italy, in particular from fortified bases such as that which they established at the mouth of the Garigliano River to the north of Naples. In 846 they even sailed up the Tiber and sacked the extramural churches of Rome, probably scattering for ever the bones of the Apostles and martyrs. Nothing like it had ever happened before or ever happened again, since even the sacks of Rome of 410, 455, and 1527 were carried out by Christians who stole church treasures, but left the saints in peace. In northern Europe, we are used to thinking of Muslim expansion as at its greatest in the early eighth century, until checked by Charles Martel at the Battle of Poitiers in 732, or in the late seventeenth century, until checked by John Sobieski's relief of the Turkish siege of Vienna in 1683; but in Italy the high point of Arab and Muslim success undoubtedly came in around 900, with Sicily successfully absorbed and raids being launched even against some of the greatest cities of the peninsula.

Despite political and military disruption, the eighth and ninth centuries saw the gradual emergence in both northern and southern Italy of great trading-towns dependent on a newly flourishing Mediterranean trade. Of these settlements, the most famous is Venice, because of its long and glorious later history; but Venice in the ninth and tenth centuries was only one of a number of new or newly rich settlements: Venice, Bari, Amalfi, Salerno, Naples, Gaeta, Pisa, and Genoa. When a late tenth-century Arab geographer described the cities of Italy, it was Amalfi that he singled out for particular praise, as, of all the cities of Italy, 'the most prosperous, the most illustrious, the most affluent and the most opulent'.

Anyone who visits Amalfi today on its rocky peninsula, or Venice in its bleak lagoon (much more remote, of course, before the draining of the mainland, the building of the rail- and road-bridges, and the emergence of the horrors of Mestre), might wonder how isolated cities with such poor agricultural hinterlands could rise to great prominence and wealth; but from the ninth century a rich living could be made from trading on the seas, and remoteness and independence could even be a substantial advantage. Cities can become great by being tied to the fortunes of a powerful state, as in the cases of ancient Rome and its port of Ostia, or London and Paris in medieval Europe; but they can also become great by standing slightly at a distance from political power, serving a trading function for a number of different masters at once. The emergent Italian seaports of our period fit into this latter category, able to trade fruitfully and profitably between the different worlds of the Arabs, the Byzantines, the south Italian Lombards, and the Franks. Italy may have suffered politically in being parcelled up between different power blocks; but these divisions may have been a boon to Italian traders, who enjoyed considerable independence and stood at the geographical and cultural crossroads of the Mediterranean.

The basic pattern of politics in southern Italy in the second half of the ninth and the first half of the tenth centuries was broadly stable; though a pattern that involved Byzantines, Arabs, and Lombard Italians, and a plethora of

VENICE from the air. This photograph, of course, shows Venice in its fully developed glory. The original settlement was much more scattered, on low-lying islands on either side of one of the watercourses snaking through the lagoon (the later Grand Canal). One early focus of settlement was at 'Rivoalto', later Rialto (at the centre of the photograph, where the Rialto bridge crosses the Grand Canal); another was around the later church of San Pietro, in the top left of the photograph (near the Arsenal). Here early houses of drystone and wood have recently been excavated.

41

largely independent principalities and duchies, all jockeying for advantage, was, inevitably, in its detail, highly complex and ever-changing. In northern and central Italy, however, the underlying pattern was changing, with the break-up of the Kingdom of Italy that the Carolingians had inherited from their Lombard predecessors. In common with Carolingian power north of the Alps, the strong kingship of the beginning of the ninth century gradually degenerated into civil war between rival claimants of the throne, exacerbated by the intervention of foreign raiders—Arabs in the centre of the peninsula, and along the western Alps and Ligurian coastline from a base at Fraxinetum in Provence, and Magyar horsemen in the Po Plain, raiding from their base in modern Hungary. In these circumstances, the kings of Italy of the late ninth and early tenth centuries were forced to buy support from their nobles and their bishops with vast grants of lands and of rights over such things as control of city-walls, of tolls, and of taxes. As an astute contemporary observer noted, 'the Italians prefer to have two kings, so that they may keep one in check by threatening him with the other'. By 950 the whole of Italy, north and south, was characterized by a fragmentation of power into units of different sizes: some quite large, like the Byzantine 'catepanate' of the southern mainland or the northern marcher duchy of Ivrea, and others very small, like the duchies of Gaeta or Venice (the latter ruled by a *dux*, or duke, later to be called a 'doge').

Ottonian and Norman Intervention; and the Dispute between Empire and Papacy (961 to the Later Eleventh Century)

Events in northern Italy in the second half of the tenth century were dominated by the emergence of a new north European super-power, the Ottonian kings of Germany. Conscious of the divisions and weakness within the peninsula and aware of the illustrious precedent set by Charlemagne, Otto I invaded Italy in 951 and again, more decisively, in 961, on this occasion having himself crowned 'king of Italy'. In 962 he intervened in Rome in answer to a papal request for help; and, in return, was rewarded with the imperial crown.

Otto's intervention began a period of German imperial interests in Italy which lasted until 1250 and beyond. From the perspective both of the nineteenth- and early twentieth-century nation-state, and of the current European Federation, these warlike sallies are not particularly appreciated. In Italy they have been viewed as one more boorish period of north European domination; and in Germany as a foolish distraction into dangerous and unstable foreign adventure, away from the serious and necessary business of forging and maintaining a strong and united Germany. Otto, and his successors, of course, did not see things in quite these terms: for them, Italy was a rich and fruitful area to tax and exploit. Also, once claimed, Italy and the imperial crown became a dynastic birthright, and abandoning them would have been seen as a mark of weakness. It is often very difficult for powers to shed their privileges with dignity, even when they have obviously become a burden; as Britain is currently finding, with its expensive monarchy and its costly seat on the UN Security Council, both inherited from an age of empire.

German kings and emperors, like all rulers, had a highly evolved sense of their own rights; and, like all ninth- and tenth-century kings, they also felt a strong sense of duty towards the Church. Both characteristics of their rule almost inevitably led to direct intervention in papal affairs. The Papacy in the early tenth century had become enmeshed in the family politics of the city of Rome, sometimes to the obvious detriment of its prestige, as when one successful claimant of the Chair of Peter exhumed the body of his predecessor and rival, and solemnly put it on trial. The re-emergence of a powerful Christian emperor to the north once more encouraged imperial action in Rome, and raised the difficult and delicate question of the division between papal authority and imperial power. On a number of occasions between 963 and 1046, German emperors intervened in Roman affairs, effectively appointing several popes and occasionally deposing previous holders of the Papacy in the process. The reasons given for deposition were always moral (the corrupt behaviour of the incumbent); and in the tenth century we see the clear emergence of a northern view of Rome and the Papacy, that was to have a long history—a hotbed of Latin intrigue and corruption, repugnant to upright north

OTTO III receiving the tribute of his Empire, in a manuscript of *c*.997 produced at Reichenau. The regions of the Empire are personified, and identified (from the front) as 'Italia', 'Gallia' (the imperial lands west of the Rhine), 'Germania', and 'Sclavinia' (the new Slav conquests, east of the Elbe). This iconography of subjects bearing tribute derives from Roman prototypes, and 'Italia' is here given special prominence, as the leading personification; but, unlike its position of privilege in the original Roman Empire, Italy is now just one more province under the control of a north-European ruler.

MILAN
Pavia
Cremona
Venice

K I N G D O M   O F   I T A L Y

Genoa

Pisa

ADRIATIC SEA

'LANDS
OF
ST PETER'

Rome

Gaeta
Capua
Benevento
Bari

Naples
Salerno
BYZANTINE
TERRITORY

Amalfi

Otranto

TYRRHENIAN SEA

Palermo

SICILY
(Arab)

M E D I T E R R A N E A N   S E A

0   200 km

ITALY IN 1000 AD

Europeans. But there were also substantial political gains to be made by German rulers from having a compliant holder of the see of Peter. In this period, and in particular during the reign of Otto III (983–1002), who chose to reside for much of his reign in Rome itself, the Papacy came close to being a mere bishopric within the control of a great secular power.

However, in the second half of the eleventh century imperial control over the see of Peter, indeed secular power over any part of the Church, increasingly came to be challenged, as a broad movement in favour of reform in the Church influenced the whole of western Christendom. The main hope of this reform was to create a pure and isolated priesthood, untainted and untrammelled by ties of family, sex, money, or secular power. Inevitably the comfortable (if often entirely satisfactory) world of the Carolingian and Ottonian Churches came to be seen by the reformers as decadent, and far too closely enmeshed in secular life, since bishops (even popes) were often appointed by a king or emperor, and invariably received their insignia of office from him.

The Papacy was more or less bound to become centrally involved in this debate. The growth of the ideal of a separate Church, as opposed to a loose confederation of national Churches under local royal control, strengthened the existence of a separate and international ecclesiastical hierarchy of which the Papacy claimed to be the divinely ordained leader. In the second half of the eleventh century the popes issued decrees both in favour of their own primacy in the Church and against secular involvement in ecclesiastical affairs, in particular against the universal practice of rulers investing bishops with ring and staff as a mark of their office. Because high churchmen were also inevitably major figures of state and because their contribution to the power of the German Empire was particularly strong, this debate inevitably caused friction between Empire and Papacy. Under two strong and determined individuals, Pope Gregory VII (1073–85) and the Emperor Henry IV (1056–1106), disagreement spilled out into a lively polemical literature, and, indeed, into open warfare.

For the development of the Papacy, the open struggle with the emperors was a heroic phase, but not necessarily of the greatest significance, since the dispute ended in a compromise, whereby lay powers abandoned the symbolic gesture of investing bishops, but retained the all-important power of appointment. More significant for the long-term history of the Church, was the slow but seemingly inexorable process whereby it became accepted that the Church should have its own law (canon law), and that the papal court should be the ultimate arbiter of this law. Appeals to Rome from all over western Christendom increased steadily through the late eleventh and twelfth centuries, and turned the papal palace at Rome into a true court, or Curia, staffed by an army of officials.

Imperial authority was challenged not only in Rome, but also in northern

Italy during the eleventh century. Indeed, already in the tenth century, there are signs that the political ground was becoming unstable, and was unlikely to sustain for ever a strong unified state. The town-dwellers of the north, at first in coastal centres like Genoa and Venice, but then also in inland towns, like Milan and Bologna, became richer and richer during the tenth and eleventh centuries. Very slowly, this economic muscle was translated into autonomous political action.

The beginnings of the decline of royal power date back even to before the German intervention, to the prolonged civil wars between rival claimants to the crown of Italy in the first half of the tenth century: in Cremona, for example, one king in 916 granted the bishop the free exercise of very extensive powers and very profitable rights. The Ottonians were only able to reverse this process in part: because so much had already been given away by solemn legal charter, and because they were anyway happy to work through the bishops, as long as they were loyal. But what is remarkable in Italy, and separates the experience of the peninsula from that of most of Europe, is that power seeped away from royal control, not only to the level of aristocratic bishops and counts, but even further down the social scale, to the level of rich citizens and traders in the cities. The stages whereby this process occurred are never chronicled in detail, and only tantalizing hints survive in the evidence: in 996, for instance, the free citizens of Cremona briefly gained an imperial grant of privilege *against* the interests of their own bishop.

Episcopal power was still formidable in the eleventh century, as was imperial power (particularly when it was backed up by the presence of an army from Germany), but in certain towns, particularly on the coast and in the Po Plain, groups of citizens were beginning to act both autonomously and effectively. In 1024 the citizens of Pavia, in an action that has rightly been seen as symbolic of this shift in politics, burned down the royal and imperial palace of the city, which had served as the seat of the kings of Italy since Lombard times. The palace was never rebuilt, and, ironically, Pavia's new-found freedom soon led to the eclipse of its early medieval greatness, in favour of nearby Milan. Some coastal towns were already in the eleventh century turning their wealth and their maritime skills to successful military ventures overseas. The Pisans, in alliance with the Genoese, ousted a Muslim overlord of Sardinia in 1018, and brought the island under their joint hegemony; in 1062 they successfully raided Palermo, the greatest port and city of Arab Sicily, and returned laden with spoils; and in 1099, with other Italian cities, they played a role in helping the First Crusade to capture the Holy Land, but only in exchange for favourable trading-rights.

In the south of Italy, the appearance of the Ottonians also had an impact, since several German emperors launched serious attempts to extend their power to the foot of the peninsula. However, none of these efforts were in the

long term successful, and some came very badly unstuck. In 982 Otto II's expedition was defeated by disease and by the Arabs so seriously that the news sparked off a massive and successful revolt of his Slav subjects back on the frontiers of Saxony. Success in Italy brought wealth and prestige that could be deployed by emperors to increase their power in Germany; but failure could bring disaster.

More significant for the long-term development of the south was the appearance of the Normans, formidable military toughs, who, like their compatriots in England after 1066, were Viking in ancestry but French in language and culture (after a century of settlement in the north-west of France). The first Normans came to Italy at the very beginning of the eleventh century as mercenaries, hired to fight in the frequent wars between the independent princes of the south and the Byzantines. However, like Hengest and Horsa in fifth-century Britain, the Normans soon discovered that their considerable military power could be used against their paymasters, as well as in their support. Slowly but surely the Normans took over the south, eliminating not only the Lombard principalities and the independent duchies, but also the two 'foreign' powers, the Byzantines in Calabria and Apulia, and the Arabs in

PISA, the cathedral complex. The buildings date from the period of Pisa's greatest prosperity and power. The cathedral was begun in 1063, a year after the successful Pisan raid on Palermo, and completed at the end of the twelfth century. The baptistery was started in 1152, and the bell-tower (the famous 'Leaning Tower') in 1173. The cemetery (the 'Camposanto'), supposedly built around shiploads of soil from the Holy Land, was added at the end of the thirteenth century.

47

Sicily: in 1071 Bari, the last Byzantine stronghold in Apulia, fell and in 1072 Palermo, the greatest city of Arab Sicily, was captured.

The elimination of Byzantine and Arab power in Italy was, as it happens, definitive, and therefore highly significant, ensuring that all of Italy became firmly a part of western Christendom (which we now identify as Western Europe), speaking a Romance language derived from Latin (not Greek or Arabic), and identifying with the western Latin Church, rather than with Islam or Greek Orthodoxy. We have already seen how things might have turned out otherwise in Sicily in relation to nearby Islamic North Africa; but it is also necessary to stress the long-term importance for mainland southern Italy of the ending of Byzantine power. Parts of the peninsula, in particular Calabria and southern Apulia, were successfully ruled from Constantinople for more than 500 years, and, through trading ports like Otranto and the widespread foundation of Greek-speaking monasteries, were well integrated into the broader economic and cultural life of the Empire. The Norman conquest of the south ended Byzantine political domination, and thereby began a process in which many of the cultural and economic links were eventually broken.

For the popes in their central Italian principality, the emergence of a new and aggressive power in the south offered both possibilities and dangers. There was the chance to use the Normans as a counterweight to the might of the German emperors, perhaps in return for legitimizing upstart Norman rule; but, as ever, a new strong ally could prove unreliable and dangerous. One pope, who attempted to oppose the Normans, was soundly defeated in battle and captured in 1053; and another, who obtained a Norman alliance, nevertheless saw the city of Rome sacked and partly burnt by his allies in 1084. By the eleventh century, the Papal State was fully organized to raise taxes and field an army, so that the Papacy could not be brushed aside quite as dismissively as Stalin did during the Second World War, when he asked how many divisions the pope had under his command. But, in the Italian pond, the popes were, none the less, military minnows alongside the Norman and German pike. Survival and independence tended to depend on alliance with one or other of these bigger fish, and on persuading the ally of the moment that the tasty titbit of the Papal State contained enough of a skeleton of spiritual power and international prestige to promise severe indigestion.

Emperors, Popes, Kings, Lords, and Communes (from the Beginning of the Twelfth Century to the Death of Frederick II, 1250)

The very title of this section well illustrates the complexity of politics in twelfth- and thirteenth-century Italy: the peninsula offers case-studies of virtually every form of power to be found in medieval Europe, and, in the Papacy and Empire, institutions with international pretensions whose claims often

Facing: ROGER II OF SICILY depicts his new kingship as a direct gift of God, rather than as a papal grant, in this mosaic (1143–8), in Santa Maria dell' Ammiraglio (the Martorana, Palermo). The church of Santa Maria, like the Norman court, was cosmopolitan. Its founder was born to Greek parents in Syrian Antioch, and came to Roger's employ via Muslim North Africa; and it was originally served by Greek nuns. Greek craftsmen almost certainly made the mosaics, and Roger is shown in Byzantine court dress, and in a Byzantine iconographical schema. The inscription is in Greek letters, but the words 'Rogerios rex' are a mixture of a Norman name (in a Greek form) and a Latin title!

overlapped those of smaller powers. Broadly, however, the pattern of Italian politics remained that of the preceding period: with a southern zone, once Arab, Byzantine, and Lombard, and now Norman; a central papal state; and a northern zone (the former Kingdom of Italy), once Lombard, then Carolingian, and now part of the German Empire, but within which city-states were increasingly wielding autonomous power.

In the south, the Norman conquerors built up a new and powerful state. This was a gradual process, since their initial conquest had eliminated most external rivals but had left much power in the hands of cities and of great lords. However, particularly under Roger II, the new rulers extended their peace and their power over Sicily and the mainland, and in 1130 Roger celebrated his undoubted strength by obtaining papal recognition to raise his countship to a kingship. On Christmas Day 1130 Roger was crowned king of Sicily, Calabria, and Apulia in Palermo cathedral. The creation of a new kingdom, though seemingly less momentous than the creation of a new empire for Charlemagne exactly 330 years earlier, in fact proved more lasting. Although occasionally split between the mainland and Sicily, and often under foreign absentee rule, the Kingdom of Sicily survived, with very much the geographical boundaries it had in 1130, until its sudden and dramatic collapse in the face of Garibaldi's Thousand in 1860. As a result, the feeling that southern Italy includes Sicily, and that central and southern Italy 'rightly' divide somewhere between Rome and Naples is still very much a feature of Italian consciousness and Italian politics (whereas in the Roman period, for instance, the city of Rome had been very closely linked with Campania, the region around Naples).

The Norman dynasty ruled the south until ousted by the German imperial family of the north, the Hohenstaufen, in 1194. In 1197 Frederick II of Hohenstaufen succeeded to the throne aged only 3. Although Frederick was of German imperial blood through the male line, his mother was a south Italian Norman and he was brought up in Italy. Italy, not Germany, was his greatest concern right up to his death in 1250, and the south was home to him and his

Achim medic̃ · Reg̃ W̃ egt̃ás · aftrolog̃ · plačť eiů Reg̃ deficit' · cappella Regia

porta panormi · confeſ · et Baroneſ · Dũſ curie

THE ILLNESS AND DEATH of King William II of Sicily in 1189, from Peter of Eboli's *Liber ad honorem Augusti*. The people of Palermo and the nobles and courtiers of the kingdom weep to hear of William's death. Above, on the right, the dead king is laid out and mourned within the palace chapel; while on the left, shortly before his death, he is attended by an Arab astrologer and an Arab doctor, examining a urine sample, identified as 'Achim the doctor'.

family: his son Enzo, during a long imprisonment in Bologna, wrote a hauntingly beautiful poem in which he sends his song and his thoughts, not north, but south to Apulia, 'là dov'è lo mio core nott'e dia' ('there where my heart is night and day'). During Frederick's reign, the normal state of affairs within the Empire was for a time reversed: Italy was temporarily at its centre, and the lands north of the Alps were merely peripheral. Whether or not this was a good thing for Italy is disputable, since (as we shall see) being at the centre of Frederick's realm meant paying for his grandiose military ambitions.

Norman and Hohenstaufen rule in the Kingdom of Sicily (the 'Regno', as it came to be called) has attracted both scholarly and romantic attention: powerful and cultured kings from the north, ruling amidst the lemon-groves and pleasure gardens of Palermo, are the stuff of legend and of dreams. The Regno has been seen both as a cosmopolitan paradise, and as a remarkably powerful and 'modern' state. There is truth in both these images; but both can also be exaggerated. Certainly the Regno retained close cultural links with the Byzantine and Arab worlds in the twelfth century, and the Norman kings kept a Chancery that made records in three different languages— Latin, Greek, and Arabic. However, some of this cultural diversity was opportunistic (it was profitable to take over Greek and Arab methods of taxation) and temporary, since gradually through the twelfth century the court and administration were Latinized. Frederick II too is famous for his free thinking and his appreciation of Islamic culture; but he savagely repressed a Muslim revolt in Sicily, and deported the survivors to Apulia, where they were concentrated at Lucera and exploited for their tax-revenue and services. Frederick's Muslim bodyguard (who accompanied him to northern Italy, and even to Jerusalem on crusade) were certainly shocking to the rest of Christendom, which in this period was becoming increasingly intolerant of all difference of opinion; but they were probably more the playthings of an autocratic ruler who enjoyed the unease of his contemporaries, than a model for a modern multicultural State.

Norman and Hohenstaufen rule in the south was undoubtedly exceptionally efficient and seen to be so by contemporary rulers elsewhere: Henry II of

SAINT THEODORE PROTECTING PAVIA in a fresco of *c.*1525. Pavia displays both the remarkable continuity of Italian towns, and the great changes which took place within them. Roman are the checkerboard of streets and the arches of the bridge; while many of the churches were originally founded when the city was capital of the early medieval kingdom of Italy. The private towers are mainly thirteenth century, and are evidence of strife within the medieval commune. The castle in the background was erected in 1360–5, to hold down the city, by Pavia's new lords, the Visconti of Milan.

MOSAIC OF THE REIGN OF THEODORIC (493–526), in San Vitale, Ravenna, showing the façade of his palace. The building is entirely Roman in style, complete with Victories over each column. After the Byzantine conquest, the church was confiscated from the Arian Goths and rededicated to Catholic use. All traces of former heretical use were carefully removed, including here a row of mosaic figures (probably Ostrogothic courtiers) under the columns; but the new mosaicists left untouched on the columns some drapery and two hands (on the third column from the left, and the second from the right).

FOLLOWING THE ARAGONESE TAKEOVER in 1442, the Kingdom of Naples began a period of political and economic expansion. In 1464, when this panel was painted, an Angevin invasion had just been repulsed, Neapolitan naval power was growing rapidly, and the refurbished Castel Nuovo, here in the foreground, symbolized a new military strength.

England, for instance, accorded one 'Master Thomas Brown', a former servant of Roger II, the singular honour of keeping a separate record of the English Crown's financial office, the Exchequer. The rulers of the south, both in Norman times and under Frederick II, were also good at presenting their power in grandiloquent terms, borrowing for the purpose both from Byzantium and, particularly under Frederick, from ancient Rome. However, under the surface, the Regno remained like other medieval states: its stability depended ultimately on the political and military unity of its landed aristocracy, and it was occasionally rocked by revolt or seriously threatened by outside interference.

It is also probably true that the south paid a very heavy price for its grand kings and its political unity. Both the Normans and the Hohenstaufen eliminated all communal stirrings within the cities of the Regno, and exercised a powerful control over trade for royal profit. While cities in the north were ruled by aristocracies intimately involved in trade and manufacture, who often used military might to extend trading opportunities (as, for instance, the maritime cities did in exchange for helping the First Crusade), cities and merchants in the south were being milked by harsh taxation, to support royal courts and royal territorial ambitions.

During the twelfth and thirteenth centuries, the north achieved the economic *sorpasso* of the south, and relegated it to a position as a provider of food and raw materials for northern populations and northern industries. While Venice went from strength to strength, Amalfi gradually sank to being the pretty fishing-town that it remained until the era of mass tourism. The legacy of this change, which was at least in part due to strong Norman and Hohenstaufen rule in the Regno, is still very much with Italy today. As indeed are some possible broader consequences. In Italy, loose government, as in the twelfth- and thirteenth-century north and as in the modern post-war period, has tended to go with economic prosperity; while strong central government, as in the south, has tended to be associated with poverty. Modern Italians have found it very difficult to achieve a balance between an excessively powerful and self-aggrandizing state (as under Mussolini) and almost complete *laissez-faire*, with all the attendant dangers of corruption, faction, and environmental and social disintegration. One reason for the difficulty is that the two extremes were set up as rival patterns for Italian life already in the Middle Ages.

For the popes in central Italy, the delicate political balance of the twelfth century, between Normans in the south and German emperors in the north,

BUST from Frederick II's 'Capuan Gate', built in about 1240 and demolished in 1557. On the bridge that received the main traffic from the papal state into the Regno, Frederick built a great triumphal archway, decorated with sculpture in a heavily classicizing style, which was certainly designed to invoke the greatness of the first Roman Empire, and with inscriptions which strongly implied that the traveller would find better rule in the Regno than what he had left behind!

FRESCO of the mid-thirteenth century, showing the Emperor Constantine (312–34) respectfully, and on foot, leading into Rome the mounted Pope Silvester. The fresco supported a papal view of the ideal relationship of Empire and Papacy, and papal claims to a grant of lands, supposedly made by Constantine after his conversion by Silvester. In 1155 the Emperor Frederick Barbarossa understandably protested at being expected to perform this same menial service for the pope who was to crown him.

was rudely upset by the successful seizure of the Regno by an emperor, Henry VI, in 1194, and by the determination of his son Frederick II to assert effective control over old imperial claims in central and northern Italy. The Papacy and the papal lands again risked being absorbed into a single powerful imperial state. Popes and Hohenstaufen inevitably became locked in a bitter war which was to end, only after our period, in the elimination of the latter.

The Papacy has always been a curious institution, and most of its oddest features are clearly apparent by the twelfth and thirteenth centuries. At one level, it was a grand international body whose power rested wholly on its ideological claim to be the primary see of the Church. This claim was ignored in the Byzantine world, but brought western clerics to Rome in increasing numbers during the twelfth century, so that the city thrived as an international ecclesiastical capital. At its most elevated, this success made the Papacy and Rome the true spiritual leaders of the Church, exemplified by Innocent III's great reforming Council of the Lateran in 1215, attended by over 400 bishops. But at another level, success sunk the Papacy and the Curia into the process of dealing with hundreds of legal appeals to Rome from all over the western Church. To become pope, it became increasingly necessary to have a training in the law, and Rome came to be viewed by those who petitioned it (in particular the unsuccessful) as yet another venal court, where money spoke, rather than truth: 'if you bring nothing in hand . . . then out you will go.'

But, while acting (for better or worse) on a grand international stage, popes were also princelings in central Italy, whose hold on power was greatly complicated by the fact that, for obvious reasons, they were unable to set up stable dynastic succession. Control of the Papacy was bitterly fought over by the rival families and factions of Rome, who stood to gain or lose considerably from the outcome. Innocent III (1198–1216) was a great pope, trained in canon law, the patron of Francis of Assisi, and the driving force behind the Fourth Lateran Council; but he was also by birth Lothar of the house of the counts of Segni, and he did not hesitate to advance his brother during his pontificate. The papal position has always contained the paradox (which is both its great strength and its great weakness) that the 'Successor of Peter' is an ordinary mortal, operating within the political constraints of his time and often with understandable concerns of his own, whether he be a medieval Italian aristocrat or a modern right-wing Pole.

In the north, the twelfth and thirteenth centuries are marked by the steady growth of the communes, and by two great periods of warfare against German emperors who sought to impose their wills on the cities, Frederick I 'Barbarossa' ('Red Beard') between 1154 and 1183, and Frederick II between 1226 and 1250. By the beginning of the twelfth century, most northern cities were not only independent, but had regularized their rule under a new form of government, the consulate. Although great rural lordships survived in many areas of Italy, such as the Veneto, during the twelfth century each commune continued a process of pacifying its *contado*, the countryside and settlements around, and of bringing it under effective rule.

In the case of the greater cities, their power extended even beyond the immediate *contado*. Venice, for instance, in 1203–4 successfully managed to divert the Fourth Crusade into first capturing the rival city of Zadar (Zara) on the Dalmatian coast, and then Constantinople itself. In an action which exemplifies the steady rise of western economic and military power from the eleventh century, Venice, once a remote duchy of the Byzantine Empire, now seized its very capital. Inland Milan's power had grown sufficiently by the mid-twelfth century to be perceived initially by some neighbouring towns as a greater threat than Barbarossa himself; one German chronicler noted with some surprise the bitter feelings of the Cremonesi and the Pavesi towards the people of Milan. As later in Italian history, strength of local feeling and local identity already had its negative side in fear and dislike of the outsider.

There are already in the twelfth century clear signs that Italy was not only breaking down into alliances of rival city-states, but that rivalry and faction were reaching into the individual cities themselves. In 1160 a Jewish traveller, Benjamin of Tudela, recorded in detail the tower-warfare that periodically broke out within the city of Genoa. The only thing that could bring any temporary unity to the north was a sustained threat from outside, as occurred under both Barbarossa and Frederick II. In 1167 a group of northern cities, including some former enemies, created the Lombard League. In 1176 the League imposed a crushing defeat on Barbarossa at Legnano. Although the enemy has changed in the twentieth century into the taxing bureaucrats of Rome, it is not surprising that the present-day symbol of the Lega Lombarda-Lega Nord is a twelfth-century knight, sword proudly raised to defend the honour and independence of the north.

What defeated Barbarossa and frustrated Frederick II, despite the enormous power of Germany and of the Regno, was temporary unity (which fell apart as soon as the imperial threat receded), and the sheer number and wealth of independently minded cities that were able to turn their money into new defences and into armed men. Northern Italy had become hydra-like: as soon as one dissenting head was lopped off, more grew in its place. Whereas in the south it was difficult, but possible, for a new dynasty to take over the kingship of another, as happened in 1194 (and later in 1266), in the extreme fragmentation of the north, success in one area prompted even greater resistance elsewhere.

The wealth and urban character of Italy is also manifested in the greatest religious movement of the Italian Middle Ages. It may at first seem strange that Francesco Bernardone, the son of a rich Assisi merchant, whom we know as St Francis, attracted through his love of Lady Poverty an immediate following amongst both the wealthy and the poor of Italy. But his attitude and his popularity, in fact, make particular sense in a society that was newly rich; just as our Green conscience makes sense in the context of our own system-

RELIEFS from two of the gates (Porta Romana and Porta Tosa), built by the Milanese in *c.*1171. When the Milanese re-occupied and refortified their city, after Frederick Barbarossa had partially demolished it in 1162, they decorated the new gates with commemorative sculpture. One scene (*below, right*) shows the triumphal re-entry of the Milanese and their allies. The female figure (*left*) is perhaps a caricature of the Empress (she is shearing her pubic hair). The Milanese had particular reason to loathe her, since for her benefit their humiliating ceremony of capitulation in 1162 was performed a second time.

atic destruction of the environment. The mission of the Order which he founded, the Franciscans, evolved to fill a gap that economic and social change had opened in Italy: to preach to the citizens of the burgeoning cities, and to assuage the consciences of the rich, by providing a means for them to buy Poverty through patronage of the Order. The paradox that ensued, of an Order dedicated to poverty attracting fabulous wealth, tore the Franciscans apart in the latter half of the thirteenth century, but is also testimony to the success and power of Francis's message.

A Postscript: The 'Middle Ages'

The concept of a 'middle age' was invented by Florentine humanists, in order to pass over the period of about a thousand years that lay between the glories of Rome and their own 'renaissance', a period in which very little happened, most of it bad. The pattern of this book, except for its brief treatment of ancient Rome, is much in the humanist tradition: one chapter for a short political outline of the 850 years from 400 to 1250, and then dual chapters, covering culture and politics over much briefer time-spans. It is as though serious events and intellectual, literary, and artistic achievement only really began with the rise of Florence and with the birth of proto-Renaissance luminaries like Giotto and Dante.

I am as guilty as anyone for this schema, since I agreed to cover the 'Middle Ages'. But it is not a satisfactory one. It ignores, perforce, the cultural achieve-

FRANCIS was a master of dramatic gestures and visual tableaux, and, unsurprisingly, representations of these played an important part in his cult. Even in early depictions, such as this mid-thirteenth-century altarpiece, the visual image and iconography were somewhat toned down. Despite his dread of material possessions, he is shown in a freshly laundered habit holding a bible; and amongst the scenes arranged around him, there is no representation of how he shared a bowl of food (and bloody pus) with a leper, nor of how he lay dying stark naked on the bare earth.

ments of Ostrogothic Italy; the sixth-century churches of Ravenna; the *Rule* of Benedict and the *Dialogues* and *Pastoral Care* of Gregory the Great; the eighth-century frescoes of Castelseprio; the ninth-century mosaics of Rome; the great Romanesque churches of Pisa, Venice, and Monreale; the medical school at Salerno; the jurists of Bologna; the rise of vernacular poetry; and even Thomas Aquinas.

What is more, it makes the one thing I have been able to cover, the essential political developments, seem like a mere prelude to the 'real' things that happened after. Only for Florence, which was a 'late developer' and whose greatest period of economic and political power really did begin in roughly 1250, does the medieval periodization of this book work well. It does not work for the south, where it was the eleventh-century elimination of Byzantine and Arab control and the twelfth-century creation of a new kingdom which were the essential elements in shaping the region. Nor will it work for Rome, where the centuries between the sixth and the twelfth were the crucial ones in the formation of the Papacy. Nor, indeed, will it work for the Po Plain, where the greatness and independence of cities like Milan and Venice were firmly established by 1150, and were soon to be crowned by successful wars against the Christian World's two empires. Nor, even, will it work for the whole of Tuscany; since, from the perspective of towns like Pisa, 1250 and the rise of Florence mark the end of their period of greatest power and prosperity.

By 1250 the basic shape of Italy had been established: a highly urbanized, politically fragmented, and very rich north, periodically threatened by powers from beyond the Alps; a central papal state, ruled by a prince who was also the head of the international Church, and who had successfully asserted his independence from the Empire; and a powerful, but less wealthy, southern kingdom which had reversed the balance of power with its former masters in the Byzantine East and Arab North Africa. It is obviously a matter of taste whether one sees these developments as the foundations for what happened after, or whether one sees events after 1250 as an interesting appendix to what had come before!

✣ 3 ✣

POLITICS AND SOCIETY
1250–1600

MICHAEL MALLETT

Political disunity is often seen as the most significant characteristic of
Renaissance Italy and the ultimate cause of the declining importance of
the peninsula in the early modern period. But in introducing the topic of politics and society in Italy in these centuries one needs to have in mind some very
clear reservations about this traditional preoccupation with disunity. In the
first place, historians of the western monarchies, of France, England, and
Spain, in this period have placed much more emphasis in recent years on the
lack of unity in their own areas, on continuing regionalism and localism, on
poor communications, on the ineffectiveness of central authority. Furthermore, the political history of Italy in the Renaissance is increasingly one of
assimilations and alliances—often of a long-term nature. The transition from
city-state to territorial or regional state has been a major area of interest to historians in recent years; one that can produce its own exaggerations but which
has fundamentally altered our perception of the political map of Italy.
Thirdly, it is possible to perceive in Italy in this period a greater degree of
social than political unity. A sense of community as Italians, a growing
together of social groups across political divides, these are insistent features of
the experience of the peninsula by 1500.

It is true, of course, that the fundamental disunity of Italy is that between
north and south. It is equally true that a major explanation of the cultural
vibrancy and authority of Renaissance Italy lies in the strength of local political autonomy. Cultural competitiveness between cities, states, and courts
was an important stimulus to artistic and literary creativity, which at the same
time contributed to the sense of superiority towards barbarian ultramontanes
which Italians shared.

A final issue which will be explored in this chapter is the role of the Papacy
and the Church in Italy. Papal domination and interference in the political
affairs of the peninsula has often been seen as one of the principal causes of
Italy's political problems. The period from 1250 to 1600 saw the position of the
pope change from dominant overlord in matters both political and spiritual,

to prominent political presence with some slight moral advantage over the rival Italian states, to, finally, a return to more spiritual preoccupations and a certain detachment from the Italian political scene in the years of the Catholic Reformation.

Popes and Communes in the Thirteenth Century

Two powerful and unique movements dictated the course of Italian history in the thirteenth century: the emergence of wealthy and populous city-states, and a new spiritual fervour and preoccupation with religious issues linked in part to the activity of the new mendicant orders. The fact that the first of these movements was fundamentally temporal in its emphasis, while the second was directed by the Church, even if the spiritual yearnings were essentially popular, suggests inevitable contradictions. They were the contradictions of the age of Dante: wide-ranging idealism confronted by small-minded fac- tiousness, inventiveness by cynicism, the worldly wise by the visionary critics and upholders of the Church. At the same time the movements were mutu- ally supportive; the cities provided political support for popes in Guelph alliances, and were the main fields of action for the Franciscans and Domini- cans as they wrestled with the problems of poverty, urban overcrowding, and heresy.

The death of the Holy Roman Emperor Frederick II in 1250 was a decisive moment in the papal–imperial confrontation. Initially supported by Innocent III because of his youth and potential position of dependence, Frederick proved to be the most powerful of emperors, committing himself to the dom- ination of southern Italy as well as of Germany. By doing this he shifted atten- tion from the ideological issues which had dominated the confrontation for two centuries to practical political control in Italy. The death of Frederick left the intensely bureaucratic and centralized Kingdom of Sicily in the hands of his illegitimate son Manfred, who, without imperial title and German re- sources, gradually succumbed to baronial rebellion and papal pressure. The key to the destruction of Hohenstaufen power in southern Italy was the inter- vention, on papal invitation, of the Angevin house. Charles of Anjou, younger brother of Louis IX of France, defeated and killed Manfred at the Battle of Ben- evento (1266) and finally dislodged the Hohenstaufen following his victory at Tagliacozzo (1268) and the capture and execution of Manfred's son Conradin. For an uneasy period the combined Kingdom of Sicily survived under Angevin rule. The 40,000 florin annuity demanded from Charles by the popes in recognition of papal feudal rights in the kingdom, and the huge profits extracted by Florentine and Genoese merchants and bankers from a virtual monopoly of Sicilian and Neapolitan markets, began a long decline of the economy of the south. They also fostered disillusionment with the Angevin regime and the violent rebellion of the Sicilian Vespers (1282). The Sicilian barons invited Peter of Aragon to take over the island, and the battle-lines for a long-term Franco-Hispanic confrontation for control of the central Mediterranean were now drawn.

To the north of the troubled Kingdom of Sicily the popes had not been relying entirely on their Angevin allies to resolve their political problems. The second half of the thirteenth century saw an increasing coherence and control established within the areas of central Italy roughly defined by the various 'donations' of early medieval emperors. The Papal State emerged not as an extension of authority by a dominant city, but as a series of negotiations, grants of privilege, and applications of papal pressure in an area of tense rivalries and confused political authority. Papal bureaucrats worked tirelessly, calling local parliaments, making deals with key cities and nobles, and dividing the area into administrative provinces. The geography of the new state was against them, split as it was by the Apennines, but by 1300 there was in place a system of administration which depended heavily on the Camera Apostolica in Rome but was also a patchwork of local alliances.

The death of Frederick also removed the threat of effective imperial intervention in the affairs of northern and central Italy. For more than thirty years the emperor had both given encouragement to local lordlings like Ezzelino da Romano to create ministates in Lombardy, and involuntarily induced a certain local unity by inspiring new Lombard Leagues of cities to oppose his authority. The vacuum created by the death of Frederick and the long-drawn-out uncertainty about the imperial succession allowed a return to the more normal fragmentation of city-state politics.

By 1300 twenty-three cities in northern and central Italy had populations of over 20,000, and as many as four hundred claimed a degree of political autonomy; that autonomy is often seen as the principal characteristic of these city-states. However, their political and social development was crucially conditioned by differing economic functions. The cities fell into three broad categories: major commercial centres, usually with port facilities, dominated by basically mercantile élites; large-scale industrial centres, producing commodities for export, and therefore including a strong industrial entrepreneurial element in their dominant groups; and cities which were essentially

ARNOLFO DI CAMBIO'S powerful statue portrays Charles of Anjou, younger brother of King Louis IX of France, who conquered the Sicilian kingdom in 1266 at the invitation of the Papacy and thus founded the Angevin dynasty in southern Italy. He was the architect and inspirer of the Guelph alliance until his death in 1285.

59

MILAN •   Brescia •

Pavia •   • Cremona   Padua • Venice •

Genoa •

Bologna •

Prato •
Pisa •   • Florence

Siena •

THE PAPAL STATE

Assisi •

Tagliacozzo •
Rome •

ADRIATIC SEA

Benevento •

Naples •   **KINGDOM**
Salerno •   **OF**   APULIA
Amalfi •   **SICILY**

CALABRIA

TYRRHENIAN SEA

MEDITERRANEAN SEA

Palermo •

0   200 km

ITALY IN ABOUT 1250

local market centres where landed interests operated alongside small mercantile and industrial groups. Venice, Genoa, and to a lesser extent Pisa, were obvious examples of the first category; Milan as an inland commercial centre, with an active river-port and a strong industrial base, was something of a hybrid; while Florence was primarily an industrial centre although strong mercantile and banking interests developed as part of the industrial structure. The distinction between these cities and the smaller centres was as much one of function as of size, although to emphasize either distinction too much can mislead. Brescia and Prato, for example, while coming into the category of smaller cities and having a prime function as local market centres, produced arms and cloth respectively for international markets.

By 1250 the map of communal Italy was fully drawn. Political autonomy had been claimed, and largely recognized, as imperial and episcopal authority declined. All the communes had developed systems of rapid circulation of executive office amongst a citizen élite, with judicial functions and the maintenance of law and order in the hands of a foreign official (the *podestà*) and foreign judges invited in for strictly limited terms of office. They had experimented with large councils and with smaller councils to enable the executive to seek advice and establish consensus. They had drawn up rules of citizenship which conferred privilege and rights of participation in public affairs on long-term residents and property-owners. They had encouraged the growth of guilds to defend the interests of individual crafts, and imposed limits on the number of members of any particular guild or family who could hold office or sit on councils at the same time. They had developed bureaucracies for the day-to-day administration of the cities, and militias of citizens for the defence of the walls and the keeping of the gates. The institutions of the city-state had become immensely sophisticated by contemporary standards. Literacy, legal expertise, record-keeping, and oratory were the skills in demand in the market-places and the council-chambers. But if the urban world of later thirteenth-century Italy was the focus of new ideas and new attitudes, this should not suggest either that the problems of the expanding urban societies had been resolved or that those societies had separated themselves entirely from the old rural and courtly world.

The cities were dependent on the countryside for food supplies, for industrial labour, and for raw materials; control of the hinterland meant control of local markets, of commercial routes, and of defence installations. Equally important was control of, or at least accommodation with, the rural nobility. The élites of the cities in the early stages of their development were largely made up of landowners; the new rich rapidly acquired land and aped the lifestyle of their more established neighbours; but in the more aggressively commercial societies the *rentier* class became suspect and tended to be excluded from public affairs. At the same time waves of immigration and expanding economic interests brought forward new families to challenge those established in power. In many cities the challenge took the form of rival institutions to those of the commune, the creation of a *popolo* with its own captain and officials and its own council. In all cities the result of these socio-economic trends was violent faction as families with similar interests grouped together in informal political and social alliances and built up support among their dependents. While some of the cities, particularly those with a large industrial sector, experienced real class friction, the damaging rivalries, particularly in the later thirteenth century, were between groups of the urban élite.

If internal rivalries were tearing the urban societies apart in the late thirteenth century, another process, that of amalgamation of cities through alliance or conquest, was in full swing. An urge to expand, to extend the *contado* and cripple or subdue neighbouring rivals, was an inevitable characteristic of the city-state. Rivalries between cities could both exacerbate and distract from internal rivalries. However, generalizations about the political development of Italian city-states are difficult to sustain, and at the same time the laying-out of particular examples tends to confuse rather than enlighten. That said, it is possible to identify a key period in the history of many of these cities in the last two decades of the thirteenth century. At that point the dominance of a more traditional élite in some cities began to point towards dominance of a particular family, and indeed of a particular leader; i.e. *signoria*. On the other hand dominance by a wealthy new élite, a *popolo*, produced a determination to exclude the traditional families from political participation, and the creation of a more or less closed oligarchy of merchants, bankers, and entrepreneurs. The establishment of the government of the Nine in Siena in 1287, the creation of the Florentine priorate and the Ordinances of Justice of 1293, and the closing of the Great Council in 1297 in Venice, were all examples of this sort of development. Each led to a long-term survival of republican institutions. On the other hand the triumphal return of Ottone Visconti to Milan in 1277, having defeated the popular faction, and Obizzo d'Este's suppression of the guilds in Ferrara in 1287, were decisive moments in the development of *signoria* in these cities. An exception to this particular generalization was the case of Padua where in 1318 Jacopo da Carrara, a leader of the popular Guelph party, was installed as captain-general in perpetuity with the consent of the nobility, in response to a grave external crisis. The extent to which this apparent turning-point in the history of the Italian city-states was linked to the beginning of an economic downturn is a question to which we must now turn.

The Problems of the Fourteenth Century

The calamities of the fourteenth century have become something of a cliché of late medieval European history; the Hundred Years War, the Black Death, the 'economic depression of the Renaissance', and the 'closing of the European frontier' are all components of a concept of a European crisis which seems to mark a dividing-line between the Middle Ages and the modern world. Like Fernand Braudel's 'long sixteenth century' the 'calamitous fourteenth century' is also seen to embrace much of the fifteenth century. However, the Italian Renaissance was firmly rooted in the fourteenth century, the century of Dante, Petrarch, and Boccaccio, of Giotto, Ambrogio Lorenzetti, and Simone Martini. It was a century of changing fortunes, periodically disastrous for some, but, particularly towards the end of the century, with strong signs of a general trend towards a well-ordered, prosperous, and positive lifestyle.

Unique to Italy in the fourteenth century was the degree of apparent political confusion. Naples and the Papal State experienced particular turmoil for reasons to which we shall return. However, it was the fate of the city-states which has particularly attracted the attention of historians. The development of *signoria*, often translated into English as 'despotism', has been seen as a retrograde step from the increasingly ordered and free life of the thirteenth-century city-republics. Arbitrary tyranny in the interests of the few replaced consensus in the interests of the many, with inevitable resistance, violence, exilings, and degradations. This black and white picture has been subjected to much criticism in recent years. *Signoria* was normally the outcome of a gradual breakdown of communal institutions; it was preceded by a narrowing of the power base in the city concerned and a growth of factional violence; it was in some respects a natural process, particularly in a small city with a traditional landowning élite. It was also a very gradual process; there were few coups or dramatic take-overs; there was little immediate violence. In widely differing circumstances an obvious leader was offered particular authority—often as *podestà* or *capitano del popolo*—for a limited period. If successful the period was extended, the powers marginally increased. The *signore* grew into his role and worked to preserve it; he cultivated support and honoured the republican institutions. Membership of traditional councils remained, alongside the growing importance of the favour of the *signore*, as indication of belonging to the city's élite. By the end of the century legitimization through the acquisition of imperial or papal title, and through the evolution of hereditary rights to his authority, were the aims of the *signore*. There were, of course, violent and arbitrary moments, just as there were such moments in the lives of the surviving republics. The Council of Ten in Venice, set up in the early fourteenth century to detect and prevent seditious conspiracies, and the Otto di Guardia, the internal security committee created by the Florentine republic, had more arbitrary power than a *signore*. The doge, appointed for life, in Venice and Genoa was a form of *signoria*. With little formal power, but immense informal influence, the doge provided continuity and experience as the new officials of the republic changed round. Florence lacked such a figure; the Gonfalonier of Justice changed, like his eight priors, every two months. Florence experimented with *signoria* twice during the fourteenth century but on each occasion drew back and reinstated a republican regime. It is at least arguable that the city went through more political turmoil and uncertainty in the middle years of the century as a result of these decisions, even if it is equally arguable that its eventual cultural dominance owed something to its continued long-term republicanism.

Thus, the political confusion which plagued northern and central Italy in the middle decades of the century owed little to signorial rule in itself. The problem continued to lie more in the fragmented political world, the rivalries between cities, and particularly the emergence of the appropriate military means to advance those rivalries. Errant mercenary companies began to make a significant appearance on to the scene in the thirteenth century. The cities, turning their attention to expansion and aggression against their neighbours and reluctant to use their urban militias in such an offensive role, proved to be ready employers of companies of hardened soldiers, both Italian and ultramontane, which began to assemble in the peninsula. The Italian expedition of the Emperor Henry VII (1312–13) was more significant for the numbers of German troops who remained as mercenaries after his departure than for the immediate political implications of the expedition itself. French companies aiming to reach the Angevin south, Catalans returning from the settlements in the Balkans, French and English bands released from the Hundred Years War after the Peace of Brétigny (1360), and Hungarians following their king in his attempt to assert rights in Naples—all added to a constant flow of Germans, to fill the ranks of the great companies which took advantage of the unsettled state of Italy in the years before 1370. The companies of this period were by no means made up entirely of foreigners; dispossessed Italian feudal nobility and urban exile groups contributed significantly to the numbers and to leadership. Nor were the companies entirely to blame for the atmosphere of infidelity and licence which prevailed as they moved rapidly from one employment to another, and from one devastated *contado* to another. Short-term contracts were devised primarily by the employing states which had no wish to pay the costs for longer than necessary, and the devastation of a neighbour's territory was always part of an official war strategy. Nevertheless, the companies were a scourge to the countryside and a drain on the purses of the citizens.

HENRY VII OF LUXEMBURG was crowned Holy Roman Emperor in San Giovanni Laterano in Rome in 1312 by cardinals in the absence of the pope, Clement V, in Avignon. The ceremonies in Rome followed one of the last major interventions by a medieval Emperor in Italy with Henry's participation in the Guelph–Ghibelline wars in Lombardy and Tuscany.

It was not just the city-states which were bullied, blackmailed, and occasionally assisted by the companies. The source of much of the political confusion lay to the south, just as did some of the main recruiting areas and many of the richest rewards. The death of Robert of Anjou, king of Naples, in 1343 was the beginning of serious problems for the Angevin dynasty. Robert, by dint of careful economic measures, had succeeded in reducing the royal debts to manageable proportions, and thus limiting the interference of the popes, his principal creditors. He was aided in this, of course, by the absence of the Avignon Papacy from Rome, and its Francophile affiliations. But neither of these factors could save his daughter Joanna I (1343–82) from a series of challenges to her rule. Rival Angevin claimants, the hostility of the Aragonese in Sicily, and eventually a challenge from the Anjou-Durazzo rulers of Hungary troubled her reign. The queen and her husband, Louis of Taranto, were excommunicated in 1355 by Innocent VI for non-payment of the annuity owed to the pope. However, the main cause of the financial stress was not so much economic weakness or decline, as a preoccupation with military strength to safeguard the dynasty. The great baronial families, which provided the armies, were courted by the Angevins rather than the cities which might have provided the wealth. This commitment to a semi-feudal structure was to have long-term consequences for the kingdom.

The absence of authority during the residence of the popes in Avignon had a greater effect in Rome itself than in the Papal State as a whole. During the thirteenth century the economy and life of the city had come to rely more and

THE PALAZZO PUBBLICO in Siena was decorated in the fourteenth century with a series of patriotic scenes depicting the successes of Sienese governments and armies. This fresco by Lippo Vanni celebrates the victory of the Sienese over the mercenary Compagnia del Capello led by Niccolò da Montefeltro at Sinalunga in 1363.

more on the presence of the fast-growing papal court and its satellite institutions. With the departure of the popes the powerful baronial families of the Colonna and the Orsini, Savelli, and Conti, which had extended their activity far into the surrounding countryside, reasserted control. Their feuding provoked a brief popular reaction in the early 1350s when the inspirational figure of Cola di Rienzo emerged to lead a communal revival. But Rome lacked any significant economic élite that might have backed a permanent restraint on noble power or sustained a popular *signoria*, and Cola's regime collapsed. However, elsewhere in the Papal State papal officials, directed from Avignon, continued to try and maintain order. Cardinal Gil Albornoz, plentifully funded from Avignon, used a combination of force and persuasion to gain acceptance of the Egidian Constitutions in 1357 which were to form the framework of the administration of the Papal State for four centuries. A part of this achievement was the creation of vicariates for the *signori* of the Romagna cities, providing them with titles as papal vicars in return for payment of census and obligations of obedience. However, a part of Albornoz's success lay in the fact that many of these lordlings, like the Malatesta of Rimini and the Ordelaffi of Forlì, were military figures who derived their income from and directed their attention to the more lucrative worlds of Lombardy and Tuscany.

In the last three decades of the century there were significant moves towards greater political control and continuity. The return of the papal court from Avignon in 1377 was in fact the least significant of such moves, as the Great Schism which followed the election of the Italian pope Urban VI in 1378 divided papal resources and distracted papal government. Nor did the accession of Ladislas I of the Anjou-Durazzo line to the throne of Naples in 1386 immediately resolve the problems of the kingdom as he was only twelve at the time, and during his minority the claims of the main branch of the Angevin house continued to fuel the factional struggles. However, to the north the new trend was much more apparent. Giangaleazzo Visconti acquired full control of the Milanese state in 1386 and embarked on a process of expansion which had the significant side-effects of strengthening his internal control in order to raise money and support for his aggression. Venice was threatened by his advance eastwards and occupation of Verona, Vicenza, Belluno, and Feltre; Florence was encircled as he took over in Bologna, Pisa, and Siena. In 1395 he acquired the title of duke from the emperor. This was *signoria* at its most decisive and influential, but the success was dependent on a good rapport with the Milanese noble and banking élite, and on retaining the services of experienced Italian military captains like Jacopo dal Verme, Alberigo da Barbiana, and Facino Cane, with their increasingly permanent companies. Nor were Visconti's main targets, the republican regimes of Venice and Florence, far behind in their rapid extension of control and resources. Venice,

finally successful in destroying the influence of its main trading rival, Genoa, in much of the eastern Mediterranean after the War of Chioggia (1378–81), responded to Visconti threat by strengthening its influence in the hinterland surrounding the lagoon, and eventually resorting to a military takeover of Padua, Vicenza, and Verona (1404–5). Florence's expansion to control much of Tuscany was a more gradual process, culminating in the occupation of Pisa in 1406. The combination of expansion of the state and increasing oligarchical control in Florence itself after the trauma of the popular Ciompi revolt in 1378, produced a regime growing in confidence and authority in the later years of the century. The view that the sudden death of Giangaleazzo Visconti in 1402 when apparently on his way to encircle and subdue Florence was the catalyst for this new-found confidence, is significantly over-simplified and takes insufficient account of the long-term factors in the creation of Florentine civic ideology.

Rapid development of the institutions of government and a growth of bureaucracy were inevitable features of this period of expansion and consolidation. Chancellors and lawyers became increasingly important figures, committees of senior politicians proliferated, and there was a growing emphasis on the holding of public office as an essential part of citizenship and a path to

THE VIEW OF FLORENCE north-westwards from the Piazzale Michelangelo emphasizes the way in which the great communal and ecclesiastical buildings of the thirteenth and fourteenth centuries, the Palazzo Vecchio and the Duomo, dominate the city.

67

honour. An extension of this control to the military world was inevitable. The northern states in the later fourteenth century moved towards more permanent defence mechanisms, with longer contracts for more carefully chosen captains. They were assisted in this by a decline in the role of foreign captains and companies in the last two decades of the century. Alberigo da Barbiana's celebrated victory over the Breton companies at Marino in 1379 was hailed as a turning-point in the recovery of Italian military prowess and the ending of the scourge of the companies. However, more significant changes were being instituted by the political regimes moving towards new contractual relationships with their captains and the creation of fiscal resources to finance these. John Hawkwood, Florence's English general through the 1380s and into the 1390s, was more significant as an example of this changing relationship between leading captains and the states which employed them than as one of the last examples of the great foreign captains.

This discussion of the problems of the fourteenth century has barely touched on the much-debated question of the state of the economy of Italy in this period and the long-term impact of the Black Death. How far were the trends that have been described affected by demographic crisis and subsequent economic depression as some historians have suggested? It is difficult to underplay the social and psychological effect of the plague which swept through Italy in 1347–8, or indeed the immediate economic disruption as towns were abandoned and fields left untilled. But in the longer term there were gains to balance the losses; per capita income of the survivors tended to increase, giving them greater purchasing power and new capital resources; a new wave of immigration into the towns brought new initiatives and newly committed groups. Some of the political and social problems of the middle years of the century can indeed be attributed to these new forces, and a decline in certain traditional trades and industries was an inevitable part of the process. However, the important point is that long before the end of the century the major centres of northern Italy were strengthening their economic position by drawing in wealth and expertise from their surrounding hinterlands, by tightening control, and by fostering the interests of a new wealthy élite. The problem was to be that the costs of government and the needs of the states were soon to outrun, not so much the economic and fiscal resources of those states, as the willingness of the economic élites to contribute on the scale required.

The Divided Fifteenth Century

The history of the Italian states in the fifteenth century is often viewed from the standpoint of the events of the 1490s, Guicciardini's 'crisi d'Italia', when foreign invaders swept aside many of the Italian regimes and forced the remainder to accept outside predominance. The failure of the major Italian states to act in concert and the comparative weakness of their military institutions are blamed for this débâcle. The century which preceded 1494 can be seen as divided in two senses: in one respect it appears as a century divided into two contrasting parts, a first half filled with wars and confrontations, and a second half apparently peaceful and harmonious. But the peace and harmony bred complacency and military inertia, and hence this view of a divided century helps to explain the eventual crisis. On the other hand, division takes the form of the traditional disunity of Italian politics, manifest in the struggles of the first half of the century but also to be seen in the mutual suspicions and watchfulness of the second half when spies and informers played a greater role than recruiters and *condottieri*. This discussion will seek to soften some of the hard lines of previous explanation and develop the idea of an increasing social disunity which was perhaps more damaging to the Italian states in the long term. One also has to test the implied view that Italian affairs in the fifteenth century were conducted in a vacuum, free of foreign interference, unaware of the developing strength of the western monarchies, and therefore helpless in the face of the predators at the end of the century.

DOGE FRANCESCO FOSCARI of Venice (1423–57), portrayed here by the sculptor and architect Bartolomeo Bon, presided over a dramatic expansion of the Venetian state in a series of wars with Milan. His abdication was forced by the Council of Ten amidst growing doubts about his mental and physical capacity.

One generalization that is certainly valid about the fifteenth century is that it was a period in which inter-state relations, 'foreign affairs', became of increasing importance in the perceptions and policies of the Italian states. Prolonged wars did indeed dominate the first half of the century: wars for control of the Kingdom of Naples between Angevin and Aragonese claimants; wars for control of peripheral territory and for economic advantage in the north between the duchy of Milan on the one side and the republics of Venice and Florence on the other. They were wars in which the armies on each side numbered over 20,000 men, in which military captains like Francesco Sforza, Carmagnola, Gattamelata, and Niccolò Piccinino made enduring names for themselves and exercised a major influence on political affairs. They were also wars which consumed and destroyed economic resources on a

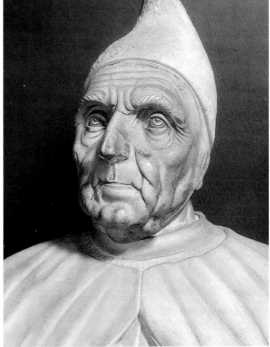

significant scale. However, they were far from continuous wars; they affected differing parts of Italy spasmodically; they contributed to moving wealth around as much as destroying it; they were themselves indicative of the extent of economic resources available to the Italian states, and above all they served to strengthen the internal administrations which managed them and to create a sense of internal unity and even patriotism in the populations which participated in them. Such wars bred alliances and bonds as well as divisions; the advent of organized diplomacy, usually seen as a product of the 'peaceful' second half of the century, was apparent in the alliances and the protracted negotiations for the cessation of war of the first half.

The change of dynasty in Milan with Francesco Sforza, the ally and protégé of Cosimo de' Medici, taking over from the Visconti (1450); the advance of the Turks and the fall of Constantinople (1453) increasingly distracting Venice from Italian affairs; and the pontificate of the humanist Nicholas V (1447–55), produced a new atmosphere in many respects. The Peace of Lodi (1454) and the much-acclaimed Italian League (1455) were a part of this; internal peace seemed both desirable and necessary; there was wide recognition that the costs of war should be avoided and the mechanisms of war controlled. However, none of this amounted to a sustained determination for peace and coexistence. After 1454 alliances and diplomacy may have seemed to predominate, but the distrust and suspicion remained; reduced but substantial armies retired to their billets and trained, paraded, and jousted until periodic but fierce short wars brought them back into action. The Pazzi War (1478–80), in which large parts of central Tuscany were seized by Neapolitan and papal armies, and the War of Ferrara (1482–4), when a substantial Venetian army occupied the northern part of the Ferrarese state, were not 'brush-fire' wars devoid of military significance. The military capacity and organization of the Italian states were relatively little impaired by the more peaceful years of the second half of the century.

However, if military weakness can be eliminated as a key factor in the impending crisis for the Italian states, the failure to achieve greater political unity was a more complex problem. The Italian world underwent a revolution in the first half of the fifteenth century with a dramatic recovery of central authority and control in the centre and south of the peninsula. Whilst the first half of the century was dominated by the struggle of the republics of Florence and Venice to control the hegemonic aspirations of the Visconti dukes of Milan, by 1450 both Naples and the Papacy had moved firmly into the power game. The emergence of Alfonso V of Aragon in 1442 as the victor in the long confrontation with the Angevins for control of the Neapolitan kingdom, not only brought an end to the era of debilitating disunity but installed on the throne a ruler who already aspired to a western Mediterranean empire. Defeated by the Genoese fleet at Ponza in 1435, he had responded by seeking an understanding with Filippo Maria Visconti in Milan, and had even apparently been promised succession to the duchy. In the last stages of the wars in the 1450s, when allied with Venice, Alfonso disembarked troops in southern Tuscany in order to open up a second front against Florence, and a Neapolitan interest in dominating this area, and particularly Siena, remained for the rest of the century. Alfonso's successor in Naples was his natural son Ferrante; this was a deliberate dynastic decision to divide the Aragonese Empire and cut the administrative links between Aragon and Sicily on the one hand, and Naples on the other. However, the hegemonic intentions of the dynasty remained; Ferrante could count on Aragonese support as he built up his fleet and military strength, and began to take the lead in Italian political affairs. Venice soon learnt to distrust the growth of Neapolitan sea-power, while the Sforza dukes of Milan, although often allied to Naples in the second half of the century, found their position increasingly undermined by Neapolitan intrigue.

However, the main focus of the aggressive intentions of the Aragonese dynasty in Naples was the neighbouring Papal State. The return of a single, universally recognized pope, Martin V, to Rome in 1420 after the Council of Constance had settled the Great Schism, led, after two further decades of internal turmoil, to determined papal initiatives to recover control of the Papal State and intervene in Italian political affairs. While it was on the whole true that papal policy was broadly defensive in this period and concerned to protect the Papal State from the powers on its immediate frontiers, Naples and Florence, the methods used were often aggressive and deliberately divisive. Sixtus IV (1471–84) and his nephew Girolamo Riario were largely responsible for the Pazzi conspiracy against Lorenzo de' Medici and the subsequent Pazzi War (1478–80); their intention was to destabilize the Medici regime in Florence and prevent Florentine interference in the Romagna where the pope and Riario were seeking to gain control through the authority of an all-powerful papal nepot. Similarly, ever-strained relations between the popes and Naples were exacerbated by Innocent VIII's support for the revolt of the Neapolitan barons in 1485–6.

The popes of this period were able to make up for their relative military weakness by the use of their spiritual authority for political purposes. Both Florence and Venice were placed under interdicts in the second half of the fifteenth century, and the granting of authority to raise crusading taxes from the clergy was used freely as a political weapon. Rome indeed became the most active diplomatic centre in Italy, and probably in Europe, by the later years of the century, as cardinals, often appointed for political reasons, linked up with foreign ambassadors in a search for papal support in political enterprises and the distribution of benefices to their co-nationals. The same popes, from Nicholas V onwards, who sought to restore the Papacy to the centre of the Italian political stage, were concerned also to make Rome a cultural and spiritual capital, a true heir to imperial Rome. The coherence of the programme set out by Nicholas V and Giannozzo Manetti in the 1450s became obscured by the self-interested preoccupations of subsequent popes, but the net effect remained imposing and, to some, frightening. By the end of the cen-

tury the Italian political and social world was centred on Rome and Naples, rather than Milan or Florence.

However, the story of Italian politics in the fifteenth century was one of determined resistance to any attempt at establishing hegemony. Political élites and patriotic traditions had become too deeply entrenched in the main states to allow the growth of any overarching authority within Italy. Visconti hegemony was opposed in the first half of the century, Venetian 'imperialism' in the second; the new political strength of Naples and the pretensions and ambitions of the popes were resisted for the same reasons. The methods of imposition of hegemony and resistance to it tended to be diplomacy and intrigue rather than war in the second half of the century. The detailed reports provided by ambassadors and informants heightened the mutual suspicions rather than dispelling them. There was little room in such a context for the sudden and effective military strike, although Venice nearly succeeded in May 1482 with its attack on Ferrara; but suspicion and distrust abounded in the so-called peaceful years which preceded 1494.

The impression of an Italy free of foreign interferences is also a misleading one for the fifteenth century. The power struggle in Naples was resolved in favour of the Aragonese; Aragonese resources and manpower sustained Neapolitan ambitions in the middle years of the century, while Alfonso still lived, and in the later years the diplomats and fleets of Ferdinand of Aragon and the new united Spanish monarchy continued to sustain his Neapolitan cousin. At the same time the Angevins intrigued and occasionally fought for a recovery of the kingdom. Angevin-led armies joined Milan against Venice and Naples in 1452–3, and marched south again in the early 1460s. The duke of Lorraine signalled his claim to the Angevin inheritances by taking service with Venice in 1483 against the league led by Naples. However, by this time the inheritance had firmly devolved on the French royal house and it was Charles VIII himself who was preparing yet another Angevin counter-attack. In Rome the revival of Italian dominance at the papal court generated by the return of the Papacy from Avignon was gradually eroded. Catalan Borgia popes and great foreign cardinals like Bessarion, Estouteville, and Balue came to preside over a court that attracted talent from all over Europe. Interest in influencing papal policy was not confined to the Italian states for obvious reasons, and embassies from France, Spain, and the emperor jostled with those of Florence, Naples, and Milan for papal audiences in the second half of the century.

The popes of the fifteenth century were no less inclined to seek outside support against Italian rivals than were other Italian governments. The intention may sometimes have been the genuine one of promoting a European crusade against the Turks, but more often the motives were more mundane. While Milan sought imperial and Hungarian support against Venice, and the Venetian government courted Savoy, France, and even Burgundy to counter-

Facing: MANTUA, ruled by the Gonzaga family in the fifteenth century, preserved its independence between Milan and Venice. Marquis Ludovico (1445–78) is here portrayed by Andrea Mantegna, his court painter, in the Camera degli Sposi, in earnest conversation, no doubt about political affairs, with his sons— Cardinal Francesco, an influential figure at the papal court, and Federico, his eventual successor.

balance threats from Milan, Naples looked inevitably towards Spain for backing, and Florence tended to rely on French goodwill and support. None of this
was seriously intended to encourage a permanent foreign presence in Italy or
to be a compromising of the fierce independence of the Italian regimes; it was
an attempt to manipulate foreign powers for Italian purposes, a strategy
which was conducted with considerable success on a number of occasions
during the fifteenth century.

However, the most dangerous of the foreign powers by the second half of
the fifteenth century was the Ottoman Empire. With the fall of Constantinople (1453) a threat which had seemed distant to many Italians became imposed
on the European consciousness. The Papacy began to derive authority from
making calls for crusading action, while Venice became increasingly involved
in direct confrontation with the advancing infidel. The long Veneto-Turkish
War of 1463–79 was seen by the other states as on the whole a useful distraction of potential Venetian aggressiveness in Italy. There were hints of covert
encouragement being given to the Turks, particularly by Florence, and certainly by the mid-1470s Venice was prepared to arrange its Italian alliances
with a view to gaining help against the Turks. However, the Turkish assault
on Otranto (1480) and the reign of terror in Apulia which followed was foreign
intervention on a new scale. The Venetians were blamed for inviting the
Turks to attack Naples and there may have been some justification for the
charges. Certainly the distraction of Naples caused by the invasion was not
unwelcome to Florence and Milan who dallied in sending support to their
ally, and Sixtus IV was able to polish up his image as a crusading leader as he
summoned European support to evict the infidel.

However, of course, it is the regimes themselves, their composition, their
aspirations, their fears which must be the capstone of the argument. The
instability and disunity which remained, despite the increased power and
improved organization of the major Italian states, was as much the result of
social disequilibrium as of feverish external relations. Regimes collapsed in
the late fifteenth century more because of a lack of internal support than
because of external pressures upon them. The main factor in this situation
was a growing élitism in Italian society; regimes which had always been fundamentally oligarchical became increasingly aristocratic during the century.
Entry into the political élites became more difficult, their privileges, mores,
and lifestyle became more exclusive. A typical example of this process was in
Florence where a republican oligarchy made up of well-established trecento
families dominating high office and public affairs through manipulation of a
sortition system, and the use of carefully chosen emergency committees and
informal discussion groups, became after 1434 a Medicean élite. Judicious use
of exiling and more systematic exploitation of now traditional manipulation
mechanisms created bonds of interdependence between the Medici family

and a stable majority of the political élite which became formalized in 1480 with the establishment of the Council of Seventy. The causes of this stasis were not so much a freezing of wealth and of economic opportunities, as a growing emphasis on family office-holding traditions and on relevant political expertise. The justification for this form of political élitism was that only those with experience of public affairs and a real commitment to the state could be trusted to lead it. Most sections of the Italian economy flourished in the first two-thirds of the fifteenth century and new wealthy groups certainly came forward; but they tended to be held on the fringes of the élite as favoured tax-payers, financial advisers, holders of specific and relevant offices, rather than admitted to the inner echelons.

The Venetian political system with its emphasis on age and experience as essential attributes for high office, its growing divisions between rich and poor nobles, its drift towards decision-making in smaller councils in conditions of carefully preserved secrecy, exhibited exactly the same traits. The Sforza dukes of Milan established the Consiglio Segreto at the heart of their regime and relied on an inner élite of nobles, bankers, military captains, and bureaucrats, many of whom were enfeoffed with estates and aristocratic privileges. In Rome a sort of curial élite was emerging as politically minded cardinals, proto-notaries, and senior papal officials fostered and extended their position through patronage and influence.

BOTTICELLI'S *Marriage Feast of Nastagio degli Onesti* completed a cycle of paintings for the Pucci family based on a Boccaccio novella. This typical representation of a Florentine élite social occasion is thought to have celebrated the wedding of Giannozzo d'Antonio Pucci to Lucrezia di Piero Bini in 1483. The probable presence of Lorenzo de' Medici is indicated by the prominent Medici arms.

75

The effect of these tendencies was inevitably to generate resentment and opposition within the societies themselves. This was not just a matter of the resentment of those who felt that they had a right to participate in public affairs through title, tradition, or wealth, but who were being excluded; it was the resentment of the ordinary population who found government becoming more remote, more arbitrary, more unfathomable. Conspiracies which hoped to attract popular support, rather than large-scale outbursts of popular unrest, were symptoms of this detachment of political élites from the rest of society. The murder of Galeazzo Maria Sforza (1476), the Pazzi and Frescobaldi conspiracies in Florence (1478 and 1481), the revolt of the barons in Naples (1485), the rising of the Colonna against Sixtus IV (1484), were such symptoms. None succeeded in raising significant popular support at the time because the cities in which government resided were well policed and their populations to some extent pampered. The real test of the effectiveness and acceptance of Italian regimes came in the wider states which they controlled in the fifteenth century. How far were regimes based in Milan, Florence, Venice, etc. able to attract the loyalty and effectively control the affairs of Parma, Pisa, or Padua? Even more importantly, perhaps, how far did the writ of the regime run into the remote countryside? Evidence suggests that the Italian states of the fifteenth century handled these problems in very different ways. The most centralist was probably Florence with the imposition of large numbers of officials from Florence, a centralized tax structure, and hints of a concern for a regional economy. Naples, and to a lesser extent Milan, relied on the traditional nobility and local urban élites to maintain control. Venice fell somewhere between these two solutions with a limited number of Venetian patricians supervising local institutions and imposing some central edicts. The extent of success depended on location and personalities; this was not 'State-building' in any coherent sense; the fate of the regime at the heart of the 'State' remained largely a matter of indifference to the bulk of the population.

It is difficult in these circumstances to talk of a creation of unity within these states. The élites had more in common with each other than with the populations over which they presided. They shared a lifestyle, a diplomatic world, and an intellectual world in which the links between élite groups and families spread across Italy. But that very process made them vulnerable to local aspirations and envy, even if superficially their regimes seemed to exude confidence and authority.

The Years of Crisis 1494–1530

In November 1494 Piero di Lorenzo de' Medici was forced to flee from Florence in the face of rising opposition both within the élite and at a popular level. The Medici ascendancy established over the previous three generations

ITALY IN ABOUT 1500

FRANCESCO GONZAGA commanded the army of the Holy League which confronted Charles VIII of France at Fornovo during his retreat from Naples in 1495. The Italians claimed victory in the battle and Gonzaga commissioned this *Madonna della Vittoria* from Mantegna and placed it in a special chapel in Mantua dedicated to the Virgin in gratitude for his survival.

collapsed and within weeks major constitutional reforms had established a more widely based republic than the city had ever previously experienced. The immediate context of these dramatic events was the advance of the French army through the Lunigiana and Piero's apparent willingness to surrender vital fortresses, including Pisa itself, in order to gain French support for the regime. However, disillusionment of the Florentine élite with the leadership which Piero had provided since the death of his father Lorenzo two years earlier, and indeed perhaps a growing feeling that, over an even longer period, the Medici had been usurping too prominent a position in the state, contributed to the débâcle. The radical and visionary preaching of Savonarola also had a role to play in creating support for the new republican regime which lasted until 1512 when the Medici were restored by Spanish troops.

The political crisis in Florence was followed within a few years by the collapse of the Sforza regime in Milan (1499) and the division of the Kingdom of Naples between France and Spain at the Treaty of Granada (1500). At that moment Venice and the Papacy, with Alexander VI of Catalan origins as pope, survived, but only by coming to terms with the invaders and accepting the destruction of their erstwhile rivals. Foreign intervention had clearly played a crucial role in these events. Charles VIII's invasion and successful occupation of Naples in 1494–5 had sparked off an inevitable Spanish reaction in support of the beleaguered Aragonese dynasty, and for the next half-century Italy was to be a battleground for the two main powers in Europe.

The questions that have to be asked about this period of crisis are why did proud Italy apparently succumb so easily to the foreign incursions, and what difference did the foreign presence, whether occupying or just threatening, make to the political and social life of the Italian states? Some of the answers to the first of these questions have already been explored in the discussion of the fifteenth century. Military incapacity was among the least of these problems: French and Spanish armies were no larger than the main Italian armies, nor were they markedly superior in training and equipment; the famous French artillery was well known and widely imitated in Italy; many of the leaders of the invading armies were soon to be Italian. The main battles of the period, with the exception of Fornovo (1495) and Agnadello (1509), were in fact fought between French and Spanish armies, with Italian contingents fighting mainly on the Spanish, and ultimately victorious, side. Those troops and their leaders played a significant role in the major advances in warfare which the wars generated.

What was missing in Italy was the will of governments and populations to resist, and particularly to resist in concert. In early 1495 the Neapolitan baronage deserted to the French in droves, and the peasants of the Abruzzi marched in their thousands to join in the overthrow of the unpopular Aragonese dynasty. In 1499 it was not just sections of the army which refused to fight for

Ludovico Sforza and the defence of Milan; the French invasion was led by Gian Giacomo Trivulzio, leader of the discontented Milanese Guelphs and one of the most experienced Italian captains, who knew the invasion routes intimately and could exploit the divisions within the state to the full. Further-

more, the French invasion was supported by a Venetian attack in the rear, and connived at by the pope, Alexander VI, who saw an opportunity to use French troops for the overthrow of his Romagna vicars and the establishment of a duchy for his son Cesare Borgia. Similarly the division of Naples in 1500 was supported by the pope, and by Venice seeking a permanent hold on the Apulian ports which it had gained when defending Naples in 1496. The League of Cambrai (1508) which plotted, and nearly accomplished, the destruction of Venice was joined by Ferrara, Mantua, and Pope Julius II; it was an attempt to settle Italian scores as much as a European power move. Venetian resistance after the defeat of its army at Agnadello was hampered by the mass defection of the nobility of the terraferma, and aided by the unexpected loyalty of the rural classes who distrusted their local élites even more than they distrusted Venetian central government.

ANOTHER ITALIAN PRINCE who played a major role in the Italian Wars was Duke Alfonso d'Este of Ferrara, the third husband of Lucrezia Borgia. He was an artillery expert and is here depicted by Dosso Dossi and Battista Luteri on the battlefield at Ravenna (1512) where he fought alongside the French.

Undoubtedly the long period of war, tensions, and pressure created its own responses of resignation and weariness. The government of Milan changed eleven times between 1494 and 1530 and it would be unreasonable to blame this febrile instability entirely on weak institutions and misguided policies before 1494. The invading powers had their own agendas, and neither the weakness of Italy nor the blandishments of Italian princes and exiles were the controlling factors in the situation. This was even more the case by the 1520s when the extension of the Habsburg Empire took the confrontation between France and Spain to other theatres of war than Italy, and the term 'Italian Wars' becomes increasingly difficult to define.

The question of the impact of the wars, particularly in socio-economic terms, is a very difficult one. Traditionally the period of the Italian Wars has been seen as a turning-point for the economy as well as the political structures of the peninsula. The sacking of cities, the devastation of the countryside, the drain of manpower and resources to the armies, the imposition of new taxes,

FED. OF
SWITZERLAND

HOLY ROMAN
EMPIRE

KINGDOM OF HUNGARY

D. OF SAVOY

Valtelline

D. OF
MANTUA

REP. OF VENICE

Aquileia

OTTOMAN EMPIRE

Milan
Bergamo

D. OF MILAN

Turin

Pavia

Verona

Padua

Venice

PR. OF PIEDMONT

D. OF
PARMA

Mantua

Istria

MARQ. OF
SALUZZO

Parma

Modena

Ferrara

D. OF
FERRARA

REP. OF GENOA

D. OF
MODENA

Bologna

Ravenna

Genoa

MARQ OF
MONFERRAT

Lucca

REP. OF LUCCA

Rimini

D. OF
URBINO

ADRIATIC SEA

Pisa

Florence

Urbino

Livorno

D. OF
TUSCANY

The Marches

Siena

PAPAL
STATE

Capitanata

CORSICA
(Genoa)

Umbria

Rome

Campania

KINGDOM OF
NAPLES

Bari

Apulia

Naples

KINGDOM
OF
SARDINIA
(Spain)

Basilicata

TYRRHENIAN SEA

MEDITERRANEAN SEA

Calabria

Palermo

Messina

Reggio

KINGDOM OF SICILY

0   200 km

ITALY IN 1559

and the looting of treasure, all took an inevitable toll. Economic historians have talked of a destruction of the industrial base, of a breakdown of commercial monopolies, and of long-term rural depression and unemployment as consequences of the crisis.

However, the destructiveness of war is always exaggerated by emphasis on disastrous episodes and contemporary accounts. Florentines complained bitterly, and with justification, that the loss of Pisa in 1494 had ruined their trade, and that the long siege of Florence in 1529–30 desolated the countryside. But Pisa was recovered in 1509 and the Florentine *contado* was as popular as ever with investors within a few years of the siege. The Sack of Rome (1527) had a particularly damaging effect on what was always a rather artificial economy, and certain areas such as Piedmont and parts of southern Lombardy where armies marched and camped incessantly clearly suffered from sustained exploitation. But after 1503 Italy from Rome southwards had little direct experience of war; the Veneto and the whole of eastern Lombardy suffered only for the limited period of 1509–17; Tuscany was only periodically affected. For much of the sixteenth century Italian local economies tended to prosper; Venetians continued to exercise commercial monopolies in the eastern Mediterranean until late in the century; Genoese merchants and bankers continued to infiltrate the Iberian economies after the dramatic volte-face of Andrea Doria in 1528 bringing his fleet over to the imperial side; Lombard industries did well throughout the century; and Florentine bankers and woollen cloth and silk manufacturers continued their business unabated in France and the Netherlands. As Fernand Braudel has convincingly argued, the long-term fate of the Italian, and indeed Mediterranean, economy is related to gradual shifts in demand, consumption, and supply problems across Europe as a whole rather than to political crises or warfare.

The social patterns of Italian life seemed to be even less affected. The political élites on the whole accommodated themselves to changes in rule, and the new rulers made use of the old élites. Both French and Spanish governors of Milan sought to work through Sforza princes until 1535, and restoration and maintenance of the Medici in Florence was always the main thrust of imperial policy. Angevin nobility in Naples suffered but that had been their fate for a long time; Colonna and Orsini continued to vie with each other in Rome despite Alexander VI's attempts to destroy both families; Venetian terraferma nobles were restored to their privileged if subordinate positions in the cities of the Veneto. The lower orders of Italian society quickly lost any hopes that French or Spanish aristocratic governors or captains would support their cause. Some historians would argue for a spiritual crisis brought about by the events of this period, a retreat into bitterness, subservience, and nostalgia; others would see such trends as inherent in the pre-1494 situation. However, these are debates which must be pursued elsewhere.

Italy in the Sixteenth Century

The coronation of Charles V by Pope Clement VII in Bologna in 1530 has been interpreted in many ways, ranging from the culmination of the subjection of Italy and the true end of the Renaissance to the end of calamities and the beginning of a new order. That the remaining years of the sixteenth century were a period of relative calm and rising prosperity for the Italian states and their societies is now generally recognized; it will be the argument of this final section of the chapter that there were important continuities which make it essential to carry the story through to 1600.

The dominance of Charles V was based not just on his ownership of Sicily and Naples, and his conquest of Milan, but more significantly on his effective assertion of imperial title to the rest of Italy. Here at last was the supreme arbiter for which Italy had been yearning, a Holy Roman Emperor who spoke Italian and to whom Italy meant a great deal. His settlement of Italian affairs in the months on either side of the coronation went far beyond reconciliation with the pope and an acceptance of the need for a Medici restoration in Florence. He recognized the integrity of the smaller states, confirming Modena and Reggio to the Este dukes of Ferrara, restoring Francesco Maria della Rovere to Urbino, raising Mantua to a duchy, and sanctioning the survival of Siena and Lucca as independent republics. In Milan he allowed authority to Francesco II Sforza until the latter's death in 1535, and he recognized Venetian rights to the Republic's terraferma possessions and promised not to interfere in its rule. Imperial ambassadors and imperial viceroys directed the affairs of Italy, although the emperor always made himself available to petitioners and complainants. The friction between the Italian states gradually died down as the emperor resolved disputes and the imperial army in Lombardy remained on guard.

In the two most independent of the Italian states, Venice and the Papal State, the continuities were most apparent. In the 1520s and under the leadership of Doge Andrea Gritti Venice continued to seek opportunities to maintain an international political role. It was finally persuaded to give up the Apulian ports by Charles, but its powerful fleet and well-maintained army ensured recognition of its political importance. However, the Turkish War of 1537–40 once again proved a distraction and from the late 1530s defence and the

Facing: THESE PROCESSIONAL SCENES celebrated the entry of Ottone Visconti, archbishop of Milan, into the city in triumph in 1277 after the Visconti faction had defeated their rivals, the Della Torre, at the battle of Desio. Ottone became *de facto* signore of the city, but Visconti hegemony was only permanently established sixty years later.

THE CORONATION OF CHARLES V as Emperor by Pope Clement VII in Bologna in 1530 marked the completion of Habsburg domination in Italy and the beginning of a period of relative peace and recovery under Imperial protection, following the Sack of Rome and the overthrow of the last Florentine Republic.

maintenance of the status quo seemed to dominate Venice's stance in Italy. The long pontificates of Clement VII (1523–34) and Paul III (1534–50), both of whom had been prominent figures of the papal court through the years of crisis and had first-hand experience of the role and advantages of nepotism, also ensured continuity. Dynastic concerns, tolerably good relations with the emperor, and a recognition of the need for gradual reform of the Church, culminating in the opening of the Council of Trent, made the pontificate of Paul III a relatively successful period of papal policy. Less successful was the brief reign of Paul IV (1555–9), a Neapolitan who used his position to challenge imperial authority and to resurrect the old tensions between spiritual and temporal, but this was a passing phase.

In Tuscany the Medici dukes, who gradually established in the 1530s a sort of mixed authority based in part on republican traditions, were firmly attached to the emperor and therefore allowed a free hand. The successful take-over of Siena, one of the most cherished of Florentine ambitions, in 1555 was carried out with imperial permission and support. This was one of the few territorial adjustments in a remarkably stable period, in which the rulers of Italy were concerned to create consensus and support through constitutional government, and above all effective government. A particular concern was the encouragement of economic recovery and growth: the building of port installations, protection for industries, improved roads, land-reclamation schemes all figured in the policies of the period. The intention was not just to generate taxable wealth but also to promote good will and satisfaction with government. The policy was particularly successful in Tuscany where the dukes (elevated to grand dukes in 1569) were able to distract the Florentine élite from their traditional political concerns by encouraging their business and landed interests.

The transfer of authority in Italy from Charles V to Philip II on the emperor's retirement in 1556 was potentially a disruptive moment. Philip, king of Spain, ruler of Naples and Milan, did not have the imperial authority; he was Spanish in a way that his father had not been and the Spanish were not popular in Italy. Philip himself, more distant and aloof, less interested in Italy, committed to Castilian rather than international advisers, appeared less likely to preside over an Italian entente. But on the whole the entente survived for the rest of the century despite some growing tensions between Philip and successive popes, and between Spain and Venice. Philip, whatever

THE OTTOMAN THREAT loomed over Italy for more than a century after the fall of Constantinople (1453). The last great naval confrontation took place at Lepanto in 1571 when Venetian, Spanish, and papal fleets combined to crush an Ottoman armada. The Christian fleet was led into battle by six great Venetian galeasses loaded with cannon.

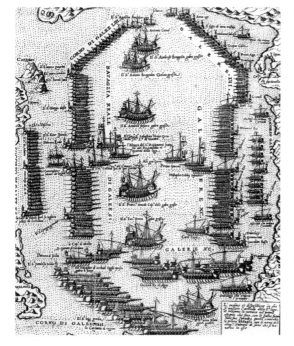

his reputation, was not an aggressive ruler and he had a genuine concern for justice and the interests of his subjects. He was determined to defend Italy and the euphoria of the great victory of Lepanto (1571) over the Turks, won by combined Spanish, Venetian, and papal fleets, survived the disillusionment and recriminations of the aftermath, as the allies pulled out in rapid succession.

Undoubtedly a key factor in preserving a degree of tranquillity and mutual understanding in Italy in the second half of the century was the temporary ending of the Franco-Habsburg confrontation with the Treaty of Câteau Cambrésis (1559). The removal of the threat of French intervention in Italy narrowed the options for Italian rulers resentful of Spanish hegemony, and reduced the military burdens on Italian treasuries. At the same time the success of Tridentine reform gave a new coherence and sense of purpose to Italian religious life and a new prestige to the Papacy. Humanism came of age in Catholic reform which is another of the continuities of this period.

By the 1590s there were signs that this Indian summer of the Renaissance was ending. The accession of Henri IV and his successful bid to end the religious wars which had so divided and distracted France, increased the likelihood of Franco-Spanish confrontation once more. Spanish taxation in Italy was rising with inflation; plague and famine had re-emerged to cull the spectacular population growth of the middle years of the century. Élites began to look askance at governments as profits started to decline. Venice was finally losing influence in the eastern Mediterranean following the loss of Cyprus to the Turks in 1571 and was approaching a new confrontation with the Papacy over ecclesiastical jurisdiction which culminated in Paul V's interdict of 1606. The Italian states and their societies had remarkably survived the crisis of the early years of the century. They had confronted the problems posed by expanding European powers, by shifting markets and routes, by extraordinary religious turmoil, with enterprise and tolerance; by 1600 the task was increasingly difficult.

✣ 4 ✣

RENAISSANCE CULTURE

GEORGE HOLMES

The Age of Dante and Giotto

The surge of cultural achievement which is evident in some parts of Italy around the year 1300 had as its most important cause the commercial success of some of the great cities, which produced a more urban civilization, different from the society which had existed earlier in Italy or contemporaneously in the rest of Europe. But there were other important contributory factors. If we think of the cities of Florence, Siena, and Pisa—all of which were in Tuscany—their intellectual evolution was affected by the memory of ancient Rome, now dead but still spiritually alive in writings of Vergil and Cicero, and in the vast monuments scattered about the city itself. An equally powerful influence was exerted by modern Rome, the city of the popes and the capital of the western Church. The civilization of Renaissance Italy had to live, easily or uneasily, with the Christian Church.

The greatest and most original of the new breed of creators was Dante Alighieri (1265–1321), the writer of the *Divine Comedy*. Serious poetic creation in the Italian tongue, unlike the medieval tongues of northern Europe, scarcely stretched back before 1250. Dante, first schooled by other gentlemen-poets of the Tuscan towns, wrote a long and complex poem which has never ceased to dominate the Italian mind as Homer did the mind of Greece. The *Divine Comedy* was composed by Dante in the years of exile between his expulsion from Florence in 1302 and his death in 1321. The three sections of Hell, Purgatory, and Paradise are entirely symmetrical in form and also linked by the fictional figures of Dante himself, who visits all three levels of the universe, and the lady Beatrice, an idol of love in the old poetic tradition, transformed into a redeemed and all-knowing inhabitant of Heaven. But the subject-matter of the poem covers a very wide variety of topics which provide a conspectus of Dante's own life and of many of the pressing concerns of his Italy. A large part is played by the political problems of strife in cities, dominated by great families and factions, and of the political claims of the popes, who wished to be theocratic emperors in Italy. Dante was probably also much influenced by the teaching of the Spiritual wing of the Franciscan Order which gave him, at least for a time, an apocalyptic expectation of the future history of the Church and the Holy Roman Empire. *Paradiso*, the last of the three *cantiche*, expressed his acceptance of the philosophical theology of the greatest of medieval Italian philosophers, St Thomas Aquinas (d. 1274), who had attempted an elaborate accommodation to each other of the rationalist philosophy of Aristotle and the revelation offered by the Bible. Aquinas had done most of his philosophizing at Paris. Italy had several important universities, including the great law school at Bologna and the university of Padua, close to Venice, famous for its devotion to Aristotle's scientific and medical works. Dante, however, was very much the product of Florence and expressed in the fullest way the new culture of the City, partially free of ecclesiastical and academic domination in its thought—Florence as yet had no university—and therefore a receptacle fitted for the spirit of the new humanism, which was to play a dominant role in Italian culture for the next three hundred years.

The culture of Renaissance Italy was to give exceptional prominence to the visual arts. Humanism was to be expressed as much by painting and sculpture as by literature. The resurgence of the visual arts began, it might be argued, as much in Rome, and in Assisi, under Roman influence, as in Florence. Siena and Pisa were also important because it was there that Niccolò and Giovanni Pisano, father and son, inaugurated the imitation of Roman sculptural remains which very quickly developed into a new kind of figural naturalism. Giovanni Pisano's figures at Sant' Andrea, Pistoia, and at the cathedrals of Pisa and Siena reached a high level of sophistication in the presentation of the human form. It was the case at several stages in the history of Renaissance art that sculpture *preceded* painting. One is inclined indeed to apply this opinion not only to Giovanni Pisano in the late thirteenth century but also to Donatello and Ghiberti in the fifteenth and to some extent to Michelangelo in the sixteenth. However this may be, much of the later Renaissance seems already present in Giovanni's pliant and vital human figures and the painters of the next generation were to some extent imitating the stone figures of Giovanni Pisano and Arnolfo di Cambio rather than nature.

Thirteenth-century painting was inseparable from the Franciscan Order, first and most successful of the new mendicant orders which flooded Italy with their friars and transformed its cities with their huge convents. The Franciscans promoted the visual presentation of the events of the life of St Francis (d. 1226) and the great double basilica built at Assisi, where the order originated, contained several series of frescoes, painted in the late thirteenth and early fourteenth centuries, which gave a powerful impulse to that type of art. Most notable was the great series of the life of St Francis in the upper basilica, providing a visual interpretation of the account written by St Bonaventure,

which became the accepted record of stories such as that of St Francis preaching to the birds.

The names of most of the painters at Assisi are unknown, those of the main series of St Francis's life totally unknown. It is generally thought that papal patronage and influence led to much of the fresco work being done by Roman painters and that thus the reconsideration of the ancient Roman traditions, which seems to have been active but whose productions in Rome itself have been largely destroyed by the rebuilding of the sixteenth and seventeenth centuries, was given a prominent place at Assisi, where it inspired artists from further north. However that may be, the great painter who was most obviously inspired by Assisi, and may have worked there, was the Florentine Giotto (d. 1337). Giotto may also have met Dante in exile at Padua; if that is so the two main founders of the Renaissance aesthetic tradition were linked. Giotto was in Padua to cover with frescoes the interiors of the Arena Chapel, his most important surviving work. The chapel was paid for by a rich man, acting on an impulse which must have owed something to the model of Assisi. Giotto produced a series of scenes illustrating the life of Christ preceded by the lives of the Virgin Mary and her apocryphal mother Anne. The series of scenes is remarkable for its dramatic quality: the episodes lead into each other to present a tragic battle between good and evil. But perhaps more important was Giotto's attempt to give each scene a spatial reality. This was the beginning of the movement which was eventually to lead to Brunelleschi's invention of mathematical perspective and Leonardo's further scientific projects. Giotto's space was by these standards primitive and his perspective rough and ready and based largely on the relationship of a few figures to a simple architectural space, often the interior of a single room. Nevertheless the leap to an art in which the figures were clearly placed in space, not simply related notionally to it and to other figures, was sudden. Also the figures were given a new discernible weight, most noticeable perhaps in the altarpiece of the enthroned Virgin and Child, the *Ognissanti Madonna*, now in the Uffizi at Florence, which made a striking advance in naturalism over the countless other panel-paintings of thirteenth-century Italy. Traditionally such altarpieces, made to stand behind altars or to be carried in processions, required by the fervent popular religion which was associated especially with the Franciscans and Dominicans and many other orders, had served a symbolic rather than a realistic purpose. That psychology was now changing.

Facing: THE CRIB AT GRECCIO from the St Francis Legend in the Upper Basilica at Assisi, *c*.1300. No one knows who was the painter of these frescoes—perhaps Giotto, perhaps someone linked with Rome. This scene shows the capacity for illustrating a story with an interior perspective setting, in this case the portion of a church behind the screen.

Sienese Painting and Petrarch

Giotto's greatest contemporary was the Sienese painter Duccio (d. 1318). Siena, though not as large as Florence, was also a notable commercial centre and, in the period before the Black Death of 1348, was able to command a visual culture of similar splendour. The Sienese, who had built their cathedral in the thirteenth century, were hoping in the early fourteenth to enlarge it into the greatest structure of that kind in the world and were prevented from doing this only by the physical instability of the site and the demographic disaster of 1348. Duccio was the artist chosen to paint the *Maestà*, a grand celebration of the Virgin, the traditional protectress of Siena, and her Son, to stand behind the altar of the cathedral. It was finished in 1311, a series of painted wooden panels, fixed together, which gave a detailed account of the life of Christ, particularly of the events leading up to the Passion and beyond. Duccio's concerns were different from those of Giotto. His interest in space and figural weight was much weaker. But he was extraordinarily successful in presenting a vivid story, in which, for example, the command of elegant figures and the grace of the structural pattern were stronger than Giotto's. The *Maestà* (1309–11) was produced almost at the same time as the Arena Chapel (*c*.1305–10). They were both ambitious works covering the life of Christ by painters whose origins were only about 50 miles apart. It is interesting—and a testimony to Italian inventiveness—that it should have been possible for two such strong, but divergent, traditions to arise in such close proximity to each other.

In the first half of the fourteenth century Siena continued to produce inventive painters. After Duccio the development of the representation of space proceeded further than at Florence, particularly in the work of Ambrogio Lorenzetti (d. 1348). His *Presentation* (1342), now in the Uffizi at Florence, shows the biblical scene taking place in an elaborate church, whose side aisles and chancel can be seen receding into the background of the picture. This carries Giotto's spatial naturalism a good deal further and in fact was not to be improved on before the next century. A few years earlier Lorenzetti had

A PORTION of Ambrogio Lorenzetti's fresco of *The Well-Governed City* (accompanied by the *Well-Governed Countryside* and *Tyrannical Government*) in the Palazzo Pubblico, Siena, done in the late 1330s as a model to the city's rulers, showing the advantages of peace. For its time it is an advanced perspective drawing of buildings, in Siena itself.

painted a series of frescoes illustrating the themes of good and bad government in the Palazzo Pubblico at Siena, which were a striking illustration of the political ideals of the republican city. Some of them are allegorical but two scenes, which are fairly well preserved, show the *Well-Governed Town* and the *Well-Governed Countryside*. The latter is in one sense a presentation of the whole *contado* of Siena, stretching to its seaport on the coast, a view of over 40 miles, of course unrealistic. But, taken as a painting of countryside, it is a daring attempt to present a realistic space of fields and hills, not defined by walls, which again was not improved on or rivalled in the fourteenth century.

Another major Sienese painter, Simone Martini (d. 1344), ended his career at the papal court in France. There the Papacy had resided since 1305 and remained until 1377. This 'Babylonish Captivity', as some regarded it, deprived Italy and Rome of the papal court and its artistic and intellectual patronage for a long time. There Simone Martini met another Italian exile, the writer Petrarch (1304–74), apparently drew Petrarch's beloved Laura, and was admired by the writer. Here then is another meeting of artist and writer, succeeding the—possibly legendary—meeting of Dante and Giotto, and foreshadowing the well-documented and very important intercourse of humanists and artists to come later. Petrarch has often been regarded as the founder of humanism, but, although he spent much of his time outside Italy, he

belongs to the tradition of lay education and learning, which existed before him and which was one of the important national peculiarities of Italian society throughout the Renaissance period. The notary, who wrote formal documents in Italian and Latin, was the Italian equivalent of the modern solicitor, and because of the importance of Latin to him, he often took an interest in the classical writings of Cicero. Petrarch was the son of a notary and partly trained as a lawyer at Bologna, to follow in his father's footsteps. Instead he gave it up to become a professional literary man.

Although he sprang out of an earlier tradition, Petrarch was a man with quite exceptional innovative creativity. It is difficult to think of any other literary artist so fecund in the invention of literary genres. He is best remembered nowadays for the Petrarchan sonnet and his Italian poetry was a powerful influence throughout the Renaissance period. But he was also the inventor of the scientific study of Latin texts and of the dialogue, wrote lives of the heroes of ancient Rome, attempted a Latin poem in imitation of Vergil, and castigated the scholastic philosophy which was prevalent in the universities. Petrarch earned his living by writing and in 1341 was crowned with the laurel on the Capitol at Rome, by order of King Robert of Naples. He was the first modern man of letters.

To grasp the nature of Petrarch's cast of mind it is probably best to look at his *Secretum*, mostly composed about 1347. This is a dialogue, the prototype of hundreds of dialogues composed later in the Renaissance, a discussion between two characters—Augustine, based on St Augustine, and Francis, based on Petrarch's name Francesco Petrarca—who represent the two tendencies struggling within Petrarch's mind. Augustine presents the austere Christian doctrine that this life is merely a preparation for death, Francis presents Petrarch's personal attachment to a life of love and glory arising from his skill as a poet. The debate is unresolved. Petrarch was both, on the one side a lover and poet, on the other a being disturbed by the fear that the monastic life was the true purpose of humanity. In the *Secretum* he gave a picture of the underlying dilemma which was to run unsolved through the whole of Renaissance culture: how to reconcile the worldly purposes based on a literary humanism derived from pagan Rome with the Christian self-denial and devotion to heaven preached by the religious orders. Both were strongly rooted movements in the Italian world and, though many made attempts at reconciliation, notably, as we shall see, Marsilio Ficino and Michelangelo, the problem was insoluble.

Petrarch's greatest literary contemporary was a very different person, Giovanni Boccaccio (1313–75), also a man of letters and precursor of more modern writers, but this time rooted in the Florentine city world, which he occasionally served as an envoy. Boccaccio is best remembered for his *Decameron*, the long series of stories imagined as told by Florentine gentlefolk in flight from the plague of 1348. The *Decameron* is a literary adaptation of city story-telling, witty, fantastic, often anticlerical or obscene, and it is written in Italian. In historical perspective it shows one way in which the Italian imagination might have developed. With Boccaccio's stories, Petrarch's poems, and the *Divine Comedy* literature in Italian had very rapidly, within a hundred years, reached a high level of success, which made it at the very least comparable with, perhaps superior to, the achievements of medieval French and German. Why not continue on this path? Boccaccio himself was an example of the tensions which turned the Italian mind in another direction for he was also fascinated by classical literature. One of his last compositions was the *Genealogy of the Pagan Gods*, in Latin, which told the classical stories in a manner which was acceptable to the Christian and was in fact to have a long celebrity as a repository of classical legend. As it turned out the next century, the fifteenth, was to see much classical humanism and little first-class writing in Italian, in one sense an impoverishment, in another an enrichment of the Italian genius.

The Humanist Revolution

The explosion of humanist scholarship and writing which took place at the beginning of the fifteenth century marked a turning-away both from city gossip and from Christianity. One of the conditions of its success was the collapse of papal authority during the Great Schism, 1378–1415, which followed the return of Pope Gregory XI from Avignon to Rome and split the College of Cardinals, leading to support for two rival popes for a whole generation. In these circumstances of papal weakness devotion to classical literature grew unchecked at Florence, promoted by a group led by the chancellor, or chief civil servant, of the city, Coluccio Salutati. After 1415, when the Papacy was reunited at Rome and papal prestige and wealth revived, the papal court became once again an important centre of patronage for Italians, which it had ceased to be in 1305, and the link between humanists at Florence and Rome was strong and important. 'Humanism' is an imprecise word which can only be taken to mean a devotion to the supreme cultural value of classical literature and thought. Though the definition is vague the instinct it represents was of very great importance to Italians for the next two centuries.

The Florentine-Roman humanist school promoted a series of original and influential literary creations which were adaptations of classical models to modern life. The simplest of these, in a sense, was the writing of a new kind of history, continuous narrative of secular events, modelled on Roman historians, as opposed to the annals and the placing of events within a providential Christian framework, running from the Creation through the Incarnation and the evolution of the Church, which had been normal earlier. One of the very prominent humanists was Leonardo Bruni (1370–1444), like Salutati chancellor of Florence, and a very prolific writer in various humanist fields. He wrote a long *History of the Florentine People* which told the story of the city, placing it, so far as it received an external framework, against the flowering of the early Roman Republic, the decline of Rome under the emperors, and the revival of Florence in modern times. This was in embryo the plan of world history seen as a series starting with classical civilization, passing through the Middle Ages, the quality of culture again reviving in the modern secular city. Bruni was therefore the inaugurator of a new trend in the conception of the past which was to become commonplace: history of civilization as opposed to providential history.

Bruni's history was concerned at its centre with the republican city. Florence was self-consciously republican, especially in opposition to the aggressive despotism of Milan. The propagandist needs of the city married with the reading of Aristotle and Cicero to produce a new republican city-state political thought, of which Bruni was again a main inventor and promoter. Like the new history this too was a break with the medieval tradition which had commonly treated political thought as a semi-theological discipline, because its main issue was the problem of the relationship between Church and State. Bruni and others were able to regard the republican city in independence as a proper subject, the aims of politics defined by the needs of citizens living in a secular community, and this gave birth to a kind of proto-utilitarianism. The new political thought was much practised throughout the fifteenth century and adapted here and there to support despotic government, which was in fact at least as common in Italy as republicanism.

In spite of its origins in its enjoyment of the pagan classics humanism did not come seriously into conflict with ecclesiastical authority, and popes, notably Nicholas V (1447–55), happily patronized the translation of Thucydides and other Greek writers into Latin with as much equanimity as they planned the rebuilding of Rome to revive ancient glories. Even the writings of Lorenzo Valla (1407–57), a Roman by origin who used his linguistic skill to criticize the Latin Vulgate translation of the Bible and the translation of Greek philosophers' words by several scholastics, did not upset the friendly alliance of classics and Christianity. The most influential of the Roman humanists was Leon Battista Alberti (1404–72) who wrote the only important humanist text of this period in Italian, *On the Family*, a work of political and social thought which was again indifferent to the old obsession with Church–State relations, and instead took as its subject the family within the context of the secular city. Alberti, however, was still more original than this. He began the crucial movement of alliance between humanism and the visual arts which was to fructify in the glorious century and a half of Italian art which started in the early fifteenth century. Alberti's book *On Painting* (1436) was a work by a rich and learned humanist inspired by the artistic craftsmen—so they were commonly regarded—of contemporary Florence. It did two things. First it established a new set of aims for painting: to reproduce scenes naturalistically, using perspective and giving figures an appearance which was true to their emotions; to use the colours of nature, avoiding decorative gold and silver, to tell a story. Secondly it proclaimed the artist to be a man of culture like the literary humanist. Florentines had adulated Giotto among their great men but now the artist was to be part of the company of cultivated gentlemen, a quite different role from that of the artisan with a physical skill. Alberti also wrote a book about architecture in which he advocated planned cities and a classical style. Again it was both in tune with the intellectual ethos of the time and an innovative book, carrying ideas unexpectedly further. As Bruni transformed the Italian mind, Alberti did more than anyone else to change the face of Italy.

LEON BATTISTA ALBERTI's self-portrait in bronze. Alberti was the learned humanist who praised and codified the practices of artists and also worked as an architect. This self-portrait (c.1435) is an exceptional creation which shows he was capable of art-work himself.

Humanism and Art

Alberti's inspiration was the revolution in the visual arts which took place at Florence. The key figures were Filippo Brunelleschi (1377–1446), architect and sculptor, and Donatello the sculptor. Again, as in 1300, sculpture advanced a little ahead of painting. The new movement would have been impossible without the assistance of literary humanists, who advised the use of classical models and helped to patronize the new work. But it also required the skill of the craftsman. Great skill was required to devise the dome which Brunelleschi managed to place above the crossing of the Gothic cathedral of Florence, in imitation of the Pantheon at Rome and the Byzantine domes of Constantinople; great skill also was needed for the complex casting of the bronze of Donatello's *Judith and Holofernes*. Florence was a rich society with many brilliant artisans and much interest in palatial decoration. The basis of the artistic evolution was also, however, a fairly sudden determination, under humanist influence, to turn to classical models.

Brunelleschi's architecture in the loggia of the Innocenti orphanage made the decisive turn from the pointed arches of Gothic, normal in Italy as elsewhere throughout Europe, to the round arches of Roman architecture. Thus it became possible to develop an architecture which was based on the circle and the square, very different from the assumptions of the Gothic past. While a medieval church had been essentially a lengthy procession towards the altar, the trend was now essentially towards the concentric church, enclosed in cupolas and rounded arches. Brunelleschi moved towards this in his Florentine churches of San Lorenzo and Santo Spirito. Later came Alberti's architecture based more intellectually on the study of actual Roman remains, which found one of its main practical expressions at Sant' Andrea, Mantua, designed by him, where the huge and heavy arches foreshadowed the later development of churches. In the next generation came Donato Bramante (d. 1514), a Lombard whose most famous work was done at Rome, who went the whole way to the completely concentric church at San Pietro in Montorio, on a hill above the Vatican. Bramante was eventually to design the new St Peter's for Julius II, and this too was intended to be a concentric church in the form of a Greek cross, without the huge nave which was added by later masters. Thus the triumph of the Roman-Mediterranean spirit in architecture was complete.

It provided a setting for sculpture, again in imitation of classical remains. Brunelleschi had a friend and collaborator in Donatello (1386–1466) who was avid in his acceptance of classical inspiration and profound in his mastery of dramatic emotion expressed in stone and bronze, perhaps the greatest of all European sculptors. Donatello produced a long series of works, stretching from the first to the seventh decades of the century, which transformed sculpture through their examination of a wide variety of human figures and forms, from the confident beauty and innocence of the *Annunciation* in Santa Croce at Florence to the sinuous attractiveness of the *Bronze David* (Bargello, Florence) and the experience of suffering in the Christ of the late *Resurrection*

DONATELLO's *Healing of the Irascible Son*, a low relief in bronze on the altar of Sant'Antonio, Padua, 1446–50. This shows Donatello's characteristic skill with low relief, sculpture approaching close to painting, and also his devotion to complex perspective drawing in the background to the miracle.

relief (San Lorenzo, Florence). Donatello was fully awake to the demands of new spatial ideas of perspective and to the adoption of motifs taken over from ancient art but he added to these an exceptional grasp of humanity, which would be difficult to parallel.

Brunelleschi was the inventor of the new method of exact perspective, arranging scenes within orthogonals leading to a vanishing-point which gave a new confidence and substance to artistic space and was quickly taken up. It had a dramatic influence on the practice of painters, first exhibited by Masaccio (1401–28) in his fresco of the *Holy Trinity* set in a completely realistic chapel, a wholly successful space on a flat surface, which now became the standard practice of painters. By mid-century a whole school of Florentine painters was practising one or other variety or extension of the science of perspective and an age of spatial naturalism was in existence.

There were other schools of painting which grew up under the aegis of local tyrants anxious to enjoy modern culture and to add splendour to their capitals. The political fragmentation of Italy meant that centres of culture grew up not only in Florence, Venice, and Rome but also in petty states ruled by tyrants with taste: the Visconti and Sforza of Milan, the Gonzaga of Mantua, the Montefeltro of Urbino, to mention only the notable families of

GHIBERTI's *Jacob and Esau*, a panel in gilded bronze for the Gates of Paradise at the Baptistery, Florence, shows several temporal stages of the story within one spatial setting. In the foreground Esau approaches Jacob, against a background of low-relief classical architecture.

Facing: LEONARDO DA VINCI's *Lady with an Ermine* is a portrait of Cecilia Gallerani, a mistress of Leonardo's employer, Duke Ludovico il Moro of Milan, about 1489. Leonardo has successfully adopted the three-quarter pose and given the face more real character than other Italian portraitists could muster.

patrons. The lords of Urbino, for example, patronized Piero della Francesca (d. 1492), a painter who was not a member of the Florentine school, though he had learned from it, an enthusiast for perspective with the mathematical interest to write treatises about it. Both Piero's great series of frescoes of the *Legend of the Holy Tree* at San Francesco in Arezzo, telling the story from the time of Adam to the rediscovery of the cross by Helena and after, and his *Flagellation* at Urbino with its elaborate and delicate perspective drawing, show that it was possible for provincial art to reach the highest levels and that the existence, for political reasons, of a very large number of centres of patronage made possible a remarkably widespread variety of artistic achievement.

It was at this period that Italy clearly outstripped the rest of Europe in the luxuriousness of its artistic life. In the mid-century Alberti's Tempio Malatestiano at Rimini—another work paid for by a provincial despot—was a completely classical piece of architecture. The chapel of the Cardinal of Portugal at San Miniato, Florence, was produced in the 1460s by the joint efforts of architect, sculptor, and painter with extraordinarily delicate luxuriance. These and other artistic works set standards which would be followed by the rest of Europe, starting at least a century behind.

Florence under Lorenzo de' Medici

In the latter half of the fifteenth century the Florentine haven of culture was presided over for nearly a quarter of a century, 1469–92, by Lorenzo de' Medici, poet, aesthete, rich banker, and political manager, who established perhaps the nearest thing to an aesthetically inspired political regime seen in European history. Lorenzo was a Maecenas with political authority. One of the men who lived under his protection was Marsilio Ficino, the most important thinker of Renaissance Italy; a curious case, it might be said, of a man who was not outstanding as a philosopher, prophet, or writer but nevertheless whose literary output earned him a dominant position in Italian—and European—thought. With Medici patronage Ficino translated the whole of Plato into Latin, making most of the works available to the West for the first time, and added to that translations of the main Neoplatonic thinkers, Plotinus and Proclus, and the hermetic corpus. Neoplatonism was the key to Ficino's importance. The Neoplatonic cosmology placed the universe in a gradation extending from matter to spirit within a celestial system centred on earth. This coherent and beautiful picture of the universe had fascinated thinkers intermittently since the end of the Roman Empire. It was, for example, the physical system accepted in Dante's *Comedy*. Ficino's revelation of the riches of Platonic and Neoplatonic thought gave it a new impetus. Moreover he linked it with a devotion to the classical gods, some of whose names were attached to the planets, a conviction of the power of reason, love, and art to

improve man's position within the heavenly hierarchy, and a belief in the therapeutic value of natural magic. Perhaps it is not surprising that Ficino's art captivated writers and artists; it forms, for example, the concluding section of Castiglione's *Courtier*, written in the next generation, and certainly influenced Michelangelo. In spite of the difficulty of reconciling it with the Christian distinction between the Creator and his Creation it remained very influential for the next century.

Lorenzo's other main literary client was the poet Poliziano (1454–94). Poliziano was a considerable classical scholar but he was also, like Lorenzo himself, an Italian poet who revived vernacular poetry by writing the *Stanze* to celebrate a jousting competition won by Lorenzo's brother and composed a play about Orpheus which was eventually, more than a century later, to inspire the beginnings of opera. The extraordinarily rich assembly of talent in the visual arts which Florence had at that time enabled Lorenzo to use the export of artists as a diplomatic weapon, sending Ghirlandaio and others to paint the new Sistine Chapel walls for Pope Sixtus IV, Verrocchio to Venice to make an equestrian statue of the mercenary captain Colleoni, Filippino Lippi to Rome to paint for a cardinal, perhaps encouraging Leonardo da Vinci to go off to Milan as employee of the Sforza. Lorenzo himself was not particularly outstanding as a patron of the arts. But he presided over a city in which art was richly cultivated and the intellectual milieu encouraged the belief that art mattered. Lorenzo's capacity as a protector was shown by the refuge which he gave to the enterprising thinker Giovanni Pico della Mirandola (1463–94) whose attempt to amalgamate Christian, Jewish, and pagan ideas in one comprehensive philosophy had earned papal disapproval. Pico was not important to artists but in a less liberal climate not only he but also Ficino might have suffered from ecclesiastical disapproval.

Lorenzo's regime thus facilitated the existence of an aesthetic society, in which much of the art was naturally religious, but the glorification of the pagan gods was also encouraged—witness Botticelli's *Birth of Venus* which was to remain for so long a symbol of female beauty—and in which the cultivation of secular values was more or less unhindered by clerical disapproval. The sinuous and exaggerated beauty which Botticelli characteristically developed in his paintings was also associated with an elevation, for the first time, of classical stories to the very highest level of art, where they were to remain in the works of sixteenth-century painters and after. This was, in one sense, a continuation of the dependence on the divided thought-world, classical and Christian at the same time, which had been marked in the writings of Dante and Petrarch. But the Laurentian aesthetic confirmed the divided loyalty and gave it a dominant place in the visual world as well as the literary, imposing a firmer stamp on the Italian, and in consequence the European, mind.

The fragility of the Laurentian regime was shown disastrously by its col-

PONTORMO's *Entombment* in a chapel of the Capponi family at Santa Felicita, Florence, about 1525, is one of the early masterpieces of Mannerism. Pontormo has painted the figures almost as if they were floating rather than standing. This emphasis on refinement rather than straightforward realism became characteristic of the Mannerists.

lapse after his death in 1492 and replacement by the dominance of the Dominican friar Girolamo Savonarola from 1494 to 1498. Savonarola reminds us of the massive and continuous importance of the mendicant friars in Italian society, which must always be remembered as a balance to the delicate aestheticism which modern observers tend to venerate more highly. Though his sway over Florence was exceptional, Savonarola was not isolated. He belongs to the line which included St Catherine of Siena in the late fourteenth and San Bernardino in the early fifteenth centuries, that is to say the class of powerful holy men and women who effectively recalled Italian cities to their religious duties, a class which included many less eminent figures. Savonarola disapproved of paintings in which the Virgin was made into a débutante. He encouraged a return to the philosophical theology of Aquinas, a member of his own order, and puritanical bonfires of ladies' vanities. Combined with the collapse of Medici power after Lorenzo's death, this halted the progress of the Florentine artistic tradition.

Facing: FILIPPINO LIPPI's *Vision of St Bernard, c.*1485–90, in the Badia, Florence. St Bernard faces the Virgin and a group of angels, looking as though they might be modelled on the children of the donor, Francesco del Pugliese. Note the nervous irregularity of the rocky background.

Venetian Art

Meanwhile at Venice a new tradition was being brought into existence. Venice did not have the long and complex history of struggle with Christian and secular values which we see in the works of Dante, Petrarch, and Ficino. Venice introduced no very great thinker on religious issues. It was further from Rome and indeed had a stronger insistence on ecclesiastical independence from Rome than we see at Florence. Venetian attitudes were therefore more easily and unconcernedly secular and this will be seen in the next century, though it remains true that a large proportion of important art was ecclesiastical. In the late fifteenth century the two most prominent artists were Giovanni Bellini (d. 1516) and Vittore Carpaccio (c.1488–1526). Carpaccio's narrative paintings, the *Scenes from the Life of St Ursula* and the *Healing of the Possessed Man*, included the most realistic and artistically up-to-date representations of the life of the city. They were painted for display in the houses of lay religious societies, the so-called *scuole*, of which Venice had many, and no doubt they pandered to the members' liking for scenes which told a story and had a recognizable physical setting. Their themes were religious but nevertheless they exhibited a secular, urban realism which makes it easy to link them in the Venetian tradition with Canaletto and Guardi more than two centuries later. As we view the gondoliers on the Grand Canal in one scene of the *Healing of the Possessed Man*, or Gentile Bellini's *Procession in Piazza San Marco*, or the ships in the harbour in the *St Ursula* series, we feel, and with some justification, that we are seeing the fifteenth-century city as it was.

Andrea Mantegna (1431–1506) and Giovanni Bellini were brothers-in-law, both important in the history of art but very widely different in their inclina-

THREE PHILOSOPHERS by Giorgione, about 1505, has all Giorgione's mellow romanticism in the landscape. The figures are shown to be philosophers by the document one of them carries. Beyond this the picture is mysterious. Are they the Magi journeying to Christ? And why is one of them apparently staring into a cave?

tions. Mantegna spent most of his life as a court artist at the Gonzaga court at Mantua. He had keen archaeological interests and was responsible, more than any other artist of the period, for promoting the antiquarian fascination with the architecture, sculpture, and dress of the Roman period. A striking example of its influence was his series of nine *Triumphs of Caesar* (now at Hampton Court) which attempted to depict a Roman military parade faithfully. Mantegna had other gifts as an artist, for example in precise portraiture, shown in his portraits of the Gonzaga family fresco at the palace in Mantua. Bellini, essentially a Venetian, seems to have been daunted by Mantegna's archaeological learning but was in fact a more thoughtful and aspiring artist whose technical developments in the management of figure, face, and landscape place him beside Leonardo da Vinci as one of the main artistic revolutionaries who enabled Italian painting to reach the heights of the sixteenth century. A good example of his devout painting is the *St Francis Receiving the Stigmata*, now in the Frick Collection, New York, which places the powerful figure of the saint in a rich landscape and expresses successfully his relation both to the natural world and to the supernatural source of the stigmata. Bellini was among the early users of oil-paint, as opposed to the tempera which had been common before, and the subtlety of his command of facial expression in this medium, exhibited in a number of madonnas, was remarkable.

Close to the end of his life (the picture was completed in 1514) Bellini was persuaded to undertake a classical subject for the duke of Ferrara. The result was *The Feast of the Gods*, now in the National Gallery, Washington, an erotic collection of figures based on a story in Ovid. It was magnificently painted with all the skill that Bellini had acquired in half a century of religious painting. It was the first picture completed for a room which was later to include important works by Titian, forming a harmonious series, and must, in spite of its somewhat vulgar subject-matter, be regarded as a historical turning-point, rather like Botticelli's *Birth of Venus*: a skill acquired in ecclesiastical art magnificently applied to a secular and pagan story and creating the dream world of Mediterranean legend which was to be so important in the new century and to provide the essential glamour of Italian art as it was to be seen by the rest of Europe.

The other great revolutionary of Venetian painting, Giorgione, had died young in 1510, leaving a puzzling collection of secular works. Two of the most

THE SLEEPING VENUS, about 1510, is thought to have been begun by Giorgione and finished by Titian. The earliest of the great reclining nudes, it has a composed, scarcely erotic character, which contrasts with other nudes of the early sixteenth century, for instance by Titian and Giulio Romano.

famous of his pictures, *The Tempest* and *The Three Philosophers*, have defied interpretation; we do not know for certain what they were intended to represent. This has not prevented Giorgione from being enormously admired for the slightly sad and dreamy romanticism which was certainly characteristic of his work, and which, like the late pictures of Bellini, helped to turn Venetian and in general north Italian art towards the exciting originality characteristic of the sixteenth century. Two paintings which may be important works by Giorgione at the very end of his life—the *Sleeping Venus* in Dresden, said to have been completed by Titian, and the *Concert Champêtre* in the Louvre, Paris, which may be by Giorgione or Titian or neither—are again important transitional works which have posed problems to the art historian. The obscurity of Giorgione is a serious obstacle to the historian of culture. All we can say with certainty is that roughly between 1500 and 1515 Venetian art was moving rapidly into an important new phase.

Leonardo, Michelangelo, and Raphael

At about the same time striking developments were taking place in central Italian art associated mainly with the three giants, Leonardo da Vinci (1456–1519), Michelangelo (1475–1564), and Raphael (1483–1520). Leonardo and Michelangelo both began as young men patronized or assisted by Lorenzo de' Medici but they developed in very different ways. Leonardo, already a very accomplished painter whose skill in facial expression and composition could be seen in the *Adoration of the Magi* which he left behind in Florence unfinished, went to work in Milan from 1481 to 1499. There he received a salary as a court painter, which gave him the leisure to experiment. Leonardo was remarkable for two things. In the first place he was a ceaseless autodidact and investigator with an interest in mathematics, the invention of machines of many kinds, and the essential nature of the physical world, as exhibited, for instance, in the eddies of water, the turbulence of storms, and the terrestrial upheavals of earthquakes. Leonardo inherited his interest in perspective and of course many Italian artists also had a reputation as military engineers. But his wide-ranging and brilliant scientific curiosity was unique, apparently unconnected with the Laurentian school. It made him an aspiring inventive genius, parallel in a curious way to his contemporary Christopher Columbus (1451–1506), also of course an Italian, from Genoa. The background of Columbus's thought is perhaps even more mysterious than Leonardo's. But it certainly owed something to Italian speculations about the shape and geography of the earth. Columbus may have had some influence from the Florentine humanist Paolo Toscanelli, who was interested in the map of the world, and it is therefore conceivable, though rather unlikely, that his and Leonardo's intellectual backgrounds were remotely linked. Of course Leonardo's chief claim to fame was as a painter and Columbus's as a navigator. But both could be said to owe much to the adventurous, speculative attitude which was so characteristic of Italy in the late fifteenth and early sixteenth centuries. Leonardo was painting the *Last Supper* (1495–7) only a few years after Columbus set foot in America (1492). The two events remind one of the astonishing fecundity of the Italian mind at this time.

Leonardo's other claim to fame was his capacity to paint with a depth and skill which outshone his contemporaries. In the animation of the individual face, in the convincing relationships which he established between figures, in the chiaroscuro with which he clothed his forms—in all these things Leonardo seemed to surpass his contemporaries. When he returned from Milan to Florence in 1500 he was already a very famous man, his work much sought after by noble patrons, and he made a drawing of the Virgin and Child and St Anne which the Florentines queued up to see. Many of his works suffered to some extent because they were so dominated by experiment: the *Last Supper* ruined by paint which did not survive, *Mona Lisa* endlessly painted so that it lost contact with the original model. He moved about restlessly between Milan, Florence, Rome, and eventually Amboise in France and rarely finished anything. But his example dominated the art of central Italy.

Michelangelo was his great rival, practising sculpture, which Leonardo expressly despised, and rating it above painting. For a time in the early years of the sixteenth century they were both in Florence and it seems probable that Michelangelo's *Doni Tondo* (1504) was intended in part to rival Leonardo's drawings of the Holy Family. About the same time they both started work on paintings for the new council chamber of the Florentine republic, Leonardo planning a furious clash of horsemen at the Battle of Anghiari, Michelangelo a group of soldiers bathing before the Battle of Cascina. Michelangelo had already sculptured the flawless *Pietà* in Rome. Now he was persuaded by Pope Julius II to work in succession on two projects which called forth his greatest skill: Julius's tomb and the ceiling of the Sistine Chapel.

The tomb was intended to be a huge construction in St Peter's. Julius lost interest in it but, from Michelangelo's many years of labour, remain the huge figure of Moses and, perhaps more interesting from an intellectual point of view, the so-called *Slaves* in the Louvre. These are figures of male bodies escaping from the bonds of clothing. Michelangelo no doubt intended them to stand for the human soul freeing itself from the bonds of earthly existence and they are results of his devotion to the philosophy of Ficino, which remained part of his religious imagination throughout his life, as his poetry also shows. The Neoplatonist conception thus penetrated with Michelangelo to the centre of the Christian world. The Sistine ceiling required painting to complete the chapel founded by Julius's uncle Sixtus IV. Michelangelo placed on it the great series of scenes from Genesis, running from the Creation to the

Drunkenness of Noah, the Prophets and Sibyls who had foretold the coming of Christ, and Christ's ancestors, a panoply of the Christian tradition. But he also included the figures of nude men, again throwing off their bonds, like the *Slaves*, which are arguably the most striking parts of the ceiling and, with their probable intellectual explanation, emphasize the extent to which the fresco was produced by a combination of Christian and classical traditions.

BALDASSARE CASTIGLIONE, painted by Raphael about 1515, was the diplomatist and scholar who wrote *The Courtier*. Raphael knew him well in Urbino and Rome and captured the gentle charm of his character in an outstanding portrait.

Apart from Donato Bramante (1444–1514), the designer of the new St Peter's, the other main artist employed by Julius II was Raphael, who painted the walls of the papal apartments and also a portrait of Julius himself. Raphael was intellectually a less serious artist than Leonardo or Michelangelo, his masters, whose styles he adapted to the most delightful figure-painting of the Italian Renaissance. He had a very wide range of sympathy and of expressive power. The *Expulsion of Heliodorus* in the Stanza d'Eliodoro in the Vatican is a story-picture emphasizing papal righteousness. Raphael gave it great dramatic force and filled it with examples of masculine and feminine grace in the series of figures involved in the chase after the thieves and in the bystanders. In a quite different mood he could paint a portrait of a delightfully attractive young woman, the *Fornarina*, or a profoundly sensitive portrait of a highly intelligent and amiable scholar-administrator, *Baldassare Castiglione*, or of the pope, *Julius II* himself, not as a hieratic pontiff but as a tired and slightly apologetic old man. The *Triumph of Galatea*, painted for a Roman banker in the Villa Farnesina, a piece of frivolous painterly entertainment which though it is not serious does illustrate a classical story, marks the complete fulfilment of the Renaissance cultivation of the body. Raphael's work was the completion of the Renaissance grasp of humanity. These three artists of the early sixteenth century, Leonardo, Michelangelo, and Raphael, achieved a command of the human form which provided a kind of summit to the Renaissance.

Literature in the Age of Ariosto

While the papal buildings at home were being rebuilt and redecorated Niccolò Machiavelli (1469–1527) was composing *The Prince* (*Il principe*), another

creation of the Italians which was to reverberate through Europe. Machiavelli's view that the successful ruler must be ruthless, if necessary immoral,
in the pursuit of political stability was the end-product of the cultivation of the
new political thought in fifteenth-century Italy and also the main vehicle in
which Italian political thought was transferred to northern politicians, ideas
first proposed with relation to the city-state often being used later on in connection with the quite different nation-state. Machiavelli had a humanist
training but he had also been deeply involved in the actual politics of Florence
and knew that the republican city-state was in deep trouble in the world of
despots and foreign kings. *The Prince* was therefore the result of a disabused
observation by one who had the highest qualifications. As the political philosophy inaugurated by the earliest humanists reached its literary summit in *The
Prince*, the writing of political history also broke through to its complete fulfilment in the *History of Florence* and *History of Italy* by Machiavelli's contemporary, Francesco Guicciardini (1483–1540), who wrote in a manner which
remains recognizable in the twentieth century as a rational portrayal of events
related to causes.

Machiavelli's greatest literary contemporary, however, was the Ferrarese
poet Ludovico Ariosto (1474–1533). His *Orlando Furioso*, which emerged in the
first edition (1516) close in time to *The Prince* and to the visual works at Rome
and Venice (another cultural concatenation to rival the trio Dante–Giotto–
Duccio), was a long poem and a new romance epic. Its subject-matter was
related to the history of the Este family, rulers of Ferrara and Ariosto's
patrons, but it essentially concerned the history of love, its pains, disasters,
and happiness, presented partly through two main love stories, that of
Orlando and Angelica whose betrayal drives Orlando to madness, and that of
Ruggero and Bradamante leading happily to the founding of the Este dynasty.
These stories are contained within an extremely complex world of other
characters and events, fantastic warfare and magic, confrontation of Christian
and pagan armies. Ariosto's world is made up partly from the romance narrative traditions which he inherited, partly from the military adventure of the
Italian world in which he played a part, but partly also from his own serious
and semi-serious reflections on the effects of love. There is thus a curious
combination of the epic, admired in courtly society, with a fuller presentation
of character and emotion which to some extent steps out of the one-
dimensional romance background.

The courtly world of the despot, for which Ariosto wrote, was also celebrated in *The Courtier* (*Il cortegiano*) by Baldassare Castiglione (1478–1529),
again written in the first version about the same time. Castiglione was a gentleman from Mantua, who was attached from 1504 to 1513 to the court of
Urbino, ruled for most of that time by Duke Guidobaldo Montefeltro. This
was the setting for his book, an Italian dialogue between courtiers. It owed

something to the more expressly erudite Latin dialogues of the humanists, in the sense of using that form for the expression of opinions about philosophical or semi-philosophical matters. But, like *The Prince* and *Orlando Furioso*, it pushed the old, inherited form forward into a more modern taste, making it more lifelike, so that some of the interchanges between the characters were in fact quite like actual conversation of a rather mannered and witty kind. It is interesting too that women play a fairly substantial part in *The Courtier*. The subject-matter is the variety of ways in which a courtier should behave: his need for accomplishment as a soldier, as a negotiator, as a player and a lover, as an adviser of the prince, his master. Castiglione's book, reflecting a world which was immediately recognizable to inhabitants of courts all over Italy and Europe, was an enormous success throughout the sixteenth century. The last section of the book presented Ficino's idealization of love, an interesting indication of the strength of that idea's hold on courtly as well as republican Italy, stated fictionally by Pietro Bembo, a very well-known Venetian patrician, who had in real life published an account of Ficino's ideas and had been a lover of Lucrezia

THE VILLA ROTONDA near Vicenza, begun by Palladio in 1550, is the most striking example of his classicism in secular buildings. It is symmetrical. The architect has paid much more attention to extravagant classicism in the columns and pediments than to the convenience of the interior, which is rather limited.

Borgia, though he later became a cardinal. Bembo was an influential arbiter of taste in the writing of Italian.

Sixteenth-Century Venice

The position of Bembo with Castiglione, Machiavelli, and Ariosto at the beginning of the sixteenth century showed that the purely Latin phase of humanism had come to an end. The vernacular Italian had now reasserted itself, absorbing the effects of the humanist movement of the fifteenth century. Paradoxically, about the same time Aldus Manutius (d. 1515) was printing his new small editions of the classics at Venice, to export them all over Europe and to give printing, first introduced into Italy in the 1460s, a very much enlarged function in meeting the demands of a mass market. Both these movements, however, testified to the great strength of bourgeois secular society at this period in raising levels of intellectual refinement which were to provide models for the rest of Europe.

After the first quarter of the sixteenth century, Venice, still a very rich republic, jealous of its independence from Rome, and the associated university of Padua, which had retained its attachment to Aristotelian science since the thirteenth century, provided the most original and interesting cultural manifestations. Renaissance architecture had had its earlier development in Florence and Rome. It was decisively taken over by Venice when Sebastiano Serlio (1475–1554) published his books on classical architecture in 1537 and 1540. Jacopo Sansovino designed the classical façade of the library of St Mark's, which still faces the Piazza San Marco, about the same time. Then came Andrea Palladio (1508–80) whose *Four Books on Architecture* was published in Venice in 1570 and became the most influential guide to the classical style in other parts of Europe, superseding Alberti. Palladio was building from the 1540s in and around Vicenza where he evolved his style for the palace or the country house, often using broad colonnades, which to some extent typify his work in this kind of building. Then, late in life, he moved to Venice and produced his famous churches overlooking the water, San Giorgio Maggiore and the Redentore. Taken as a whole Palladio's buildings symbolize the classicism of Venice in its golden age, when economic decline had only just set in, the splendour both of the city itself and of the fine houses which its nobles built on the mainland.

At the same time Titian, Veronese, and Tintoretto were creating the painting of classical Venice. Titian (*c.*1485–1576), like Michelangelo long-lived, and even more endlessly productive, left masterpieces which expounded supremely both the intense religious enthusiasm of the Italian world and its capacity for classical eroticism. His farewell to art was the Pietà which had to be finished by Palla Giovane after his death. Before a broad classical niche the dead Jesus lies on his mother's knees. On one side Titian himself approaches kneeling to the dead Christ; on the other side the Magdalene walks out with raised proclaiming hand, making an affirmation of the tragedy and glory of religion and life. This dramatic religious scene is placed in a classical setting. Titian had painted many powerful religious scenes, for example the *Martyrdom of St Lawrence* (*c.*1548–57), a terrifying portrayal of the saint burning on the gridiron, turning for spiritual hope to the angelic saviours appearing from heaven above him. But Titian was also much patronized by nobles and princes. There were the pictures done for the Duke of Ferrara's *Camerino* in the 1520s, following Giovanni Bellini's *Feast of the Gods*, including the delightful *Bacchus and Ariadne* in the National Gallery, London. These established a capacity for treating secular subjects of classical legend. Later in his long life Titian worked for Pope Paul III, the Emperor Charles V, and Philip II of Spain. Philip's orders included several pictures of events in the life of the huntress Diana, including, for example, *Diana and Actaeon* in the National Gallery, Edinburgh, where Actaeon appears to surprise Diana and her ladies naked beside the bathing pool. These sensuous pictures continued the process of adapting painting gradually to secular stories, in which Titian was perhaps the

THE TRANSPORT OF THE
BODY OF ST MARK
exhibits some of Jacopo
Tintoretto's character-
istics as a painter, in
particular the deep
perspective vista and
the eerie colouring
resulting from the
lightning, which is
supposed to have caused
alarm, permitting the
flight of the body.

greatest master, and his combination of religious and mythological art was
the most splendid expression of the duality of the Italian imagination.

Titian's younger contemporaries, Veronese (1528–88) and Tintoretto
(1518–94), were both painters on a grandiose scale, partly a result of the primacy of colour in Venetian art as opposed to drawing in Florentine art. The
Venetian style probably facilitated rapidly sketched work on a very broad canvas. Veronese's penchant was for grandeur, exhibited in rising sweeps of dizzy
perspective or more ordinarily in plain architectural vistas. His leaning to the
ceremonial was exhibited in a very large number of canvases, but he was also

capable of a delicacy of expression which was rather more tender than Titian's. The two characteristics appear for example in *Alexander and the Family of Darius* (1565–70) (painted, incidentally, when he was temporarily in exile because of a brush with the Inquisition) where the high, arched bridge is in the background and both Alexander and the kneeling ladies have real expressions. Tintoretto painted some even larger pictures: witness the enormous and not very successful *Paradise* (1588, completed by his son) for the council-chambers in the ducal palace, a building which offered big opportunities to Venetian artists. His paintings covered most of the walls of the Scuola Grande di San Rocco, the house of a wealthy lay confraternity, and his instincts were on the whole distinctly more religious than Veronese's. His most striking gift was for the perspective view, to which distance added excitement and colour, and light, together with much darkness, gave both mystery and charm. The *Transport of the Body of St Mark* in the Accademia at Venice is a very striking example in which an air of mystery is created by the perspective and the obscurity of the figures, seeming to link the painting almost with modern surrealism. In spite of his strong religiosity Tintoretto painted with an inventive freedom which was one of the clearest indications of the enormous changes in Italian control of visual art since the thirteenth century.

The wealth of Italian visual art in the sixteenth century was overwhelming and it would be impossible in a short chapter even to list major figures. The wealth of Italian literature was less impressive but still considerable. The aim in this account has been only to indicate the most dramatic innovations at times when the Italian mind was particularly original because social development carried it into hitherto unknown fields of human experience. The early sixteenth century in Italy had been one of the great creative periods in human history. The later sixteenth century was somewhat less interesting for two reasons: first because Italian economic supremacy was waning and, second, because the decline of republican regimes and the new strengthening of ecclesiastical authority limited the possibilities of full inventiveness. Nevertheless, at the end of the century Italy was able to produce an Annibale Carracci (1560–1609) and a Caravaggio (1571–1610) in painting. Torquato Tasso (1544–1595), like Ariosto a poet associated with the Este court at Ferrara, wrote the *Gerusalemme liberata*, which carried the epic style into an account of the crusading capture of Jerusalem. Giovanni Palestrina (d. 1594) bore church music to new heights at Rome, and the great revolutionary Monteverdi was approaching maturity when the century ended. There was plenty of innovation to come.

⟡ 5 ⟡

ITALY 1600–1796

STUART WOOLF

The Forgotten Centuries

For contemporaries, as for later historians, the two centuries between the Peace of Câteau Cambrésis (1559) and that of Aix-la-Chapelle (1748) marked a low point in Italian history, as negative as the centuries that followed the collapse of the Roman Empire. Contemporaries, like Francesco Guicciardini, inevitably looked back to the golden age of cultural leadership in Europe of the Italian city-states, which heightened their sense of humiliation at the transformation of the peninsula into the battlefield and colonial supply-line of foreign powers. Historians, on the other hand—from Cesare Balbo to Benedetto Croce—by looking forward to the epic of the Risorgimento accentuated the darkness of the preceding centuries of Habsburg domination.

Even allowing for the literary flourishes of metaphors of decadence, in political and economic terms Italy in the seventeenth and eighteenth centuries undoubtedly moved on a different, and lower, level than in its earlier age of glory. But it would be erroneous to belittle the significance of these centuries, as the impact of the Counter-Reformation, on the one hand, and the aristocratic restructuring of society, on the other, were to leave a lasting imprint and constraint on Italy's subsequent evolution.

Italy under Foreign Domination

The wealth of Italy had attracted the initial invasion of foreigners and the prolonged duel between France and Spain until Câteau Cambrésis. By 1600 the political geography of the peninsula had acquired firm contours, which were only subjected to relatively minor modifications until the succession wars of the following century. Possession of the duchy of Milan and the kingdoms of Naples, Sicily, and Sardinia were crucial for Spain's pursuance of its imperialist ambitions in Europe, first as the route to Flanders, then for intervention in the Thirty Years War. The presence of so great a power constrained the freedom of action of the other Italian princes, even if initially, in the age of Philip

II and Lepanto, their naval forces still provided a margin of autonomy. The contemptuous disregard of their sovereignty by mercenary armies during the European wars provided constant evidence of the weakness of the princes. Their sophisticated diplomatic skills, once so eulogized by Machiavelli, were rendered impotent, to the point that by the mid-seventeenth century Torquato Accetto, in his tract *On Honest Dissimulation* (*Della dissimulazione onesta*, 1641), could caution Italy's rulers to hide their *virtù*.

In the north, Spanish garrisons and troops in Lombardy provided a constant reminder of their vulnerability to the Republic of Venice and the dukes of Savoy; Habsburg imperial troops besieged and sacked Mantua in 1630, on the excuse of contesting the succession of the last Gonzaga duke. In central Italy, the grand dukes of Tuscany were firmly boxed in by the Spanish creation of a garrison state on the Tuscan coast (the state of the Presidii: Piombino, Elba, and the Argentario promontory). The Republic of Genoa was tied by the umbilical cord of its loans to the kings of Spain, at least until the Spanish bankruptcy of 1627; and the Papal States by the reliance of successive popes on the military arm of Spain to uphold and enforce the Counter-Reformation.

The territory of Italy was as important to European statesmen in terms of the balance of power as were its cultural artefacts to European élites on the grand tour. Moreover, it was a territory in which it was relatively easy to intervene, not least because of the claims to feudal suzerainty of pope and emperor, ultimate legacy of the great medieval conflicts. Feudal devolution provided legitimation for the annexation of states on the extinction of their dynasties: the Papacy seized Ferrara (1598) and Urbino (1631) on the deaths of the last Este and Della Rovere; the Habsburg emperor confiscated Mantua during the lifetime of the last Gonzaga duke (1708). The presence of imperial and papal fiefs within their territories weakened the efforts of the various Italian rulers to impose exclusive authority over their subjects.

Even after the end of the Thirty Years War (1648), when Spain's decline was apparent to all, the Italian princes remained powerless, dependent on decisions taken elsewhere. For even without the dubious legitimation of feudal devolution, the great powers had no scruples in decreeing the destiny of the Italian states, disposing of them as if they were colonies. In the first half of the eighteenth century, control of Italy and possession of Spain's Italian provinces were essential elements in the complex settlements that followed the three succession wars. The Austrian Habsburgs succeeded their Spanish cousins in Italy, in compensation for their loss of Spain (1713), despite the protests of the Papacy; Tuscany was assigned to the Empress Maria Theresa's husband, Francis Stephen of Habsburg-Lorraine, on the death of the last Medici (1737). From protagonist of the European scene in the Middle Ages and Renaissance, Italy had become a passive object of international politics, a condition in which it was to remain until the Revolutions of 1848.

JACOPO TINTORETTO's *Susanna and the Elders* (1557) is an exception to the religious scenes commonly painted by him. Susanna's is an apocryphal religious story, but it was used by Tintoretto and others as an excuse for the painting of the female nude, here in a rich garden, painted with the accomplishment of Venetian art at its height.

Only one dynasty, the Savoy rulers of Piedmont-Savoy, tried to exploit the rivalry of France and Spain through a hazardous policy of constant change of alliances and intervention in the wars in exchange for expansion of its territories. Despite its ultimate success, this highly militaristic dynasty remained a client state, dependent on the favour of the great powers, as was made evident in 1720, when Victor Amadeus II was forced to renounce the Kingdom of Sicily for the impoverished island of Sardinia.

The Crisis of the Economy

If politically the Italian states lost their autonomy following the invasions and establishment of Spanish rule, economically Italy plunged from its major role in Europe during the crisis of the seventeenth century.

During the later sixteenth century, northern and central Italy experienced an industrial boom: production and export of mainly luxury goods—textile cloths, ironware, firearms, crystal glass, ceramics, printing, quality soap, leather—had increased to unprecedented levels in Venice, Milan, Florence, and a multitude of smaller cities. Venice's production of fine woollen cloths rose from 1,310 pieces in 1503 to 28,729 in 1602; Milan had 3,000 silk looms in 1606; Florence more than doubled its production of woollen cloths between 1553 and 1572, from 14,700 to 33,312 pieces. Southern Italy, which included major artisan centres in Naples and Salerno, was closely integrated to the manufactures further north through its export of raw materials, from the

Facing: URBINO is the supreme example of the Court as city, with Federico of Montefeltro's great castle dominating the city. The castle palace incorporated and exhibited all the needs and virtues of the prince, from the practical demands of administration to the famous *studiolo* of the humanist philosopher. Urbino city was in every sense subservient to the palace, as can be seen in this aerial view.

crude silk of Calabria to the wool of the vast transhumant sheep flocks passing through the *dogana* of Foggia, and the cereals and olive oil of Apulia, shipped to Venice.

Northern and central Italy remained one of the most developed industrial areas of Europe into the first decades of the seventeenth century. Its strength lay in the scale of its exports of manufactured goods and banking services to the Levant and across all Europe. The turning-point came with the commercial crisis of 1619–22. All the indicators, from levels of production to customs revenue or numbers of artisans in the guilds, then confirm a sharp and irreversible decline: Florence only produced about 6,000 cloths around 1650, Venice a mere 3,820 in 1680. Only industries directly related to the military operations in northern Italy—construction of fortifications and armaments—remained buoyant until the mid-seventeenth century.

The industrial decline of Italy was the result of the loss of its export markets to the competition of the cheaper, lighter new draperies produced in northern Europe. Whereas across the Alps the economic depression of the seventeenth century had led to a relocation and restructuring of the textile industries in the countryside, in Italy the guilds, closely identified with the civic authorities, proved too rigid, insisting on quality of product, high wage levels, and the monopoly of production within the cities. The English, the Dutch, and soon the French, taking advantage of Venice's wars against the Ottoman Empire in defence of its colonies, penetrated the Mediterranean. Venice's decline was Leghorn's gain, as the free port, established by the grand dukes of Tuscany in the 1590s, became the supply base for foreign ships.

By the eighteenth century the consequences for the Italian economy of this long process of decline were everywhere visible. From exporter of manufactures, Italy had become a major market for import of foreign manufactured goods and exporter of primary and semi-finished produce. Nowhere was this more visible than in the silk industry, where northern Italy, once the major exporter of silk brocades and cloths, now only managed to continue to export few and cheaper items, like ribbons, while expanding its production of crude silk as the main supplier to the Lyons silk industry. Major cities, like Venice, Florence, or Naples, became consumption centres, dependent on their administrative role as capitals, their courts, and the rising flow of tourists; many smaller cities, once famed for their manufactures, like Como, Pavia, Cremona, or Lecce in Apulia, became provincial backwaters. Perhaps only the building sector retained a certain resilience, still visible today in the ubiquitous baroque churches and palaces of Italy.

The complementarity between the two areas of the Italian economy was irrevocably broken with the drastic fall in demand in the north and centre: in the south, market-oriented products vanished, like Calabrian crude silk, or retracted, like Sicilian vines. The economic circuits within the peninsula, which had boosted internal demand and provided a certain unity to the Italian economy, broke up into a multitude of local markets.

As urban production collapsed, from the later seventeenth century rural textile and metalworking activities developed in northern and central Italy, and on a more limited scale in the south. As elsewhere in Europe, they tended to be concentrated in areas of smallholdings, subsistence agriculture, and abundant population, such as the foothills and lower valleys of the Alps, from Venetia to Piedmont, the Ligurian Apennines, or the Salernitano. But, in contrast to the high-quality urban manufactures of the sixteenth century, such cheaper-quality artisan production was now primarily oriented towards local markets, or carried abroad in small quantities by pedlars and chapmen.

Population and Plague

Italy was among the more densely inhabited areas of Europe, where pressure on agricultural resources was periodically relieved, in Malthusian style, by famine or plague. By the mid-sixteenth century Italy's population had finally recovered to the pre-1348 plague level of 11 million; by 1600 it had increased to 13.3 million. Already before the industrial crisis, the limits of a generally traditional agriculture in feeding a rapidly rising population had become apparent. The traditional granaries of Sicily were no longer capable of making up the shortfall in northern Italy, as was demonstrated in the terrible famines of 1590–1. Plague then diminished demographic pressure. But nearly two centuries later, when the population had once more risen to 15.5 million, the traumatic famines of 1764–6 led to sharp increases of mortality among the peasantry of southern Italy and incited the Tuscan physiocrats to radical measures of reform.

The regression of the urban economies in northern and central Italy was accompanied, and certainly accentuated, by the devastating plagues of 1630, immortalized in Alessandro Manzoni's novel *I promessi sposi* [The Betrothed]. The plague, while erratic in its incidence, killed between a third and a half of the inhabitants of many cities and villages, including the capital Milan. In 1656 an outbreak of plague, of similar intensity, attacked the vast metropolis of Naples (the most populous city of Europe at the end of the sixteenth century, with 250,000 inhabitants), and spread across the southern mainland. But it was not just the plague that was responsible for the overall fall in Italian population; for many towns barely touched by the plague, like Macerata, experienced repeated mortality crises throughout the seventeenth century, coincidental with poor harvests and high wheat prices.

Overall, the population of Italy only recovered its 1600 level a century later, more rapidly in the north than in the south, but still far behind the demographic growth of northern Europe. As significantly, when population began

THE PLAGUE AT NAPLES, by Domenico Gargiulo (1656). By the seventeenth century the plague occurred ever less frequently, but with greater intensity. After its prolonged passage in the Po plain in 1630-1, its outbreak in 1656 in so densely populated a city as Naples was predictably devastating. Gargiulo dramatically renders in apocalyptic overtones the sense of disordered urgency of the living to distance themselves from and dispose of the infected corpses and their bed-clothing.

to increase more rapidly during the eighteenth century, rising to 18.1 million in 1800, this did not affect the cities, whose populations remained stagnant. The sole exception was Naples, whose population doubled in the eighteenth century to over 400,000 through constant immigration, confirming the growing pressure on subsistence levels of rural population growth.

Spanish Italy

Spanish rule in Italy was based on the same principles as applied to the component states of the monarchy in Spain, and more generally to early modern European monarchies: acceptance of the sovereign's authority by the traditional representatives of the nation in return for recognition of their privileges and rights. In formal constitutional terms, these representatives varied from state to state, from the senate of Milan to the parliaments of Sicily and Sardinia or the municipal *seggi* of Naples. In practice, they consisted of powerful and wealthy nobilities, whether feudal (in the southern Italian states) or of urban patrician origin (in the State of Milan). The major innovation was the establishment of the Spanish Inquisition in the two islands of Sicily and Sardinia, closely allied to the viceregal administrations.

In Italy, as in Spain, such an arrangement failed to develop into the contours of the early modern absolutist state, on the model of France or Prussia, because of the financial implications of the Most Catholic monarchy's continuous involvement in European-scale wars. Under Charles V, and still under Philip II, the policy of alienating fiefs established a tacit equilibrium by which state control over large areas of the provinces was delegated to local powers. In the first half of the seventeenth century the spiralling exactions to sustain the costs of the wars increased the presence of the state, but also accentuated its reliance on the support of the élites in the periphery.

In the State of Milan, citizens and patricians, as well as peasants, were taxed ever more heavily; the city of Cremona, for example, increased its 'civil tax' from 70,000 lire in 1565 to 1,359,000 lire in 1630. The central administrative institutions did little more than coordinate the fiscal, military, and provisioning obligations of the individual cities. The huge increase in levies overlapped with the economic depression. But it was compensated in part by the receipt of financial subsidies, from both Madrid and Spain's other Italian states, because Milan was the only Spanish possession that experienced military campaigns.

The other Italian provinces were forced increasingly to contribute to Spain's wars without any counterpart. In Sardinia, the poorest region, parliament was forced to increase its 'voluntary' contribution of 15,000 ducats sixfold between 1613 and 1626. Sicily sent 10 million scudi to Milan between 1620 and 1650. The Kingdom of Naples, second only to Castile in terms of money raised for the wars, increased its contributions from 835,000 ducats in 1616 to 11,709,000 in 1645.

Inevitably such huge levies had devastating economic, social, and political consequences. No administration was able to exact these vast sums from its populations. New taxes were invented, state and communal revenues were alienated, noble titles and feudal properties sold. Loans were raised from local families and foreign bankers, until the accumulated debts led to official bankruptcies. In the State of Milan, the market in fiefs of the 1640s reinforced the position of the old and new nobility. In Sicily and Naples, Genoese and Tuscan financiers took advantage of the crisis in public finances until, following the bankruptcies, they were replaced by local speculators and wealthy nobles. In these southern kingdoms, old feudal dynasties and new families exploited the difficulties of the government to increase their pressure on the peasantry on a scale unknown in Lombardy.

The financial exactions finally sparked off political revolt. The most spectacular instance, which aroused the attention of contemporaries across Europe and was rapidly transmuted in historical memory, was the revolt of Naples in 1647. The image of the revolt is indissolubly linked to the name of its fisherman leader Masaniello, who led its first, brief phase of a genuinely pop-

THE NEAPOLITAN
REVOLUTION of 1647
struck the contemporary
imagination, to judge
by the gazettes and
prints, because of the
charismatic figure of
the fisherman leader
Masaniello, and his
capacity to arouse the
popular classes of Naples
against the great power
of Spain. This engraving
by Micco Spadaro, with
Vesuvius as backcloth,
stresses this popular
aspect.

ular and ritualistic rising in the name of the Virgin of the Carmine against tax collectors, speculators, and unpopular ministers. Popular religiosity, as the revolt showed, could be turned against established authority. But the spread of the revolt to the provincial cities, with a strongly anti-feudal colouring; the obscure machinations of a French aristocratic adventurer, the duke of Guise; the proclamation of a republic; and the deep, social divisions between capital and provinces, peasantry, feudal barons, and royal magistrates, were all evidence of the divisive aftermath of the collapse of royal authority. Repression of the revolt and restoration of royal authority were dependent on the collaboration of the baronage, whose fiefs were recognized as part of the administrative structure of the state.

In Sicily and Sardinia, the escalating fiscal exactions also underlay political revolts against Spanish power. The Neapolitan revolt had been anticipated by the revolt of Palermo and other Sicilian towns in the same year. Here too popular attack on noble privileges and the proclamation of a republic brought together the viceregal administration and the feudal barons of Palermo. The revolts in 1672 and 1674 of the mercantile city of Messina re-enacted the same social antagonisms between privileged nobles and the 'popular' guilds, but were confined by the traditional rivalry of the capital Palermo. In Sardinia, the refusal of Madrid to respect redress of grievances in return for parliamentary grants finally led to open revolt by feudal barons (1668).

The longer-term consequences of Spain's utilization of its Italian provinces for its European wars, and the opposition this provoked, was definitively to remove the possibilities of imposing more centralized authority within these Italian states. Stability demanded recognition of the existing order, on the part of both viceroys and privileged bodies. In Sicily the administration would rely on the Spanish Inquisition as a counterweight to the baronage. In Naples magistrates and lawyers close to the administration would contest papal claims of suzerainty. But throughout Spanish Italy the power and privileges of the landed aristocracy, whether feudal or patrician, were consolidated in the later seventeenth century.

The Counter-Reformation

Although Spain was the paladin of the Counter-Reformation in Europe, it would be mistaken to attribute to it any direct role in the diffusion of the Counter-Reformation. On the one hand, it was only able to establish the Spanish Inquisition at Palermo and Cagliari, former possessions of the crown of Aragon, and was unable to overcome the resistance of the local élites at Naples. On the other hand, Spain's representatives in Italy followed Madrid's rejection of Rome's pretensions to jurisdictional privileges. In Naples in particular (where the popes claimed feudal suzerainty), already at the beginning of the seventeenth century a royal lawyer was elaborating on the doctrine of the kingdom's autonomy in a conflict between secular and ecclesiastical courts, a theme which was to re-emerge forcefully from the 1680s and culminate in Pietro Giannone's great *Civil History of the Kingdom of Naples* in 1723.

The Counter-Reformation was so successful in Italy because of the remarkable ability of the Catholic Church to respond to and direct the undoubted demands for the reform of the Church that had affected Italy as much as other parts of Europe in the first half of the sixteenth century. Fear of heresy had dominated the immediate phase following the Council of Trent. The danger of Protestantism had been blocked in the Aosta Valley and generally in northern and central Italy

GALILEO GALILEI (1564–1642) belonged to the great scientific tradition of Pisa university. Although Tuscany offered a relative haven from Counter-Reformation pressures, Galilei was forced to abjure his public espousal of Copernico's heretical views. But this saved his life, whereas Giordano Bruno was burnt at the stake.

by visitations and persecution, with the sole exception of the old-established Waldensian settlements in west Piedmont. But the price of religious uniformity was high: entire villages of Waldensians—or *Valdesi*—in Calabria had been massacred (1561). The small Jewish communities of Italy had been segregated in ghettos. The substantial numbers of Muslim slaves in southern Italian cities (10,000 in Naples around 1640) were subjected to intense efforts at conversion.

From the 1570s until the 1630s a succession of vigorous popes—from Pius V (1567–72) to Urban VIII (1623–44)—imposed, in highly centralized fashion, the application of the decrees of the Council of Trent. The hierarchical Church became the Church militant, exclusive repository of doctrinal truth. Politically, this new self-confidence explains the pope's arrogant and unsuccessful attempt to exploit spiritual arms in Church–State relations in the Interdict of Venice (1606). Socially, there were multiple implications, both immediate and longer term, for the fragmented, stratified, and conflictual societies of seventeenth-century Italy in this unified *reconquista* of civil society to a single faith.

In the country where humanism had flourished only a few decades earlier, where the formalized but unbound exchanges of high culture between laymen and clergy had led to new levels of intellectual and moral commitment, the boundary between acceptable and unacceptable discussion was set unilaterally by the Church—as Galileo discovered to his humiliation in 1633. Literati were not only excluded from the Church's sphere, but were obliged to declare their acceptance of elementary doctrinal principles, and warned against public mockery or criticism of the elaborate rituals and ceremonies devised for the people. Already by the end of the sixteenth century, they had accepted their subordinate role and learnt to practise the virtues of prudence and patience.

Within the Church, now staffed exclusively by clergy, a renewed Catholic culture was forged and imposed on Italian society. It was a socially and hierarchically structured culture, with the message adapted to the level of education, in which ignorance was equated with peasants and artisans. The great reforming bishops of the later sixteenth century and the Jesuits had shown the way, through their strong awareness of the need for seminaries to train priests as the new class of ecclesiastical intellectuals responsible for indoctrinating the ignorant, and colleges to educate the children of the lay aristocratic élites. The religious orders, particularly the new ones, played a major role in spreading the word, because of the relative shortage (and lack of preparation in the south) of secular priests. But the parish priest, supported by the new confraternities of the Christian Doctrine and Sacred Sacrament, firmly under the control of the diocesan bishop, was the ideal central figure, trained through the Roman catechism to hear confessions and deliver socially appropriate sermons, to guide and control the faithful from birth to death.

The links of the Church with the nobilities of Italian society remained inti-

Facing: CHAPEL OF THE HOLY SHROUD, in Turin Cathedral. G. Guarini (1624–83) was one of the most original baroque architects in Italy and Europe, who worked almost exclusively in Turin and Piedmont. A Theatine priest, he used his mathematical skills to launch audacious constructions reaching for the heavens, nowhere more visibly than in this extraordinary chapel built to house the Holy Shroud.

MONSTRANCE OF THE HOLY SHROUD at Turin, 1613. The shroud in which, it was claimed, the body of Christ was wrapped, was venerated from the fourteenth century in Champagne. It was moved from Chambéry to Turin in 1578 by Emanuel Philibert (1559–80) in order to enhance the role of the Savoyard dynasty. In this engraving by A. Tempesta, the monstrance is set in the central piazza of Turin in front of the royal palace.

mate: the ecclesiastical hierarchy (especially the now predominantly Italian body of cardinals) was recruited from their ranks; their children were educated by the Jesuits; they continued to control benefices and nomination of priests. Above all, the Church's vision of society was intimately hierarchical, from its organization of religious ceremonies and processions along lines of social standing to its sermons to the people on the duties of obedience, respect, and resignation, and the expulsion of the poor from the sight of the well-ordered society: in the later seventeenth and early eighteenth century Jesuits successfully preached the need to erect enormous hospitals to segregate and enclose the poor, the sick, and other marginal groups in most of the capitals of Italy.

But whatever its material and mental closeness to the lay nobilities of Italy, the Church successfully represented itself as a body apart from and superior to lay society in the course of the seventeenth century. From cardinals and bishops to religious and secular clergy, the figure of the priest was exalted and distinguished from laymen by cassock, speech, and behaviour. The baroque churches and sanctuaries of Italian Catholicism were a flamboyant and aggressive manifestation of the Church's superiority. The enormous growth of its properties and incomes was evidence—like the increase in the number of convents, conservatories, and charitable institutions—of the Church's success among the wealthy classes.

The massive spread of new forms of popular religiosity provided as strong evidence of its success among the people. In the Kingdom of Naples, from the end of the sixteenth century, missionaries from Jesuit, Barnabite, and the other new orders, modelling themselves on the Jesuit experiences among the South American Indians, set out to preach the word; their activities extended in a slightly later period to northern and central Italy. The missions were followed by more permanent congregations, confraternities, and oratories, recruited from the nobility and higher bureaucracy.

Throughout Italy the message of the Catholic reform was carried in multiple ways. It was a carefully filtered message, to the point of imposing tight procedural control from Rome over local initiatives to create saints. Rome, with its holy years, together with Loreto and Assisi, attracted religious tourists on an unprecedented scale; Marian sanctuaries, reliquaries, and saints' bodies provided the local structures for networks of pilgrims. Paintings in churches, like prints of pious images in the home, offered continuous reminders of the influence of the supernatural on everyday life. Religious books, particularly hagiographies, were printed in increasing numbers until the mid-eighteenth century, in Venice as much as in Naples: written for clergy and the educated faithful, they were passed on in sermons and spiritual gatherings to the illiterate masses. The *bizzocche*, tertiary sisters too poor to enter convents, spread the cult of images, saints, and reliquaries among the women of their neighbourhoods.

By the eighteenth century a popular Catholicism had taken root among the illiterate masses in Italy, as much in the cities as in the countryside. Selectively incorporating and redirecting earlier popular rites and traditions, it was structured around the cult of the Virgin and saints, increasingly identified as direct intermediaries with the divine. It was a collective, theatrical expression of faith, symbolized by the new cult of the rosary, a public gesture of devoutness, a visible accompaniment to the litany of processions.

G. BOLLANDO, *Acta Sanctorum*. Belgian Jesuits were responsible for the publication of the lives of the saints. The initial purpose was to refute Protestant contestations by the philological methods deployed in publishing documents and comments. But the successive volumes relating to all the saints according to the liturgical calendar amounted to a celebration of the Counter-Reformation church.

The Formation of Regional States

Machiavelli's concern with the need for the Prince to 'sink roots' highlighted the difference in the historical evolution of northern and central Italy from that of the European states across the Alps: the absence of dynastic loyalties rendered the transformation of republican city-states into *signorie* insecure. The invasions and wars in Italy had accelerated a radical process of natural selection among the *signori* thrown up in the precocious developments of the late fourteenth–fifteenth century and again in the final phase of pre-Tridentine papal nepotism.

By the end of the seventeenth century regional states were firmly established in Italy. Italian (like European) historiography has long interpreted such a development as part of the inevitable process of formation of the modern state. But the very fragmentation of power among a multiplicity of territorial and social bodies that had characterized the earlier period presented a different dimension to the institutional problem of the centralization of authority. The evidence of this was the inability or reluctance of even powerful new states in the sixteenth century to develop strong, centralizing administrative structures: Milan and Naples, like Spain's protégés, the restored Savoyard dynasty and the Medici, were no different in this respect from the republics of Venice and Genoa, the Papacy, the Este of Modena, or the upstart Farnese of Parma-Piacenza.

From the fifteenth century already, the dominant capitals—such as Rome, Milan, or Venice—were affirming their monopoly over taxation, challenging at least some of the traditional privileges of the subject-cities over their *contado*, and beginning to impose controls over the local communities. But they remained dependent, for the enforcement of their rule within their territories, on the collaboration of the existing élites, whose support had to be attracted. Centralizing measures were introduced with extreme discretion and caution, for example through the creation of new magistracies, alongside formal confirmation of the existing liberties and rights of the established local élites. Florence never challenged the exclusive monopoly of the noble *riseduti* of Siena, any more than did Venice that of the Veronese patricians. The emergence of regional states was the result of a continuous process of transaction and opportunity, certainly not of the imposition of a superior centralized authority.

Where there was a threat of political opposition from parliaments, feudatories, or subordinate cities, the prince took appropriate measures: the estates of Piedmont were simply not summoned by Emanuel Philibert; Duke Cosimo of Tuscany built the *fortezza da basso* to ensure the obedience of the citizens of Florence; the Farnese dispossessed the great feudatories and controlled and marginalized the city council of Parma. But such examples were exceptions. Over the long period from the mid-sixteenth to the eighteenth century, the norm was for a compromise to be reached by the different parties. From the point of view of the state, administrative advantages help explain the practices of negotiation and transactions. The sale of fiefs in the Milanese, with powers of civil and criminal justice, reduced the costs of maintaining order and administering the law at the local level; fiscal concessions by Venice to the feudatories of Friuli and the valleys of the Bergamasco and Bresciano ensured the Serenissima of their loyalty.

Slowly, during the course of the seventeenth century, through the creation of new magistracies and the growth of administrative personnel, the governments began to centralize some judicial and fiscal activities. They exploited the traditional hostility between cities and *contado*, feudatories and peasants, by offering alternative procedures that emptied, without formally removing, local privileges. But the process of extension of the state's presence was negotiated in each instance, thus accentuating the heterogeneity and dissimilarity of conditions and privileges that was characteristic of the Italian states.

The growth of regional states was facilitated by the acquisition of landed properties by the patriciates of the dominant cities. Perhaps it is not surprising that this was most visible in the Republic of Venice, where the government was exclusively identified with the Venetian nobility: the strong presence of Venetian landowners on the terraferma accompanied the Serenissima's growing institutional role. But the phenomenon was more general: Florentine citizens were second only to Pisan citizens as landowners in the Pisan *catasto* of 1622; virtually all the wealthiest landowners in the Pavia *contado* in 1756 were Milanese citizens.

Most important in the formation of the regional states was the deliberate policy of the princes to attract the support of the nobility. It is possible that the oligarchical republics of Venice, Genoa, and Lucca were at a disadvantage compared to the princes, as they were too jealous of their prerogatives, closed in their attitudes, and lacking the symbolic and material advantages of a court. The princes went out of their way to attract the feudatories and patriciates to their service. In Tuscany the grand dukes created fiefs and a chivalric order as a means of engaging the nobility in their service. In Piedmont, the house of Savoy consciously developed a large army and traditional military values in order to attract the feudal barons into the ducal orbit, where they successfully maintained their value-system despite the vast influx of newly entitled bankers, army suppliers, and bureaucrats. In Parma, the Farnese followed a consistent policy of controlling the great landed feudatories by repression, attendance at court, and later restitution of confiscated patrimonies, while promoting the urban patriciate through office and titles. By the eighteenth century, regional states had been created, moulded around the courts, and characterized by the permeation of society with aristocratic values.

The Courts

The symbol and instrument through which the princes affirmed their power and constructed their regional states was the court. The court in Italy not only anticipated the experiences of Versailles and the absolute monarchies of Europe, but politically exercised a more direct function, presumably through the smaller dimensions of the Italian states. For it was through the exaltation of the court that the Italian princes redefined their new role and restructured their relationship with the multiple sources of power with which they were confronted.

Courts, of course, had existed as long as monarchies. But unlike, for example, the Burgundian court, or the Aragonese in the kingdoms of southern Italy, the Renaissance *signori* were successful in spreading the values of an idealized court style of life. This was the explanation of the enormous success, in Italy and across the Alps, of Castiglione's *Courtier* (1528) until the French Revolution. It would be otiose to decide whether the courts in Italy corresponded to, or were responsible for, a society with a strong taste for theatricality,

128

where appearances were judged as important as reality, where largesse and magnificence, pomp and splendour, ostentation and grandeur were stressed as necessary or at least appropriate values for status. Certainly the courts met these criteria, whether within the cities, like Mantua or Florence, or outside, like the Caserta Palace of Charles III Bourbon of Naples, or the Stupinigi hunting-lodge of Victor Amadeus II in Piedmont. They were one of the sources of the extravagance and layout of the more grandiose palaces and gardens of the nobility, such as Villa Aldobrandini at Tivoli. But the functions of the courts were far broader, and embraced administration and office, networks of social relations and personal influence, artistic patronage and remodelling of urban space, religious symbolism and aristocratic models.

Even if fifteenth-century Urbino or Ferrara offered supremely sophisticated examples, the geographical area of the princely courts was not confined to that of the *signorie*, but extended from Palermo and Naples to Rome and Turin. In many ways Rome offered an exemplar of the symbolic identification of court and prince. From the late fifteenth until the mid-seventeenth century, the complex of Vatican buildings was expanded to accommodate the bureaucracy required in the drive to exert control over the Papal States, and to ensure an appropriately decorous setting for the Papacy's revived international role. Contemporaneously, the city of Rome as capital was repeatedly restructured, with monumental avenues to enhance the approach to the Vatican; palaces and villas for pope and cardinals; squares, fountains, obelisks, churches, and public buildings constructed, all for the greater glory of the papal monarchy and head of the Counter-Reformation Church.

In the sixteenth century the fortified palace had been replaced by the princely court conceived as an enclosure, separate from the citadel, and marked off from the city as a distinct and self-sufficient complex. In the seventeenth century public affairs were regarded as necessarily close to the person of the prince; the seats of administration and justice were thus to be located in the vicinity of the palace, if possible with internal communications, like the Vasari corridor between the Uffizi and Palazzo Pitti in Florence. Courts grew in size and formality: there were thirty-nine officials on the payroll of the Medici court in 1550 and 797 in 1692.

Administration and ceremonial were intimately linked in the distribution of space both within the palace and in the adjoining city. Within the palace, the sacral role of the prince was underlined by the protected isolation of his private quarters, chapel, and garden. Increasingly, the capital was replanned or remodelled in relationship to the palace. Rectilinear roads converged on the palace as the focal point of the city, broad enough to cater for carriages and processions, and decorated with statuary, coats of arms, plaques, and other symbols of the prince's power. The cathedral was utilized to emphasize the sacred quality of the ruler, even, as it were, annexed to the palace, as at Turin.

The courtiers were encouraged to build palaces near the court and were expected to make them available for the prince's guests, should the number or quality of the latter not match the court's standards.

The court triumphed in seventeenth-century Italy because it proved so effective an instrument for the affirmation of the princes' superiority. It was through the court that the Farnese curbed the great feudal barons and transformed the urban patriciate of Parma into a titled aristocracy; and that the Savoy turned the army into a financial and social market, capable of absorbing their inflationary sale of titles.

But the effectiveness of the court in turn derived from the advantages and opportunities it offered to the élites. Because of the close identification of administration with the prince, the court was the location for the distribution of resources—magistracies and offices, ceremonial positions and titles, military appointments and ecclesiastical benefices, provisioning contracts and licences to create feudal villages. Noble families were probably encouraged by the seventeenth-century economic crisis to repair or reinforce their patrimonies and resources through service to the prince. They were certainly conscious of the centrality of the court as the meeting-place of social relations of

MANTUA, under the Gonzaga dynasty, became a typical Court city. This 1628 engraving by G. Bertazzolo shows clearly the dominance of the Court over the city, with the ducal complex of buildings occupying the entire central part of the city; an elevated corridor between the palace and the cathedral facing it on the large central piazza can be seen (centre, bottom). The sack of the city two years later marked its irrevocable decline.

130

STUPINIGI was the hunting lodge of the Savoy dynasty, built close to Turin in 1729–31 for Victor Amadeus II. Designed by F. Juvarra, its spectacular approach and scale offered an appropriate monument to the new kings of Sardinia.

FOR THE GREAT ARISTOCRATIC FAMILIES of Italy in the seventeenth century a visible social role was a necessary accompaniment to their economic wealth. The wealth, importance, but also the sobriety of this Lombard family (the Spinola, in origin a Genoese family) emerge in this painting by C. del Cane, in which the austere but elegant clothing contrasts with the foods and wines.

MASKS OF VENICE, about 1614. Venice tempered its ever more archaic constitution, jealously preserved by an aristocratic oligarchy, with festivities, increasingly an attraction to the élites of Europe. Carnival was the peak moment of Venice's season, when the wearing of masks accentuated the temporary suspension of the rigid conventions of social comportment.

all kinds, from recommendations to marriage alliances. The seventeenth century witnessed a flood of treatises that debased Castiglione's respect for the dignity of the intellectual as courtier into opportunistic advice on how to obtain pensions and benefices through adulation of the prince.

The Power of the Nobility

The process of recomposition of social relations that underpinned the consolidation of regional states and their courts was based upon acceptance, indeed encouragement, of a new and leading role for the nobility within the Italian states. It was through such a compromise that the rulers were able to attract into their service and amalgamate the multiple and often conflicting groups that held local power. By the mid-eighteenth century the Habsburg rulers and Enlightenment reformers were confronted by a powerful and often wealthy aristocracy, more capable of defending its privileges than a Church that had lost its intellectual monopoly. Over the longer term, the consequences were to prove negative, even after the Revolutionary–Napoleonic experiences, for the presence of Church and nobility was to impose heavy social constraints on the future evolution of Italy.

Such a development might appear in some ways surprising, at least in northern and central Italy, given its earlier history. For if feudal aristocracy was of the essence of the southern kingdoms, the history of communal Italy was based on its defeat and replacement by an urban patriciate. But, as we have seen, albeit expelled from the cities and their immediate *contado*, feudatories remained characteristic of the countryside, where they could assert fealty to different parties (emperor, pope, local state, or other), according to circumstances or whim.

By the sixteenth century there were thus two wholly separate sources of nobility: feudal and urban patrician. In the latter case, there were considerable uncertainties and extreme differences about what constituted nobility; at one extreme, the great Venetian merchant ruling class had long since closed its ranks in a golden book of nobility; at the other, the Florentine patriciate remained reluctant to accept noble titles—at least from the Medici grand duke (although not from foreign rulers)—even in the seventeenth century. By then the sources of nobility had multiplied, primarily through the creation of new titles in return for service to the prince, or simply for cash; or by acceptance into one of the papal-protected chivalric orders, like the Order of Malta, or the Tuscan Order of Santo Stefano; or as a corporate qualification of particular professions, such as notary or doctor.

In a Europe where the ideology of nobility was steadily reinforced in the seventeenth and eighteenth centuries, it is hardly surprising that the recognition of nobility by the princes corresponded to the demand of the local Italian oligarchies. Even the Florentine patricians acknowledged the utility of a title in the eyes of foreigners. By the later sixteenth century the urban patriciates had closed their ranks throughout the cities and towns of Italy; the grant of a title merely confirmed their institutional role and status, if not their real power.

An outflow of publications appeared in mid-sixteenth-century Italy on how to define a gentleman and a noble. The cult of genealogies dated from the same decades, when coats of arms also began to be displayed on the outside of palaces. By the seventeenth century the earlier humanist insistence on virtue as the qualification of true nobility had vanished, replaced by a science of chivalry, regulating the practice of honour as a value in its own right. Status, precedence, heredity, military posturing, search for princely pensions, private violence, and contempt for inferiors became the hallmarks of the Italian aristocracy. Whatever the resentments expressed in private—the unresolved conflicts between birth and wealth, between feudal-military origins and exercise of an office—a noble ideology was constructed through the convergence of interests of the princes, the urban patriciates, and the newly entitled. Distinctions of origin were replaced by negative definitions of behaviour incompatible with the status of noble—definitions, for example, of 'vile' arts that changed over place and time according to the activities of each noble patriciate.

The ideology of nobility was probably strengthened by the shift of economic interests of the urban patriciates away from manufactures, trade, and banking to the land. Only in Genoa did the investments of the oligarchy remain in international finance. The aristocracy of Venice, Florence, Milan, and elsewhere became primarily landowners. Such a structural shift does not necessarily explain Italy's economic decline, and in part was certainly the consequence of the risks and declining returns of trade. Nor can one conclude that investment in land was evidence of an abandonment of an entrepreneurial mentality, given the numerous examples of response to market opportunities, from the massive drainage works by Venetian nobles, to the expansion of rice cultivation in Lombardy, the shift to sheep-raising for the Roman market by the papal aristocracy, or the development of sharecropping by the Tuscan noble landowners. Land provided the basis for collateral financial activities, particularly loans at exorbitant (and ecclesiastically prohibited) rates of interest to impoverished states, rural communities, and peasants. Urban landownership and the growing commercialization of agriculture certainly worsened the living conditions of peasant families. But undoubtedly land also reinforced pretensions of noble status.

In the republics of Venice, Genoa, and Lucca the price paid by the ruling nobility, as by the patriciates of the subordinate cities in most Italian states, for their jealous monopoly of power was a dramatic fall in their numbers through restrictive matrimonial policies. Transmission of property and rising levels of dowries encouraged high levels of celibacy among both sons and daughters. At Venice, the most notorious case, the number of nobles fell from 6,439 in 1586 to 4,457 by 1642 and 3,557 by 1766. But a demographic decline of similar proportions has been documented for many other cities, such as Milan, Florence, and Siena. By the eighteenth century such civic oligarchies had difficulties in meeting their institutional obligations. Within these republics, wealth was a condition of power, because of the rising costs of office. Venice was forced to provide education and charity for poor nobles to ensure they upheld their status. Political divisions between the wealthy oligarchy and poor nobles and periodic crises characterized the history of seventeenth- and eighteenth-century Venice and Genoa.

In contrast to the republics, or to the nobility of individual cities within their domains, the cohesive power of the princes lay in their capacity to formalize recognition of noble status, irrespective of difference or uncertainty of origin. The policies followed by the Farnese dukes of Parma and Piacenza, a state created for his family in 1545 by Pope Paul III in a region of particularly powerful feudatories and communes with a strong civic tradition, are exemplary.

But in Parma, as in the other states, there was a price to be paid. For the policies of the princes consolidated the economic power of the nobility, without necessarily creating a cohesive class, and even less one that could be employed

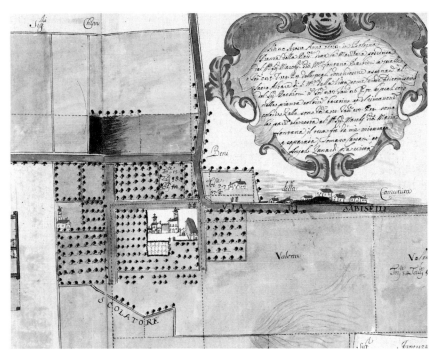

CABREO, 1682. The consolidation of aristocratic privileges and properties led at least the more efficiently organized noble families to pay increasing attention to the management of their estates. By the later seventeenth century, inventories and land maps were drawn up, like this *cabreo* of an estate at Medicina (near Bologna), in which pictorial elegance perhaps counted more than rack-renting.

usefully in the service of the ruler. In Parma, the different segments of the ducal aristocracy did not fuse but continued to follow a logic of distinction in their matrimonial policies; in Piedmont, the military nobility retained its sense of superior distinctiveness. Whatever the interdependence between noble families and rulers, the interests of the family remained pre-eminent. Indeed, the deliberate encouragement of the aristocratic restructuring of Italian society reinforced the priority assigned to the conservation of the family patrimony. Aristocratic wealth, power, and ideals were consolidated in all the states; economically and socially the nobility had become the most powerful class.

Only from the early eighteenth century did criticisms begin to emerge. Scipione Maffei, a noble from Verona, where myths of feudal origin were particularly marked, cast ridicule on the chivalric virtues of the nobility. Enlightenment writers—in the Habsburg territories, although hardly in Piedmont—attacked the traditional privileges of the aristocracy and its absence from service to the monarch. Ultimately, the limits to the Enlightenment in Italy derived in good part from the power of the nobility.

PETER LEOPOLD OF TUSCANY (1765–92) was emblematic of Enlightened despotism. The younger son of Empress Maria Theresa, as grandduke of Tuscany he led one of the major experiences of reforms, from free trade in cereals to the attack on ecclesiastical privileges. In 1790 he succeeded his more radical brother Joseph II as emperor.

The Enlightenment

The Enlightenment would not have been conceivable in Italy but for the radical political changes in the peninsula's role in Europe. The end of Spanish rule and the succession wars brought new rulers to Italy: the Austrian Habsburgs to Lombardy and Tuscany, the Bourbons to Naples, Sicily, and Parma. The Italian princes remained even more impotent than before, as the great powers disposed of their territories in war and peace: Francis III Este of Modena owed his succession in 1737 to his career fighting the Turks in the Habsburg armies, as in the sixteenth century Emanuel Philibert of Savoy had recovered his states through his success as a general in the Spanish armies in Flanders.

But there were major differences from the period of Spanish rule. For a pacific settlement of Italy was finally achieved through the agreement by the major powers that neither Habsburg nor Bourbon should retain his Italian possessions if he acceded to the throne of Vienna or Madrid: Charles III was obliged to renounce Naples and Sicily in 1759, Peter Leopold abandoned Tuscany on the death of his brother Joseph II in 1790. Only Lombardy remained part of the Austrian Empire, albeit at the price of losing to Savoy ever more of its western provinces in the three succession wars. The formal separation of the Italian states from the great rival dynasties of Europe brought a period of peace of unprecedented length, from the Treaty of Aix-la-Chapelle (1748) to the invasions of the French Revolutionary armies (1796). Peace was a precondition for the Enlightenment reforms.

Austrian Habsburg rule in the eighteenth century was also fundamentally different from the earlier period of Spanish domination in that it brought the Italian states into direct contact with the major current of Enlightenment reformism. If Italian intellectuals turned primarily and constantly to Paris, as the power house of Enlightenment debate and ideas, the administrators and reformers of the two most advanced states—Lombardy and Tuscany—never lost sight of the reforms elaborated in the Vienna of Maria Theresa and Joseph II. The Enlightenment in Italy was lived by its protagonists as a return to Europe.

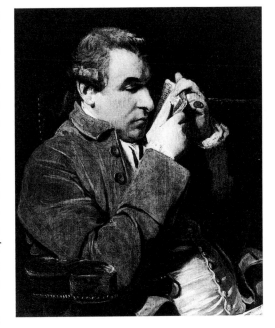

GIUSEPPE BARETTI (1719–89) was a minor but significant literato of the European Enlightenment. His journal *Frusta letteraria* was too polemical for the Venetian government, which forbade its publication. Baretti then settled in London, where he was a well-known figure, as testified by this portrait by Sir Joshua Reynolds.

The origins of the Enlightenment in Italy were complex. They can be dated back to the crisis of the European absolutist conscience at the end of the seventeenth century, on the one hand in a renewed interest in scientific and philosophical developments outside Italy, and on the other in an increasingly determined struggle against the suffocating dominance of the Church. The ideas of Newton and Locke played their part in the elaboration of a new critical approach and scientific methodology and mentality, that rapidly expanded into faith in the potential of science for man's progress, a predilection for 'useful' science, and an optimism about the practicality of rational reforms to improve public felicity. The attack on the Church derived directly out of jurisdictional conflicts in Naples and Piedmont into a challenge against the monopoly of thought imposed by ecclesiastical censorship and the Inquisition, and finally into an assault against the Jesuits.

By the mid-eighteenth century Pietro Verri and Cesare Beccaria in Milan, Pompeo Neri and Francesco Maria Gianni in Tuscany, and Antonio Genovesi in Naples were at the centre of a thriving movement of intellectual debate. The intensity of the discussions among Italian intellectuals, which formed part of the broader European debate but focused on the specific problems of each Italian state, depended on the attitude of the political authorities: favourable in Lombardy, Tuscany, and Parma, accepted in more limited fashion in Naples, but making little headway in Modena, Venice, the Papal States, Piedmont, and Sicily through the hostility of both authorities and local society; the Republic of Genoa simply prohibited any political discussion.

Whatever the differences among the intellectuals, what united them was their sense of what they saw as the appalling backwardness of the Italian states

AUSTRIAN EMPIRE

SWISS CONFEDERATION

Geneva

K. OF FRANCE

D. OF
SAVOY

Como
D. OF
Vigevano
Turin
SARDINIA
PR. OF PIEDMONT

Bergamo
Milan
MILAN
1714
to Aust.
Pavia
D. OF
MANTUA
D. OF
PARMA
1735 to Aust.
1748 to Sp.
Parma
Modena
D. OF
MODENA

Susa

K. OF

Brescia
Trent
Rovereto
Vicenza
Padua
Este

Belluno
Udine

Trieste

Fiume

REPUBLIC OF VENICE

Venice

Pola
Zara

ISTRIA

DALMATIA

Spalato

REP. OF
RAGUSA
1718 Indep.

Nice

Finale
Oneglia
PR. OF MONACO

REP. OF GENOA
Pontremoli
Spezia
Massa
Pisa
REP. OF LUCCA
Florence

Ferrara
Bologna

EMILIA

ROMAGNA

Ravenna
Cesena
REP. OF SAN MARINO

Urbino

Ancona

Livorno
GR. D. OF
TUSCANY
Siena
1737 to Habs
Lorraine

PAPAL
STATES
Camerino
Spoleto

ADRIATIC SEA

CORSICA
to Genoa
Ajaccio

Piombino
ELBA
STATO
Orbetello
DEI PRESIDII
1714 to Austria,
1735 to Spain

Orvieto
Viterbo

PATRIMONY
OF
ST PETER

Rome
Velletri

Chieti

Pontecorvo
Gaeta
Capua
Benevento

Foggia
Barletta
Bari

K. OF NAPLES
1714 to Aust.
1735 to Spain

Sassari

K. OF
SARDINIA
1720 to Savoy
Monte Reale
Cagliari

Naples
Salerno
Amalfi

Taranto
Lecce
Brindisi

Otranto

Cosenza

Catanzaro

TYRRHENIAN SEA

MEDITERRANEAN SEA

LIPARI IS.

Seminara

Trapani
EGADI IS.

Palermo
Messina
Reggio

K. OF SICILY
1720 to Austria, 1735 to Spain

Caltanissetta
Terranova

Catania
Siracusa

PANTELLERIA IS.

GOZO
MALTA
1530–1793 to Knights of St John

Boundary of the
Austrian Empire

0   200 km

ITALY IN 1748

compared to the progress of Europe (by which they meant western Europe). Superstition and privilege, as much as Italy's past, were seen everywhere as blocking reform. Increasingly, where the princes were active, the intellectuals turned to them as the necessary and ultimately the sole agents of change. The function of the intellectuals was to win the support of public opinion. Once the princes started to impose changes, the reforms extended to ever-wider fields, from rationalization of the machinery of government to subordination of the Church and the removal of obstacles to the development of the economy.

The collaboration between reforming princes and intellectuals reached its peak in the attack against the Church. The Church had lost its earlier driving force already in the later seventeenth century and easily appeared as an amorphous mass of privilege, ignorance, and anachronistic moral censorship. Its wealth and the 'idleness' of the regular orders made it particularly vulnerable. In unison with Austria, France, and Spain, all the Italian states launched an onslaught against the Church, suppressing monasteries, prohibiting mortmain, confiscating properties, expelling the Jesuits, and finally—in Lombardy and Tuscany—even attempting to impose Jansenist reforms and state control over the training of priests. By the 1790s the Church had lost most of the economic, juridical, and cultural advantages it had enjoyed in Spanish Italy. But Counter-Reformation popular piety remained intact and was to show its political potential in the reaction against the French Revolution.

For both intellectuals and reformers, economic reform was seen as the most effective instrument for progress. All agreed on the need to unify the domestic market by removing internal tolls and barriers, lay and ecclesiastical privileges. Tuscany became a model state in the European Enlightenment debate when Peter Leopold put into practice physiocratic doctrines, allowing free export of cereals as a means of stimulating production. Private property was an issue of faith, like economic individualism, and encouraged the attack on communal properties in all the states. There can be little doubt that a consequence of Enlightenment reforms was further to weaken the bases of peasant self-sufficiency. On the other hand, the ideological beliefs and measures in favour of productive property blunted the potential effects of the reforming movement's critique of noble privilege and power. In Naples landowners were encouraged to become more commercially oriented, but were allowed to retain their feudal privileges. In Tuscany, where landowners lost fiscal exemptions, they benefited from the abolition of institutional or traditional blocks to production (such as the obligation to supply the domestic urban market), but successfully resisted government attempts to protect smallholders or peasants.

After a decade of active and fruitful collaboration, by the later 1770s the intellectuals began to express reservations about their earlier confidence in the prince. Too much depended on the humours of the prince: Peter Leopold and Joseph II had become too radical for many of the intellectuals, Ferdinand IV of Naples and Victor Amadeus III of Savoy too weak or bigoted. Even where the ruler was active, resistance to change was seen as proving too great. In Naples and Sicily, at Rome and Modena, Enlightened reformism arrived too late, when the earlier optimism had already dissipated, replaced by a sense of growing disillusionment.

The French Revolution abruptly ended the Enlightenment experience, as the rulers abandoned all reform. To a degree the Enlightenment had undoubtedly transformed the Italy of Spain and the Counter-Reformation. Italy was once more part of Europe. But there were many Italies, socially as much as politically. The reforms themselves had accentuated the divisions. The Revolution was to deepen them further.

✤ 6 ✤

CULTURE IN THE AGE OF BAROQUE AND ROCOCO

ROBERT ORESKO

The Unity of the Arts in Opera and Architecture

On 6 October 1600 *Euridice*, a dramatic text by Ottavio Rinuccini (1562–1621) with music by Jacopo Peri (1561–1633), was performed at Palazzo Pitti, Florence, as part of the wedding celebrations of Henri IV, king of France, and the grand duke of Tuscany's niece, Maria de' Medici. This date has traditionally been used to mark the birth of a new form of cultural expression, opera, and, although it is clear that *Euridice* certainly had immediate predecessors to which it bore striking resemblances, it remains true, as Tim Carter has observed, that 'Few genres in the history of music have their origins fixed with such apparent precision as opera'. It could be added that few forms of cultural expression in general emerged so definitively at the beginning of a new century, so that the history of opera assumes a critical and central role in the history of seventeenth- and eighteenth-century Italian culture in the broadest sense. One fundamental reason for the importance of opera is its guiding principle of cultural combination; it remained, above all, a collaborative effort, and as such it implicitly challenged the notions of individual genius and expression which had been codified in the previous century by Giorgio Vasari in the *Vite*. This collaboration was not simply aesthetic, it was cultural in the widest definition of the term, for opera drew on the abilities not only of poets and musicians, but also painters and architects for the scenery, scientists for stage machinery, classical scholars and historians for subject-matter, court officials for the practicalities of the staging and for placing the performance within festival cycles, and, ultimately, the power-brokers, including the prince himself, who used the new genre for straightforward and easily understandable political purposes. However much we now associate specific operas with specific musicians, in the seventeenth (seicento) and eighteenth (settecento) centuries, opera became the crossroads, the common meeting ground, for most forms of cultural activity. However diverse the settings for the presentation of opera subsequently became—private performances in aristocratic households, churches and colleges for the sacred, didactic operas sponsored by the Jesuits, and the public opera-houses opened to a fee-paying audience with the aim of making a profit—it is striking that the roots of opera were deeply implanted in dynastic, court culture: the earliest recognizable operas grouped around Medici court festivities were complemented in 1607 by the performance at the court of Mantua of *La favola d'Orfeo*, with music by Claudio Monteverdi (1567–1643) to a text by the court secretary Alessandro Striggio (d. 1630), emphasizing the overlap between the worlds of politics and culture.

In addition to focusing on the concepts of combination and collaboration, opera has a second prime importance for what we now think of as specifically 'Italian' culture. It provides a rare example of cultural unity in an otherwise fractured and particularist peninsula. However diverse the forms of Neapolitan opera developed from those of Venetian opera, however slow such expanding courts as that of Turin were to adopt opera as the central form of entertainment, opera in general, at least during the seicento, could be viewed as a uniquely Italian innovation, and it was treated as such in the non-Italian world. In Paris, the Italian-born Cardinal Jules Mazarin made repeated attempts to introduce Italian opera at the French court, culminating in his commission to Francesco Cavalli (1602–76) for an opera, *Ercole Amante*, to celebrate Louis XIV's wedding (1660; opera not performed until 1662). The failure of this cultural campaign spurred on native French attempts to establish an indigenous operatic canon, but even the origins of these were directed by Jean-Baptiste Lully (1632–87), the Gallicized name of the Florentine musician who governed the king's music. Throughout the eighteenth century knowledge of Italian opera, inclusive of all its many strands, was as much a common cultural language amongst élites as French had become for diplomatic parlance.

The perception of this cultural operatic unity is vitally important because the very notion of an 'Italian culture', indeed of 'Italy' itself, was more coherent to non-Italian observers (and to nineteenth- and twentieth-century historians) than it was to the artists, writers, musicians, and patrons living in the peninsula during the seicento and the settecento. One of the outstanding hallmarks of Italian culture during these two centuries is its regional diversity, the very lack of homogeneity, of internal unity, which Risorgimento apologists strove to impose as part of a cultural justification for political unity following 1870. The immense differences, even between neighbouring cities, in formalistic cultural expression and its practical organization, while deriving in the first, simplistic instance from geographic specificity, were fundamentally the expression of the varied patterns of power-holding. The dense implantation of dynastic courts in the north and the centre—Turin, Modena, Mantua, Parma and Piacenza, Florence—generated different forms of cultural patronage from those of their republican neighbours, Venice, Genoa, and Lucca.

Not only was the artistic ideology different, so was the balance between official culture and private culture, though even such a supposedly centralizing court as that of Turin by its very vigorous expansion created multiple centres of princely and aristocratic patronage within the same capital. A dramatically different form of the mixture of official court culture and unofficial élite culture is provided by the examples of Milan, Naples, and Palermo, all of which were ruled by foreign governors or viceroys, but all of which were socially structured by grandee families of long pedigree who sustained the arts over centuries regardless of the identity of their always-temporary ruler.

The cultural patronage of papal Rome is an extreme case of the diversity of the Italian peninsula. The pope was the head of the Catholic Church, but also a temporal prince, and pontifical patronage reflected the duality of his spiritual and worldly roles. The emergence of opera around 1600 was not the only major cultural phenomenon which marked out the significance of the very first decade of the seicento. The assertive pontificate (1605–21) of the Borghese Pope Paul V brought a final resolution to the questions of the internal distribution of space, with all its liturgical implications, and the outward appearance, literally the façade, of the heart of Catholicism, the new basilica of St Peter, of which Pope Julius II had laid the foundation stone as far back as 1506. The sixteenth century, as generation of artists succeeded generation of artists, had been replete with debates over the ecclesiological and aesthetic benefits of a centralized Greek-cross plan as opposed to those of the extended Latin-cross. In 1605, at the very beginning of his pontificate, Paul V awarded the commission to realize the fabric of St Peter's to Carlo Maderno (c.1556–1629), whose initial projects, including the long nave which stamped the Latin-cross solution upon the ground plan, the façade, and the portico, were completed during the course of the next decade and rapidly became the instantly recognizable and external image of Catholic Christianity.

This bold solution to a long-standing problem focused papal patronage upon the basilica, for once the basilica stood intact it generated new problems of its internal decoration and the distribution of the urban space surrounding it. Many of the choices posed by the 'nude envelope' of the new St Peter's were considered during the long pontificate (1623–44) of the Barberini Pope Urban VIII and the rapid emergence as his principal artistic counsellor of Gian Lorenzo Bernini (1598–1680), who became responsible for much of the internal appearance of the basilica, notably the celebrated *baldacchino* (1624–33) erected over the tomb of the Apostle Peter and the cathedra Petri, the very heart of pontifical authority, both spiritual and temporal. Bernini's career offers a number of insights into the practical functionings of Italian culture during the early modern period.

The central concept in Irving Lavin's work on Bernini is the unity of the visual arts, the inability to identify sharp divisions between his activities as a sculptor, an architect, and even a painter, a field in which Bernini had notably less acclaim. This unity was fostered by Bernini's highly theatrical concept of three-dimensional forms and of space, pointing once again to the key role played in Italian cultural life by opera, which, like Bernini's own achievements, was based upon the combination of multiple forms of artistic expression. The crossing of the basilica of St Peter's and the oval piazza in front of it were literally conceived as stages for the papal theatre of ceremony and etiquette and their appearance and form, their iconography of sculpted relief to be 'read' and understood, were all determined by function, the need to present and to display the head of Catholic Christianity in the most dramatically visible means possible. The determination of Urban VIII to concentrate as much power as possible in Bernini's hands, to emulate the directive sweep of Michelangelo's authority at the Vatican in the previous century, signals another characteristic figure of Italian culture, the artist as courtier and the artist as the member of a bureaucratic administration, as Filippo Juvarra would become in Turin and of which Rubens, Velázquez, and LeBrun provide non-Italian variants.

Involvement in court politics inevitably meant rivalry, both personal and

professional, another critically important mechanism of Italian culture in the seicento and settecento. However dominant the individual figure of Bernini may seem in early seventeenth-century Rome, the sheer scale of the task to embellish the new St Peter's forced him to collaborate with other Barberini favourites, for example Pietro da Cortona (1596–1669), and to deal with declared rivals belonging to other factional camps, most notably Francesco Borromini (1599–1667). The concepts of rivalry and competition had been well established in Italian culture during the sixteenth century, but during the seicento and settecento they confirmed their central role in the organization of Italian culture, in the public and frequently acrimonious debates about form, not only the form of buildings but also the form of opera and theatre, conducted in printed literature, pamphlets, and news-sheets, and in the institutionalization of the officially organized *concorsi*, those competitions for designs for general types of buildings or for a specific architectural commission for which rival entries were invited. In Rome and elsewhere, competition stood at the opposite pole from collaboration to define the magnetic field of cultural patronage, and the Piazza Navona, frequently described as the private forum of the Pamphilj family, which had produced Pope Innocent X (reigned 1644–55), presents a prime example of an artistic unit which had evolved as the result of an effectively enforced collaboration of rivals. Borromini designed the gallery of the Palazzo Pamphilj and from 1653 the Pamphilj family's adjacent and private church of S. Agnese, to which he gave a characteristically concave façade, while Cortona, by this point one of the great European practitioners of dynastic decorative cycle painting, provided the fresco for the gallery, the story of Aeneas (1651–4). At the same time, Bernini, who had initially suffered an eclipse of favour following the death (1644) of the Barberini pope, was working on the fountains of Piazza Navona, notably the Fountain of Four Rivers (completed 1651). This great monument of seventeenth-century urbanism is, therefore, attributable to no one hand; it combines several of the arts and sciences—architecture, sculpture, hydraulics, painting, classical scholarship—yet its practical purpose was to produce a three-dimensional statement of the rise of the family who had the resources and force to commission it.

Piazza Navona was not an official Vatican commission; it was undertaken on the private initiative of the pope and his family, the main beneficiaries, but its elaboration in the 1650s sheds much light on the intricacies and complexities of papal cultural patronage. There was no juridical role for women at the papal court, and certain forms of cultural expression requiring or associated with women, notably secular theatre and opera, were accordingly banned. Critical parts of papal patronage were, therefore, shifted to the palace of the pontiff's family, frequently, as the construction of Piazza Navona shows, with the active encouragement of the pope himself. The use by Urban VIII's fam-

Facing: PIAZZA NAVONA, Rome. Much of Italian urbanism was consciously programmed from central authorities, from the expansion of Turin, dictated by the court of Savoy, to the construction of new towns, Pienza in the fifteenth century, Valletta (in Malta) and Sabbionetta in the sixteenth and Noto (in Sicily) in the eighteenth, all touching upon the key concept of 'the ideal city'. The expansion of Rome, however, was largely dependent upon individual initiative, that of the religious Orders, the resident 'Nations', and the great families, such as the Pamphilj, who created Piazza Navona on the site of the Circus of Domitian as a visual reply to the building activities of the Barberini clan during the previous papacy.

ily of its large theatre, seating 3,000, at Palazzo Barberini for the presentation of opera and other forms of court entertainment not admissible, for canonical reasons, at the Vatican, established the central role of their urban power-base in the cultivation of the new idiom of music theatre. Many of those artists closely associated with official papal patronage were employed here, on what was, juridically, a private commission. The building itself had been begun in the late 1620s to designs by Carlo Maderno and Borromini, but, following Maderno's death (1629), Bernini succeeded him both at the Vatican and, at least effectively, at Palazzo Barberini, while the task of creating the fresco ceiling of the room which became the iconographic centre-piece of the decorative scheme was awarded to Cortona. Bernini also became involved in opera production at Palazzo Barberini where he designed stage sets, combining his skills as pictorial draftsman and architect. All these artists, therefore, moved between the worlds of public and private patronage, both Bernini and Cortona openly associating themselves with the Barberini family as members of the social and financial patronage system. The perils of such baronial affiliations were made clear by Bernini's temporary eclipse, when Borromini, now his arch-rival, seemed poised to benefit from the new Pamphilj pontificate, whose pro-Spanish sympathies he shared.

Public and Private Patronage

The importance of social networks and local loyalties in shaping artistic careers had been obvious during the brief Ludovisi papacy of Gregory XV (reigned 1621–3), who turned to his native Bologna for painters to work at St Peter's. The precipitous return from Bologna to Rome, where he had previously been employed on major commissions, of Domenichino (Domenico Zampieri: 1581–1641) and the extraordinary displacement from Cento, near Bologna, of Guercino (Gian Francesco Barbieri: 1591–1666) were prompted by expectations that a Bolognese pope would favour Bolognese artists. Domenichino was put in charge of the Vatican palace, while Guercino received two of his most significant commissions from Ludovisi hands: the altarpiece of St Petronilla (now in the Capitoline Museum, Rome) for St Peter's, an example of official papal patronage, and the Aurora ceiling fresco at the Villa Ludovisi, a private commission from the papal family. Domenichino and Guercino painted in very different and highly distinct styles, but they benefited from the same networks of patronage, because of their close links to Bologna.

Traditional historians of culture and of art have attempted to explain seventeenth-century Italian culture in terms of formalistic adjectives and antitheses. Mannerism is opposed to classicism which, in turn, is opposed to baroque, only to be supplanted, once it has decayed into *barococo*, by neo-classicism; naturalism is pitted against idealization, and tenebrism against clarity of

THE CHURCH OF S. IVO DELLA SAPIENZA, Rome. Born in the helvetic Ticino, Francesco Borromini was one of the most significant 'imports' for cosmopolitan Roman culture. Borromini was the official architect of the institution that would eventually become the University of Rome, a papal appointment. His design for its chapel and courtyard reflects the architect's mathematical sophistication— the geometric designs on the forecourt—while his learnedly technical virtuosity was matched only by Guarino Guarini's domes for S. Lorenzo and the SS. Sindone in Turin, for the audacity of swirling forms and the bold use of concave surfaces.

palette. Most of these concepts and terms would have been unrecognizable to painters and architects of the seicento, whose major concern was not the articulation of a specific aesthetic, the expression of the 'self', but the securing of employment, any more than the major princely, aristocratic, and ecclesiastical patrons were exclusively guided by a personalized taste. These power-brokers needed to maintain their own service systems, and, for artistic patronage, this dictated the flow of commissions to those painters, architects, and musicians closely tied to them by means of clientele, money, positions, generalized favour.

The group of Bolognese artists provides a good example of this phenomenon of cultural and social history. Bologna, a city with a strong native political, aesthetic, and intellectual tradition, had been firmly incorporated into the Papal States only during the first half of the sixteenth century, and because of the special status it enjoyed, it was able to provide adequate élite patronage for its indigenous artists. On the death of Gregory XV, Guercino returned to Cento and spent the remainder of his long career there and in Bologna. As his fame grew, major European patrons approached him with commissions which did not require him to leave his home, and in this way Guercino's career prefigures that of the paradigm of the renowned but geographically static artistic celebrity Francesco Solimena (1657–1747), who operated almost exclusively from Naples, choosing commissions as he saw fit, sending canvases abroad and exercising a wilful dictatorship over princely patrons who wished to own his work, a key figure in the evolution of the concept of the artist as entrepreneur. Guercino's decision also reflects retrospectively the virtual renunciation of Rome and the withdrawal to Bologna after 1614 of Guido Reni (1575–1642), frequently presented as one of the master practitioners of a Bolognese classicism. The careers of Reni and Domenichino, however different their use of colour in their paintings, had striking similarities; with Guercino they shared a strong home-base in Bolognese patronage, which made them only fitfully reliant upon papal Rome, depending upon the identity of the pope and other major patrons. Both were encouraged by the protection of the Carracci family of painters, associated with the major work undertaken by Annibale (1560–1609) in the gallery of Palazzo Farnese, and, with him, figure prominently among the 'heroes' of Cesare Malvasia's *Felsine pittrice*, published in 1678, the standard compilation of the lives of the outstanding Bolognese painters, which emphasized the achievements of Emilian

FRANCESCO SOLIMENA, *Self-Portrait*. As Solimena's European renown increased, so did his reputation as a difficult client for even the most hierarchically august patrons. Dangerous as it is to read a personality from an image, this carefully contrived self-presentation, in a characteristic palette of livid greens and only partially defined backgrounds, captures the public success of an artist who operated with exceptional independence and helped to define the role of the cosmopolitan painter as a financial entrepreneur.

painters while continuing a tradition of biographical assemblages initiated by Vasari and making a significant contribution to the historiography of Italian culture.

In the retrospective vision promoted by Malvasia, this group of artists, tied to one another through links of friendship and protection, associated with the Carracci circle and with the patronage of Cardinal Scipione Borghese, one of the great prototypical cardinal-nephews in the history of patronage, can seem remarkably homogeneous and coherent. Rivalries, notably that between Domenichino and Giovanni Lanfranco (1582–1647), can shed a different light. Born in Parma where he had studied the Correggio church decorations, Lanfranco was also part of the Carracci team working at Palazzo Farnese, to which he doubtless had his own special access, as the Farnese family were the sovereign dukes of Parma. Thus, despite sharing similar protectors, the disputes between two such dramatically different artists—Lanfranco traditionally depicted as a master of baroque vigour, Domenichino as the less interesting colourist emulating Raphael—need not have been grounded exclusively in aesthetic diversity and may have equally originated in the antagonism arising from their different cities of birth. Emerging from the patronage of ducal Parma and despite his Carracci training, Lanfranco simply did not belong to the same local circle as Domenichino, Reni, or Guercino.

CARAVAGGIO, *The Calling of St Matthew.* Painted in 1599–1600, Caravaggio's first public commission demonstrates most of the pictorial elements of early seicento tenebrism—the dramatic shaft of defining light, equivocal adolescents in elaborate dress—which attached the artist's name to an entire European tradition of tavern-life painting. It is one of two paintings—the other depicting St Matthew's martyrdom—in the Contarelli chapel in S. Luigi dei Francesi. The italianized name of the chapel's founder, the French Cardinal Cointrel, is another reminder of the multiplicity of foreign patrons providing employment in Rome.

147

Stylistic diversity, exaggerated by twentieth-century historians of art and culture, had never been, moreover, a barrier to coexistence within the same building. The prime example is given by Palazzo Barberini where the ceiling depicting the allegory of *Divine Wisdom*, painted by Andrea Sacchi (1599–1661) along rigorously Raphaelesque lines, contrasts dramatically with Cortona's allegory of *Divine Providence* in the central salon, rightly perceived as a triumph of illusionistic ceiling painting and dynastic celebration. The rooms which house these two ceilings are disposed opposite each other around the grand entrance staircase, and despite the theoretical disputes between the individual painters, the point remains that for the patrons, the Barberini family, the message of these two wildly divergent ceilings, the glorification of Urban VIII's pontificate and of his family, remained more important than the painterly style by which it was transmitted. A similar stylistic collision is presented in the church of S. Luigi dei Francesi, in which two startlingly different chapels, one by Domenichino, the other by Michelangelo Merisi da Caravaggio (1573–1610), seem to confront each other across the nave.

Caravaggio's itinerant career initially appears distinct from the Bolognese and Neapolitan patterns of Reni, Guercino, and Solimena. Born in Lombardy, Caravaggio made a boldly innovative contribution to the typology of painting with one of the earliest independent Italian still lifes (Galleria Ambrosiana, Milan) which stands as a progenitor of an important tradition in the visual arts. His tempestuous career, moving to Rome, then to Naples, Sicily, and ultimately Malta, was largely dictated by the constant need to change patrons as his irregular behaviour—several assaults and one murder—necessitated rapid departures from cities where he was no longer welcome. In this way alone, Caravaggio helped to feed the development of the image of the artist as an outsider, a social renegade whose fluorescent life-history was directly reflected in the heightened tenebrism, the starkly menacing gestures, and the direct sexuality of his painterly and compositional style. Seen in this way, Caravaggio's career seems closer to that of certain musicians than it does to painters such as Guercino, comfortably settled at Cento, and it suggests parallels between creativity and experience that have frequently been outlined in the Romantic vision of cultural expression as revelatory of and dependent upon the tortured self. In this mode, both the madrigals and the ecclesiastical responsoria for Tenebrae of Carlo Gesualdo, Prince of Venosa (*c*.1561–1613), are depicted as his only possible psychological means of dealing with his celebrated double murder of his adulterous wife and her princely lover, while the career of Alessandro Stradella (1644–82) has similarly been presented as reflecting the elopements and sexual adventures which ended with his own murder at the hands of hired assassins in Genoa.

The relationship between Stradella's cantatas and Caravaggio's paintings and the public awareness of their disordered private lives, which has been, and

Facing, above: DOMENICHINO, *St Cecilia Distributing Alms to the Poor.* Painted in 1611–14, in the same church as Caravaggio's Contarelli chapel, Domenichino's decoration of the Polet chapel, derived from the life of St Cecilia, rapidly established itself as an icon of Bolognese classicism, and was openly discussed in terms of its pictorial debt to Annibale Carracci. The importance of the specifically Bolognese presence in circles of Roman patronage of culture was somewhat mitigated by the consciously Roman subject of the five paintings comprising the sequence. Here St Cecilia distributes the wealth of her husband and his brother to the poor of Rome.

Facing, below: EVARISTO BASCHENSIS, *Still Life with Musical Instruments.* Baschensis (1617–77) adopted the north-Italian still-life rhetoric established by Caravaggio, but infused it with more erudite allusions to the world of music. His use of musical instruments, frequently as foreshortening devices to create the illusion of three-dimensional space, directs attention to the virtuosity of the great creators of stringed instruments based around Cremona, near Bergamo, the centre of Baschensis's artistic activity.

Facing: MARCO RICCI, *The Opera Rehearsal.* Marco Ricci established himself in London where he formed part of a network for cultural exchange between the Protestant north and the Italian south, based upon the success of Italian opera—singers, ·musicians, and sceno-graphers—during the London social seasons of the 1720s and the commercial promotion of such painters as Cana-letto and Marco's own celebrated uncle, Sebas-tiano Ricci. This system was facilitated in Italy by the presence of British diplomats interested in the arts, Joseph Smith in Venice, Horace Mann in Florence, and William Hamilton in Naples, not neglecting the shadowy figure of the Irish adven-turer Owen McSwinney, all of whom played key roles in exporting Italian culture.

which continues to be, given considerable currency, is reiterated far too frequently by commentators eager to tie accepted masterpieces to specific moments of crisis and anxiety. Stradella and Caravaggio shared with the much more placid Guercino a capacity to live independently, not as members of the household of a prince or an eminent aristocrat, but drawing instead on a range of patrons. The artist and the musician became, in effect, cultural entrepreneurs, and while the static model of Guercino and Solimena held great attraction for artists disinclined to abandon their native base, Caravaggio and Stradella demonstrated that, for whatever private reasons, such activity could be effectively conducted through geographical mobility, amongst the various Italian courts, underscoring the pluralism of Italian cultural patronage, and eventually, as became the case during the settecento, north of the Alps.

The very cosmopolitanism of Rome encouraged fluidity of various types and models of cultural consumption. In addition to the Vatican court, the households of papal nephews and papal families, Rome offered a dramatically varied array of foyers for cultural patronage. Returning to the stylistically opposed chapels of Caravaggio and Domenichino, the church of S. Luigi dei Francesi provides a prime example, for it was specifically the French national church, the importance of which indicates that in the seventeenth and eighteenth centuries Rome was, as the centre of Catholicism, a collection of international communities, each of which pursued its own cultural patronage, frequently helping to sustain colonies of non-Italian artists working in the papal capital. In this sense the careers of Nicolas Poussin and Claude Gelée, 'Claude Lorrain', who spent most of their productive lives in Rome, belong as much to the history of painting in Rome as they do to the history of French art, for which they have been exclusively and so remorselessly claimed by generations of chauvinistic writers based in Paris. Such painters should, at least, be seen as much within the context of Roman culture as they are presented as fabricators of a grand, French, classicizing style.

Queen Christina of Sweden in Rome

This openness to outsiders found an extreme, if telling, example in the royal establishment of Queen Christina, who, following her abdication of the Swedish throne and conversion to Catholicism, settled in Rome (1655), where she effectively created her own court. Christina's life in Rome helps to elucidate several structures in Italian cultural history in general. Gesualdo's madrigals were reported to be her favourite music—thus confirming the theme of princely irregularity in cultural expression—and music played a central role in all her activities. Here she prefigured another exiled queen, Maria Casimira Sobieska of Poland, installed in Rome following her husband's death in 1696,

and maintaining a private opera-house in her palace, for which Filippo Juvarra provided designs. Juvarra also worked for the other leading operatic patron in Rome during the early eighteenth century, Cardinal Pietro Ottoboni, another cardinal-nephew (actually the great-nephew of Pope Alexander VIII), whose household included musicians of the distinction of Arcangelo Corelli (1653–1713) and Alessandro Scarlatti (1660–1725), the first a predominantly instrumental composer, the second the creator of Neapolitan opera, and to whom works by Antonio Caldera (1670–1736) and Tommaso Albinoni (1671–1736) were dedicated, suggesting ties of clientele. Such a varied assemblage of composers suggests cultural heterogeneity within a single residential establishment, and as secular music in Rome had, by definition, to be private, almost domestic, music—specifically not associated with the papal court—two, amongst many other, distinctly prominent types of patron are highlighted: the exiled prince and the cardinal-nephew.

Christina did not come to Rome empty-handed. She brought with her the collections which she generously deemed to be her own private property, not entailed to the Swedish crown, and this included much of the artistic loot seized by the Swedish armies during the Thirty Years War. On one level, Christina's importation is representative of a larger Italian cultural phenomenon, the migration of collections. Many of the most significant Italian collections were either enriched or impoverished by the mobility of sales or inheritances in block, either amongst the Italian sovereignties or from abroad. The celebrated Gonzaga collection of pictures was sold to Charles I of England in 1627, but the dukes of Mantua promptly started to create a second collection which, itself, was dispersed in 1708. The equally famous Urbino collection was inherited by the Medici grand dukes of Tuscany as the sole tangible compensation for Ferdinand II's marriage (1637) to the Della Rovere heiress and was consolidated into the holdings in Florence. Charles Emanuel III of Savoy acquired the collection of pictures in Vienna of his kinsman Prince Eugene of Savoy, following his death in 1736, a family arrangement which dramatically enhanced the reputation of the royal gallery in Turin, while in a reverse transalpine direction, Duke Francesco III d'Este of Modena sold (1745) a substantial portion of his collection to the Saxon elector and king of Poland, Augustus III, who had been closely advised by Francesco Algarotti (1712–64), one of the most successful popularizers of neoclassical aesthetics. This was not the first displacement of the Este collection, as much of it had already been moved once before, from Ferrara to Modena following the papal sequestration of 1597. The Farnese collection is a special case, for when Elisabetta Farnese's eldest son became (1734) king of Naples, he moved his ancestors' pictures, sculptures, and archives south from Parma, of which he had been duke, to embellish his new court at Naples. Such mobility in the life of immensely prestigious collections was emphasized by Duke Francis Stephen of Lorraine, who stripped bare his palace at Lunéville following his accession (1737) as grand duke of Tuscany, transferred all his possessions, including the *boiseries* of his Galli-Bibiena opera-house, to Florence, but then moved the assemblage once again to Vienna following his father-in-law's death in 1740. The decision of the last of the Medici, Anna Maria Ludovica, to fix at her death (1743) her family's collections, by testamentary bequest, in Florence, as a museological monument to her dynasty and native city, stands out as an instance of stability in the volatile world of the history of collecting in the early modern period.

Christina's collection itself had only an ephemeral presence in Rome, and following her death (1689) it passed eventually to the Odescalchi family and most of it was then sold (1721) to the Orléans regent in Paris. However temporary its installation in the queen's Roman palace was, such a celebrated collection inevitably drew artists and amateurs to her residences, as did Christina's own personal fame. Access to such juridically 'private' collections, especially before the fully developed concept of the public museum, was relatively easy for any person of condition, but Christina herself positively encouraged the creation of a cultured entourage of artists, including Bernini, and men of learning, and as early as 1656, only shortly after her arrival, she established a private academy of letters, followed by her own theatre. In 1690, the year after the queen's death, this academy formally constituted itself as the Accademia dell' Arcadia, traditionally presented as a pioneering precursor of eighteenth-century naturalism. The Accademia dell' Arcadia posed one of the most serious challenges to the baroque literary aesthetic of the Neapolitan Giambattista Marino (1569–1625), whose narrative poem *L'Adone* (1623), while continuing the cinquecento epic traditions of Ariosto and Torquato Tasso, evolved an elaborate style of rhetoric and of erudite imagery which had become a model for much Italian literature of the seicento.

Academies and Universities

The impact of Arcadia went far beyond formalistic literary debates and extended into the world of theatre, antiquarianism, and history, but it was also representative of an essential feature of Italian cultural life in the early modern period, the private academy, founded under princely protection, and subsequently transformed into a quasi-public institution for the organization of a wide variety of forms of humanistic and scientific erudition. The sixteenth century had seen the consolidation of such academies as an important force in Italian intellectual life, while the seventeenth witnessed their vigorous expansion.

One of the most notable, the Accademia dei Lincei in Rome, was founded in 1603, again during the culturally fertile first decade of the seicento, by the Prince Federico Cesi. The Lincei had a strong disposition to the physical and natural sciences, and included among its members Cassiano dal Pozzo (1588–1657), whose 'paper museum' of drawings (some of which were commissioned from Pietro da Cortona) of antiquities and of botanical and biological specimens did much to encourage archaeological research and to shape subsequent definitions of the function of public museums. One of the epic moments in the history of the Lincei was, however, its defence of a most celebrated member, Galileo Galilei (1564–1642), the son of a Florentine musical theoretician and lutenist, who emerged, with the publication of his *Dialogo sopra i due massimi sistemi del mondo* (1632) and his *Dialoghi delle nuove scienze* (1638), as a defender, of truly European stature, of the Copernican solar-based astronomical system. Recent research has directed the study of Galileo's career back to the practical context of employment and protection. Initially Galileo was linked to the world of the university, first that of Pisa and then that of Padua, moving from there to the Florentine court of the grand dukes of Tuscany, tutoring the Medici princes, and eventually benefiting, like Bernini, from Barberini patronage and from the support which the papal family gave to the Accademia dei Lincei. An even closer parallel exists with the career of Cortona who, like Galileo, drew his patronage from a combination of the Roman Barberini clan and the Florentine Medici rulers, settling in the Tuscan capital (1637) to design the so-called 'Planetary Rooms' of Palazzo Pitti as the ceremonial enfilade for the Medici state apartments. Based upon a programme devised by Francesco Rondinelli and working with craftsmen in stucco, Cortona's combination of painting, scenographic architecture, and literary allusion provides yet another illustration of the collaborative aspect of seicento creativity and served as a model for European ceremonial rooms. The links with Galileo continue in the iconographic emphasis upon the teaching of princes in Rondinelli's and Cortona's project, while the notion of astronomical themes is also related to Galileo's discovery of the satellites of the

planet Jupiter, even though, in a paradox which has been frequently noted, the planetary system adopted for the decoration of the Pitti rooms is Ptolemaic rather than Copernican. Such criss-crossings of patronage structures bringing artists, musicians, and men of learning into the same social systems, such decorative collaborations between poets and historians, painters, architects, and *stuccatori* all serve to emphasize the futility of separating early modern Italian culture into rigid compartments.

Galileo's enormous intellectual stature, ranking him with Bernini as one of the most revered figures of early modern Italian culture, also directs attention to the singular combination of his sources of support. At various points in his career, Galileo was sustained by all three of the fundamental institutions of cultural organization: the university, the court, and the academy. Many of the subsequent giants of the physical sciences relied upon the universities. Although he published many of his significant discoveries through the Royal Society in London and although he enjoyed papal favour—he was appointed (1691) official physician to Pope Innocent XI—Marcello Malpighi (1628–94) conducted much of his revelatory research on the capillary system, supporting William Harvey's theses on blood circulation, from his professorial posts at Messina, Pisa, and Bologna. The University of Bologna, where Copernicus had studied and which sustained a tradition of scientific cosmopolitanism, also provided the institutional structure for the experiments on electricity conducted by Luigi Galvani (1737–98). Similarly, the University of Pavia fostered both Lazzaro Spallanzani (1729–99), who made dramatic breakthroughs in the study of digestion and human fertilization, and Alessandro Volta (1745–1827), with Galvani the second great figure in the history of early modern Italian, and indeed European, electronics.

Notwithstanding the massive contributions to experimental science carried out under the aegis of a university system, it is impossible to underestimate the importance of the academic tradition, which extended itself from the world of learning and of letters to embrace the visual and plastic arts as well as music. The founding of the Accademia di San Luca in Rome in 1593 prompted the creation of other similarly named academies for the fine arts and architecture among the Italian cities. The Roman academy was strengthened in 1676 by its merger with the French academy in Rome, another indication of the importance of foreign 'colonies' in the papal capital, and eventually (1710) by the absorption of the Accademia Clementina in Bologna, underscoring Bologna's importance in the institutionalization of culture. The competition (*concorso*) became a central activity of such academies, setting generalized themes of paintings or buildings for which submissions were invited and prizes awarded. Such competitions codified the various aesthetic disputes which had previously been conducted outside the official establishments, and, moving from the general to the specific, introduced the notion of

Facing: THE TREVI FOUNTAIN, which has become one of the immediately identifiable symbolic emblems of Rome, inscribes itself in the long-standing papal tradition of providing water for the pontifical capital. Nicola Salvi's successful design underscores the importance of the officially organized competition, as does the award in 1732 to Alessandro Galilei for the façade of S. Giovanni in Laterano, the cathedral church of the pope as bishop of Rome. Both projects demonstrate the continuing vitality of architecture in Rome and of papal patronage of culture well into the eighteenth century.

the competition as the means for awarding commissions for individual projects. The competition system clearly challenged in the early eighteenth century the functional notion of artists and architects winning commissions on the basis of affiliation to a familial clientele, and both the façade of S. Giovanni in Laterano, built in 1733–5 by Alessandro Galilei (1691–1736), and the Trevi Fountain, erected by Nicola Salvi (1697–1751) after a hotly contested competition of 1732, two of the major pieces of pontifical patronage of architecture in the settecento, resulted from public *concorsi*, opened to all, whether Italian or not.

Culture at Turin

Important as the various academies in Rome and Bologna (part of the Papal States) were, their widespread proliferation throughout the Italian sovereignties can, like opera, be viewed as a rare instance of cultural homogeneity on the peninsula. But, again, as with opera, the clear-cut distinctions between the academies in different cities point back to the diversity of cultural identification in what is still thought of as a homogeneous Italy. The academies in Turin provide an important example of those moulded to respond to the needs of a seat of a court. During the highly significant regency (1675–84) of the Duchess Maria Giovanna Battista, the court of Turin actively supported a number of initiatives to organize cultural life and the world of learning. An academy of painters, sculptors, and architects was founded, and the duchess herself created a literary academy for both French and Italian writers, reflecting the polyglot nature of the states straddling the Alps which she governed in her son's name. Maria Giovanna Battista was also a patron of the Jesuits and was instrumental in their establishment of a Collegio dei Nobili, an institution which, with its parallel foundation in Parma, underscored the importance of the Society of Jesus in shaping court erudition and, with the Collegio Romano in the papal capital, its central role in élite education.

The architect of the Jesuit Collegio dei Nobili (1678) in Turin was Guarino Guarini (1624–83), a Theatine priest, generally credited with initiating a golden age of architecture in Piedmont. Rudolf Wittkower observed that 'in matters of architecture Turin became the most advanced Italian city' with a successive triad of Guarini, Filippo Juvarra, and Bernardo Vittone, to which the name of Benedetto Alfieri should be added. Guarini's career followed the itinerant model. Born in Modena, he worked in Messina, provided designs for a church in Lisbon (which he may have visited), and settled in Paris, before accepting the summons to Turin. The proximity of music to theoretical mathematics was paralleled by architects such as Guarini whose audacious structures, particularly his domes, of the church of S. Lorenzo and chapel of SS. Sindone (housing the most valued relic of the House of Savoy, the Holy

Shroud), were dependent upon a technical mastery of scientific theory without which their exposed and open criss-crossed ribbing would have been impossible. The broken profiles of his domes and his use of oval interior space and of concave, undulating façades rank Guarini with Borromini as one of the most innovative and experimental architects of the seicento. Moreover, both Borromini and Guarini stand as early prototypes of the figure of the virtuoso which came to characterize so much of eighteenth-century Italian culture, the artist, in the broadest sense of the word, who by his intellectual knowledge and by his personal bravura and daring realized the seemingly impossible, a concept which would have profound implications for the history of theatre and the history of music, as well as the history of art and architecture.

Filippo Juvarra (1678–1736) did not arrive in Turin until 1714, following his engagement in Messina by Victor Amadeus II, who was in Sicily for his coronation as king. Previously Juvarra had worked in Rome, gaining a reputation as a scenic designer for the operas staged by Cardinal Ottoboni and the dowager queen of Poland. Once installed in Turin, Juvarra acquired a dominant role in shaping the visual culture of the court, working, as usual, with teams of *stuccatori*, painters, and sculptors, ordering decorative paintings from leading Italian artists in other capitals and continuing his activities as a scenographer. His classicizing vocabulary, clearly derived from Roman palace and ecclesiastical architecture, aimed at reflecting the newly acquired royal dignity of the House of Savoy. It was most clearly expressed in his basilica of Soperga (begun 1717), placed on the hill above Turin on which Victor Amadeus had vowed to erect a church should he lift the siege (1706) of the city by the French. The clear silhouette of arching and unbroken dome flanked by two bell-towers dominates the city from afar, and its selection as the site of the dynastic necropolis emphasized its political message.

Juvarra died in Madrid, technically on loan from the service of Charles Emanuel III to his brother-in-law Philip V of Spain and his second wife Elisabetta Farnese, for the construction of the new royal palace. Thus, there were certain striking parallels between his career and that of Guarino Guarini: neither was indigenous to Piedmont but had been imported; both had ecclesiastical affiliations (Juvarra was an abbot); both had Messina in common and both had some contact with the court of Lisbon, indicating a growing cosmopolitanism of a larger Mediterranean culture. Yet there were also significant differences. Although he carried out work of the highest importance, notably the façade of Palazzo Madama (begun 1718), one of the supreme European expressions of classical palace design, for Maria Giovanna Battista, who was operating in naked artistic rivalry with her son, Juvarra was fundamentally a client of the court, principally managing the growing cultural machine of Victor Amadeus, even if participating in family fissures. Guarini certainly worked for the Savoy crown, but was technically in the employ of

the duke's cousins, the princes of Carignano, for whom he designed (1679) their urban palace. Even at a court such as Turin, the centralizing and absolutist tendencies of which have been overemphasized, many different foyers of cultural patronage coexisted: the dynasty and its different branches, the secular clergy and the religious orders, the municipality and the great court clans, for instance the Dal Pozzo family, the elder, much wealthier, and powerful cousins of the overcelebrated Cassiano, who assembled an important collection of more than 500 pictures. Apart from the difficulties in studying Italian culture in general, each individual centre within the Italian ambit proves itself more heterogeneous in its cultural activities than neat and tidy homogeneous models would suggest, and the tensions between a set of specific cultural identities, defined city by city, and the fractured rivalries within each urban unit can only highlight the difficulties and contradictions in studying the seicento and settecento.

The court culture of Turin, like that of the popes and the grand dukes of Tuscany, and indeed most other Italian sovereigns, was structured by the politics of display and expenditure. The city of Turin itself did not expand naturally, but was extended, by the court, in a series of stages to create an imposing capital designed along intersecting axial lines with dramatic architectural viewpoints, a classic instance of political theatre and political urbanism. Such imperatives also shaped architecture in Piedmont later in the eighteenth century, when Bernardo Vittone (1702–70) was virtually shunned by the court (and forced on to ecclesiastical and private patrons for the realization of his centralized church plans) in favour of Benedetto Alfieri (1699–1767), whose creation (1738–40) of the Teatro Regio, and its subsequent publication, served, with the creations of the Galli-Bibiena family, as a model for court theatres throughout Europe. Alfieri frequently worked closely, in another model of collaboration, with the cabinet-maker Pietro Piffetti (c.1700–77), one of the towering figures in the history of furniture design. Piffetti's manipulation of seemingly unyielding wood into etiolated yet architectonically sustaining forms places him squarely amongst those central cultural figures who defined the concept of the virtuoso, but his close collaboration with Benedetto Alfieri drives attention towards another crucial aspect of cultural expression, the use of expensive, luxury materials as a means of hierarchical validation. Working in tandem, Alfieri and Piffetti combined large mirrors, gildings, and expensive fabrics with the various elements of surface-coverings for Piffetti's furniture, precious woods with inlays of mother-of-pearl and tortoiseshell. Such expressions of 'conspicuous consumption' can be viewed as a response to the same policy of cultural patronage adopted by the Medici grand dukes of Tuscany, the sumptuous, illusionistic Cortona Planetary rooms, but also the furnishings, the mighty tables of gilded wood supporting tops composed of *pietre dure*, the hard, semi-precious stones cut and arranged to create an illusionistic

Facing: THE BASILICA OF LA SOPERGA commemorated one of the great iconographic events in Piedmontese history, the lifting of the siege of Turin in 1706. Filippo Juvarra's classicizingly rhetorical architectural language—the strikingly silhouetted dome and the colonnaded portico—aimed to distance the court of Turin from a local idiom and, by placing its buildings in a broader European context, to support its royal, as distinct from ducal, rank. La Soperga, a complex of votive church, monastery, and dynastic mausoleum referred clearly to Philip II's Escorial, outside Madrid.

pictorial image. The Medici Opificio delle Pietre Dure had been founded in 1588, and its creations of compositions which combined highly skilled technical facility with the use of precious materials helped to forge the link in Italian, and later European, courts between expertise and luxury. Only courts of specially elevated status aimed to produce such artefacts.

Naples

Like the House of Savoy, the Medici family, throughout the seventeenth century, had attempted to secure recognition as a specifically royal dynasty, but by the early eighteenth century it was clear that the Medici, in common with many other indigenous Italian sovereign families, were doomed to extinction. The acquisition of the Kingdom of Sicily in 1713 (exchanged for that of Sardinia in 1720) guaranteed the royal position of the court of Turin, but opposition from a different quarter emerged in 1734 with the re-establishment of the independent Kingdom of Naples under Charles VII (from 1759, Charles III of

Spain). Eager to establish the cultural credentials of his new royal court, Charles transported the bulk of the Farnese collections from Parma to Naples in order to compensate for the inevitable failure of relatively short-term, foreign viceroys to create a royal Neapolitan collection during the previous two centuries. In the same fashion that a celebrated picture-gallery had become an essential element of court culture, a royal ceramics factory had also emerged as a significant emblem of sovereign status. Charles's consort was a Saxon princess, fully attuned to the European prestige which her father's hard-paste manufactory of Meißen attracted to the court of Dresden, and the foundation in 1743 of a soft-paste porcelain manufactory in the grounds of the palace of Capodimonte reflected the wider European phenomenon of the institutionalization of the various branches of the applied arts,

both for the practical use of the court and as a signifier of its hierarchical status. The use of Capodimonte porcelain, particularly for a room at the palace of Portici (now in the Museo di Capodimonte) should be seen, in its profuse display of expensive materials, as a Neapolitan response to the rooms created in Turin by Benedetto Alfieri and Piffetti for the kings of Sardinia, and

Charles's own blatant cultural rivalry with the court in Madrid of his parents Philip V and Elisabetta Farnese, designating a triangle of tense artistic competitiveness between Naples, Spain, and Piedmont which enlarged the ambit of Italian patronage of painting and architecture. The beginning of work on the massive palace of Caserta, just outside Naples, in 1751 to the designs of Luigi Vanvitelli (1700–73), with its celebrated garden cascade, was yet another element in a conscious political policy to assemble all the elements viewed as essential for a royal court, as was the creation of a new opera-house, S. Carlo, erected (1737) adjacent to the royal palace in Naples and fostering a tradition of *opera buffa*, of which *La serva padrona* (1733) of Giovanni Battista Pergolesi (1710–36) was a precursor and *Il matrimonio segreto* (1792, but first performed in Vienna) of Domenico Cimarosa (1749–1801) the culmination. Neapolitan opera henceforth challenged the dominance of Venice for primacy of the Italian lyric stage.

The determination to create a specifically Neapolitan court culture can also be detected in the nomination in 1735, the year following Charles's installation as king, of no less a figure than Giambattista Vico (1668–1744) as the royal historiographer, another essential component of court erudition. Vico's enormous European reputation as a historicizing philosopher propounding theses of cyclical change in the nature of political regimes, along with the fame of his *La nuova scienza* (three editions: 1725, 1730, 1744), and his autobiography, was a subsequent phenomenon, but his rapid official absorption into the new Bourbon cultural system indicates Charles VII's determination to use patronage of the arts and of learning as a tool to establish his own European standing. In this, the king was representative of a specific princely type, for Rinaldo I d'Este, duke of Modena, had previously engaged (1700), as his librarian, Ludovico Antonio Muratori (1672–1750). Muratori's *Antichità Estensi* (1717, 1740) was an obvious attempt to celebrate and to validate his sovereign's family, while making, at the same time, a vital contribution to the developing science of archaeology and to the evolving notion of history as an evidential, rather than revelatory, branch of erudition. Muratori's *Rerum Italicarum Scriptores* (1723–50) and his *Annali d'Italia* (1744–9) were subsequently praised as pioneering works of scholarship which established a firm documentary basis for the study of the past, while being claimed by the Risorgimento as precursors of a generalized Italian cultural consciousness. The posthumous reputations of both Vico and Muratori should not weaken the brutally practical observation that both scholars, particularly Muratori, looked for support to a court culture, the needs of which inevitably shaped their writing.

In assembling his new court at Naples, Charles VII had been able to draw upon a strongly Neapolitan cultural self-identity, preserved during the centuries of viceregal government by, amongst others, painters who had evolved an audaciously fluid, but also highly learned, style for covering the surfaces of

Facing: GIUSEPPE GRICCI, *The Portrait*. Queen Maria Amalia of Naples, with her two sisters, the French Dauphine and the Bavarian electress, helped to diffuse the enthusiasm for their Saxon father's hard-paste porcelain production at Meißen through their own encouragement of soft-paste manufactories at the courts into which they married. The Capodimonte ceramics works in Naples drew upon broader Italian themes of domestic life as depicted in the paintings of Longhi and the plays of Goldoni and referred to the even wider European theme of rococo gallantry evident in the compositions of Watteau and the writings of Marivaux.

PIETRO DA CORTONA, *Divine Providence*, Palazzo Barberini, Rome. Cortona's composition was the largest decorative fresco executed in Rome since Michelangelo's work at the Sistine Chapel. It announced a new sophistication in pictorial illusionism which reached its apogee with the nave paintings by Giovanni Battista Gaulli, 'il Baciccia' (1639–1709), at the Church of the Gesù and by the Jesuit Father Andrea Pozzo (1642–1709) at S. Ignazio. Papal families advertised the extent of their cultural patronage by direct reference to their dynastic symbols and emblems. The Barberini bees, adopted by the Bonaparte clan in the early nineteenth century, immediately identified works of art and buildings associated with Urban VIII's kinship network.

walls. Luca Giordano (1634–1705) was a prototypical figure. His sobriquet of 'fa presto' ('do quickly') associated his career with the elaboration of the notion of the virtuoso, in this instance, a painter able to produce metres of pictorially convincing painted space within an erudite iconography of images and, indeed, of colours. Such easily worn facility was acquired only by profound application, both technical and intellectual, and this became a hallmark of official Neapolitan painting. Giordano's period at the Spanish court (1692–1702) heralded, as well, the concept of the exportation of Italian culture during the eighteenth century, Italian artists who were able to implant themselves abroad thanks to their reputations gained in the service of the diverse range of Italian patrons. Francesco Solimena (1657–1747) has frequently been presented as a natural successor to Giordano, and, without moving from Naples, he created key, essential decorative canvases, for major schemes at both the royal palace in Turin and the Doges' Palace in Genoa, underscoring the importance of a painter based in the south for both the royal and republican imagery of northern Italian sovereignties. Thus, when Charles VII installed himself in Naples, a tradition of courtly painting, objects to decorate rooms rather than to serve as small, framed museum-pieces, was fully established.

Equally set in place was its accompanying historical ideology. The *Istoria civile del regno di Napoli* was published by Pietro Giannone (1676–1748) in 1723, more than a decade before the complete independence of the Kingdom of Naples. Historians of intellectual thought and of scholarship are increasingly convinced of the need to place the great classical writers within the context of immediate, political imperatives. Both Muratori and Giannone were pushed to develop a new form of historical research, based upon what they viewed to be incontrovertible evidence, because of the pressing needs of the sovereignties of which they were subjects. Muratori, in close epistolary correspondence with Gottfried Leibnitz, skewed his history of the Este dynasty to a greater German, specifically Guelph, tradition, stressing the prestige of the family's transalpine links, while Giannone was primarily concerned to write a history of Naples which argued for the independence of the kingdom from direct papal control. Both scholars, by insisting upon evidential proof, made major contributions to the evolution of the writing of history as a scientific exercise, but both as well had specific political cases to argue, thus blurring, once again, the divisions between the history of culture and the history of power.

Venice

The obvious model for both Muratori and Giannone, as historians working within the structure of high power politics, was Paolo Sarpi (1552–1623), the apogee of whose work, his history of the Council of Trent, was, in a smuggled

version, first published in London in 1619. Sarpi provides a classic instance of a major scholarly mind, endowed with access to fundamental primary sources, placing his talents at the service of his native state, in this case the Republic of Venice. As with Vico and Muratori, Sarpi held an official post, as the historiographer of Venice and its archival adviser; as with Muratori and Giannone there was a clear political agenda underpinning his research: the substantiation of the claims of the Republic of Venice to be totally independent from both the Pope and the Holy Roman Emperor, an argument which acquired a sharpened edge with the papal interdict imposed upon Venice in 1606. Sarpi's career crystallizes the intersection between a new form of historical research, constantly insisting upon the value of supposedly neutral evidence, and the utilization of such research for the needs of the State, be it dynastic or republican in nature. By the nineteenth century Sarpi, a subject of assassination plots, and Galileo, the victim of the Inquisition, not to mention Giordano Bruno, burnt alive in 1600 in the Campo dei Fiori in Rome, had been adopted as the most prominent intellectual martyr-heroes by the anticlerical ideology of the unified Risorgimento Italy. Sarpi is a prime example of a polemical scholar, supported and protected by his State, who drove forward the scientific basis of historical writing while serving openly political goals, and his published works became the canonical basis for the cult of Venetian particularity.

The intense sense of local cultural identity obvious in capitals as diverse as Turin and Naples, significantly the two Italian cities which registered obvious demographic growth during the early modern period, was even more clearly articulated and defined in Venice, as Hugh Honour, despite his use of anachronistic terms, sharply perceived: 'No culture was more self-consciously national, one is tempted to say isolationist, than that of eighteenth-century Venice. Every effort was made to maintain its integrity.' As examples, Honour cites two leading figures of Venetian literary and theatrical culture, Carlo Goldoni and Carlo Gozzi, specifically for their skill in using various types of Venetian dialect in their plays as a means of sustaining forms of culture which were, like the various city-scapes painted by Venetian artists, so topographically specific that only the mastery of a highly specialized and local vocabulary, either visual or linguistic, can provide entry to an enclosed world of coded references and sophisticated allusion. Appreciation of the achievement of Carlo Gozzi (1720–1806) has been clouded, during the late twentieth century, by the remarkable enthusiasm evinced for Goldoni's plays, spearheaded by the pioneering productions of Giorgio Strehler and Luchino Visconti. The rivalry and public competition between the two writers established itself as one of the great cultural debates of eighteenth-century Europe, another variant upon the theme of artistic competition, fuelled by the academic structure of Italian intellectual life, as Gozzi used the Accademia dei Granelleschi

THE TOELETTA DELLA REGINA, Palazzo Reale, Turin. Created within the 'private' space of the court of Turin, this combined effort of Benedetto Alfieri and Pietro Piffetti crystallizes both a distinctively Italian concept of 'magnificence' and an immediately identifiable mode of Piedmontese decorative arts. Piffetti himself was at the forefront of the creation of a 'school' of Sabaudian furniture-makers, the eighteenth-century arch of which was realized by Giuseppe Maria Bonzanigo (1745–1820). His virtuosity in working wood and utilizing precious materials demands comparisons with the great instrument-makers living further to the east but still within close distance of the River Po, the major fluvial artery of cultural exchange in northern Italy.

(founded 1747) as a means for attacking Goldoni's aesthetic. Both Gozzi and Goldoni drew heavily upon the tradition of the *commedia dell' arte*, but both interpreted this static body of popular theatrical device in strikingly different ways. Gozzi belonged to a broad European tradition of collecting and reassembling the deceptively simplistic stories of folklore, and his *fiabe drammatiche*, dating from the early 1760s, *L'amore delle tre melarance* [The Love of Three Oranges], *Turandot, Il re cervo*, and *L'augelin belverde*, were dependent upon a grasp of metaphor and imagistic genealogy.

Although they also drew heavily upon the conventions and character types of the *commedia dell' arte*, the much more directly narrative plays of Carlo Goldoni (1707–93), which had at their heart the practicalities of human dilemmas—love, sex, and money, along with much reference to local Venetian customs—stood out in stark contrast to Gozzi's assemblage of a highly refined and reworked literary expression of what was essentially an oral tradition of moral allusion, albeit one as deeply rooted in Venetian culture as were Goldoni's comic masterpieces. It is surely striking that while Gozzi's plays received their supreme operatic translations only in the twentieth century, at the hands of Puccini, Prokofiev, and Henze, Goldoni's plots entered, and immediately enriched, the standard choices of libretti for his contemporary composers, including Baldassare Galuppi (1706–85), with whom he had a fifteen-year-long collaboration, and Antonio Salieri (1750–1825), ultimately a fixture at the court of Vienna, another example of Italian cultural exportation.

Carlo Goldoni is, indeed, one of those key cultural figures whose career sheds so much light on the artistic structures of his own time. On the most basic level, his plays of erotic confusion and social and financial advancement, such as *La locandiera* (1753), which furnished the theme for an opera by Salieri, were obviously precursors of the libretti provided by Lorenzo Da Ponte (1749–1838), eventually the founder of Italian studies in the United States, at Columbia University in New York, for Mozart's *Le nozze di Figaro* (1786), *Don Giovanni* (1787), and *Così fan tutte* (1790). Goldoni, like Guercino or Guido Reni in Cento and Bologna or Solimena in Naples, was immediately identifiable with a specific urban culture, that of Venice, but like Caravaggio and Juvarra, he ultimately (1762) assumed a more mobile existence and moved to Paris.

Goldoni crystallizes the intense contradictions in Venetian artistic life between the obsessive cultural structure of self-reference and its role, in sharp competition with Turin and Rome, as the leading Italian representative of European cosmopolitanism. Goldoni's departure for Paris contributed to a fundamentally important phenomenon of early modern history, the exportation to and diffusion of Italian culture throughout both Catholic and Protestant Europe in the eighteenth century. The celebrated journey (1665) of Bernini to Paris for the unrealized designs of the Louvre façade had been an early, if uninspiring, precedent, but by the eighteenth century Goldoni was

merely one of many major cultural figures who settled permanently abroad. Another of the greatest Italian playwrights, Pietro Metastasio (1698–1782), also a member of the Arcadian Academy, accepted (1730) the post of imperial court poet at Vienna, where he remained for the rest of his long life. Metastasio's reworking of classical mythology and history could scarcely have been more distant from the social world of Goldoni's 'realistic' comedies, but it is highly significant that so much of what is now considered to be canonical Italian theatrical literature was initially produced for audiences in non-Italian cities. In a strikingly similar fashion to the musical means by which the Goldonian canon entered a wider European cultural consciousness, the texts of Metastasio owed their currency to their suitability as opera libretti, and they were set to music at least 800 times during the course of the settecento, most durably perhaps *La clemenza di Tito* (1732), which formed the basis of Mozart's last opera (1791).

Export of Culture

Such permanent transplantings were common in all aspects of Italian cultural and intellectual activity. The Piedmontese geometer and astronomer Giuseppe Luigi Lagrange (1736–1813) helped to found the scientific academy in Turin but then entered the employment successively of Frederick II of Prussia, Louis XVI of France, and, following the revolutionary upheavals, Napoleon, displaying a dexterity for surviving changes of political regimes. A cluster of strong-minded women played a major role in the Italianization of European court culture, two successive queens-consort of Spain, Elisabetta Farnese and Maria Barbara of Bragança, and two near successive empresses of Russia, Elisabeth Petrovna and Catherine II. Despite the pronounced francophile affinities of the two Russian tsarinas, the visual appearance of the newly created capital of St Petersburg was largely the work of Italian architects, the distinctly nordic rococo of the buildings of Bartolomeo Francesco Rastrelli (1700–71), Elisabeth Petrovna's favourite architect, yielding to the neo-classical language of the members of Catherine's clientele system, including Giacomo Quarenghi (1744–1817). Catherine's position as a correspondent of leading French *philosophes*, an open display of mutual esteem which the empress took pains to conduct with the maximum publicity, should not disguise the extent to which she continued Elisabeth Petrovna's patronage of Italian artists. Music, as well as architecture, had a distinct Italian flavour, as Catherine engaged (1776) as her *maestro di cappella* Giovanni Paisiello, whose *Il barbiere di Siviglia* received its first performance at Saint Petersburg in 1782, before the composer returned to the Bourbon court in his native Naples and subsequently provided music—yet another example of Bonapartist engagement of Bourbon artists—for the great set pieces, including the emperor's coronation, of the Napoleonic court in Paris. Napoleon, with his intimate links to the Italian peninsula, appreciated the unique capacity of its culture to validate innovatory political arrangements.

Spain provided an equally telling example of Italian cultural colonization in the eighteenth century. The disastrous fire of Christmas Eve 1734 which gutted the royal Alcázar of Madrid necessitated the construction of a new royal palace, which, with the decoration of the dome of St Paul's Cathedral in London and the design of the façade of S. Giovanni Laterano in Rome, emerged as one of the three great European architectural and decorative commissions of the first half of the eighteenth century. The installation of a team of Italian architects and artists, headed by Filippo Juvarra, has been interpreted as part of Queen Elisabetta Farnese's conscious policy to mould the visual culture of the Spanish court along Italian lines and thus define its distinction from the ponderous model of Versailles, where her husband Philip V had been raised. The engagement of Corrado Giaquinto (1703–1765) from Naples and eventually the Venetian Jacopo Amigoni (1682–1752) as the creators of the painted decorative space for the new seat of the Spanish court was a clear indication of this aesthetic orientation, while the later employment of Giambattista Tiepolo (1696–1770) and his son Giandomenico (1727–1804) confirmed the

Italophile tendency. Giambattista Tiepolo was one of the major figures in the history of painting in eighteenth-century Venice, reviving the technical skills of large-scale fresco composition and the larger-than-life decorative schemes of such cinquecento predecessors as Veronese, while realizing a unique combination of recondite imagery and allusion with a fluent painterly style which owed no little debt to the illusionistic grandeur of Cortona's ceiling and wall decoration. The Cortonesque tradition had been perpetuated in Rome with commissions associated with the Society of Jesus, notably two famous illusionistic ceilings in Rome, that of the Gesù by Giovanni Battista Gaulli, 'il Baciccia' (1639–1709), and that of S. Ignazio by Andrea Pozzo (1642–1709), the two master-coordinators of scientific perspective realized on two-dimensional surfaces. Tiepolo combined these skills with a range of colour associated with the international rococo idiom, and his career, like those of Pozzo and Amigoni, can be understood as a case-study in Italian cultural exportation. All three worked at a number of northern courts, and Tiepolo, indeed, created what were, arguably, his signal decorative masterpieces (begun 1750) in the Kaisersaal and grand staircase of the palace of the prince-bishop of Würzburg, one of the most grandiose examples of Italian visual culture in a transalpine setting.

Queen Elisabetta Farnese was also responsible for luring to Madrid Carlo Broschi, called 'Farinelli' (1705–82), the best-known of the soprano *castrati*. The *castrato*, with his technical vocal capacity for singing intricate music at high pitch, became one of the most distinctive emblems of the Italian cult of virtuosity, but it would be grossly misleading to represent a highly refined musical facility as exclusively linked to opera. Queen Maria Barbara was the leading patron of Domenico Scarlatti (1683–1757), most of whose keyboard sonatas, numbering over 600, were written for her. Domenico Scarlatti stands as a prime eighteenth-century example of a composer of purely instrumental music, a tradition stretching back at least to Girolamo Frescobaldi (1583–1643), whose collections of works for a variety of keyboards, including the organ, established themselves as canonical classics. Alongside this tradition of keyboard virtuosity existed a second strand of technical proficiency and musical pyrotechnics, one for the violin. Pietro Antonio Locatelli (1695–1764), who settled permanently in Amsterdam in 1729, another cultural export, helped to establish the image of the virtuoso violinist, and the very title of one collection of his published compositions, *L'arte del violino*, underscores his desire to define the capacities of his instrument and to establish its place in the musical hierarchy based upon its potential for virtuoso display. Significantly, Locatelli had been born in Bergamo, close to Cremona, where the celebrated Stradivari family (Antonio Stradivari: 1644–1737), along with the Guarnieri and Amati clans, established European-wide reputations as makers of stringed instruments. Without this tradition, combining mathematical precision with the skills of working wood, in itself an example of technical virtuosity, performances of virtuoso violinists would have been impossible.

Strong as these traditions of purely instrumental music were, hard and clear-cut definitions are difficult to impose. Music could be non-vocal but still programmatic, linking it to the worlds of painting, theatre, and literature. The experiments in both sonata and concerto forms, essential for subsequent developments in instrumental music, made by Arcangelo Corelli, have largely, with the exception of the *Christmas Concerto*, escaped descriptive titles, although Corelli, admitted to the Arcadian Academy at the same time as the leading opera composer Alessandro Scarlatti, was clearly a man of considerable literary culture. More representative of the overlap of genres are the compositions of Francesco Geminiani (1687–1762), another expatriate—he died in Dublin—whose purely instrumental *La foresta incantata* (1754) was indebted to the literary images of Torquato Tasso, and the prime example Antonio Vivaldi (1678–1741), who self-consciously baptized collections of his concerti with rhetorical titles: *L'estro armonico* (1711) and its assumed successor *La stravaganza* (of uncertain date). Vivaldi's almost-too-famous *Four Seasons*, from *L'estro armonico*, is perhaps the most obvious instance of the elision between instrumental music and literary and visual image.

Like Frescobaldi, who composed both purely instrumental pieces and sacred vocal music, Vivaldi defies neat categorization, since he wrote secular operas, music for the Church, and concerti for an impressively wide variety of instruments, including the bassoon. Such multiplicity of musical expression reflected the very mixed nature of Venetian patronage. A republic with aspirations to royal rank but without a fully elaborated court, buttressed by a group of powerful élite families and endowed with a range of ecclesiastical foundations, Venice had, in addition, a highly developed tradition of a fee-paying public, which could encourage private cultural speculation for financial gain. This was the situation one century earlier which faced Claudio Monteverdi. Having left the service of a ducal court, Monteverdi composed *Il combattimento di Tancredi e Clorinda* (1624) for the Mocenigo family before profiting from the truly remarkable inauguration of four public opera-houses—totally distinct from the concept of the court opera—between 1637 and 1641 for the realization of *Il ritorno di Ulisse in patria* (1640) and *L'incoronazione di Poppea* (1643, the year of the composer's death). The late twentieth century has reserved for these works, after long neglect, a central position in the broad tradition of European cultural history, but the practical backgrounds to their creation were rooted in Venice's special role as an entrepreneurial emporium of artistic activity.

Painters based in Venice were quick to grasp the potential of the city's position. While using the indigenous centres of patronage as their operational base, they extracted maximum profit from Venice's particular allure for foreign clients. Venice had throughout the seventeenth and eighteenth centuries a privileged relationship with the Protestant north, based upon its geographical accessibility and its nearly unrelenting jurisdictional disputes, represented by the works of Sarpi, with papal Rome. The European fame of its pre-Lenten carnival was a powerful magnet, and, along with such other high points of Venetian ritual as the Wedding to the Sea and those central elements of Venetian social life, the summer retreat to the villa (the *villegiatura*) or the frequentation of the gambling casino (the *ridotto*), it appears in the plays of Goldoni, the paintings of Pietro Longhi (1702–85), and the sequence of city-scapes by a succession of artists who created a tradition of topographical auto-celebration. Longhi's genre scenes, with their meticulous documentation of Venetian dress and residential interiors, have, indeed, often been interpreted as the visual equivalents of Goldoni's domestic comedies.

The popularity in northern Europe of such images of a specifically Venetian culture encouraged many of the most celebrated Venetian painters to try their fortunes on the far side of the Alps. Sebastiano Ricci (1659–1734), with Giambattista Tiepolo, responsible for the revival of the grandiose historico-mythological decorative style codified in the cinquecento by Veronese, spent time in Vienna (1701–3) and then, around 1712, when well into his fifties, journeyed to London to join his nephew Marco Ricci (1676–1729), who had made his British career with the invention of scenery for Italian opera. Upon returning to Venice, Sebastiano Ricci, although disappointed with his failure to secure the commission for the decoration of the cupola of St Paul's Cathedral, nevertheless retained his links with London through a cycle of commissions from the British consul Joseph Smith. Smith himself was largely responsible for one of the great cultural marketing exercises of the eighteenth century, the creation of the international career of Giovanni Antonio Canaletto (1697–1768). With his virtual contemporary, Gianantonio Guardi (1699–1760), the brother-in-law of Giambattista Tiepolo, Canaletto marks the culmination of the tradition of Venetian view-painting, with sequences and cycles of paintings, subsequently engraved, recording, not always with strict topographical accuracy, the idealized appearance of the city and purportedly characteristic details of urban life. Although Canaletto came to England in 1746, the density of his paintings in British collections owed much to Joseph Smith's single-minded promotion of his protégé in acquiring commissions for him, normally for series—several pictures rather than one single composition—of depictions, all easily recycled for other clients, of the classic and celebrated Venetian city-views.

Other Venetian painters embarked upon careers which were so peripatetic that they can be seen as cultural progresses which played a major role in the dissemination of the Venetian pictorial idiom. Giovanni Antonio Pellegrini (1675–1741) produced decorative paintings, strongly influenced by Sebastiano

LOUIS-JEAN DESPREZ, *The Visit of Gustavus III to Tivoli in 1784*. The visit was an act of homage to the proto-Romantic cult of 'the Sublime', which ran in a not always easy tandem with contemporary notions of academic neoclassicism, a tension which this highly atmospheric composition fully captures.

Ricci, for a number of northern European courts and capitals, while his sister-in-law Rosalba Carriera (1675–1758) established her fame as one of the leading portraitists in pastel of her day through an itinerant career which brought public celebrity (and commissions) in the leading cities of Europe. Family ties were fundamentally important in the organization of Italian cultural life and its exportation. Canaletto's nephew Bernardo Bellotto (1720–80) transported his own sharply defined version of Venetian view-painting north to Vienna, Dresden, and Warsaw, while various members of the Bolognese-based Galli-Bibiena family (two brothers, Ferdinando (1657–1743) and Francesco (1659–1739), who sired three generations of scenographers and theatre architects) created a network of theatre and stage designers across the continent which made a major contribution to the cosmopolitanization and, indeed, homogenization of European court culture in the eighteenth century. As with the realized buildings of Borromini and Guarino Guarini, the Galli-Bibiena family based its work upon meticulously thought-out mathematical theories of visual perception, another aspect of the intensely strong scientific tradition of Bologna. In its fictive stage architecture, therefore, the Galli-Bibiena family pushed the boundaries of perspective to a new level of refinement and precision, while Ferdinando's son Giuseppe (1695–1747) transmitted, through the, happily, still-intact opera-house at Bayreuth, the sumptuousness of Italian theatrical space into transalpine Europe.

Cultural traffic did not move, however, in only one direction, for with the increasing secularization of European society, the grand tour established itself as a supplement, at times a replacement, for more formal modes of education amongst the Protestant élites. Fear of Catholic contamination eased to such a point that Gustavus III, king of the very Lutheran Sweden, could visit Rome, meet the pope, and even, incognito, attend Mass at St Peter's. One additional and vital encouragement to the extension of such itineraries southwards, towards Rome and Naples, was the astounding archaeological excavations begun in 1738 at Herculaneum and then Pompeii, which added considerably to the cultural prestige of the newly established royal Neapolitan court, which, in its turn, jealously regulated access to them.

BÉNIGNE GAGNERAUX, *The Interview of Pope Pius VI with Gustavus III, King of Sweden, in the Museo Pio-Clementino on 1 January 1784.* In this commission from the Swedish court, Gagneraux took considerable liberties in depicting the space of the papal museum, but his cool and detached painterly style, totally unlike that of Desprez, reflected the cultural commitment of the papal court to neoclassicism and the preservation of the Antique heritage. Lest that message be lost, the poses of Pope Pius and King Gustavus mirror inversely the two statues against the back wall, 'the Apollo Belvedere' for the pope and 'Antinous' for the young king.

Archaeology and Neoclassicism

The revelations at Pompeii, with its well-preserved examples of antique painting, had European repercussions of the greatest weight for the development
of a neoclassical aesthetic and for the organization of the archaeological past.
The adoption of a classicizing canon for nearly every branch of the Italian
visual arts, from painting to furniture design, was deeply indebted to two
transalpine imports, Anton Raffael Mengs (1728–79), from Dresden, whose
painting *Parnassus* (1761) for the Villa Albani, outside Rome, represented a

truly revolutionary break with the Italian decorative tradition of the preceding centuries, and Johann Joachim Winckelmann (1717–68), born a subject of the king of Prussia but also closely attached, as librarian, to the Albani family, a late eighteenth-century reminder of the critical role played by cardinal-nephews in Roman cultural life. Winckelmann's writings (1755, 1764) on antique Greek art were written in German but were rapidly translated and became the most obvious literary point of reference for the cause of Hellenistic classicism.

The massive importance of archaeological studies and their impact upon a

GIOVANNI BATTISTA PIRANESI, 'The Campo Vaccino' from the *Vedute di Roma*. Piranesi's career divides itself between the history of the visual arts, the history of archaeology, and the history of publishing. The wide diffusion of his prints made a critically important contribution to the politics of neoclassicism, but while some of his etchings were 'fantastical' and totally unhistorical reconstructions, others, such as this view of the so-called 'Campo Vaccino' have the immediacy of a 'snap-shot', and indicate the enormity of the task—the arch half-buried in urban detritus—facing the papal authorities in restoring and in excavating Antique Rome.

range of aesthetic forms which closely imitated their findings, spurred on by the concept of the novelty and freshness of only recently excavated antique artefacts, found its most eloquent representative in Giovanni Battista Piranesi (1720–78). Born near Venice, where he absorbed the tradition of city-scapes, Piranesi settled in Rome, where he became a leading voice in favour of Italian classicism against the Greek ideal, another in the sequence of public controversies which defined Italian cultural life. Piranesi's etchings ranged from the meticulously archaeological (which made a profound impact upon the decorative arts) to the fantastical, notably the *Carceri* or imaginative prison scenes (1745–61), passing by a combination of these two modes, in his celebrated and immensely popular views of both ancient and modern Rome, which contained strong elements of imaginative reconstruction. Piranesi's attempts to organize and to catalogue in printed form the glories of classical antiquity found their parallels in the systematization of collections of surviving artefacts from the ancient world, notably the Museo Pio-Clementino established within the Vatican itself and named after the two popes, Clement XIV (reigned 1769–74) and Pius VI (reigned 1774–99), who had been largely responsible for the acquisition of the pontifical antiquities and their display and presentation in a way which marked a critical transition-point between the private princely or royal collection and the nineteenth-century phenomenon of the public museum organized along lines dictated by contemporary scholarly opinion. The lucid and uncluttered space designed for the Museo Pio-Clementino by Michelangelo Simonetti (1724–81) provided an important model for subsequent museum architecture.

The neoclassical movement, varied, factionalized, and riven with jealousies as it was, is too frequently presented by Anglo-American scholarship as, primarily, a development in visual culture. The plays of Metastasio established a literary canon of classical history and mythology for the stage, while his close imitator, Raniero Calzabigi (1714–95), another itinerant writer and another member of Arcadia, entered into a close working relationship with the composer Christoph Willibald Gluck, to produce a number of operas, notably *Orfeo ed Euridice* (1762), which revolutionized lyric theatre by reorientating it towards a fusion of classical declamation and austere musical expression. The Piedmontese playwright and poet Vittorio Alfieri (1749–1803), nephew of the architect Benedetto Alfieri, with his tragedies based upon biblical and classical history also drew upon the antique past, albeit by means which have too frequently been presented as heralding the Romantic movement. All three authors, however distinct from one another, provide literary counterparts to the interest in the plastic culture of the ancient world. Although interest in Vittorio Alfieri's grandly tragic theatre is reviving, his most enduring literary monument remains his memoirs, the *Vita* of 1799–1803. Here Alfieri reached back to one of the strongest traditions in Italian literary history, the autobiog-

Facing: THE PIEDMONTESE POET AND PLAYWRIGHT, Vittorio Alfieri, was the first non-Tuscan celebrity to be buried in Santa Croce, the pantheon of a specifically Florentine view of Italian cultural history. Commissioned by Alfieri's mistress, the countess of Albany, the one-time wife of the Stuart pretender, this tomb effectively commemorates two of the leading figures of the northern Italian Enlightenment: Alfieri himself and the sculptor Antonio Canova, who played a major role in establishing the visual and monumental forms of European neoclassicism.

raphy, enunciated in the sixteenth century by Benvenuto Cellini and elaborated and refined in the eighteenth century by Vico, Goldoni, Da Ponte,
Gozzi, and the adventurer Giacomo Girolamo Casanova (1725–98), who, like
Goldoni, wrote down his recollections in French. Such autobiographies
inevitably put the individual artist or thinker at the centre of his own personalized universe, and they were shadowed by the perpetuation of the Vasarian
model of viewing the history of art as a collection of biographies: the *Vite de'
pittori, scultori et architetti moderni* (1672) of Giovanni Pietro Bellori (1615–96)
and Malvasia's highly political and virtually contemporary attempt to emphasize the importance of his native Bolognese tradition of painting, *Felsine pittrice* (1678).

When Vittorio Alfieri died (1803), his long-term mistress, Louisa of Stol-
berg-Stolberg, countess of Albany, commissioned a monument for him in the
Florentine church of Santa Croce from the most prominent Italian classiciz-

ing sculptor of the day, Antonio Canova
(1757–1822), settled in Venice from 1768.
Canova's absorption of the visual rhetoric of
antique sculpture helped him to produce a
sequence of mythologically inspired statues,
including those of *Eurydice* and *Orpheus*
(1773–6; both in the Museo Correr, Venice),
reflecting the collaboration of Calzabigi and
Gluck of the previous decade, and brought
him the post of inspector-general of papal
antiquities. His monumental pieces with
unmistakable references back towards the
ancient vocabulary of style and form made
him an ideal candidate, as were, in the
fields of music and of science respectively,
Paisiello and Lagrange, for incorporation
into the new regime of Bonapartist Europe,
to which he gave a highly idealized three-
dimensional expression of historical validity
and tradition.

Equally prepared to make this political
and social transition was the Milanese writer
and reformer Pietro Verri (1728–97), who,
with his younger brother Alessandro
(1741–1816) and their friend Cesare Beccaria
(1738–94), founded the combatively named
Accademia dei Pugni (the Academy of Fists),
a further indication of the vitality of the Ital-

ian academic tradition. Beccaria's *Dei delitti e delle pene* (1764) made him a figure of enormous stature in the European Enlightenment, aligning him specifically with the concern to define the structure of human nature and to press for juridical and penal reform. The Verri brothers defended Beccaria's views on civil crime and punishment in their journal (founded 1764), *Il caffè*, the very title of which points to the central role played by the coffee-house in the intellectual life of northern Italian cities. Unlike other members of the Lombard aristocratic élite, however, Pietro Verri remained in his official governmental positions following Bonaparte's entry (1796) into Milan, thus associating one of the city's leading cultural figures with the new regime. The bronze version of Canova's massive, nude, and heavily imperial statue of Napoleon as Mars, the god of war (the marble version is in Apsley House, London, the residence of the duke of Wellington, as a cultural trophy for one of Napoleon's most formidable adversaries), now stands as the centre-piece of the courtyard of the Brera Museum in Milan. Commissioned for Milan in 1807 by Napoleon's stepson, it signals the suitability of Bonaparte's choice of the Lombard capital, in preference to other Italian cities, as the capital for his projected Italian kingdom, the first of a sequence of attempts in the nineteenth century to impose political and cultural unity on the collection of radically diverse sovereignties and traditions composing this highly individualistic peninsula.

7

ITALY 1796–1870: THE AGE OF THE RISORGIMENTO

JOHN A. DAVIS

Introduction

The Revolution in France in 1789 marked the start of a period of foreign occupation, political upheaval and revolution in the Italian states that lasted until a unified and independent Italian monarchy was created in the mid-nineteenth century. The changes precipitated by the Revolution were to play a major part in this process, most obviously because they brought about the rapid collapse of the *ancien régime* principalities in Italy: by the time that Napoleon's Empire finally unravelled, every Italian state had been remodelled in some degree along lines originating from the Revolution. When the Italian rulers returned from exile in 1814, they found themselves masters of centralized and autocratic states immeasurably more powerful than the limited *ancien régime* monarchies they had abandoned.

The old order had been changed, but not effectively replaced. Along with new forms of autocratic government, the Revolution had also given new force to ideas of political democracy and representative government. From this dual legacy came the struggles between autocracy and liberalism that dominated political life in Italy in the decades that followed (Italy was the theatre for major revolutions and insurrections in 1820–1, 1831, 1848–9) and which were only resolved through the process of political unification that resulted in the creation of a single constitutional monarchy in Italy under Victor Emanuel II of Savoy.

In that respect, the political struggles in Italy in these years were part of a more general process of political change in Europe. But in Italy they took a particular form because political change was inseparable from independence. For two decades after the Revolution, the political destinies of the Italian states were governed by France. Then in 1814 the Congress of Vienna made Austria the dominant power on the peninsula. Prince Metternich's famous claim that Italy was 'a mere geographical expression' could not disguise the fact that Vienna was the power behind every Italian throne and the unifying force behind the otherwise untidy mosaic of dynastic principalities. Political

ITALY IN 1797

change was therefore inseparable from independence from Austria, providing Italian reformers of widely different political colours with a common enemy.

Austrian rule provided Italians with a common enemy, but not a common cause. For an older, nationalist historiography, unification was achieved through a concerted will to create an independent nation-state, an idea that survives in the term *risorgimento* that identifies the 'resurrection' or 'rediscovery' of a sense of national identity as the driving force behind the process of unification. But this imposes unities of intent on the political struggles of the period that are anachronistic. Probably a majority of politically aware Italians favoured independence by the mid-nineteenth century, but with little agreement as to how this might be achieved or what political form it should take. For most Italians, an independent confederation of existing states seemed the likeliest outcome. If this did not happen it was because political conflicts forced the struggles for independence into wider geographical, diplomatic, and political arenas, that in 1860 resulted in the formation of a single Italian state whose existence few had anticipated or desired, and whose political form—a constitutional monarchy—disappointed many of the most ardent nationalists.

These struggles for political reform and independence engaged the energies of only a small minority of Italians, however, and were never the only cause of unrest in the Italian states. By the mid-nineteenth century the propertied and educated classes constituted scarcely 2 per cent of the population—roughly the number that gained the right to vote in the new Kingdom of Italy. The vast mass of Italians were peasants and rural labourers, and it was here that the most serious social tensions were to be found. As in many other parts of Europe, the causes lay in the expansion of commercial agriculture, enclosures and encroachments on public lands that threatened the existence of entire rural communities. The twin forces of commercialization and institutional change caused grinding poverty and insecurity to prevail throughout rural Italy, generating tensions and conflicts that formed a constant backdrop to the political struggles of the nineteenth century. Striving to fend off the forces of economic, institutional, and political change that the middle classes wished to accelerate, popular protest often came into conflict with the programmes and objectives of the reformers and nationalists. These social conflicts imposed critical constraints on the actions of middle-class reformers, but none the less popular protest did as much to undermine the existing political order in Italy as the more articulate conspiracies of the liberals and democrats. Indeed, the inability of the existing governments to contain or remedy popular discontent helped persuade many conservative Italians that there could be no political stability without a new political order.

The struggles for political change in Italy took place against backgrounds of persistent and often violent social conflict, but they were played out against an international backdrop as well. For as long as Austria remained the corner-stone of a European system of alliances, the international constraints on political change in Italy were formidable. That would not change until the 1850s, when the revival of French imperial ambitions under Napoleon III and the realignments that followed Britain's alliance with France against tsarist Russia in the Crimea created a revisionist climate in European international relations in which political change in Italy once more became a possibility.

Italy in the Era of the French Revolution and Napoleon (1789–1814)

The French conquest of Italy after 1796 was rapid, and in the Treaty of Campoformio of 1797 Austria gave up the Po Valley, the strategic key to the entire peninsula, to France. In 1798 a French army occupied Rome, and in January 1799 General Championnet entered Naples. The withdrawal of the French armies from Italy in the spring of 1799 caused the collapse of the Italian republics, but Bonaparte's decisive victory at Marengo (14 June 1800) opened the way for a more permanent and comprehensive reorganization of the Italian states.

The French armies were accompanied by many Italian exiles who had escaped political repression in Italy after 1789. With the Italian patriots, they helped set up provisional republican governments that provided the first opportunities for open political debate in Italy. The debates revealed wide gulfs between radicals and more moderate reformers, but in their acceptance of the general principle of popular sovereignty the short-lived Italian republics (1796–9) marked a decisive break with the political world of the *ancien régime*.

In 1799 the French armies withdrew and the Italian republics were swept away in a violent wave of popular counter-revolutions. The royalist restorations were vengeful but short-lived, and after Marengo Italy's political geography was redrawn under Bonaparte's personal supervision. In January 1802 the former Cisalpine Republic was reconstituted as the Italian Republic: its capital was Milan and it included the territories of the former Cispadane Republic south of the Po River (Modena, Reggio Emilia) and those of the former Republic of Venice. In September Piedmont was annexed to France.

Following Napoleon's coronation as emperor (2 December 1804), the Italian states were transformed into appanages for the imperial family. The Italian Republic now became the Kingdom of Italy (May 1805) governed by Eugène Beauharnais as the emperor's viceroy. After the victories at Ulm and Austerlitz (December 1805), Napoleon deposed the Bourbons of Naples, and in March 1806 a French army installed Joseph Bonaparte on the throne of Naples. Two years later Joseph was moved to Spain and replaced in Naples by Joachim Murat, the husband of Caroline Bonaparte. In February 1808 French armies occupied Rome, which was annexed to France a year later: in 1811 Napoleon's son by Maria Luisa of Austria was crowned king of Rome. In 1807 Tuscany was annexed and entrusted to Napoleon's sister Elisa Baciochi, while in 1805 another sister, Paolina Borghese, became ruler of the duchies of Parma, Guastalla, and Piacenza, which were subsequently annexed to France in 1808. By 1806 only the islands of Sardinia and Sicily—the refuges respectively of the legitimist rulers of Piedmont and Naples, the latter under the protection of the British Mediterranean fleet—remained outside French control.

Neither the new dynastic system nor Italy's revised political geography outlived the empire, but the institutional reorganization of the Italian states proved more durable. As in France, the abolition of feudalism did away at a stroke with the pretensions to power-sharing and privileged exemption that were inseparable from the *ancien régime* monarchies, and established instead the absolute sovereignty of the state. This was the essential juridical premiss for the creation of new centralized and bureaucratic administrations, with hierarchical chains of command stretching out from the centre to every province, locality, and community. Institutional reform was consolidated by the intro-

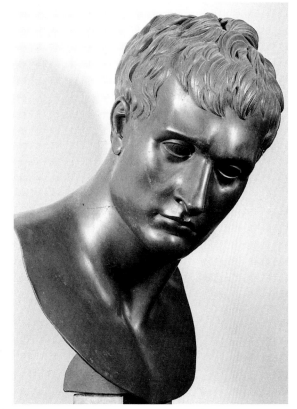

CANOVA'S BUST OF NAPOLEON BONAPARTE illustrates that the cult of the Emperor was as forceful in the Italian satellite states as in France. Bonaparte's sober and imperious gaze appropriately captures the authoritarian tone of French rule in Italy.

duction of the French Civil Code, which standardized and regulated civil law and administrative procedures. It was also accompanied by a new, interventionist style of government that looked to standardize, regulate, control, and police in ways that were unknown to the *ancien régime* monarchies.

In the south, where feudal jurisdiction had survived and where feudal land tenures remained extensive, the impact of these changes was especially great. The abolition of feudal land tenure did away with the multiple use-rights that had previously attached to feudal estates, to public and communal lands. Direct taxes were reorganized around a single land tax, while throughout Italy the sale of the lands of religious houses and former royal domains enabled the French rulers to redeem the debts of the *ancien régime* rulers, reorganize public finances, and float new consolidated national debts.

The impact of these reforms was profound, but not always in ways that the reformers had anticipated. The abolition of feudal land tenures, the sales of land owned by religious houses, and the partition of feudal lands and village

GERMAN CONFEDERATION

SWITZERLAND

TYROL

AUSTRIAN EMPIRE

Geneva

Alto Adige

SAVOY

Aosta

Bolzano

Varese

Sondrio

Trentino

Como

Udine

Gorizia

K. OF

Milan

Brescia

Vicenza

Treviso

Trieste

Turin

Pavia

LOMBARDY

Verona

VENETIA

PIEDMONT

Cremona

Padua

Venice

ISTRIA

Fiume

SARDINIA

Mantua

Rovigo

CROATIA

Parma

Ferrara

FRANCE

Cuneo

D. OF

PARMA

Bologna

LIGURIA

Genoa

D. OF MODENA

Ravenna

OTTOMAN

EMPIRE

Nice

PR. OF MONACO

MASSA

LUCCA

Pistoia

Forli

REP. OF SAN MARINO

Pisa

Florence

Ancona

Livorno

Arezzo

GR.

Siena

THE MARCHES

ADRIATIC SEA

D. OF

ELBA

TUSCANY

Perugia

PAPAL

Elba

Grosseto

STATES

CORSICA

UMBRIA

Teramo

Ajaccio

Aquila

Civitavecchia

LAZIO

ABRUZZO

Chieti

Rome

MOLISE

Foggia

Gaeta

Caserta

Benevento

Bari

K. OF

Sassari

Capua

Naples

SARDINIA

Salerno

Potenza

Taranto

Brindisi

Eboli

Lecce

BASILICATA

Monte Reale

Sapri

Cagliari

K. OF THE

TYRRHENIAN SEA

TWO SICILIES

Cosenza

Catanzaro

Cotrone

CALABRIA

LIPARI IS.

MEDITERRANEAN SEA

Trapani

Palermo

Messina

Reggio

EGADI IS.

Calatafimi

Marsala

SICILY

Catania

Caltanissetta

Girgenti

Siracusa

TUNISIA

━━━ Boundary of Northern Italy

ALGERIA

GOZO

MALTA

0

200 km

ITALY IN 1815

commons were intended to stimulate agriculture and create a mass of new small peasant properties. But the prime beneficiaries were those who already owned land, while rural communities that lost their former rights to graze animals, grow crops, hunt, fish, gather firewood, or glean after the harvest were threatened with disaster. Not surprisingly, the struggles to retain or regain lost use-rights would remain a major cause of unrest in rural Italy throughout the early nineteenth century.

Conditions for broader economic growth remained unfavourable throughout the Napoleonic period. There was some increase in demand for raw materials from France and attempts at import substitution expanded the volume and range of textile production, but almost uninterrupted warfare in the Mediterranean and Napoleon's Continental System seriously disrupted trade. The commercial treaties which Napoleon imposed on the Italian states were weighted exclusively to France's advantage, while the Italian satellites were obliged in addition to pay heavy cash tributes and to provide for the emperor's unrelenting demands for men and materials.

This caused resentment amongst the propertied and educated classes, although in many ways French rule had much to offer these groups. As landowners they had benefited from the abolition of feudalism, while the expansion of public administration offered important new opportunities for professional employment. Education and training rather than birth or social status became the prerequisites, and the establishment of new technical training schools for civil engineers, architects, agronomists, veterinary and medical practitioners, and others signalled the emergence of a new professional class. Service in the emperor's armies also offered attractive careers for many young men from wealthy Italian families.

Yet although the French rulers did seek support from wider social groups than their predecessors, the attempt to establish a political alliance with the propertied classes proved the most fragile aspect of French rule in Italy. After the upheavals of the republican era, the political tone of the Napoleonic states in Italy was conservative and authoritarian. Former Jacobins were carefully excluded, and at Lyons in 1802 Napoleon famously cut off debate on the constitution of the Italian Republic. The Italian élites rallied to the promise of law and order, but grew increasingly resentful at the lack of real power. The French political strategy was to replace the privileged political orders of the *ancien régime* monarchies with a broader regime of notables, but the weakness of the formula was that it did not delegate real power. As in France, provincial assemblies of notables were created that did have important administrative responsibilities (for example, distributing taxes and conscription quotas) but had no consultative rights.

Among the Italian élites, opposition to French rule took the form of demands for constitutional government. The closest the French rulers came to granting a constitution was in the south, where Joseph Bonaparte had promised to establish a national parliament before leaving Naples for Spain in 1808. Murat never honoured that commitment, though he did come under increasing pressure to do so when in 1812 first the British revived Sicily's medieval parliament and then the Spanish national assembly in Cadiz proclaimed a constitution based on universal suffrage and a single chamber parliament. The 'Spanish Constitution' of 1812 was both a declaration of national resistance to France and also a clearly articulated liberal political alternative to the autocratic, hierarchic, and highly centralized organization of the Napoleonic State: for both reasons, the Italian liberals quickly adopted the Spanish Constitution as their own.

In 1814 Joachim Murat defected from the empire and made a bid to create a new dynastic state for himself in Italy, and his Neapolitan generals immediately demanded a constitution as the condition for their support. Their action also reflected the growing influence of the secret societies in the army. Descended from the Masonic lodges that had offered the provincial gentry and intelligentsia opportunities to exchange ideas in secret during the Enlightenment, the secret societies increased rapidly after the French occupation. One reason was that the French armies included many former Jacobins and dissidents whose politics were out of place in Napoleon's France. The French governor of Calabria, Jean-Pierre Briot, for example, a former Jacobin and a staunch opponent of the Napoleonic regime, established the first Carbonari lodges in southern Italy. These became the principal rallying-point for opponents of Murat's government and provided supporters of the constitutional movement with an extensive network of clandestine contacts.

Support for representative government was not limited to the south, and Gian Domenico Romagnosi's essay *The Constitution of Representative Monarchy*, published in Lombardy in 1815, reflected expectations that the Restoration would widen political representation. But constitutional government could be interpreted in many different ways, and had a strong appeal for many sections of the old élites who hoped to regain the political influence they had lost with the fall of the *ancien régime* monarchies. French rule ended in Lombardy in 1814, for example, when a group of noblemen seized power in the expectation that Austria would restore their traditional role in government. But this did not happen, and hostility to Austrian rule in Lombardy after 1815 originated with the resentments of the aristocracy and great landowners who were excluded from the new Austrian administration. This exclusiveness was characteristic of the administrative autocracies of Restoration Italy more generally, making them vulnerable to opposition from sections of the old élites as well as from liberals and democrats. This opposition exposed the fragile basis of the political solution that had emerged from the crisis of the *ancien régime* monarchies and the years of French rule and reform in Italy.

The Restoration Governments (1814–1830)

The ideology of the Restoration was embodied in the Holy Alliance signed in September 1815 by Tsar Alexander I, the Emperor Francis I of Austria, and King Frederick William of Prussia. The aim was to shut out the ideas of the Revolution which, it was believed, had brought upheaval and disaster to Europe. To that end, Austria, Prussia, and Russia took it on themselves to restore the principles of legitimate monarchy, deference, and religion.

In practice, this proved impossible and the break with the immediate past was more apparent than real. Even Italy's political geography could not simply revert to the boundaries that had existed before 1789. The ancient republics of Genoa and Venice were absorbed respectively into the subalpine territories of the House of Savoy and the new Habsburg kingdom of Lombardy-Venetia. Through its viceregal government in Milan and its standing army in the fortresses of the Quadrilateral, Austria was master of the whole of Italy. South of the Po River, the duchies of Parma and Modena and the grand duchy of Tuscany were Austrian clients. As the principal Catholic power in Europe, Austria was also the leading protector of the pope's extensive temporal dominions, including the Legation cities of Bologna and Ferrara. The Neapolitan Bourbons looked on Vienna as their principal ally, as did the only other Italian rulers that enjoyed some real degree of diplomatic autonomy, the House of Savoy.

The news of the fall of Napoleon's Empire had been received in the Italian states as a death foretold, and the principal concern of the propertied classes was to ensure a peaceful transfer of power and avoid the anarchy of the 1790s. This was also the policy of the Austrian government although it was not shared by all the Italian rulers, most notably Duke Francis IV (1815–46) of Modena who set out to delete every trace of the French occupation, and Victor Emanuel I of Savoy (1802–21) who revoked all French legislation in the subalpine territories of the kingdom of Sardinia and banished those like Cavour's family who had 'rallied' to the French regime. In Rome, Pope Pius VII (1800–23) restored the Jesuits and the Inquisition and abolished toleration for Jews, although Cardinal Consalvi did attempt to maintain the impetus of administrative reform. In the duchy of Parma, on the other hand, the former empress of France, Maria Luisa of Austria (1815–47), retained French institutions, while in Tuscany the younger brother of the Emperor Francis, Archduke Ferdinand III (1790–1824), also looked for continuity. In Naples, Ferdinand IV (1815–25) only regained his throne after Joachim Murat had been defeated at the Battle of Tolentino (3 May 1815). Here, too, Prince Metternich was keen to avoid any repetition of the royalist purges of 1799 in Naples and ensured that extreme reactionaries like the Prince of Canosa were kept out of power. Initially at least, the Neapolitan Bourbons not only held out an olive-branch to the supporters of Murat's government and retained the majority of the French reforms, but through the creation of a new unified monarchy actually extended the reforms to Sicily as well. When in 1816 Ferdinand IV, king of Naples and Sicily, changed his title to Ferdinand I, king of the Two Sicilies, Sicily lost its centuries-old autonomy as a separate kingdom.

Neither reconciliation nor reaction brought political peace, however, and in 1820 and 1821 Naples and Turin were both targets of revolution. The Italian revolutions took their cue from Spain, following an attempt early in 1820 to restore the Spanish constitution of 1812. Ominously for the Italian rulers, both revolts began in the armies. In Naples, an insurrection by a group of army officers in July 1820 quickly spread throughout southern Italy and forced Ferdinand I to concede a constitution. In Sicily, the leaders of the revolution in Palermo at once demanded the restoration of the island's autonomy that had been abolished in 1816. The great landowners were the main force behind the revolution and their separatist demands quickly brought the Sicilian revolutions into conflict with the liberal government in Naples. On the mainland Mezzogiorno too (i.e. Italy south of Rome), the provincial notables also demanded greater autonomy from Naples.

Vienna was considering an appeal for help from Ferdinand of Naples when new insurrections broke out in Piedmont. The initiative again came from a group of army officers, some of whom were in contact with the king's cousin, the prince of Carignano (and later king), Charles Albert (1831–49). In March 1821 an insurrection that started in Alessandria spread to other Piedmontese cities. Victor Emanuel abdicated and his successor Charles Felix (1821–31) fled to Modena. Charles Albert made cryptic statements in support of the rebels, then changed his mind and also fled. But Charles Felix returned at the head of an Austrian army that defeated the liberals led by Santorre Santarosa in a brief engagement near Novara. By mid-April the revolution was over and for two decades Piedmont would be ruled by reaction and repression. Another Austrian army was despatched to Naples, where it brought the revolutions to an end and remained billeted for eight more years at the expense of the Neapolitans.

In Lombardy, too, the early *rapprochement* between the government and the Lombard notables withered as the nobility and the professional classes grew resentful at their exclusion from power. In response, the Austrian authorities tried to stifle all forms of independent cultural activity, including in 1819 *Il Conciliatore,* a distinguished literary and philosophical journal that had become a mouthpiece for the conservative Lombard intelligentsia. Following the revolutions in Piedmont and Naples, the repression became even more fierce and targeted some of the most distinguished noble families in Lombardy. When they were later published, the prison diaries of the saintly Silvio Pellico (*Le mie prigioni,* 1832) provided the anti-Austrian cause with a martyr of impeccable conservative and Catholic credentials, while the denunciation of foreign oppression implicit in Alessandro Manzoni's great masterpiece *I promessi sposi* (*The Betrothed*, 1827) was further evidence that Austrian rule had not won the hearts of the Lombard patriciate.

Even reactionaries understood that the Restoration settlement rested on precariously narrow foundations. Both the Neapolitan prince of Canosa (1763–1838) and the Savoyard ultra-conservative Joseph De Maistre (1753–1821) believed that the loss of the authority enjoyed by the Church and the aristocracy in the *ancien régime* monarchies was responsible for an irreversible decline in deference and piety. Although the legitimist rulers had partially restored the power of the Church, the ultra-conservatives believed that the Restoration had compromised fatally in preserving the French reforms. While in theory more powerful than their predecessors, the new 'administrative monarchies' lacked a coherent political base. The legitimist rulers looked to the Church as their protector, but were not willing to restore the powers that their eighteenth-century predecessors had wrested from Rome nor the lands and assets seized by the French. Nor had they restored the former privileges of the nobility, leaving them reliant on the handful of aristocrats they co-opted as ministers and on their patrons in Vienna. Events in Naples and Turin in 1820–1 had shown how the absence of a true royalist aristocracy made even dynastic armies breeding grounds for revolution. For Canosa, only a full-blooded restoration of the old feudal aristocracies would remedy this, but as a stop-gap he recommended that the rulers should harness the innate royalism of the peasants who in 1799 had risen spontaneously in defence of throne and altar against the French invaders and their Italian sympathizers. He busied himself organizing counter-revolutionary secret societies and legitimist militias, but their lawlessness led to his expulsion from Naples. In 1830 he was employed by Francesco IV of Modena to organize a popular counter-revolutionary militia, and subsequently by Cardinal Bernetti to form another peasant militia known as the Centurioni to hunt down liberals and political subversives in the Papal States.

The political insecurity of the Italian rulers may explain in part the apocalyptic climate of repression after the revolutions of 1820–1, in which only Tuscany remained as a relative haven of tolerance. In 1821 Gian Piero Vieusseux founded the *Antologia* in Florence, and for a decade the Tuscan capital replaced Milan as the centre of cultural activity in Italy. Elsewhere, the Restoration autocracies entrusted their police and the clergy with invasive controls over public as well as private life in an attempt to block the circulation of ideas and stifle all forms of opposition and nonconformity. The clergy tightly monopolized what little education was available and was responsible for the censorship of all printed materials, public performances, theatres, and meetings. When not pursuing the secret societies, the police and their spies were also hard at work seizing the novels of Sir Walter Scott and similar publications deemed to be injurious to the principles of religion and public order.

Preparing the Revolutions (1830–1848)

The Spanish rising of 1820 had triggered the Italian revolutions of 1820–1, and the July Revolution in Paris in 1830 was the cue for the next wave of insurrections in Italy. While visiting Rome in 1830, Louis-Napoleon (the future Napoleon III) had been in contact with certain members of the secret societies, and in the belief that Louis-Philippe's new government in France would give support, Ciro Menotti and Enrico Misley began planning an insurrection in Modena. In February 1831 the ringleaders, including Menotti, were arrested, though not before insurrections had spread from Modena to Bologna and other parts of central Italy. Pope Gregory XVI requested Austrian intervention, and although French support for the risings did not materialize, on the pretext of deterring a permanent occupation of the Papal States by the Austrians, the French government did send a detachment to Ancona. By the end of March, however, the Austrians had regained control and on 26 May Ciro Menotti and other conspirators joined the growing ranks of martyrs to the cause of independence.

Fears that the insurrections and France's intervention might drag the European powers into war resulted in an international conference. The British government was concerned that France seemed intent on regaining a foothold in Italy, and did not wish to see Austria's control over the region weakened. However, the British representatives also insisted that papal misgovernment was the real cause of political unrest in central Italy, and called on Vienna to use its influence to reform the papal administration.

For Giuseppe Mazzini (1805–72), however, the insurrections in central Italy were further evidence of the need for a revolution that would sweep away the existing Italian rulers. While the revolutions showed the strength of support for Italian independence, Mazzini also blamed their failure on the inability of the secret societies to provide effective leadership. This was precisely what Mazzini wished to offer, and in his *Manifesto of Young Italy* in the previous year he had called on Italian revolutionaries to abandon secrecy and work openly for a single cause: the creation of a single Italian nation. Young Italy was founded in Marseilles on 14 August 1831, and Mazzini at once attempted to put his revolutionary ideas into practice. But his correspondence was intercepted (not for the last time), and in 1833 his associates in Turin, Chambéry, Alessandria, and Genoa were arrested by the Piedmontese police. All were tortured, a number were executed, and Mazzini was sentenced to death *in absentia*. Not deterred, he resumed planning an invasion of Savoy to coincide with a rising in Genoa (1834), which would have involved Giuseppe Garibaldi (1807–82) had it materialized. When this plan too had failed, Mazzini left Switzerland for London in 1837.

After 1833 Mazzini was almost permanently in exile, and returned to Italy only in 1848–9 and in 1860. His followers in Italy were dogged by censorship and police harassment, although insurrections planned or inspired by Mazzini and Young Italy continued through the 1830s and 1840s and into the 1850s. But Mazzini's influence was also divisive. Young Italy had been set up to counter the influence of the secret societies, and in 1834 Mazzini quarrelled with Filippo Buonarroti (1781–1837), the leading champion of the French revolutionary tradition in Italy. His own views owed more to the writings of Saint-Simon and were permeated by a deep and mystical religiosity. For Mazzini, nationalism was a higher, ethical cause that transcended questions of material equality and imposed duties more than rights, and in the *Duties of Man* (1860) and other essays he polemically rejected the revolutionary tradition that derived from the *Declaration of the Rights of Man*.

Mazzini's hostility to the Jacobin tradition and especially to material equality as the goal of political action estranged him from those Italian radicals like Giuseppe Ferrari (1811–76) and Carlo Pisacane (1818–57) who were closer to the ideas of the French socialists. Ferrari, like the Milanese liberal Carlo Cattaneo (1801–69), believed that a federal solution would be better suited to the cultural, physical, and material diversities of the Italian peninsula than Mazzini's single republican state. Others argued that the people rather than Mazzini should determine the political form of a new state, while to many southern liberals and radicals Mazzini's republic looked remarkably similar to the centralized Napoleonic state they wished to overthrow. When Mazzini refused to support a rising in Sicily in 1837, one of his close collaborators, the Modenese nationalist Nicola Fabrizi, founded the Italian Legion in Malta that cut its ties with Mazzini and became the principal focus for southern revolutionaries.

Despite these rivalries and divisions amongst the radicals, Mazzini's programme for Young Italy for the first time explicitly made the struggle for independence from Austria the premiss for a wider political revolution designed to sweep away the existing Italian rulers, including the pope, and create a single Italian national state. This radical and intransigently revolutionary programme forced Mazzini's opponents and critics to define and formulate their own positions.

Facing: MAZZINI AND GARIBALDI. The two heroes of the struggle for Italian independence were later frequently portrayed as brothers in arms, although direct contact between the two was quite rare. Giuseppe Mazzini (1805–72) was born in Genoa and Giuseppe Garibaldi (1807–82) in Nice, and both were influenced by the ideas of Saint-Simon. In 1849 Garibaldi and Mazzini were both actively engaged in the government and defence of the Roman Republic, but afterwards they moved further apart as Garibaldi became a convinced supporter of Victor Emanuel II. Both were deeply disillusioned by the political form of the new Italy they had helped to create.

PRINCESS CRISTINA TRIVULZO BARBIANO DI BELGIOIOSO (1808–71). In the iconography of the Risorgimento, women appear mainly in submissive and supporting roles, but the aristocratic Cristina Trivulzo di Belgioioso was a flamboyant exception to the rule. After separating at an early age from her husband, she financed Mazzini's attempt to invade Savoy in 1834 and then went into exile in Paris where she launched two nationalist journals, the *Gazzetta Italiana* and *Ausonio*. In 1848 she returned to Milan, and in the following year helped organize hospital facilities during the siege of Rome. In exile again in the 1850s, like many other former republicans she became a convinced supporter of Cavour's strategies. Hailed as a heroine of the struggle for unification after 1860, her emancipated lifestyle and the radicalism of her early politics were played down.

After the early upheavals, however, the 1830s proved to be a decade of relative economic expansion and stability, encouraging hopes that reform was imminent. Agricultural markets improved, new manufactures and industries were established, new financial institutions multiplied. In 1839 the first railway line on the peninsula was inaugurated in Naples, and discussions were held on railway projects in Lombardy and the Veneto. Commercial revival was accompanied by new signs of cultural and social activity. Periodical literature was still dominated by religious and devotional publications and remained subject to close censorship, but new journals devoted to agriculture and economics started to appear. These included Cattaneo's *Annali Universali di Statistica* (1832–6) and the *Politecnico* (1839–44) in Milan, Vieusseux's *Antologia* and *Giornale Agrario Toscano* in Florence, as well as numerous other short-lived publishing ventures. The terrible outbreaks of cholera that struck Ancona, Naples, Rome, Catania, and Palermo in the winter of 1836–7 led to more open debate on matters of public concern, and this went a step further when in 1839 the first meeting of the Congress of Italian Men of Learning (Congresso degli Scienzati) was held in Florence.

These developments reflected a more open cultural climate, and also the presence of a new urban middle class that as yet lacked an independent voice but was none the less visible. During the opera season, for example, theatres offered the élites a daily meeting-place for exchanging news and gossip which the old aristocracies now shared with representatives of new wealth and the professions. They were present, too, in the numerous new philosophical societies, agrarian associations, and cultural and recreational clubs that signalled new forms of urban sociability. Horizons were broadened as foreign visitors began to return to Italy, while wealthy and educated Italians had greater freedom to travel.

Despite these signs of change there was no relaxation in the reactionary and autocratic political climate. In Rome, Pope Gregory XVI's encyclicals *Mirari vos* (1832) and *Singulari vos* (1834) condemned attempts to reconcile Catholicism and liberalism. In Piedmont the new king, Charles Albert, adopted an intransigently reactionary stance that showed no sign of bending until the following decade. In Naples the reverse happened and although things initially looked promising when Ferdinand II (1830–59) came to the throne and dismissed the corrupt ministers who had surrounded his father, hopes that this would lead to more substantial concessions were never fulfilled.

There was no opportunity for political dissent, but criticism of commercial

THE BELLELLI FAMILY. The subject of this enigmatic family portrait by the young Edgar Degas (1834–1917) is the painter's aunt Laura Degas, her Neapolitan husband, Baron Gennaro Bellelli, and their daughters. Bellelli was a wealthy banker who had been exiled for his support of the liberal government in Naples in 1848. Degas's portrait emphasizes the respectability of the Italian revolutionaries, at the same time illustrating how the affluent Italian middle classes shared the manners, tastes, and furnishings of the European bourgeoisie of the day.

Facing: THE ELECTION of Cardinal Giovanni Mastai Ferretti as Pope Pius IX (1846–78) aroused hopes that the papacy would at last drop its intransigent opposition to reform. These hopes were dashed when Pius IX denounced the war against Austria in April 1848. In the decade that followed Pius opposed Cavour's attempts to reduce the secular power of the clergy in Piedmont. Relations between Rome and Turin finally broke when Piedmontese forces invaded the Papal States in September 1860. Pius IX defended the rights of the deposed legitimist rulers and denounced the new Italian monarchy. The 'Syllabus of Errors' (1864) and the declaration of papal infallibility (Vatican I, 1869) asserted the Church's intransigent opposition to liberalism. When Italian troops finally entered Rome on 20 September 1870, Pius withdrew to the Vatican city, condemned the occupation as 'unjust, violent, null and void', declared himself to be a 'prisoner', and excommunicated Victor Emanuel II (*Respicientes*, 2 October 1870). The rift between church and state was not repaired until Mussolini's Lateran Agreements of 1929.

policies did become more open. In Lombardy and Venetia, Vienna's preference for Trieste over Venice and Austrian commercial regulations that restricted access to other Italian states caused resentment, while the refusal of the Neapolitan government to relax its high protectionist tariffs brought it into conflict both with the southern landowners and with its principal trading partner, Great Britain. As a result, the principles of economic liberalism began to find support even amongst groups that had hitherto shown little interest in politics.

Among the professional classes, poor career opportunities were also an important cause of resentment. Opportunities for a career in the military were limited after the revolutions of 1820, while the Church had few attractive openings for educated men. Openings in law, medicine, architecture, civil engineering, accountancy, and agricultural and commercial services were growing, but not fast enough to keep up with demand. But the rulers were eager to limit the expansion of their bureaucracies and to restrict access to the professions. In Lombardy, for example, the Austrian government gave preference to Austrians and Hungarians in public employment and made entry more difficult for Italians by extending the length (and hence cost) of the university courses required for entry into public service. In Naples, university courses were available only in the capital where students were closely watched by the police and the government repeatedly refused requests that additional universities be established in the provinces.

For women, there were as yet no public careers that were considered respectable, and for the women of the emergent Italian middle classes opportunities for any kind of public career were if anything narrower than they had been for their aristocratic predecessors. The small number of women who featured in liberal circles were aristocrats, while amongst the middle classes women's education was generally confined to moral and spiritual training provided by nuns.

Middle-class resentments were less threatening than those of the rural populations, however. Commercial expansion and population growth combined to exacerbate the desperate land-hunger of the rural poor, which was compounded by new legislation in the Kingdom of the Two Sicilies, the Kingdom of Sardinia, and Lombardy in the 1830s that extended the privatization of former feudal estates and village commons. The intervention of all these governments to accelerate the processes of privatization and commercialization in the agrarian economy, while still adhering to the anti-modernist ideological principles of the Restoration, revealed all too clearly the contradictions confronting the legitimist regimes.

Even before the 'Hungry Forties' brought further suffering to rural Italy, anticipation of renewed political unrest was rising and provided the setting for the first public debate on the political alternatives open to the Italian states.

This was opened by Vincenzo Gioberti's two-volume treatise on *The Moral Primacy of the Italians* which was published abroad, in Brussels, in 1843 but quickly ran through many editions and despite police and censors was widely read throughout Italy. A Piedmontese priest and formerly a follower of Mazzini, Gioberti (1801–52) set out a programme that had a compelling attraction for moderate and conservative supporters of independence: he proposed that the Italian rulers should imitate the medieval Guelph party, that is to say make an alliance with the pope and then negotiate with Austria the formation of an independent confederation of Italian princes. This idea received strong endorsement when a Piedmontese aristocrat and royalist, Cesare Balbo, set out a similar programme in his *Hopes of Italy* (1844) that also involved creating an independent confederation of Italian rulers through negotiation with Austria.

The enthusiastic reception of these proposals indicated that many conservative Italians now acknowledged that some form of independence from Austria might defuse more radical demands for political change, and believed that this could be achieved by negotiation and hence without conflict. Those beliefs were now strengthened by two quite different sets of events. The first was the revival of the insurrectionary movement. In 1844 two Venetian brothers, Emilio and Attilio Bandiera, attempted to start a revolt in Calabria that ended tragically, but set off a fresh wave of insurrections in the northern Papal States. The growing disorder in the Papal States greatly alarmed many moderates like the Piedmontese nobleman Massimo D'Azeglio (1798–1866) who believed that Charles Albert was sympathetic to the nationalist cause. D'Azeglio had close contacts with the liberals in central Italy, and in a series of pamphlets designed to reach a wide public and make the political debate open (*Recent Events in the Romagna* (1846), *A Programme for National Public Opinion* (1847), and following the Austrian occupation of Ferrara *A Protest at Events in Ferrara* (1847)) he warned the revolutionaries that their aims would best be achieved gradually and through the force of public opinion which he referred to as a 'conspiracy in open daylight'. To strengthen his case, D'Azeglio added that in a personal audience in October 1845 Charles Albert had declared a willingness to support the national cause.

Fear of revolutionary upheaval added to the appeal of the moderate programme, but its greatest fillip came when on 17 June 1846 Cardinal Giovanni Maria Mastai-Ferretti was elected pope as Pius IX. After an uninterrupted sequence of reactionary pontiffs, the election of Pius IX seemed little short of providential and the new pope's liberal reputation was enhanced by the decision to amnesty political prisoners in Rome. In March 1847 the papal government also took the lead in relaxing censorship and entered

Facing, above: VICTOR
EMANUEL II AND NAPO-
LEON III ENTER MILAN.
Five days after their
victory at the battle of
Magenta (4 June 1859)
the French and Pied-
montese rulers entered
Milan. This image
demonstrates how this
was represented as a
royal victory: every
attempt had been made
to prevent nationalist
volunteers and irregu-
lars taking part in the
operations against the
Austrian forces. But the
French Emperor's uni-
lateral decision to make
peace with the Austrians
before Venetia had been
liberated soon soured
the victorious alliance.

Facing, below: BATTLE OF
CALATAFIMI. Garibaldi
and his 'Thousand'
volunteers landed at
Marsala in western Sicily
on 11 May 1860. This
highly romanticized
painting depicts what
was in reality only a
skirmish that took place
four days later as
Garibaldi advanced from
Marsala towards
Palermo. With their
lines of communication
threatened by a general
insurrection on the
island, the commanders
of the large Bourbon
force decided not to
engage. The decision
proved momentous and
left Garibaldi free to join
the insurgents in
Palermo.

into a customs union with Leopold II of Tuscany and Charles Albert of Piedmont.

The conservative dream of an independent confederation of Italian rulers
under the titular leadership of the pope seemed to be at hand. But events
would quickly and brutally dispel that illusion. By the summer of 1847 Pius's
government was already losing control and from Rome the agitation for
reform was spreading throughout central Italy. The situation became even
more inflamed when Austrian troops occupied Ferrara. In the hope of forestalling growing unrest, Archduke Leopold II tried reviving a consultative
assembly in Tuscany in August but instead the disturbances grew worse.
In Lombardy and Venetia the provincial assemblies petitioned for self-
government as collective acts of civil disobedience to the Austrian authorities
intensified. As in much of the rest of Europe, by the autumn of 1847 the question in the Italian states was not so much whether revolution would occur, but
where and when.

The Revolutions (1848–1849)

When it did come, the storm broke at the point most distant from Vienna.
Rioting that started on 2 January in Palermo during the processions in honour
of the city's patron Santa Rosalia turned into the first of the European revolutions of 1848. On 29 January Ferdinand II granted a constitution in an attempt
to prevent further disturbances and the other Italian rulers followed: Leopold
of Tuscany on 17 February, Charles Albert on 4 March, and Pius IX on 14
March. In each case, the concessions were designed to buy off the opposition
by granting limited voting rights to small groups of property-owners, but the
flimsy conservative provisional governments immediately came under attack
from more radical elements and from leaders ready to mobilize the discontents of urban workers and peasants.

Pressure for wider political reforms grew after the revolutions in Paris in
February and, above all, in Vienna on 13 March. With Austria apparently on its
knees and Prince Metternich in flight from the capital, the situation in Italy
changed dramatically. In Venice, the Austrians withdrew and a moderate
republican government headed by the lawyer Daniele Manin was established
on 23 March. In Milan, however, the 81-year-old Austrian military commander
Field Marshal Radetzky tried to hold firm and turned his artillery on one of
the most densely populated working-class districts of the city. This barbarous
attempt to shell Milan into submission provoked a popular rising which after
five days of fierce street-fighting (18–22) forced Radetzky's army to withdraw.

The Piedmontese monarchy now entered the lists in an attempt to gain
control over the nationalist movement. On 23 March Charles Albert's government declared war on Austria and a Piedmontese army entered Lombardy at

the request of the Milanese moderates who feared that the democrats might seize power. Charles Albert's commitment to the struggle against Austria initially won the support of radicals like Carlo Cattaneo and Mazzini, who had hurried to Milan from England. But when his government insisted on the speedy annexation of Lombardy, fears grew that Charles Albert's real concern was to increase the size of his own kingdom. The Lombard democrats mobilized against fusion with Piedmont, but Charles Albert's position was strengthened by votes in favour of annexation to Piedmont in Piacenza, Parma, Modena, and Reggio in May, followed by Lombardy and the Venetian provinces in June, and finally by Venice in July.

Cattaneo accused Charles Albert of gathering votes while Radetzky was collecting soldiers, and on 24 July the Piedmontese army was decisively defeated at the first Battle of Custoza. Charles Albert withdrew across the Ticino and sued for an armistice, while the Austrians occupied Milan, Modena, and Reggio Emilia. But even before Custoza, the Piedmontese monarchy's attempt to lead a national crusade against Austria had run into severe difficulties. On 29 April Pius IX denounced the war against Austria and shattered the conservative illusion that independence could be achieved in alliance with Rome. On 15 May Ferdinand of Naples staged a counter-revolution, suspended the Neapolitan parliament, and withdrew from the war against Austria.

After Custoza Mazzini proclaimed that the war of the princes would give way to the war of the people, and as the Austrian troops reoccupied Lombardy the radicals began to take power. In October a radical government led by Giuseppe Montanelli came to power in Florence, and in December Vincenzo Gioberti headed a government with radical sympathies in Turin. But most important of all, Pellegrino Rossi, the leader of the conservative provisional government in Rome, was murdered on 15 November; on the twenty-fourth, Pius IX and his cardinals fled to Gaeta and put themselves under the protection of Ferdinand of Naples. This gave the democrats their first real opportunity. Elections were held in January for a Constituent Assembly which met on 5 February and four days later proclaimed the Roman Republic. On the same day Leopold II fled from Tuscany and a provisional government headed by Giuseppe Montanelli and Francesco Domenico Guerrazzi called for the declaration of a republic and alliance with Rome and Venice. In early March Mazzini reached Rome and the Roman Republic voted for unification with Tuscany.

By now the Austrian counter-attack was imminent and Charles Albert made a final bid to regain the political initiative. But the Piedmontese army was forced to surrender at Novara (23 March 1849), leaving the Austrians in command of northern and central Italy. Charles Albert abdicated and the armistice was signed by his son and successor, Victor Emanuel II (1849–78).

Facing, above: FEW ITALIAN PAINTERS were more successful than Giuseppe De Nittis in successfully absorbing the French Impressionist style. Born in Puglia in 1846, the artist created vibrant images of street life in Paris and London, but this *Dinner at Posillipo* reveals his nonchalant ease in evoking more intimate scenes.

Facing, below: ONE OF THE MOST POTENT IMAGES ever devised of a restless proletariat, Giuseppe Pelizza da Volpedo's *Il quarto stato* (1901) was painted during a period of civil disturbance and economic instability in Italy, whose atmosphere of pessimism, uncertainty, and social fragmentation pervaded the nation's cultural life.

GARIBALDI IN ROME. Giuseppe Garibaldi's defence of Rome against the French expeditionary force led by General Oudinot that laid siege to the city at the beginning of June 1849 was one of the most inspiring episodes of the Risorgimento. When resistance was no longer possible, Garibaldi organized a masterly retreat that enabled the majority of the defenders of the Republic to escape. The defence of Rome established Garibaldi as the most charismatic of the nationalist leaders, and thereafter his battle-cry was 'Roma o Morte' ('Rome or Death').

But just as the Austrian victory at Custoza had floored the conservatives in 1848, the second Piedmontese defeat at Novara in 1849 now doomed the radicals. In Genoa they tried to reject the armistice, but the rebellion was put down by Piedmontese troops. The revolution collapsed in Tuscany too, and to avoid an Austrian invasion the moderates and conservatives invited Archduke Leopold to resume his throne (28 July). Only Rome and Venice were left. In Rome, the Republic delegated power to a triumvirate consisting of Giuseppe Mazzini, Carlo Armellini, and Aurelio Saffi, while Giuseppe Garibaldi took charge of the city's defence. Both Naples and France had sent armies to restore the pope, and in June General Oudinot's forces laid siege to Rome. The defence was organized by Garibaldi and lasted until early August, when he led a masterly retreat that enabled some 4,000 defenders to escape. In Venice, Manin also held out until August, even though the city was under constant bombardment, blockaded by the Austrian fleet, and suffering from cholera.

In the south the revolutions had followed a different pattern. After Ferdinand II's coup of 15 May the revolutions swept through the mainland provinces, but by the autumn had been crushed. In September a Neapolitan army disembarked at Messina to end the separatist revolt that had started in Palermo in April, and when Neapolitan forces entered Palermo in May 1849 the revolution in the south from which all the others had started was finally over.

After the Revolutions

In Italy, as in the rest of Europe, the revolutions ended in defeat for liberals and radicals alike, but brought about changes that were to prove irreversible. Hatred of Austria was even more intense and now was sanctified by new symbols of heroism and martyrdom. Most important of all, the struggle for independence had now acquired a new legitimacy through the participation of the Piedmontese monarchy.

Rather than uniting them around a common cause, the events of 1848–9 had also shown how deeply Italians were divided. As well as struggles between moderates and radicals, between urban reformers and rural unrest, the revolutions had also unleashed a spate of violent municipal rivalries. Indeed, it might seem that the struggles for greater municipal autonomy that set Genoa against Turin, the cities of the terra firma against Venice, Livorno against Florence, the Legation cities of Bologna and Ferrara against Rome, the provincial towns of the southern mainland against Naples, and Sicily against Naples were more important than the struggle against Austria. But these reflected more than petty local rivalries, and above all the strength of resentment to the centralization of power that had resulted from the French reforms. The demands for greater provincial and municipal autonomy were an essential element in the reform programme.

The revolutions had proved especially divisive for the radicals. The defeats of 1849 led to recriminations and Mazzini, in particular, came under increasing criticism. To the attacks levelled from the federalist camp by Cattaneo and Ferrari were now added those of the Neapolitan democrat Carlo Pisacane who blamed Mazzini for failing to address the grievances of the peasants, in his view the only revolutionary force in Italy. In place of Mazzini's endless and unsuccessful urban conspiracies (another would end in disaster in Milan in 1853), Pisacane proposed a programme of agrarian reform that would transform the struggle for national independence into a peasant guerrilla war similar to the Spanish War of Independence against Napoleon.

These arguments touched on one of the bitterest experiences of the revolutions for many radicals. In many parts of Italy the peasants had initially rallied to the revolutions, but once it became clear that neither the liberals nor the radicals had any intention of redressing their grievances rural Italy turned against them. In Lombardy, for example, some disillusioned peasants welcomed the returning Austrian armies in 1849, while in the Veneto, Tuscany, the Papal States, and the south rural unrest either shook off all political control or took a counter-revolutionary turn.

If the radicals had proved unprepared for these spontaneous outbursts of rural protest, the resulting violence and disorder caused many landowners in the Veneto, Lombardy, Tuscany, Emilia, Romagna, and Lazio to wait anxiously for the Austrians to restore order. The legitimist governments tried to exploit these fears by playing the card of law and order, and in the Austrian territories military tribunals meted out summary justice to peasants who had taken part in the revolutions in an atmosphere of judicial terror and reprisal. But this was no longer enough. The violence of the repression after 1849 left Italy increasingly out of line with other European states. William Gladstone's ringing denunciation of the appalling conditions in which Ferdinand of Naples had imprisoned the Neapolitan liberals was only one example of the ways in which Italian absolutism now struck European liberals as a perverse anachronism. Within Italy, the violence of the restoration did as much as the turmoil of the revolutions to persuade growing numbers of Italians that without independence there could be no political stability in Italy. But while the revolutions had dispelled the myth that independence could be achieved in alliance with the Papacy and without fighting Austria, they had also shown that the nationalist cause could be channelled towards conservative political ends.

This was why the establishment of a constitutional monarchy in one of the oldest and most conservative principalities in Italy proved to be the most fundamental and decisive change brought about by the revolutions. The endorsement of the nationalist cause by the House of Savoy turned the struggle against Austria from a subversive and revolutionary cause into a conservative but progressive one. After 1849 Piedmont's constitutional monarchy stood as an open affront to every other Italian ruler, making Turin a haven for nationalists, liberals, and democrats from all over Italy. If the revolutions left the radicals divided, they had given the moderate nationalists a new sense of solidarity and purpose. Victor Emanuel II's proclamation of 20 November 1849 from the castle of Moncalieri in which he undertook to preserve the constitution, providing that the new parliament in Turin ratified the armistice with Austria, laid the basis for a programme around which the expansionist ambitions of the House of Savoy and the political aspirations of the Italian liberals could converge.

The Cavourian Decade

But convergence was by no means automatic. Even by contemporary standards, the Piedmontese constitution of 1848 (which after 1861 would remain the *statuto* of the Kingdom of Italy until it was revoked by Mussolini in 1925) was a narrow instrument that reserved wide powers for the king, including command of the armed forces and control over foreign policy. The responsibility of the king's ministers to the parliament was ill-defined, the powers of the parliament limited, and the suffrage was tightly restricted by high property qualifications. But given the size of the Piedmontese propertied classes this was almost inevitable, and the constitution would none the less enable a minority of liberals and radicals to embark on a programme of commercial and political reforms that within a decade had transformed one of the most backward states into one of the most dynamic economies in Italy.

The success of this progressive minority was largely due to Count Camillo Benso di Cavour (1810–61). Cavour became prime minister for the first time in 1852 and thereafter dominated Piedmontese politics whether in or out of office until his early death in 1861. Well-known in Turin before 1848 through his editorship of the liberal review *Il Risorgimento*, Cavour first held office in 1850 as minister for agriculture and commerce in a conservative government headed by Massimo D'Azeglio. He immediately introduced reforms that liberalized and expanded Piedmontese trade, encouraged the development of infrastructures needed for growth (canals, roads, Alpine tunnels, railways, and banks), and not least succeeded in attracting conspicuous flows of foreign investment.

Implementation of a wider liberal programme was facilitated by the fact that many conservatives were willing to support not only economic development but also measures to modernize the Piedmontese State. D'Azeglio, for example, introduced the package of legislation known as the Siccardi Laws in 1850 that reduced the extensive civil jurisdictions exercised by the Church. These first steps towards secularization provoked fierce resistance from more intransigent conservatives, and when in 1852 Victor Emanuel refused to support a bill to introduce civil marriage to avoid conflict with the Papacy, D'Azeglio resigned and Cavour became prime minister. Not wanting to be distracted from his reform programme, Cavour dropped D'Azeglio's bill, but the battle over secularization was only postponed. In 1855 it reappeared on different grounds and caused Cavour's first resignation when Victor Emanuel refused to support a bill to nationalize the convents of minor religious orders proposed by Urbano Rattazzi (1808–73), the leader of the Piedmontese radicals and since 1852 Cavour's principal parliamentary ally. Rattazzi's bill was motivated, however, as much by the need for revenues to fund the reform programme as by ideology, demonstrating that secularization was inseparable from the wider programme for modernizing the Piedmontese State.

Defence of the privileges of the Church mobilized a powerful reactionary opposition, however, that looked to the king for leadership. To counter this, Cavour's great political achievement lay in creating a broad alliance of conservative liberals, moderates, and radicals. These eclectic cross-bench

Facing: VICTOR EMANUEL II became King of Sardinia when his father Carlo Alberto abdicated following the Austrian victory at Novara (23 March 1849). Fearful of provoking French intervention or strengthening the nationalists, the Austrians insisted that Victor Emanuel maintain the 'statuto' (constitution) of March 1848, which he agreed to. Never more than a reluctant constitutional monarch, Victor Emanuel's dynastic ambitions led him to abandon the Piedmontese reactionaries and support Cavour's nationalist programme. On 17 March 1861 at the age of 41 Victor Emanuel II was proclaimed king of Italy.

alliances earned him a reputation for opportunism that was undeserved, and in the absence of clear-cut party or political allegiances in the new parliament the effectiveness of these coalitions derived from the coherence of Cavour's programme for institutional modernization, commercial expansion, and nationalism.

Victor Emanuel, however, sympathized with the reactionaries, was grudging in his acceptance of constitutional constraints and eager not to offend the Church, but the outbreak of war in the Crimea in 1854 forced him to choose between the liberals and the reactionaries. The king was keen to exploit the collapse of the European system of alliance and to enter the conflict on the side of Britain and France, but since he could find no ultra-conservative willing to risk war with Austria there was little choice but to reappoint Cavour as prime minister. Dynastic ambitions forced the king to distance himself from the reactionaries and align with the liberals, making the Crimean War a critical turning-point as foreign policy took a new priority in Piedmontese politics after 1856, but it marked a broader turning-point in the struggle for Italian independence. The alliance between Britain and France against Russia had brought to an end the anti-French coalition that had dominated European international relations since 1814, leaving Austria adrift between former allies and former enemies. For Italian nationalists the implications were enormous and Austria's uneasy neutrality put the whole issue of independence on a new footing.

Piedmont's intervention in the Crimea as an ally of Britain and France did not produce immediate diplomatic rewards at the peace conference (February 1856), but it did confirm Victor Emanuel's leadership of the nationalist movement in Italy. Expectations grew that the war against Austria would soon be resumed, giving the cue for new conspiracies and insurrections. In July 1857 Carlo Pisacane hijacked a steamer belonging to the Rubattino shipping company and landed with his followers at Sapri in the Cilento. The expedition was a disaster, Pisacane's appeals to revolt were ignored by the local people, and he and his followers soon surrounded and killed. None the less, the Sapri expedition gave the sign for a new wave of insurrections and galvanized the moderates into pre-emptive action.

This was the purpose of the Italian National Society that was formed in August 1857 by Daniele Manin, Giuseppe La Farina, and Giorgio Pallavicino. Its declared aim was to organize support for Victor Emanuel and prepare for a new war against Austria. Although eager to convert former radicals, the National Society was concerned to set a 'sterner plan for Italian unification' by thwarting challenges to Piedmontese leadership be it from the radicals, the federalists, or from the south, where in Naples many liberals favoured the idea of an independent constitutional monarchy under an heir of Joachim Murat; while the Sicilians remained as always staunch separatists. Despite the

National Society's strongly monarchist stance, both Garibaldi and Mazzini—the latter for purely tactical reasons, the former from loyalty to Victor Emanuel—gave their support. But the National Society's principal energies were directed at establishing networks among the propertied classes, so that when the war came pro-Piedmontese notables in central Italy would be ready to seize power and forestall the Mazzinians and others.

The War against Austria (1859)

The revival of French expansionist ambitions under Napoleon III's otherwise conservative government led to closer contacts between Turin and Paris. Austria's diplomatic isolation renewed French hopes of regaining influence on the peninsula, while Felice Orsini's attempt to assassinate Napoleon III in January 1858 illustrated the dangers that Italian discontents posed for other European states. In July of the same year French intervention was discussed in detail when Cavour and the emperor met secretly at the resort of Plombières on Lake Geneva. France offered military assistance in case of an Austrian attack on Piedmont, and agreed to the creation of an independent Italian federation consisting of an enlarged Kingdom of Sardinia, the Papal States, and the Kingdom of Naples, presided over by the pope. In return, France would receive Nice and Savoy, and make a dynastic alliance with the House of Savoy. In January 1859 Joseph Napoleon signed a secret treaty on behalf of France in Turin and was married to Princess Maria Clotilde of Savoy.

Expectations of war now ran high, but the Austrians were not provoked into issuing an ultimatum until 23 April. The war ended on 8 July when Napoleon III and the Austrian Emperor Francis Joseph signed an armistice at Villafranca. The Austrians had abandoned Lombardy, and although they still held Venetia the terrible casualties suffered by both sides at the Battles of Magenta (4 June), Solferino, and San Martino (24 June) discouraged Napoleon III from continuing the war. Victor Emanuel was not a signatory to the armistice and Cavour was not consulted: when he received the news on 11 July he resigned.

Even before the fighting began, the moderates had been working to secure their political objectives. In April Archduke Leopold II fled from Tuscany, and a hurriedly constituted provisional government offered Victor Emanuel the title of dictator. Maria Luisa of Parma and Francesco V of Modena also fled in early June, Bologna rebelled, and the rest of the Papal States were in tumult. Influential notables like Baron Ricasoli (1809–80) in Tuscany and Luigi Carlo Farini (1812–66) in Modena took control and by means of carefully orchestrated 'revolutions' succeeded in circumventing the terms of the Treaty of Villafranca which had confirmed the tenure of the legitimist rulers. The fake revolutions gave the pretext for the popular plebiscites by which Tuscany and

Emilia voted overwhelmingly for annexation to the Kingdom of Sardinia in March 1860.

In January Cavour had returned to office and despite the set-back of Villafranca by the spring his strategy seemed to have prevailed. A new Italian kingdom embracing Piedmont, Lombardy, Parma, Modena, Emilia, Romagna and Tuscany was now in being. Napoleon III's hopes of creating a French satellite state in Tuscany had been blocked by the action of the moderates in central Italy. In diplomatic terms, the settlement looked more solid when Palmerston's government warned Austria against any attempt to restore the legitimist rulers and effectively recognized the new State. The radicals had also been outmanœuvred. The alliance with France had ensured that the war was fought with regular troops, removing the need for volunteers and relegating Garibaldi's irregulars to marginal operations. Although Mazzini denounced the royal war against Austria, the first elections in the newly enlarged Kingdom of Sardinia held on 25 March 1860 were a huge victory for the moderates.

None the less, the premature cessation of hostilies before Venetia was liberated provided the nationalists with an emotive cause as fresh volunteers continued to flood into Piedmont. In this tense atmosphere the announcement in April that Nice and Savoy were to be annexed to France created an uproar. The nationalists were dismayed, not least Giuseppe Garibaldi who had been born in Nice. It was against this background that the decision to send a volunteer expedition to join forces with a revolution that had started in Palermo in April 1860 was taken. The aim was to raise the standard of revolt throughout the south and march to liberate Rome, and thereby transform the royal war of independence into a wider, popular war for national unification.

Garibaldi and the Expedition of the Thousand

On 6 May Garibaldi embarked his famous Thousand volunteers at Quarto near Genoa, and after evading the Neapolitan navy landed at Marsala in western Sicily on 11 May. Three days later Garibaldi took the title of dictator in the name of Victor Emanuel, and after engaging a Bourbon detachment at Calatafimi his forces entered Palermo at the beginning of June. After a final engagement near Milazzo, the Bourbon forces abandoned Sicily. On 18 August Garibaldi crossed the Straits of Messina and entered Naples on 7 September. The young king Francis II, who had succeeded his father the previous year, withdrew to defensive positions on the Garigliano and Volturno Rivers where the Bourbon army prepared to block Garibaldi's route north to Rome.

The success of Garibaldi's expedition to the south contrasted strikingly with the failure of previous attempts. Garibaldi was an experienced irregular soldier and had more men than Pisacane or the Bandiera brothers, although

GERMAN CONFEDERATION

SWITZERLAND

AUSTRIAN EMPIRE

SAVOY
(Fr.)

FRANCE

Turin •   PIEDMONT

• Milan

LOMBARDY

Trieste

Venice

LIGURIA   EMILIA

• Genoa

ROMAGNA

Nice

Florence •

TUSCANY

Ancona

OTTOMAN
EMPIRE

DALMATIA

ADRIATIC SEA

CORSICA
(Fr.)

UMBRIA

PAPAL STATES

Rome •

Gaeta

Sassari •

Foggia •

APULIA

Bari •

SARDINIA

BASILICATA

Naples •
Salerno •
Potenza •

Brindisi •

Cagliari •

Sapri •

TYRRHENIAN SEA

Cosenza •

CALABRIA

MEDITERRANEAN SEA

Palermo •

Milazzo •

Messina •
Reggio •

Calatafimi •

Marsala •

SICILY

Catania •

Girgenti •

ALGERIA

TUNISIA

——— Boundary of Northern Italy

MALTA (Br.)

0   200 km

ITALY IN 1861

BARRICADES AT PALERMO (1860). After the battle of Calatafimi, Garibaldi advanced to Palermo where an insurrection had started in April. After three days of fighting, Garibaldi's irregulars entered the city on 1 June and five days later the Dictatorial government declared Sicily's independence from Naples. But Palermo at once became the focus of bitter struggles between Cavour, Garibaldi, his followers, and rival Sicilian political interests.

they were poorly equipped and precariously supplied. Even so, the chances of success would have been slight had it not been for the revolutions and peasant insurrections that threatened the Bourbon army's lines of communication in Sicily.

Once the Bourbon army had retreated, however, Garibaldi found himself at the centre of a complex political situation. His principal adviser was the Sicilian revolutionary Francesco Crispi (1818–1901), who as his Secretary of State was responsible for most of the political decisions and decrees issued on Garibaldi's behalf. Crispi favoured delaying annexation to Piedmont in order to organize the meeting of popular assemblies. This aroused opposition from the conservative Sicilian élites who favoured speedy annexation to Piedmont, since this offered them the opportunity at last to break free from Naples and the Bourbon monarchy.

This was Cavour's objective too. He had followed the progress of the Thousand with mounting concern over the influence of the radicals and the danger of war with France if the expedition succeeded in reaching Rome. In June he sent Giuseppe La Farina to Palermo to demand immediate annexation to Turin. Garibaldi responded by expelling La Farina, but mounting opposition in Palermo had already forced Crispi's resignation. Pressure from the Sicilian landowners also now forced Garibaldi to abandon the sweeping promises of land reform that had been instrumental in winning the support of the peasants. Now that the Bourbon army was no longer a threat, the Sicilian landowners made it clear that their continued support was conditional on the restoration of order. On 4 August one of Garibaldi's lieutenants, Nino Bixio (1821–73), opened fire on peasant rebels in the village of Bronte, an action that was repeated in other parts of Sicily, sending out the unmistakable message that the redshirts were defenders of order, not harbingers of revolution. Bixio's musketry resonated across the Straits, where the landowners were already preparing for Garibaldi's advance by taking over local government and arming National Guard units to prevent the popular upheavals that had occurred in Sicily. The alliance with the landowners guaranteed the collapse of the Bourbon State, but emptied Garibaldi's expedition of its radical political aims.

Cavour made a final attempt to organize a pre-emptive moderate revolution in Naples to forestall Garibaldi's advance. When this failed, he adopted a more direct and dangerous strategy. Warning Paris of its intentions, Turin issued an ultimatum to the papal government on 11 September and two weeks later sent an army into Umbria and the Marches. Led by Victor Emanuel, the Piedmontese force crossed the Papal States and cut Garibaldi's route to Rome. In one of the most famous encounters of the Risorgimento, the king and Garibaldi met on 26 October at Teano just inside Neapolitan territory and Garibaldi loyally surrendered his command.

Cavour's strategy had succeeded: the risks of armed confrontation with Garibaldi's followers and of French military intervention to protect the pope had both been averted. The radicals had once again been out-manœuvred and Cavour pressed to consolidate the position. Despite the attempts by Crispi and others to hold out for the organization of popular political assemblies, two weeks earlier the Turin parliament had already decreed the unconditional annexation of the southern provinces. Plebiscites in the Marches, Umbria, and Sicily in early November completed the process of political unification that had begun with the War of Independence against Austria in 1859. The revolutionaries

GARIBALDI AND VICTOR EMANUEL AT TEANO (26 October 1860). Cavour's decision in September 1860 to send a Piedmontese army through the Papal States to cut off Garibaldi's advance on Rome after the liberation of Naples had risked open confrontation with the nationalists. In this engraving, however, the tense meeting between Garibaldi and Victor Emanuel II at Teano, close to the frontier of the Papal States, on 26 October 1860 is transformed into a scene of loyal comradeship. Neatly overlooking the deep political conflicts that had shaped the struggle for Unification, such images celebrated the mythical unity of the new unified state.

and the radical nationalists had been able to force the struggle for independence into a wider geographical arena, but not to change its political character.

The Difficult Decade 1861–1870

On 17 March 1861 the first Italian parliament proclaimed Victor Emanuel II of Savoy king of Italy, but few considered the new Italy to be complete. Venice and Venetia were only ceded to Italy after Austria's defeat by Prussia in 1866, while the nationalists repeatedly attempted to liberate Rome. In 1862 Garibaldi tried to revive his expedition but was met with cold hostility by the Sicilian landowners: his small force was easily cornered by a Piedmontese detachment in the Aspromonte mountains of Calabria. In 1867 another attempt to invade the Papal States ended in disaster at Mentana. It was not until Napoleon III's defeat at the battle of Sedan removed the pope's protector that Italian troops finally entered Rome on 20 September 1870, although many Italian-speaking territories in the north and east remained under Austrian control.

The aftermath of Unification was bleak. In the south, the landowners' seizure of power in 1860 provoked unrest that by 1862 had turned into full-scale insurrections. Supporters of the former Bourbon monarchy and the radicals attempted unsuccessfully to exploit conflicts that were in reality the last act in the long-drawn-out war between landlords and peasants. The authorities used the term 'brigandage' to disguise the scale of the disturbances, but the restoration of order required a major military operation over three years that cost more lives than all the wars of independence combined. The rebellion in the south also caused plans for regional autonomy to be abandoned in favour of a rigidly centralized administrative system that provoked another separatist revolt in Palermo in 1866 and was widely resented by the élites of northern Italy.

To add to these difficulties, the new State was massively encumbered with debts arising from the wars of 1848–9 and 1859, the military operations in the south in 1860, the subsequent repression of brigandage, and the war of 1866.

Facing: THE SEAMSTRESSES OF THE RED-SHIRTS. A good example of the ways in which the national revolution was portrayed in contemporary art, this striking painting was done shortly after Garibaldi's second attempt to liberate Rome had ended in failure at Aspromonte in 1862. In this lavishly detailed interior, the dignified bearing and suffering features of the women, seated below a portrait of Garibaldi and sewing red shirts for the volunteers, link the nationalist movement with the values of order, sacrifice, duty, and domesticity.

Left: BARON BETTINO RICASOLI (1809–80) oversaw the transition of power in Tuscany from Archduke Leopoldo II to Victor Emanuel II in 1860. A wealthy landowner and head of one the most influential aristocratic families in Tuscany, Ricasoli was briefly prime minister after Cavour's sudden death in June 1861, and headed a second short administration in 1866. Ricasoli's sober conservative bearing, deep religious convictions, and keen commitment to economic development within the limits of a paternalistic, agrarian society personified the moral and social values of the new Italian ruling classes.

EXECUTED BRIGAND
(1864). Between 1861
and 1864 the southern
provinces were the
theatre of a full-scale
civil war, which the
authorities of the new
state tried to disguise as
brigandage. By 1864 over
116,000 troops were en-
gaged in operations
against the 'brigands', of
whom 5,212 were killed,
as many arrested, and
another 3,600 surren-
dered. Sicily was also
subject to military law in
1863, and in 1866
Palermo was the theatre
of a major separatist
revolt.

For most Italians, Unification meant higher taxes and greater austerity. In 1866 the government suspended convertibility of the currency and raised new revenues through wholesale auctions of former church and public land at prices that offered a real bonanza for landowners. At the same time, the extension of Piedmontese free-trade tariffs to the rest of the kingdom in 1861 caused the collapse of many industries and high unemployment, especially in the south.

The difficulties of these first years resulted in serious infringements of the civil liberties and freedoms of speech and association that the liberals had fought to achieve, and the new Italy had many fierce critics. Mazzini, Garibaldi, and other democrats denounced Cavour and his successors for betraying the ideals they had sought to realize, while successive governments treated the radicals and nationalists as enemies of the new State. But the radicals had never succeeded in developing a coherent alternative to Cavour and the Piedmontese monarchy. Many followed the lead of Francesco Crispi who in 1864 publicly renounced his republicanism on the grounds that 'the monarchy unites us, while the republic will always divide us', although a minority drifted towards anarchism and armed rebellion.

The new State was also the target of bitter attacks from conservatives, and above all from the Church. Foreshadowed in the clashes over secularization in Piedmont in the 1850s, the rift between the Church and the new State became irreversible from the moment when Piedmontese troops invaded the Papal States in 1860. Pius IX denied the legitimacy of the new State, forbade Catholics from holding office or voting, and allied the Papacy to the lost cause of the legitimist monarchies. With the *Syllabus of Errors* and the declaration of papal infallibility, Pius IX's onslaught on the new State assumed the tones of an intransigent crusade against liberalism in all its forms, which the Italian bishops and clergy reiterated from their pulpits. But although damaging in many respects, the break with the Church did reinforce the secularizing mission of the new State and made it attractive to religious minorities, especially Protestants and Jews.

The relatively young and inexperienced ruling class of the new State found itself under attack from right and left, but this was neither surprising nor unusual. The fact that there were losers as well as winners revealed that Unification had brought about a political revolution and created a new rela-

tionship between State and society. The constitutional formula that had first been hammered out in Piedmont in the 1850s finally removed the principal causes of political instability in Italy by aligning the interests of the propertied classes more closely with those of the State. For that reason, despite the difficulties that faced it and despite the loss of Cavour in 1861, the new political class was not deterred from extending Cavour's programme of economic, institutional, and political liberalism to Italy as a whole.

What made Italy unusual in mid-nineteenth-century Europe was that property, wealth, and education were still concentrated in the hands of the mere 2 per cent of Italians that acquired the right to vote in 1861. This was offset by a wider participation in municipal and local government elections, but clerical influence in the countryside and the Church's rejection of the new State limited opportunities for extending the popular franchise. Together with Italy's weak economy, apparent lack of internal integration, and vulnerable international position, the relatively narrow character of the new political class made the task of nation-building difficult, especially once Unification had removed the common enemy. But this did not weaken the process of State-building, and in creating a political system that was able to guarantee relative domestic stability and independence, the liberal revolution provided Italians with significant new resources with which to confront the unrelenting, albeit often painful and divisive, challenges of economic, social, and cultural change.

IDLENESS AND WORK. Painted in 1862, this bucolic scene, contrasting hard-working peasants and an idle vagrant, won warm official approval and was selected for inclusion in an exhibition of Italian art in Paris. The theme reflects the enterprise values of the new Italy, but also the attachment to an older, patriarchal agrarian order.

8

NINETEENTH-CENTURY ITALIAN CULTURE

JONATHAN KEATES

The Napoleonic Age

At the beginning of *La Chartreuse de Parme*, his fictional evocation of early nineteenth-century Italy, Stendhal recalls 'the vast inrush of happiness and pleasure' occasioned by the descent of Napoleon's army on Lombardy in 1796. Though the terms in which this invasion is portrayed, that of a joyous coupling between two destined partners, may echo the writer's own nascent Italophilia, he was shrewd enough to understand the extent to which Italian culture was already imbued with French ideas, as well as being able to grasp the irony and ambiguity in the subsequent cultural response of Italians themselves to incorporation within the Napoleonic Empire.

Even if the French lost no time in carrying away a considerable number of important works of art, including major paintings by Raphael, Titian, and other Renaissance masters, several of which have since remained in France, their impact on the architectural profile of various Italian cities was generally beneficent and in certain cases crucial in its aesthetic significance. At Venice, for example, the basilica of St Mark may have been shamefully despoiled of its four antique bronze horses, removed in 1797 as trophies to Paris, but the square in front of the church assumed a greater consequence by the creation by Giuseppe Soli in 1810 of the so-called Ala Napoleonica, intended both to link the Renaissance arcades of the Procuratie Vecchie and Nuove on either side and to replace the demolished church of San Geminiano with a more homogeneous close to the western vista across the piazza.

No city was more obviously marked by French cultural influence during this period than Milan, the capital of the newly established Kingdom of Italy, under the viceregal government of Napoleon's stepson Eugène de Beauharnais. While the Enlightened traditions of literature and journalism which had distinguished Milanese culture under Austrian rule during the late eighteenth century were inevitably constrained by Bonapartist censorship and the government's utilitarian approach to education, the viceroy's court was not without its sophistications, and Eugène himself drew up ambitious plans for redeveloping the central urban layout. Little of this was actually executed, but in such features as the Foro Bonaparte (replacing the outer ramparts of the Castello Sforzesco), the adjacent sporting Arena and white marble Arco della Pace, as well as in the founding of the Brera gallery in a palace formerly occupied by a Jesuit college, the city's sense of metropolitan self-consequence was signally reinforced.

Such symbolic importance in the cultural life of nineteenth-century Italy was equally apparent in Milan's development as a national centre for publishing, a role it continues to enjoy to this day. Where desirable, in the case of scientific and technological publications linked with imperial government policies, the viceregal administration actively assisted with subsidies towards the cost of printing and distributing new works, but even without such support the attraction of Milanese publishers for Italian authors was strong. A potent addition to the first serious stirrings of nationalism in Italy during the Napoleonic occupation was the systematic issue, by the Società tipografica dei classici italiani, of Italian literary and historical works of past centuries by those authors who 'through the importance of their chosen themes and their purity of language helped to propagate the knowledge and use of Tuscan speech'.

The issue of the Tuscan idiom as an appropriate discourse for Italian writers as heirs of Dante, Petrarch, and Boccaccio was to play a notable part in Milanese literary debate for the next twenty years. The Lombard capital rapidly became a magnet for younger poets, critics, and dramatists from all over Italy, led by the politically ambiguous but artistically influential Vincenzo Monti. A veritable Vicar of Bray among writers, Monti had made his name as a poet while still living in Rome, by celebrating the murder at the hands of an enraged mob of the French Revolutionary commissioner Nicholas Hougon de Bassville in 1793. Arriving in Milan in 1797 he curried favour with the new military government, earning the notice of Napoleon, whose victory at Marengo three years later he celebrated in the spirit-stirring ode 'Per la liberazione d'Italia'. In 1814, having lost his various official posts—professor at Pavia University, laureate to the viceroy, and historiographer—he hastened to ingratiate himself with Milan's restored Austrian rulers, spending his last years in dignified and politically harmless linguistic research.

Monti's career is instructive, especially when we contrast its profile of serene opportunism with the tempestuous life of Ugo Foscolo, another adoptive Milanese and the one contemporary poet who succeeded in eclipsing him. Descended on his father's side from a Venetian noble family, Foscolo was born to a Greek mother on the Ionian island of Zakynthos, a dual inheritance he successfully exploited in his fragmented but always fascinating literary *œuvre*. A proto-romantic whose career embraced a substantial period as a soldier in the French army, a series of highly coloured love affairs with Lombard noblewomen, and, after his escape to Switzerland in 1815, a prolonged final phase of poverty-stricken exile in England, he embodied for his contemporaries the fearless acceptance of all those ethical challenges Monti had carefully avoided.

Foscolo is far better remembered today as a poet than for the critical writings which later earned him admiration in London literary circles or for the enormous impact made by his epistolary novel *Le ultime lettere di Jacopo Ortis*, a work which brought him international celebrity. His immortality, somewhat dubiously guaranteed by inclusion among authors prescribed for study in modern Italian schools, rests on a single poem, the marmoreally beautiful 'I sepolcri', printed at Brescia in 1807 and occasioned by Napoleon's decree, issued the previous year, forbidding church burial or the erection of funerary

THE RESTLESS CHARACTER of the Italo-Greek poet Ugo Foscolo is evoked by the sitter's preoccupied gaze in this portrait by François-Xavier Fabre. The painter evidently sought to capture Foscolo as the Romantic prose-writer of the popular *Ultime lettere di Jacopo Ortis*, in contrast to his nowadays more familiar incarnation as the neo-classical poet of *I sepolcri*.

monuments. Here, as in *Le ultime lettere di Jacopo Ortis*, it is the uncompromising individuality of tone which validates the writer's claim to greatness. However obstinate and quarrelsome Foscolo himself might have appeared, his artistic integrity made him something of a role model for the rising generation of Italian writers.

The poet's response to Bonaparte and his empire was one of measured enthusiasm balanced against a downright rejection of the regime's more authoritarian postures. Elsewhere in Italy, reaction among artists to the French invasion and occupation had been more ardent and uncritical, and at least one major figure in the world of the visual arts was destined to contribute significantly to that wealth of icons through which painters, sculptors, and engravers were able to project the image of the first consul and emperor as genius, demiurge, and warrior. The relationship of the sculptor Antonio Canova, not only with Napoleon himself, but with the entire Bonaparte family, was more in the nature of a successful collaboration than an orthodox mutual dependency between a creator and his patrons. Early works in Venice and Rome established his reputation as the most eloquent interpreter, in the world of the fine arts, of that neoclassical spirit evoked during the later eighteenth century by European connoisseurs, antiquarians, and writers on aesthetics, passionate in their search for the indwelling soul of antique sculpture. It was natural enough, therefore, that Napoleon should have invited him to Paris to carve an official portrait bust, followed some years later by an immense full-length statue, in which the emperor was given the form of a nude Olympian god. The bust, as the more manageable of the two, became one of the most popular of imperial likenesses, and it has been estimated that reproductions issued from the marble quarries of Carrara (part of the domain of Napoleon's sister Elisa Baciocchi) at the rate of 500 a year.

Far from falling with Napoleon in 1815, however, Canova achieved his own kind of heroic status thereafter, both as an artist of international celebrity, a visit to whose Roman studio became *de rigueur* for distinguished foreign tourists, and as the principal agent in the complex operation of recovering the looted art treasures of Italy after the war had ended. Even if several of his younger contemporaries chose to place him among those who had not necessarily made their peace with legitimism and the political dispositions of the Congress of Vienna, he made no significant alignment with dissident elements, having accepted a papal knighthood and designed a funerary monument for a Habsburg archduchess. A continued allegiance to neoclassicism was entirely typical of his single-mindedness, which extended to the creation of his own mausoleum, the dignified *tempietto* at Possagno in his native Veneto.

Italian music, as well as poetry and sculpture, played its part in furthering the cause of French-influenced revolution or else in pleasing the ears of the

Bonapartes themselves. Two major composers of the late eighteenth century, Giovanni Paisiello and Domenico Cimarosa, became seriously compromised through involvement in the Neapolitan revolt of 1799. The former, though restored to favour at the Bourbon court on its return to the capital, left for Paris in 1802 to become director of music in the imperial chapel, while the latter, driven into exile, died in poverty at Venice, leaving his opera *Artemisia* unfinished. Elsewhere musicians seized what opportunities lay to hand among the various Bonaparte courts of Italy to further their careers, among them the violin virtuoso Niccolò Paganini and the composer Giovanni Pacini, both of whom achieved early success as protégés of Elisa Baciocchi. Italian audiences had by now yielded almost entirely to the thraldom which opera had begun to exert over musical life throughout the peninsula during the previous century, and it was by no special irony that Paganini, as a purely instrumental performer, was to acquire his greatest fame elsewhere in Europe.

Opera: The Age of Rossini

The role of the opera-house in nineteenth-century Italian cultural life cannot be too highly emphasized. In the half-century between the end of the Napoleonic War and the ultimate phase of unification, the number of theatres throughout Italy doubled or perhaps even trebled. Towns as small as Pienza, Castelfranco Veneto, Bagnacavallo, and Montefalco saw the creation of these characteristic horseshoe-shaped spaces, their tiered boxes adorned with gilt stucco-work beneath a frescoed ceiling allegory, and their proscenium arches adorned with drop curtains illustrating a suitably important event in the locality's history.

Performance seasons at such theatres were limited to a few months, or maybe only a few weeks, during autumn and winter. In many cases a crowded box became a preferable source of warmth, comfort, and social intercourse to the *salotto* of a draughty palace heated by an inadequate stove or brazier. To foreign visitors Italian audiences seemed noisy and inattentive, though criticism of the performance, freely offered without regard for the singers' susceptibilities, made it clear that the major phases of a particular score had at any rate been audible. The higher a composer's reputation the more respectfully, of course, his work was received. It was deemed a sufficient indicator of Verdi's importance, for example, that the première of his *Il trovatore* at the Roman Teatro Apollo in 1853 should have been marked by a reverent silence, broken only by applause at the end of each act.

Only a few of the larger houses, most notably La Scala at Milan, the San Carlo at Naples, and the Venetian La Fenice, regularly commissioned new works, though lesser-ranking theatres such as Florence's La Pergola were often able to present a *novità assoluta* with the help of an enterprising impre-

sario. As artistic manager, the impresario hired singers and conductors, contracted librettists, and engaged composers. Many of the best-known examples of nineteenth-century Italian lyric drama derive their individual outlines from the specific circumstances imposed via this *ad hoc* system. The entire operatic medium needs to be understood in terms of an exigent audience, fond of novelty but largely uninterested by musical developments elsewhere, concerned with vocal personalities rather than compositional ideas, and using the theatre itself as a place in which to underline assertions of status, politics, and social relationship.

Opera was now Italy's major cultural export, and all the principal composers in this so-called age of bel canto spent significant periods abroad. In the case of Gioacchino Rossini the experience was to prove both liberating and ultimately destructive of his talent. Prodigious early success with heroic dramas such as *Tancredi*, presented to enormous acclaim in Venice in 1813, was consolidated by the swift evolution of an unparalleled talent for comic opera, culminating in the triumph, after initial disaster, of *Il barbiere di Siviglia* in the same year. By the age of 25 when he embarked on a superb sequence of serious works for the Teatro San Carlo at Naples, Rossini had established himself

THIS VIEW of the Teatro San Carlo in Naples shows several characteristic features of nineteenth-century opera performance. The orchestra sits on a level with the audience, the conductor directs from a chair, male spectators in the stalls wear their hats, and the exits are guarded by uniformed gendarmes.

as a composer of genuine originality, attuned, at an almost uncanny level, to the moods of his age. His alertness to instrumental sonorities in original combinations made him one of the century's most inspired orchestrators, and his careful construction of individual scenes was to have a pervasive effect on operatic form throughout Europe, an impact acknowledged by musical contemporaries as distinct from him in creative personality as Beethoven, Schubert, and Wagner. Wagner was among several composers who visited Rossini during his prolonged final period of retirement in Paris, after the creation of his last opera *Guillaume Tell* in 1829. Written to a French libretto based on Friedrich Schiller's German drama describing the Swiss hero's struggle to free his country from the Austrians, the score was responsive to the availability of an excellent orchestra at the Théâtre de l'Opéra where it was first produced, and to the theatre's readiness to engage a first-rate cast for the première. Though its length eventually counted against it with Parisian audiences, *Guillaume Tell* represented a landmark in the development of nineteenth-century opera, marking a dignified close to its composer's career.

Romanticism

Rossini lived on for nearly forty years, showing (despite his last opera's revolutionary theme) an almost total indifference to the political upheavals currently engrossing Italians and not altogether in sympathy with the later phases of that Romantic movement his works had helped to popularize in Italy itself. The issue of what was or was not Romantic, together with a controversy over the political soundness inherent in espousing a Romantic standpoint, came to dominate Italian culture during the decade immediately following the fall of Napoleon in 1815. Once again Milan was the focal point, partly through its centrality as the first major stopping-place on the route taken by the horde of international travellers now crossing the Alps, partly also for its closeness to Switzerland, where the exiled Madame de Staël in her villa on Lake Geneva had acted as a tutor in German and English Romanticism to visiting Italians. There was perhaps also a strong sense, among several of the younger Milanese literati, that they were simply continuing a tradition of debate and polemic established by an earlier generation, that of Parini, Beccaria, and the Verri brothers, with whom their parents and grandparents had been friendly.

Enhanced by the occasional presence of influential foreigners such as Henry Brougham, founder of the *Edinburgh Review*, and Lord Byron, arriving in 1817 at the beginning of a self-imposed exile following his notorious divorce, the Romantic enthusiasm mobilized many of the most promising younger poets, critics, and journalists living in Milan during this period. While Giovanni Berchet, in his *Lettera semiseria di Grisostomo al suo figlio* (1816), promoted a poetic populism, condemning the neoclassical vein as essentially deadening to original inspiration, Pietro Borsieri, in his *Avventure letterarie di un giorno* published the same year, urged his countrymen to turn their attention to the contemporary literature of other nations, emphasizing the recommendation already made by Madame de Staël that Italians should relinquish their sterile preoccupation with classical paraphernalia in favour of translating foreign authors. Potentially the most influential of early Italian Romantic apologists was De Staël's friend the young Piedmontese aristocrat Ludovico di Breme, who reinforced the arguments made by Berchet and Borsieri in favour of a modern, internationalist artistic idiom with his *Discorso intorno all'ingiustizia di alcuni giudizi letterari italiani* (1816). His easily assumed role as patron, enabler, and host to men of letters (including Byron, for whom he gave a dinner at which Monti, Pellico, and Stendhal were present) allowed him to review the cultural situation of modern Italy in the *Grand Commentaire* (1817), an intellectual autobiography written in French and published in Geneva, not the least controversial of whose affirmations lay in the simple words 'J'aime mon pays . . . ni plus ni moins que la vie.'

It was inevitable that Italian Romanticism should have aligned itself from the outset with political dissent and criticism directed with increasing openness at the restored Habsburg administration controlling Milan as capital of the Austrian province of Lombardy. The ultimate test of the regime's tolerance came with the publication in 1818 of the first issue of *Il Conciliatore*, a review in the mould of the English literary magazines of the period, pioneered by Di Breme and fusing the talents of Berchet, Borsieri, the critic Ermes Visconti, and the poet and dramatist Silvio Pellico. Though the initiative was abruptly halted by the intervention of the imperial censor in 1819, a valuable point had been established among Italians of all political shades by the *Conciliatore*'s brief existence as a vehicle of liberal opinion. It was no accident that two years later most of its leading contributors should have been implicated as sympathizers with the abortive Carbonarist uprising in Piedmont. The severe measures taken by the Milanese government in 1821 to deal with all suspected dissidents resulted in a wave of arrests, imprisonment, and exile which included Pellico and Berchet among its more distinguished victims, along with Princess Cristina Trivulzo di Belgioioso, a young Milanese aristocrat whose salon in Paris, where she eventually settled, became an important forum for Italian expatriates during subsequent decades.

It is perhaps worth mentioning here that as a result of his suspected involvement with the Carbonarists, Stendhal, who had lived in Milan since 1816 and ardently espoused the new Romanticism, was forced to return to his native France, where he did much to promote the movement away from traditional classic literary modes. Where the Italian revolutionary diaspora itself was concerned, the principal benefit conferred by the exiles' arrival in cities like London, Paris, and New York lay in the chance to promulgate national culture as a symbol of the urge towards unification. While such distinguished fugitives as Giuseppe Mazzini, whose critical writings form a notable part of his extensive *œuvre*, or Antonio Panizzi, creator of the domed reading-room at the British Museum, fostered awareness of the Italian literary heritage, a reciprocal interest in Italy itself among European tourists brought about the expansion of those expatriate colonies which had developed in various cities throughout the peninsula during the previous century. Rome, for example, became the favourite haunt of artists, especially the French, whose academy at the Villa Medici offered annual prizes for Italian study to painters and musicians. Florence, host to a more mixed variety of cultural tourism, witnessed an important, if gradual, revolution in art history throughout the century, based on a discovery of medieval and early Renaissance Tuscan civilization, embracing such key figures as Giotto, Masaccio, and Fra Angelico. Largely pioneered by northern European historians, critics, and connoisseurs, it was to have notable effects on the modern tourist economy of Florence and its surrounding region.

Though the tradition of fine painting in Tuscany had more or less died out by the nineteenth century, the patronage of its restored Habsburg-Lorraine grand dukes encouraged a number of excellent architects throughout the duchy. Both Agostino Fantastici at Siena and Pasquale Poccianti, making additions to the ducal Palazzo Pitti in Florence, exercised an austere elegance and linear harmony which appealed to a venerable local sense of architectural appropriateness in the context of the Tuscan landscape and helped to influence design in the public buildings of other Tuscan centres such as Leghorn, Arezzo, and Prato. In the field of sculpture, meanwhile, Florence witnessed

DOYEN OF FLORENTINE ROMANTIC SCULPTORS, ruling his students at the Accademia with a rod of iron, Lorenzo Bartolini was much in demand among foreign visitors to Tuscany. Dated 1837, this monument to Princess Zamoyska seems typically classical in inspiration, but its style also reflects the period's growing interest in medieval sculpture and decorative art.

218

the success of Lorenzo Bartolini, a blander, more provincial version of Canova, appointed superintendent of the Carrara Academy in 1820. His marble monuments in Florentine churches, more especially Santa Croce and Santa Maria Novella, always flawless in their modelling, represent a comfortable synthesis between Bartolini's inherited international neo-classicism and a dawning interest in the Renaissance styles reflected all around him.

The city's revived cosmopolitanism during the 1820s and 1830s, under the comparatively benign rule of the grand dukes, meant that it could assume, at least to some degree, the role of liberal focal point which Milan had been forced, for the time being, to relinquish. In this context the dynamic figure was Gian Pietro Vieusseux, a Ligurian of Swiss parentage whose bookshop, printing-press, and reading-room—the famous Gabinetto Scientifico-Letterario which formed the nucleus of the much larger library in use today—occupied premises in Piazza Santa Trinita. In 1821 Vieusseux founded the *Antologia*, a worthy successor to *Il Conciliatore*, which, though carefully avoiding any obvious political alignment, brought together the best of contemporary Italian writing and scholarship, and in the work of major contributors like the nonchalantly accomplished Lombard literary critic Giuseppe Montani, addressed once again the issue of a unifying national language which had preoccupied Foscolo and Monti in the preceding decade.

Leopardi and Manzoni

One of those who frequented Vieusseux's reading-room during the 1820s was a frail-looking young aristocrat from the Marches who had come to Florence partly for his health, but mostly to escape from the stifling provincialism of the small town of Recanati where he had spent his early years. The childhood and adolescence of Giacomo Leopardi have become a byword, in the annals of Italian literature, for unhappiness and repression, largely through the potent spell cast by the poetry he distilled from this youthful experience. Its principal figures, a bookish but intensely reactionary father, a strangely unloving mother, and their half-blind and physically deformed son whose life was centred upon the voluminous library in his family's *palazzo* assume an almost legendary hue, but the inherent fatalism of Leopardi's outlook undoubtedly found its origins in such an atmosphere of gloomy, friendless remoteness.

His poetic gifts were accompanied by a conscious view of the world as a battleground between humanity's aspirations and illusions on the one hand and the ruthless interventions of reality on the other. Underlying the philosophical and satirical prose of his notebooks and essays is a strong awareness, perhaps influenced by the surrounding disenchantment among Italian patriots during the 1820s, of the inherent vanity in the Enlightenment's expectations of progress. Such a bleak hollowness combines with the impassive cruelty of existence as a whole in creating a perpetual struggle between man and nature.

Leopardi's own adult life merely exacerbated this idea, plagued as he was by continuing ill health and unsatisfactory personal and professional relationships. The result was a series of poems, 'La ginestra', 'Il tramonto della luna', 'Le ricordanze', 'A Silvia', and others, which gave utterance, in language of marmoreal sublimity, to his sense of the annihilating emptiness encompassing the spirit on earth, unrelieved by any special pledges of Christian redemption. Considered from a purely technical aspect, these works, written in various forms either as free-flowing odes or in strictly patterned strophes, consummated the stylistic achievement of earlier poets such as Monti and Foscolo, working towards a more muscular, less pedantic use of the literary language. Leopardi himself more than fulfilled those expectations of a new and original vernacular poetry raised among Milanese critics prior to 1821. In some sense, however, his effect on Italian poetry was curiously limiting, and a Leopardian romantic sombreness of mood even today marks the dominant idiom among Italy's poets.

The primacy of Tuscan as a literary medium was not asserted by Leopardi alone. Between 1825 and 1827 Alessandro Manzoni had issued the first edition

FIFTEEN SITTINGS were required for this portrait of the novelist, poet, and ideologue Alessandro Manzoni, painted by Francesco Hayez in Milan in 1844. The most abundantly gifted and long-lived of nineteenth-century Italian artists, Hayez made his name as a history painter before a burgeoning talent for portraiture enabled him to create some of the Risorgimento era's most memorable icons.

of a novel entitled *I sposi promessi*, set against the background of seventeenth-century Milan under Spanish rule. He himself was Milanese, an aristocrat, grandson of Cesare Beccaria and thus theoretically linked with the same liberal traditions as those inherited by the *Conciliatore* group. Temperamentally, nevertheless, he had kept his distance from them, separated not so much by aesthetic considerations as by the fervour of his Christian spirituality, based on a renewal of Catholic faith following the conversion of his wife Henriette Blondel, originally a Protestant, whom he married in 1808. His early *Inni Sacri* and the two tragedies *Il Conte di Carmagnola* and *Adelchi* (published posthumously), though tinged with Romantic sentiment and promoting Italian patriotism, are more noteworthy for their Christian morality, urging religion as the sole antidote to worldly adversity and disappointment.

Manzoni was convinced that the language of Florence rather than Milan should be the binding national idiom of modern Italians. He therefore substantially overhauled the text of his novel—'dipping its rags in the Arno' as he called it (again a Florentine visit was crucial here)—and re-issued it in 1840 as *I promessi sposi*, the version best known today and taught in Italian schools as a standard classic. The work's significance was thus three-fold. Memorably poetic in descriptive technique, it proposed a new and flexible prose medium to Italian narrative writers, while its theme, the adventures of two lovers whose romance is continually beset by the forces of history, appealed to the growing awareness of a parallel between former oppression by foreign overlords and the modern imposition of Austrian rule, direct or indirect, throughout Italy. More important still, the book had the effect of establishing fiction among Italian readers and writers as a viable literary mode. *I promessi sposi* was by no means the first national novel, but its masterly handling of the form already made popular throughout Europe by Sir Walter Scott, brought Manzoni worldwide recognition, setting an aesthetic standard against which Italian novelists throughout the nineteenth century continued to measure their achievements.

Some of the admiration accorded *I promessi sposi* in its second, definitive incarnation was undoubtedly linked with the growth during the 1830s of Italians' sense of a shared historical past. Continuing discussion of the language issue as a means of unification gained further vitality through a focus on the Middle Ages and the Renaissance as a time during which Italy's leading artists and poets had flourished among small states resolutely resistant to foreign interference. Not surprisingly, Manzoni's novel inspired similar works from writers more obviously wedded to the cause of nationalism, tales in which a liberal fervour, resurgent after the Carbonarist débâcle, could gather stimulus from the romantic address to a past Italian greatness waiting to be re-awakened.

Opera: The Age of Donizetti and Bellini

Fiction in Italy was never destined to achieve the popularity it enjoyed elsewhere during the nineteenth century. To bypass Austrian, Bourbon, or papal censorship by offering thinly veiled analogies with the political status quo, the picturesque adaptation of history required a more accessible medium in order to make its true impact. Opera, a 'democratic' entertainment despite the social divisions imposed on the audience by theatre architecture, offered the ideal showcase for such broad-brush parallels between past and present, sharpened as they often were by the revolutionary sympathies of the various poets who furnished composers with libretti. It is not strange to discover that among those who worked with Giuseppe Verdi before the first major phase of Italian unification was completed in 1860, two were involved in the heroic if ultimately abortive Venetian uprising of 1848, one was a noted Milanese liberal whose wife welcomed dissidents to her salon, and the others all maintained a perceptibly nationalist alignment. Ironically, neither Gaetano Donizetti nor Vincenzo Bellini, the leading opera composers foreshadowing Verdi, showed marked patriotic sympathies. Each was quite content, on the other hand, to follow the trend which sought out bold historical melodrama as a vehicle for musical expression in preference to the reshaping of materials from classical mythology which had engaged earlier generations. Even a work like Bellini's *Norma*, one of the most influential of nineteenth-century operas and generally regarded as his masterpiece, made skilful concessions to contemporary political sentiment by locating its story of two women in love with a faithless man in the context of the Roman occupation of Gaul and the resistance to the invaders by the Druids. In *I Puritani di Scozia*, last of the composer's works before his premature death from cholera in Paris in 1835, the libretto, ostensibly a harmless excursion into the territory sanctified for contemporary European readers by Scott's novels, features a duet 'Suoni la tromba' whose 'liberty or death' message could hardly be misinterpreted by Italian audiences.

Bellini's *œuvre*, limited to nine operas whose careful gestation owed as much to his morbid resentment of possible rivals as to grander aesthetic considerations, is traditionally seen as the purest essence of Italian operatic Romanticism. It was Donizetti, however, less scrupulous and more prolific, whose remodelling of standard scenic forms led to an increased alertness, among international audiences, to convincing motivation and dramatic coherence, in operas such as *Lucia di Lammermoor*, *Lucrezia Borgia*, and *La Favorite*. Fluent as Donizetti was in the bel canto idiom, his fertile genius also produced the last great examples, in *L'elisir d'amore* and *Don Pasquale*, of the Italian *opera buffa*, a comic genre stretching back, via Rossini, to the eighteenth century of Cimarosa and Mozart. Composed in 1843, *Don Pasquale* was one of the last works completed by Donizetti before his mental collapse brought about by tertiary syphilis, a tragic end to what had been one of the most productive and brilliant careers in the history of Italian musical theatre.

MOST PORTRAITS OF GAETANO DONIZETTI show the composer in a relaxed, informal pose. The slightly stiffer manner adopted here indicates the respect in which he was held during the 1830s as a prolific and versatile master of bel canto lyric drama and *opera buffa*.

Literature and the Risorgimento

The Romantic invocation of the past as a metaphor for contemporary events was enhanced on stage by the development of scene-painting techniques in the hands of Alessandro Sanquirico, La Scala's most accomplished designer during this period. An undeniable element of operatic theatricality spills over, what is more, into the work of the best Italian studio painter of the early nineteenth century, whose long life spanned the Napoleonic era, the Risorgimento, and the new industrialization of the 1880s. Described by Mazzini as 'the great Italian idealist', Francesco Hayez began his professional training at 7 years old among the ruins, as it were, of republican Venice, his birthplace and a constant point of reference in his art. A friend of Rossini and Canova, hailed as a rising genius by Stendhal, he renounced neoclassicism in favour of a style more overtly linked with the aspirations of the Milanese Romantics among whom he moved as a young man, a style which sought to reclaim the tonal and compositional language of the Renaissance masters. His most potent early achievement in this manner was *The Inhabitants of Parga Leaving their Homeland*, commissioned in 1826 by the Brescian nobleman Paolo Tosio. The subject, involving a recent tragic episode in the Greek War of Independence, was plainly 'patriotic', as Hayez later acknowledged, but its background, anything but modern in feeling, is essentially that of a Venetian altarpiece from the age of Bellini and Cima da Conegliano.

To a modern sensibility these set pieces, arresting as their *mises-en-scène* and subtle colouring always appear, possess a more limited appeal than Hayez's remarkable portrait studies of his great contemporaries, several of which have achieved archetypal status among images of the Risorgimento era. His skill as a portraitist, for which he deserves to be much better known outside his native Italy, was to reinterpret a sturdy Lombardo-Venetian tradition stretching back via Fra Galgario to Tintoretto, Titian, and the Brescian school of Moroni and Savoldo. Despite an intrinsic sensuality in his handling of details in dress and female *coiffure*, Hayez's approach to his sitters is fundamentally austere, with backgrounds kept to the simplest and emphasis placed on the inherent strength of facial contour and expression. Working in an age when studios such as those of Alinari in Florence and Anderson and Spithöver in Rome were busy promoting the new craft of photography, he felt a need to reassert the primacy of his art in definitive icons ranging from the elderly Manzoni, a dignified amalgam of senator and hermit, to the siren-like Cristina Belgioioso posed in telling juxtaposition to an antique female bust.

The intensity of feeling aroused by the Risorgimento left hardly any area of Italian art untouched during the central decades of the nineteenth century. In their voluminous writings, ideologues of independence such as Giuseppe Mazzini, Vincenzo Gioberti, and Carlo Cattaneo carried on the work begun in the pages of the *Conciliatore* and the *Antologia* of promoting a concept of national revival, invoking medieval and Renaissance points of reference while simultaneously responsive to the hopes and doubts raised by what elsewhere in contemporary Europe had become known as 'the Italian Question'. None of these figures, though a discussion of their work belongs more appropriately within a political than an artistic context, was narrowly confined to an analysis of current historical developments. Mazzini was an accomplished literary critic and musical amateur; Gioberti, a chaplain to the king of Piedmont, had immersed himself in comparative philosophy; and Cattaneo found an outlet for the astonishing catholicity of his enthusiasms by publishing a monthly review, *Il Politecnico*. Central to the achievement of each, nevertheless, lay varying strands of idealism which both dictated and echoed the mood of the hour, mirrored more crudely in patriotic poems and songs, such as Goffredo Mameli's famous 'Fratelli d'Italia', which eventually became the Italian national anthem, or the sentimental anthology favourite 'La spigolatrice di Sapri', Luigi Mercantini's verses occasioned by an abortive incursion by northern revolutionaries into Calabria in 1857.

What *risorgimentale* high-mindedness and the efficiency of reactionary censorship between them seem to have suppressed, for the time being at least, was the Italian genius for satire. Neither the great Milanese dialect poet Carlo Porta, scourge of vanity and prejudice among his fellow-citizens during the Napoleonic era and the Habsburg Restoration, nor the phenomenally prolific Giuseppe Gioacchino Belli, whose 2,000 sonnets in Roman dialect had captured life in the papal capital during the 1820s and 1830s with scarifying realism, had emboldened potential rivals or imitators. In the mid-century a single name stands out, that of the Tuscan Giuseppe Giusti, whose verse seems more original for eschewing the standard post-Leopardian solemnity and romantic introspection. Immensely self-critical, Giusti, a martyr to ill health, requested that after his death only some two dozen of what he called his 'scherzi' should be published, but the brilliant aptness of his satirical inventions at the expense of Italy's repressive sovereigns, in poems such as 'La guigliottina a vapore' [The Steam Guillotine], 'Il Re Travicello' [King Log], and 'La chiocciola' [The Snail], caused much of his work to be widely circulated beyond the confines of Tuscany during his lifetime. His is the most pungently subversive voice among writers of the Risorgimento, a fascinating anticipation of a species of political humour we might be more inclined to associate with twentieth-century Eastern European writers under Communism.

Verdi

The best-loved of Giusti's poems, 'Sant'Ambrogio', is a memorably ironic analysis of the way in which the impact of a work of art succeeds in temporarily blurring the hostile divisions between alien authority and its victims. The music to which the poet listens in a Milanese church, standing beside an Austrian soldier who shares his emotional response, is a chorus from Giuseppe Verdi's opera *I Lombardi alla prima crociata* (1843). Of all the artistic figures associated with the struggle for nationhood, Verdi remains the most accessible, a composer whose popularity, invincible on the basis of a handful of master-pieces while he was alive, has since been enhanced by our enthusiastic redis-covery of his early works, written as a jobbing maestro serving his theatrical apprenticeship during what he called his *anni di galera* (variously rendered as 'prison' or 'galley' years).

Musicology has sought to play down Verdi's links with the Risorgimento, but a glance at the material he selected for operatic treatment soon reveals a gallery of characters either at odds with political authority or else marginal-ized by an established society whose rules are either morally flawed or patently evil. The protagonists of his three most popular operas, *Rigoletto*, *Il trovatore*, and *La traviata*, are respectively a hunchback, a gipsy, and a courte-san, while for the hero of his last stage work he chose Shakespeare's lord-of-misrule Sir John Falstaff. Several of his operas feature moments of popular insurgence, and at least one, *La battaglia di Legnano*, arose directly from the Roman revolt against papal government in 1848–9. Yet more popular with patriotic audiences than the chorus referred to in Giusti's poem were those in *Ernani*, 'Si ridesti il leon di Castiglia', and *Nabucco*, 'Va pensiero sull'ali dorate', the latter becoming an unofficial Italian national anthem, sung most notably by those gathered to witness the reopening of the Teatro alla Scala in Milan after the bomb damage of the Second World War.

The son of well-to-do Emilian farming folk, Verdi united a powerful feeling for his native region (he was eventually able to purchase a handsome estate at Sant'Agata near Parma) with a reserve and asperity deriving partly from a sense of unease with the sophistications forced upon him by professional success. The triumph of his late works, such as *Otello*, *Falstaff*, and the revised *Simon Boccanegra*, owed much to a fruitful collaboration with the would-be composer Arrigo Boito, but almost from the outset of his career he had shown a consistent single-mindedness in contriving that librettists should fall in with his overall concept of the piece in hand. No other Italian composer of the second half of the nineteenth century rivalled him in terms of a life in art whose aims were all successfully accom-plished, and it was inevitable that his countrymen, of all classes and backgrounds, should consider him in terms of what is nowadays called 'a living national treasure'.

Always grudging with any hint of self-revelation,

OF ALL GIUSEPPE VERDI'S LIBRETTISTS, Arrigo Boito is thought to have had the closest understanding of the composer's intentions. His texts for *Otello* and *Falstaff* show acute sensitivity to their Shakespearean originals, enhanced by Boito's own musical interests. Both men are shown here in the garden of Verdi's publishers Giulio Ricordi.

Facing: ONE OF THE DISTINCTIVE FEATURES in Turin's skyline, the Mole Antonelliana, begun in 1878, was originally a synagogue. Its bold design, by the architect Alessandro Antonelli, aptly symbolizes the significant Jewish contribution to Italian cultural life in the wake of political unification.

Verdi was never prevailed upon to write his memoirs and thereby join the throng of Italians whose sense of the sheer momentousness in those revolutionary decades later encouraged them to document their experience. The rich literature of autobiography in Italy during the Risorgimento period has been insufficiently studied, but its range includes such widely differing works as Silvio Pellico's *Le mie prigioni*, a deeply spiritual account of his imprisonment by the Austrians in the Moravian fortress of Spielberg, and the lapidary *Memorie* of the politician, novelist, and diplomat Massimo D'Azeglio, closely involved in the establishment of Piedmontese supremacy among the Italian states moving towards unification. As a complete contrast with each of these stands Luigi Settembrini's *Ricordanze della mia vita*, the story of a Neapolitan lawyer gaoled for his part in the revolt of 1848, one of those political incarcerations which occasioned William Ewart Gladstone's famous anathema of the Kingdom of Naples as 'the negation of God erected into a system of government'. Witty, spiced with telling detail, and vigorous in their narrative sweep, Settembrini's *Ricordanze* represent one of the most consistently engaging Italian prose works of the nineteenth century.

A northern counterpart to Settembrini's book was Giovanni Visconti Venosta's *Ricordi di gioventù 1847–1860*, a panorama of liberal and artistic circles in Milan during the last years of Habsburg occupation. The critical traditions initiated among the Milanese in the 1800s by Berchet, Di Breme, and others were effectively renewed by the founding in 1850, at the instigation of Visconti's friend Carlo Tenca, of the weekly journal of arts and letters *Il Crepuscolo*, notable, among its other features, for a rigorous refusal to mention anything connected with Austria in its regular round-up of current affairs. Government censorship was wholly unavailing against this silent variety of political protest. Tenca, a *habitué* of the salon conducted by Verdi's confidante Clara Maffei, was a powerful influence on the stylistic refinement of Italian criticism of the arts, praised alike for his versatility (he was himself a novelist and poet) and for the impartial severity with which he reviewed the work of his literary acquaintances. Under his direction *Il Crepuscolo* fixed a benchmark for serious magazines in Italy and its example was widely copied during the latter half of the century.

IN HIS REVIEW *Il Crepuscolo* the Milanese critic Carlo Tenca conducted a skilful campaign against Habsburg censorship during the 1850s, while promoting younger talents and encouraging Italian writers to look more closely at their literary heritage.

The armed conflict of the Risorgimento claimed its distinguished victims in the world of the arts. Before his death at sea while on a military mission to Sicily in 1861, Ippolito Nievo, then aged 29, had experimented successfully in

verse satire, tragedy, and political journalism, as well as producing an arresting series of *novelle*, set mostly in his native Friuli, which anticipate the Sicilian
tales of Giovanni Verga in their realistic treatment of rural life. His major
work, composed in a mere eight months during 1857–8, is the majestically pro-
portioned *Le confessioni d'un italiano*, a novel whose background—the fall of
Venice and the Austrian ascendancy—is merely a historical gloss on characters and predicaments of Nievo's own time. The narrative's striking intimacy
and freedom of engagement emphasize the tragic loss to Italian fiction, in the
generation after Manzoni, of one of its few genuinely original practitioners.

Working like Nievo in a Venetian ambience and sharing his fervent patriotism was the painter Ippolito Caffi, last of the great *vedutisti*, those artists
whose images of Venice and its lagoon kept alive the eighteenth-century tradition of Canaletto and his school. Caffi had an amazing sharpness of vision,
choosing to work on small canvases in which tiny areas of vivid colour were
used to individualize his various city-scapes (he also created memorable
images of Florence and Rome). Pencil and watercolour sketchbooks now in
the Museo Correr form a vigorous record of his life on the front-line barricades during the siege of Venice in 1848, and it was as a naval volunteer in the
war of 1866 that he perished when his ship was torpedoed by the Austrians at
the Battle of Lissa.

Architecture and Art

Mostly for financial reasons, the rulers of the Italian states during the
period between 1815 and 1860 had done little to alter or improve the
architectural character and layout of the principal cities in their
dominions. Venice, indeed, seems to have been the deliberate victim
of an Austrian policy of downgrading it as a port so as to promote the
fortunes of its Adriatic rival Trieste. None of the grandiose schemes
proposed for developing the Riva degli Schiavoni as a planned
complex of hotels and government offices was carried into effect,
and though the city was linked to the mainland by a road-and-
rail causeway in 1846 it never regained a mercantile importance. Elsewhere, apart from the grand duchy of Tuscany,
where the house of Habsburg-Lorraine had made sincere
attempts at developing the commercial profile of cities such
as Leghorn, laying out adequate roads, and introducing
English and French engineers to create the nucleus of a rail
network, new urban projects were few. Though Pietro
Bianchi's San Francesco di Paola in Naples and the rebuilt
Teatro San Carlo in the same city are often adduced in connection with this supine phase of Italian architecture, each is

more interesting in itself than for any other initiatives it may have helped to inspire.

A period of drastic change in the atmosphere of Italian cities inevitably followed the creation of the new kingdom after 1860. Many towns, in the immediately succeeding decades, lost their walls, replaced by leafy *viali*, and within the centres new squares and arterial thoroughfares were hewn out of the medieval labyrinth surrounding an ancient central piazza. The most obvious casualty of such ruthless modernizing was Rome, which became capital of Italy in 1870 and lost in consequence that half-rustic, half-ruined charm in which foreign travellers had formerly delighted. Under Pius VII, it is true, significant additions had been made, such as Piazza del Popolo and the Pincio gardens, the work of Giuseppe Valadier, an architect highly sympathetic to the city's essential character and a major influence in restoring and embellishing Roman monuments under both papal and Napoleonic regimes. During the last thirty years of the nineteenth century, however, such sensitivity yielded to the imperatives of reshaping Rome in the image of an appropriate capital for an aspiring European power. The result was the present infelicitous combination of a historic city, made visually more arresting by the symbiosis of antique, Renaissance, and baroque styles and building materials, with the pompous triumphalism and suburban drabness which characterized the accelerated urbanization of the new kingdom. An inevitable accompanying

GIOVANNI FATTORI'S *La Maremma* reflects the abiding fascination of the Tuscan countryside for the so-called 'Macchiaioli' painters. Peasant life, whether presented realistically or sentimentalized, also became an obsession with Italian writers of the period, disillusioned with the prevailing mood of the newly created kingdom of Italy.

factor was the alteration for the worse in the Roman micro-climate through the extensive clearance of trees and gardens.

Not all the architecture of late nineteenth-century Italy was without distinction and elegance. Creations like the Galleria Vittorio Emmanuele in Milan; the various pump rooms, casinos, and hotels in spa towns such as Salsomaggiore and San Pellegrino; certain of the more fanciful railway stations—Assisi and Perugia offering outstanding examples—and the eccentric but memorably distinctive spires designed by Alessio Antonelli at Turin and Novara all bear witness to a renewed imaginative energy among architects after a prolonged neoclassical doze. Yet even neo-classicism found an inspired reinterpreter during this period, in the person of the Florentine architect Giuseppe Poggi, whose main projects, some of them begun while Florence was briefly (1862–70) the Italian capital, included the colonnaded Piazza Beccaria and the panoramic layout of Piazzale Michelangelo, with its connected Viale dei Colli strung out among the gardens, olive-groves, and pine-woods above the Arno.

Florence may be said to have gained rather than lost by the transference of the government to Rome. The revaluation of medieval Italian culture from the age of Dante and Giotto and an intensifying scholarly interest in every aspect of the Renaissance enhanced its hallowed status as an art city among foreign visitors to Italy, and by the century's end a significant international

community, composed largely of English, Germans, and Americans, attracted alike by aesthetic pleasures, beauty of setting, and relatively low living costs, had established itself on the hills of Bellosguardo, Fiesole, and Settignano. Modern Tuscan painting, meanwhile, had acquired a new strength of purpose among a group of artists nicknamed the 'Macchiaioli' (literally 'spot-makers'), often linked with the French Impressionists, but for the most part independent of them, though inspired by similar imaginative approaches to light and colour. The leading figure here is Giovanni Fattori, who began his career in fairly orthodox fashion as a history painter before moving, via several vigorously conceived scenes associated with the recent wars of liberation, towards a more contemplative treatment of landscape, agricultural life, or small groups of figures considered in tonal relationship to their surroundings. Telemaco Signorini was another whose unsentimental handling of genre scenes and thoughtful glances at the Tuscan countryside earned him a national reputation, heightened by various works recording his travels in France, England, and Scotland, where his sober, painterly apprehensions of the alien scene offer striking comparisons with those of his more free-flying French contemporaries Claude Monet and Camille Pissarro. The third major figure in this most dominant of nineteenth-century Italian schools was Silvestro Lega, whose refined synthesis of elements from contemporary life and landscapes alluding, not always obliquely, to those in the backgrounds of Renaissance canvases, makes him perhaps the most appealing of this Tuscan group.

Literature and Culture at the end of the Century

If the Macchiaioli, during the 1860s and 1870s, constituted a school with many pupils, the simultaneous literary revolution (as it saw itself) known as 'La Scapigliatura' was far more obviously a movement, demanding the loyalty of committed adherents in its passionate iconoclasm and rejection of the household gods set up by Risorgimento culture. The embourgeoisement of northern Italy, as the industrialization of Piedmont and Lombardy gathered momentum, created a corresponding disaffection among younger writers and journalists, for whom Milan yet again offered a rallying point. Literally translated, *scapigliatura* means 'dishevelment', but its broader implications were those of a loudly expressed disdain for established values of piety and patriotism as conveyed by Manzoni in *I promessi sposi* (a favourite target of the Scapigliati), a hankering after French decadence and the naturalism and psychology currently fashionable among Parisian novelists, as well as a deliberately anticonformist stance in the handling of various literary forms.

Certain of the Scapigliati seem to have shaped their careers according to a determined pattern of picturesque self-destruction, most notably the poet

Emilio Praga and the novelist Iginio Ugo Tarchetti, archetypes of early promise withered by existential gloom and debauchery. The multi-talented Boito brothers, longer lived, were no less bitter and world-weary in mood, at least initially. Arrigo's poetic talents were soon to be memorably channelled into creating three outstandingly effective opera texts for Giuseppe Verdi while Camillo, who became professor of architecture at Milan's Brera Academy, crowned his exceptional achievements in the relatively new genre of the Italian short story with *Senso* (1883), an astonishingly bold portrayal of anarchic female sexuality, given a much-admired cinematic treatment in our own century by Luchino Visconti. Most original of all the young voices clamouring for audience among the Scapigliatura was that of Carlo Dossi, whose experimental prose writing, anticipating many of the techniques associated with modernists such as Proust and Virginia Woolf, is still insufficiently valued and investigated by Italian readers.

That passionate embrace of the new which so powerfully conditions cultural response in Italy displayed itself, as the century neared its close, in an increasingly emphatic shift towards what was loosely labelled 'verismo', an acclimatization to Italian contexts, whether in fiction, opera, or drama, of the methods and approaches adopted in France by Flaubert, Zola, Daudet, and their imitators. It was in the region which had once formed the Kingdom of the Two Sicilies, rather than among the Scapigliati of the north, that this concentration on detailed realism, influenced by wider European perspectives on

IN THE AFTERMATH OF THE RISORGIMENTO many Italian artists sought to recapture its heroic moments in scenes like this one by Silvestro Lega, entitled *'Bersaglieri* with Austrian Prisoners', painted in Florence in 1861. Lega soon afterwards moved away from 'national' themes, preferring to concentrate on gentler subjects taken from nature and everyday life.

technological progress and the theories of Hegel, Marx, and Darwin, found its most vital expression. The long-lived Neapolitan Francesco De Sanctis, a profound influence on the Italian critical mainstream who had begun his career in revolt against the Bourbons, propounded ideas of Italian literature as essentially 'progressive' in overall character, nurtured rather than distracted by ideas from abroad. His theories were well exemplified, meanwhile, in the work of two gifted young Sicilian novelists, Luigi Capuana and Giovanni Verga. The former, having dedicated his first novel *Giacinta* to Émile Zola, devoted himself thereafter to the writing of what were essentially fictional case-histories whose protagonists, mostly female, are considered in relation to the social and psychological factors restricting them, a sequence culminating in the masterly *Il marchese di Roccaverdina* (1904), an unsparing portrayal of life in rural Sicily, its modern manners and customs those of a sclerotic medieval feudalism. For Verga, also, the Sicilian countryside provided a lethally effective backdrop for stories and novels depicting the struggles of the peasantry against the forces of bureaucratic exploitation and corruption at work in the island, forces legalized by the government of the new Italy, yet in reality perpetuating structures of control established under Sicily's various

TURIDDU REJECTS SANTUZZA, a scene from an early performance of Pietro Mascagni's *Cavalleria rusticana*. Based on Giovanni Verga's tale of a village tragedy in rural Sicily, the opera, first produced in Rome in 1890, quickly became a classic of the so-called *verisimo* style, via which Italian writers and composers of the *fin de siècle* could effectively explore subjects and characters taken from everyday life.

rulers in previous centuries. Large-scale works such as *I Malavoglia* (1881) and *Mastro-don Gesualdo* (1888) drew praise for their acid-sharp definitions of character and motive in terms of economic self-interest, family aggrandizement, and the paying-off of old scores between aristocracy and bourgeoisie. Verga's talents as a prose stylist of positively Flaubertian refinement lent him equal significance as a short-story writer, and D. H. Lawrence was among twentieth-century authors in various countries who consciously embraced the manner purveyed by the taut little episodes in *Novelle rusticane* and *Vita dei campi*.

Two of Verga's tales, *La lupa* and *Cavalleria rusticana*, were subsequently adapted by their author for the stage. If nothing has been said so far in this chapter about non-operatic Italian theatre, it is because the drama, in comparison to other arts during the period, occupied a decidedly unimportant role. Hardly anything of real substance was produced which might rank with the work of Goldoni, Gozzi, and Alfieri from the previous century, though several writers, Manzoni, Pellico, and Nievo among them, produced passable verse tragedies in the classic French mode. The Venetian actor-manager Giacinto Gallina and the Neapolitan *verista* Salvatore Di Giacomo meanwhile kept alive the dialect traditions so closely allied with their respective regions.

Otherwise *la prosa*, legitimate theatre, was continuously overshadowed by *la lirica*, opera, whose stages it often shared and whose methods of production it mostly employed. In the latter respect, indeed, there has been little advance in Italy during the past hundred years. No national company for the performance of spoken drama has been formed, and it is only owing to the initiative of certain inspired and enterprising directors that theatres have been able sporadically to develop a house style and a repertory system. Productions continue to be based around barnstorming stars and to operate on a touring basis, much as they did during the later nineteenth century, when the Italian stage was dominated by the presence of two great actresses, Adelaide Ristori and Eleonora Duse.

Ristori, celebrated for her interpretations of Alfieri, Racine, and Shakespeare, was as well known abroad as in her own country, and the testimony of such distinguished London theatre-goers as Charles Dickens, Matthew Arnold, and Queen Victoria bears out an impression of her as the finest international tragedienne between Rachel and Sarah Bern-

THOUGH THE SPOKEN DRAMA in Italy languished during the age of bel canto opera, certain great Italian actresses achieved an international reputation. Adelaide Ristori thrilled audiences throughout mid-nineteenth-century Europe in roles such as Alfieri's Mirra and Shakespeare's Lady Macbeth. Here she appears in a French play as Marie Antoinette preparing to face the guillotine.

hardt. Duse, during a sensational career which included well-publicized affairs with Arrigo Boito and the poet Gabriele D'Annunzio, effectively revolutionized the role of the serious actress by the insouciant naturalness of her stage manner, whether in comedy as Goldoni's *Mirandolina* or in sombrely tragic incarnations as the heroines of Ibsen and Verga. Both Anton Chekhov and Bernard Shaw acknowledged her impact on their respective concepts of drama, and her performances contributed crucially to the modernization of acting styles across Europe.

Without the certainties empowering writers, artists, and musicians during the Risorgimento, Italian culture at the end of the nineteenth century appears fascinatingly diffuse in its lack of focus and direction. It is tempting to see such blurring as a clear consequence of the political and social unrest which beset the nation as a whole during the 1880s and 1890s, but the relationship is not so simple. While a painting such as Pelizza da Volpedo's famous *Il quarto stato* deliberately sets out to echo the mood of discontent among the new urban working class, the stance adopted by the young Gabriele D'Annunzio in his 'decadent' novels of the 1890s is anything but critical of their aristocratic protagonists from a moral or sociological angle. One of the period's most consistently original talents, that of the Piedmontese sculptor Medardo Rosso, seems at first as though emerging directly from the everyday life of the boulevards of Paris, Milan, and Turin which inspired his more haunting images. Yet his attempt to embody the essential fluidity of movement within each figure through a distinctively unfinished modelling in bronze or wax sets these sculptures apart from the sort of contemporary authenticity which artists in other fields were so keen to register.

Paradoxically the age's loneliest voice belongs to its most public poet. By the time he died in 1907, Giosué Carducci had become a national institution, Italy's unofficial laureate, apparently unquenchable as a writer of verse, let alone as an essayist, editor, and critic. Whether he succeeded in his aim of making Italians more aware of their historic heritage or merely blew the earliest trumpet blasts of what would eventually triumph as Fascism is a debatable point, and his stock has declined drastically among Italians since 1945. Much of his verse directly linked with the historical past now appears faded and bombastic. It is the quieter, more reflective Carduccian muse, associated with his lonely childhood in the Tuscan Maremma, which emphasizes the disharmony within the *fin de siècle* Italian soul, the alienation between Italy's noisy attempts to establish its new significance on the world stage as an imperial power, and the survival, on the other hand, of immutable human values amid the peace of the countryside.

Younger artists shared little of Carducci's inherent unease as to the relationship of the individual with the surrounding socio-political turmoil or as to the correct modes of confronting it. *Verismo* had stirred a new generation of opera composers, who were also heavily influenced by the Wagnerian enthusiasm fostered in the recently reformed Italian music conservatoires. In the works of Pietro Mascagni and Ruggiero Leoncavallo, a more candid treatment of sexual passions is set against less socially exalted backgrounds than those which framed the operas of the bel canto, and the most promising of these younger talents, Giacomo Puccini (1858–1924), found himself moving in the same direction. Puccini was inspired by a performance of Verdi's *Aida* in 1886, but his style was influenced by Verismo and Wagner. Before the end of the century he had produced *Manon Lescaut* (1893), *La Bohème* (1896), and *Tosca* in 1900. He had been hailed by the aged Verdi as 'keeper of the seal of Italian music', and it seems appropriate to end this survey of the cultural scene in nineteenth-century Italy with Verdi's death in 1901. The loss of the 88-year-old composer shook the entire nation, as if a portion of its soul had been cut away.

❊ 9 ❊

POLITICS AND SOCIETY, 1870–1915

ADRIAN LYTTELTON

Church, State, and Society

THE occupation of Rome on 20 September 1870 reinforced the shaky prestige of the new Italian State. Less obviously, it strengthened parliamentary government. Victor Emanuel II had wanted to fight Prussia in alliance with France, and it was the civilian cabinet which held him back. When the French evacuated Rome, the government's political line was vindicated and the king's penchant for intrigue was curbed. On the other hand, the threat to the monarchy was reduced, as the republican followers of Mazzini lost their best rallying-cry ('Rome or Death!'). Mazzini himself died in 1872, deeply disillusioned with the new Italy he had done so much to make.

In the long term, however, the occupation of Rome raised as many problems as it solved. It finally buried any hope of a reconciliation between the new Italy and the Papacy. The 1871 Law of Guarantees gave the pope many of the rights of a sovereign. Envoys to the Vatican were to enjoy full diplomatic status. But the Law of Guarantees did not have the force of a treaty; it was an internal law of the Italian State and could be revised or repealed. For the Papacy, anything short of full territorial sovereignty was unacceptable. Pius IX declared that there could be no compromise between Christ and the Devil, and papal apologists denounced Italian unity as an unnatural and fictitious pretence. In the face of this unflinching hostility, it was difficult for the government to remain faithful to Cavour's ideal of 'a free Church in a free State'. The Law of Guarantees was a compromise; it recognized the Church's freedom to appoint bishops, but in practice retained a right of veto by making access to their property subject to government approval.

After the Vatican Council and the declaration of papal infallibility in July 1870 the liberal opposition within the Church itself was crushed. In 1871 the Vatican ruled that it was 'not expedient' (*non expedit*) for Catholics to vote in parliamentary elections. In practice, the ban on voting was widely ignored, but its effect was to make impossible the formation of a Catholic party in parliament. Having excluded itself from national politics, the Church devoted its

THE ITALIAN
OCCUPATION OF ROME
put an end to the
temporal power of the
popes as rulers of the
Papal States, but the
spiritual authority of the
pope as head of the
Catholic Church
remained intact. In the
view from *Punch* in 1870:
'Papa Pius (to King of
Italy): "I must needs
surrender the sword,
my son; but I keep the
keys!!"'.

attention to the conquest of civil society. This could only be achieved by the active involvement of the laity. The Opera dei Congressi was founded in 1874 to coordinate local Catholic initiatives in education and social work. By the middle 1880s a dense network of parish committees covered Lombardy and the Veneto, which was to remain the heartland of modern social and political Catholicism. The intransigents' aim was to organize the Catholic laity as a separate subculture in opposition to the liberal State and its principles. But they did not speak for all Catholics active in politics. The *non expedit* instruction did not apply to local elections, and many important cities, including Rome itself, came to be governed by 'clerico-moderate' alliances of Catholics and conservative liberals. The success of the Catholic movement in the south was much more limited. The bishops distrusted the idea of giving independence to the laity, and the parish clergy's ties to the local landowning élites made them reluctant to undertake social initiatives on behalf of the peasants. Piety continued to be expressed in the more traditional forms of the pilgrimage, the procession, and the festival in honour of the patron saint.

The conflict with the Church lay at the root of the liberal ruling class's sense of isolation. It encouraged the growth of a defensive siege mentality. How could the loyalty of the masses be won, or social stability preserved, without the help of the clergy? Sixty per cent of the Italian population were dependent on agriculture, and for the peasants and farm-labourers the new Italian State had brought few benefits and many hardships. It was associated with conscription, high taxation, and a free hand for landowners in local government. Even expenditure on elementary education was widely resented, as most peasants relied on the labour of their children in the fields. In 1871 only 31 per cent of the Italian population were literate, and in parts of the rural south the proportion was as low as 5 per cent. Ten years later, 43 per cent of children between the age of 6 and 12 were still not attending school. In these circumstances, the clergy were often the only source of information about the wider world. An enlightened young liberal of the right, Sidney Sonnino, wrote that the Church provided the only ideals which illuminated the grim misery of peasant life. The appropriation of Church lands and wealth by the State generally worsened the peasants' position. In some fertile areas, where fruit or

A RELIGIOUS PROCESSION in the Abruzzi. The mountainous region of the Abruzzi was famous for the intensity of popular religious devotion. Processions and festivals were an important way of affirming the identity of the local community, often in rivalry with its neighbours, and, unlike other public activities, they allowed women to play a leading role.

PEASANTS AT GENAZZANO, east of Rome. Most peasants, particularly in the south, viewed the new Italian state with hostility or indifference. Poor communications maintained the isolation of rural communities; the mule was the essential form of transport.

wine could be profitably produced for the market, a minority of rich peasants benefited from the sale of Church lands. But for the majority, the change of ownership meant harsher tenancy terms and greater difficulty in access to credit. In southern Italy municipal governments plundered the resources of the Monti di Pietà (grain banks set up to make loans to the peasants at a low rate of interest).

Agriculture and Industry (1870–1896)

There is much evidence for a generally worsening standard of living in rural Italy between 1870 and 1900. On average, three-quarters of the income of peasant households was spent on food, and their diet was often barely sufficient to avoid starvation. In northern Italy, where the staple food was *polenta* (cornmeal, made from maize), vitamin deficiency caused an increase in the terrible disease of pellagra, which led to insanity and death. The south did not suffer from this scourge, but in many areas, particularly the coastal plains, malaria was endemic. Deforestation, erosion, and consequent flooding caused the disease to spread further than before. It was reckoned that two million people suffered from malaria every year, and in the south it accounted for about a quarter of all deaths. The first serious inquiries into social conditions in the south and Sicily revealed a picture of general misery and exploitation. The 1870s and the 1880s were the years of the discovery of the 'real Italy', and the reality was often profoundly depressing. The monumental parliamentary inquiry into agriculture by the Jacini Commission provided evidence of the backwardness of agricultural techniques and the slow rate of improvement in most regions of Italy. Some areas, however, did experience a rise in prosperity as the building of railways and free trade promoted specialization and production for export. The wine-producers of Apulia and the growers of oranges and lemons in Sicily were among those who profited.

Even the modest progress of the first decades after Unification was put in jeopardy by the agricultural crisis of the 1880s, marked by the falling price of wheat and other staple products. Consumers benefited from lower prices, but unemployment rose as the profits of landowners and farmers disappeared. The origins of the crisis lay in the reduction in shipping charges which allowed the produce of North America and Argentina to flood the European market, but this also facilitated the response of mass emigration. Before the 1870s only the seafaring Ligurians had emigrated to the Americas in any large numbers. In the first decade of the agricultural depression the north, and particularly the Veneto, provided most of the emigrants. The majority travelled only a short distance to France, Switzerland, or Germany. But between 1885 and 1896 there was a mass emigration from the northern regions to the American continent, where Argentina and Brazil were the most favoured destinations.

Along with the peasants, there was a sizeable contingent of middle-class Italians seeking their fortune. Buenos Aires became one of the cities of the world most heavily populated by Italians. But emigration from the south to the Americas grew even more rapidly; by the 1890s 60 per cent of all transoceanic emigrants were southerners, and in the 1900s the proportion rose to 70 per cent. Most southern emigrants went to the United States. Among the emigrants men greatly outnumbered women, and many male emigrants returned to get married or to rejoin the families they had left behind in Italy. The stream of cash remittances from emigrants to their families was a vital resource for the Italian economy. Together with the income from tourism, it allowed Italy to compensate for a negative balance of trade and to purchase the raw materials and machinery needed for industrialization.

The crisis of the 1880s destroyed the lingering illusion that agricultural development could be the key to future prosperity. One of the leading priorities of the first Italian governments had been the construction of a national railway network: between 1861 and 1870 the length of railway track almost trebled. But Italian industry was too weak to profit from the demand this generated for rails and rolling-stock. After 1876 the governments of the left proved more receptive to the demands of industry. Piedmont and Lombardy were the leading regions of textile production, but the largest and most modern industrial firm in the country was created by the wool-manufacturer Alessandro Rossi at Schio in the Veneto. Rossi ran Schio like a little kingdom, taking care of everything from town-planning to education and the theatre. A pious Catholic, who criticized liberalism for its indifference to social issues, he was also a tireless lobbyist for tariff protection. The Depression gave Rossi a chance to ally with agricultural interests. Astutely, he threw his weight behind the demands of the wheat- and rice-growers of northern Italy for a high tariff on imports. The third element in the protectionist alliance, along with the cotton- and wool-manufacturers and the grain-producers, was the industrialists in iron, steel, and heavy engineering.

In the age of iron and steel, Italy's large merchant fleet of sailing-ships was faced by obsolescence. Shipowners and shipbuilders, heavily concentrated in and around Genoa, appealed successfully for government subsidies and contracts to help them modernize. The shipbuilders' strongest argument was that their industries were essential for national defence. They found an ally in the ambitious navy minister Benedetto Brin. Brin was a brilliant naval engineer, who was personally responsible for the revolutionary design of the ironclad battleship *Duilio*, launched in 1876. Even the British were impressed by the size of its cannon and the thickness of its hull. When Brin became navy minister for the second time in 1884, he embarked upon a construction programme which almost doubled the size of the Italian fleet and by 1890 had made Italy into the third naval power in the world. According to Brin, national security demanded that not only the ships but also the steel should be Italian. He sponsored the creation of a large steelworks at Terni, in southern Umbria. The site, far from the coast and from adequate supplies of iron ore, was chosen for military rather than economic reasons, and the Terni firm remained heavily dependent on navy contracts for its survival. The naval-industrial complex contributed only a small percentage of Italy's total industrial production, but it exercised a political influence out of all proportion to its size.

Between 1881 and 1888 industrial production grew at the rate of 4.6 per cent a year, but this advance rested on shaky financial and political foundations. The protectionist tariff of 1887 was followed by the breakdown of negotiations for a new commercial treaty with France. The disastrous tariff war of 1888–90 halved Italian exports to France, and the worst sufferers were the southern producers of wine, olive oil, and fruit. The most dynamic sector of southern agriculture regressed, while inefficient, low-yielding grain production was sheltered by the tariff. Even large landowners, except in Sicily, had not been enthusiastic about protection, but they could adapt to the new situation more easily than the peasants. Nor, in the short run, did the tariff bring the expected gains for industry. The indirect results of the tariff war helped to provoke a major financial crisis in 1889. The withdrawal of foreign capital and the slump in the property market led to a general collapse of the banking system, which culminated at the end of 1893 with the crash of the two leading commercial banks in Italy, the Credito Mobiliare and the Banca Generale. Industry was badly hit by the credit shortage and by forced reductions in State expenditure, and production remained stagnant until 1896. The effects of the banking crisis on the political system were equally serious, as we shall see.

The Left in Power: From Depretis to Crispi

The years from 1861 to 1882 were the only period in Italy's parliamentary history when a kind of two-party system prevailed. The elections were seen as a

Facing: THE STATUE OF THE WEAVER, in Schio (Veneto), dedicated by the wool manufacturer Alessandro Rossi to his workmen. The statue illustrates Rossi's paternalism, typical of Italian textile industrialists of the first generation, and his attempt to promote the work ethic through the idealization of the thrifty, honest skilled worker.

GERMANY

SWITZERLAND

AUSTRIA

FRANCE

Trento

FRIULI

VENETO

Trieste

Turin

Milan

LOMBARDY

PIEDMONT

Mantua

Venice

LIGURIA

Modena

Ferrara

Bologna

Genoa

EMILIA

ROMAGNA

Ravenna

DALMATIA

Nice

PR. OF MONACO

Pisa

Florence

REP. OF SAN MARINO

Livorno

TUSCANY

Ancona

Perugia

UMBRIA

THE MARCHES

ADRIATIC SEA

CORSICA
(Fr.)

Aquila

ABRUZZO

Rome

MOLISE

Foggia

APULIA

Bari

Sassari

Naples

Potenza

BASILICATA

SARDINIA

Cagliari

TYRRHENIAN SEA

Cosenza

CALABRIA

M E D I T E R R A N E A N   S E A

Trapani

Palermo

Milazzo

Messina

Aspromonte

Marsala

SICILY

Catania

Girgenti

——— Boundary of Northern Italy

TUNISIA

0   200 km

ALGERIA

MALTA (Br.)

ITALY IN 1870

confrontation between left and right, even if in reality both parties were deeply divided, not least by regional differences. The main weakness of the right was in the south, where its policy of centralization and fiscal rigour was made still more unpalatable by the prevalence of northerners in the administration. The southern middle classes complained of discrimination in the distribution of taxation and in the allocation of public expenditure. In the elections of 1874 a heavy defeat in the south reduced the right's majority to a margin of forty-two. The right's fall in 1876 was caused by the defection of a large group of Tuscan deputies, with strong financial connections, who voted against the government's plan to nationalize the entire railway system. They had previously been angered by the refusal to compensate Florence for the transfer of the capital to Rome. So the right's policy foundered on the opposition of regional and financial interests. The victory of the left was also a victory for the professional middle classes over the landowning aristocracy. Whereas the latter often disdained active campaigning, trusting in their inherited influence and social prestige, a new class of ambitious lawyers made politics into a second profession.

The 1882 electoral reform gave the vote to all men who could prove literacy and trebled the electorate. But the leader of the parliamentary left, Agostino Depretis, was afraid that the reform might give too much influence to the radical and republican opposition. Rather than using the reform to consolidate the ascendancy of the left, Agostino Depretis opted for an alliance with Marco Minghetti and the moderate right. This was the origin of the celebrated system of *trasformismo*. At the time there was a widespread belief that the old distinctions between the parties had become obsolete. However, *trasformismo* soon became a synonym for corrupt compromise. There had been a tendency on both left and right to strengthen local political associations and to try to coordinate them at the national level. *Trasformismo* reversed this tendency. Henceforward, majorities were to be formed by governments, not parties. The change did not bring about a strong, united centre bloc as hoped. The majority coalition was a loose conglomeration of local and personal groups, held together by patronage and Depretis's skill in mediation. The 1880s saw the flourishing of anti-parliamentary polemics. Most of the critics came from the old right, and their views were undoubtedly coloured by resentment at their defeat. But their criticisms had substance. Minghetti and Silvio Spaventa attacked the partisan interference of politicians in the workings of justice and administration, and the young Sicilian intellectual Giovanni Mosca, the founder of élite theory, exposed the mechanisms by which small cliques of 'grand electors' determined the choice of candidates. However, it was not the right which benefited from the growing disillusionment. Revulsion against the system of *trasformismo* allowed the leader of the intransigent left, Francesco Crispi, to take over from Depretis in 1887.

In contrast to the cautious Depretis, the Sicilian Crispi personified eloquence, passion, and the patriotic heritage of Garibaldi. He brought a new energy to government, and his first administration carried through an impressive programme of reforms. The State acquired new powers to regulate public health and charitable institutions. Tighter control over the Opere Pie (Catholic charities) satisfied both social reformers and anticlericals. The Council of State was reformed in an attempt to check administrative abuses. The local electorate was doubled, to match the national suffrage reform of 1882, and for the first time mayors were made elective instead of being nominated by the government. At the same time, however, the control over local administration by the prefects was strengthened, and so was the latter's dependence on the minister of the interior. The increase in grass-roots democracy was balanced and circumscribed by an increase in centralization. The progressive minister of justice, Zanardelli, introduced a new penal code which abolished the death penalty, reduced prison sentences for many other offences, and confirmed the right to strike. But here again liberal innovations were counterbalanced by stronger controls over associations and an extension of the system of police detention.

In spite of Crispi's past opposition to *trasformismo*, his victory did not lead to a restoration of the two-party system, but to a reinforcement of the government bloc. Between 1881 and 1887 the south had given strong backing to the dissident left opposition of Crispi and Giovanni Nicotera; after 1887 it became a reservoir of support for all governments, whether they were of the left or the right. The southern deputies were finally appeased by ready access to government patronage. They acted as mediators between the central government and their constituents. It was vital for their success that the flow of patronage should not be interrupted. In addition, the minister of the interior (who was usually also the prime minister) had other means of persuasion at his disposal. Through the police and the prefects he could intervene directly in local politics, by transferring government officials and magistrates, by sanctioning electoral fraud, and by outright intimidation. Elections did not make governments; the government made elections.

In Campania and Sicily the success of government candidates was often due to an alliance with the organized crime networks of the Camorra and the Mafia respectively. In Naples, the influence of the Camorra on the city administration declined after 1900, thanks to a muck-raking campaign in which the Socialists played a leading role. The Mafia, on the other hand, preserved its sinister power intact. The attempt of the governments of the right to suppress banditry in Sicily by orthodox police methods had met with failure, because of the lack of cooperation of local landowners and notables, who relied on the Mafia for protection. The governments of the Left, instead, came to accept that the Mafia was indispensable for the preservation of a minimum of social order, as well as for electoral support. The Mafia's own informal system of justice was certainly more effective than that of the State. The price, however, was high. On the eve of the war, the homicide rate in the Sicilian province of Agrigento was thirty times that in some northern provinces. In return for their protection of landlords, mafiosi, as leaseholders and middlemen, took the lion's share of profits. They continued to organize cattle-rustling on a large scale. The Mafia's attitude to crime and social order was essentially ambivalent; mafiosi acted as arbitrators between criminals and the police, peasants and landlords, and posed as the guardians of Sicilian pride against government intrusion.

The Triple Alliance and the Beginnings of Italian Colonialism

For the governments of the right, the need to balance the budget and to consolidate Italy's international legitimacy had dictated a cautious foreign policy. They had avoided binding commitments or alliances. The first governments of the left followed their example, but in the agitated period which opened with the Eastern crisis of 1875–8, it became harder to follow a policy of neutrality. A vocal public opinion demanded that Italy be compensated for the gains of other powers. Competition with France for economic and political influence in Tunis provoked the French government to establish their protectorate in 1881. The shock caused by the French occupation of Tunis drove Italy into the arms of Bismarck. While sectors of the left hankered after the unredeemed territories of Trento and Trieste (*terra irredenta*) and still saw Austria-Hungary as the main enemy, King Umberto exercised decisive pressure for a conservative alliance with the two emperors Francis Joseph and William I. The Triple Alliance between Germany, Austria-Hungary, and Italy, signed in May 1882, was the complement in foreign policy to *trasformismo* in domestic politics. It divided the moderate left from the republicans and the irredentist enemies of Austria, isolated republican France, reinforced the prestige of the monarchy, and opened the way for an expansion of the armed forces. In the next four years military expenditure increased by 40 per cent. While parliament could control internal policy, the Triple Alliance allowed the monarchy to reassert its constitutional right to have the last say on foreign and military affairs. Treaties did not have to be submitted to parliament, and the terms of the Triple Alliance remained secret.

Until 1881 Italian governments had regarded colonies as a costly extravagance, but in the era of the scramble for Africa, it was impossible to isolate public opinion from the imperialist fever. After Tunis, the acquisition of a colony seemed a cheap way to appease nationalist opinion and to confirm Italy's new status as a great power. The British government viewed the establishment of an Italian presence in East Africa with favour, as a counterweight to the French, and in 1885 Italy occupied the port of Massaua. But the local military command blundered into a confrontation with the Ethiopians, and in January 1887 a column of 500 Italian soldiers was wiped out at Dogali. The impact of the disaster can be compared with that of the death of Gordon at Khartoum on England two years earlier. There is nothing like a good massacre to excite patriotic opinion, and the catastrophe had a fundamental role in bringing Crispi to power. Dogali was also important because it consolidated the association of corrupt parliamentary government at home with timidity and incompetence abroad.

Crispi had abandoned his republicanism because he came to believe that the monarchy was an indispensable guarantee for Italian unity. However, he was convinced that to survive the monarchy had to be transformed. It had to abandon its exclusive Piedmontese and aristocratic traditions and become genuinely Italian and popular. Crispi was an enthusiastic promoter of initiatives designed to foster a popular cult of the monarchy. It was he who proposed the burial of Victor Emanuel II in the Pantheon, and in 1884 he attacked Depretis for putting obstacles in the way of a mass pilgrimage to the king's tomb. But in the age of imperialism, something more was required to establish the prestige of the monarchy on a secure foundation: overseas expansion and the display of military strength.

Crispi was determined that Italy should no longer be a passive junior partner in the Triple Alliance. He strengthened ties with Germany, and in 1888 a military convention was signed under which Italy undertook to send five army corps to the Rhine in case of a war with France and Russia. Crispi's well-advertised friendship with Bismarck, his aggressive rhetoric, and Brin's naval building programme combined to raise tension with France to dangerous heights. The repercussions were very serious. Apart from the tariff war and the closure of the French financial market to Italian loans, the reconciliation between Leo XIII and the Third Republic revived fears of French interference in the Roman question. In the same years, popular anti-French feeling was aroused by the frequent outbursts of xenophobia towards Italian immigrant workers. These culminated in the riots of Aigues-Mortes in 1893, in which eight Italians were killed.

Financial Crisis, the Bank Scandals, and the Failure of Crispi

In parliament, the continuous growth of military expenditure came under increasing criticism from both left and right. The conservative Stefano Jacini attacked Crispi's 'megalomania', while the Radicals drew attention to the role of taxation in depressing popular living standards. Although the left had kept its promise to abolish the notoriously unpopular tax on flour-milling, taxes on consumption had nevertheless risen considerably. 'Carefree finance' had produced a serious budget deficit. The financial question precipitated Crispi's fall in 1891. A new government was formed under the Sicilian aristocrat Di Rudinì, the leader of the dissident right, with thrift as its watchword. But Rudinì's programme of economies foundered on the refusal of the king and the ministers of war and the navy to agree to cuts in military expenditure. To the general surprise, he was replaced by Giovanni Giolitti, who had won a reputation as a financial expert. He owed his elevation to the backing of the minister of the royal household, Urbano Rattazzi, King Umberto's *éminence grise*; Giolitti, a former bureaucrat, was the first prime minister not to have played an active role in the Risorgimento, and he was attacked on this count, as well as for being a creature of court intrigue. Throughout his career, his refusal to engage in high-flown patriotic rhetoric made him vulnerable to the accusation of lacking ideals. More justifiably, he was criticized for using particularly heavy-handed methods to secure a majority in the elections of 1892. But Giolitti was far more than the grey bureaucrat and corrupt manipulator that his enemies made him out to be. He was genuinely convinced of the need to alleviate the suffering and discontent of the masses. This could only be done by restraining unproductive expenditures, lightening the burden of taxation, and adopting a more tolerant attitude to working-class and peasant organizations. This last policy, however, was too advanced for the times.

Under Socialist leadership, a vast peasant agitation broke out in Sicily in 1893. By the autumn it seemed to be turning to outright revolt, with the burning of tax-offices and other acts of violence. Giolitti's refusal to authorize wholesale repressive measures lost him support both in parliament and at court. But he was brought down for less creditable reasons. The crisis of the banking system precipitated the greatest scandal in Italian political history until the outbreak of *tangentopoli* a hundred years later. Regional interests had blocked the creation of a single central bank with a monopoly of note-issue. The right to print banknotes was shared between six different banks. A parliamentary investigation revealed that one of them, the Banca Romana, had exceeded its legally permitted circulation by almost 100 per cent, and that large sums from the surplus had been used to bribe politicians and journalists. As the prime minister in office, Giolitti bore the brunt of the scandal. He had almost certainly used the bank to buy support, and he had promoted its president Tanlongo to the Senate. But ironically Crispi, who returned to power in December 1893, was even more deeply and discreditably implicated. Unlike Giolitti, whose personal honesty was beyond question, Crispi had accepted money directly from the Banca Romana to pay his debts.

Crispi's new government combined reaction at home with adventure abroad. He lost no time in proclaiming martial law in Sicily and sending 40,000 troops to restore order. He suggested, and perhaps believed, that behind the upheaval there was a French intrigue designed to separate Sicily from Italy. It is only fair to say that Crispi did not believe that he could solve Sicily's problems by repression alone. He tried to introduce a major measure of land reform to compel the owners of the large estates (*latifondi*) to grant their peasants long leases. Predictably, however, the reform was blocked by landlord opposition. In October 1894 Crispi dissolved the Socialist Party and arrested its deputies. To obtain a more manageable electorate, he disenfranchised over 800,000 voters, almost a third of the total. When the truth about his involvement with the Banca Romana surfaced at the end of 1894, he prorogued the Chamber of Deputies, and kept it closed for five months, before 'making' new elections. Crispi did not conceal his conviction that parliamentary government in Italy was impossible, and he almost succeeded in reducing it to a mere façade for the absolute rule of the executive. Yet he was not able to silence parliamentary opposition, or even to eliminate dissent within his own cabinet. This increased his need for a spectacular success abroad.

Crispi had come to power with the promise to avenge the shame of Dogali. Italian diplomacy seemed to have triumphed in 1889 when the new emperor, Menelik, signed the Treaty of Uccialli. This allowed Italy to occupy additional territory and to proclaim the official foundation of the colony of Eritrea in 1890. But the Italian claim that the treaty established a protectorate over the whole of Ethiopia was deliberately not made clear in the Amharic version of the text. Angered by the deception, Menelik repudiated the treaty in 1893. Faced with the failure of his diplomacy, Crispi was prepared to give the military a free hand. At the same time the conservative minister of the treasury, Sonnino, insisted on the need to limit expenditure. The result was that the army lacked the troops and the resources necessary to overcome the reaction of the Ethiopian Empire, whose strength had been grossly underestimated. On 1 March 1896 an ill-planned advance led to the destruction of the Italian force of 17,000 near Adowa by the huge Ethiopian army. It was by far the worst disaster ever suffered by a colonial power in Africa. Crispi expected the king's support, but, faced with mass demonstrations in the streets and strong opposition even in the conservative Senate, Umberto decided to make him the scapegoat. It was clear, none the less, that the monarchy had been seriously weakened, and its role and future became the central theme of Italian politics during the next four years.

Italy's first bid for empire in Africa had failed because it was launched at a time when the crisis in State finances and the general poverty of the nation made it impossible to mobilize resources on a sufficient scale. As in other countries, colonialism was a mythical solution to real problems. A key motif in colonialist propaganda, which had considerable appeal in the south, was that colonies would absorb mass emigration. Crispi declared that Ethiopia would provide an outlet for 'that overflowing Italian fecundity which now goes to other civilized countries . . . and is lost to the motherland'. The enlightened conservative Leopoldo Franchetti tried to promote peasant colonization in Eritrea to help to relieve the pressures of the agrarian crisis. But his effort, which was not backed by the colonial authorities, was a total failure. During the period 1890–1905 three and a half million Italians emigrated, and at the end of that time the Italian population of Eritrea numbered about 4,000, mostly soldiers and their families.

The Rise of Socialism

The denunciation of the Paris Commune in 1871 by Mazzini alienated many of his younger intellectual supporters. They formed the general staff of the First International in Italy, which followed the anarchist principles of Bakunin. Bakunin, who had lived in Naples between 1865 and 1867, believed that the prevalence of brigandage was a symptom of the revolutionary potential of the Italian peasants. However, the Italian anarchists were no more successful than the Risorgimento revolutionaries in rousing the peasants. Instead, the anarchists had considerable success among urban artisans, particularly in the Romagna, the Marches, and Tuscany. The failure of their attempts at insurrection led to a decline of anarchism after 1878, but the persistence of the anarchist tradition helps to explain why these regions remained the breeding-ground of revolutionary socialism and subversion.

Meanwhile artisans, factory-workers, and some peasants acquired the habit of organization through the mutual aid societies. These were promoted by both moderate liberals and Mazzinians. They embodied the principle of self-help, and provided minimal benefits to meet the costs of funerals and sickness. They also organized night-schools and reading-rooms. By the 1880s the mutual aid societies in the more industrialized regions of Italy were becoming increasingly independent and resentful of bourgeois patronage. Meanwhile, the first long-sustained industrial strikes had broken out among the wool-workers of Biella, in the Alpine valleys of Piedmont. Many of these workers owned small plots of land, and liberals were disconcerted to find that this did not make them more conservative, but, on the contrary, gave them the resources for continued resistance. These developments, and the expansion of the suffrage, helped the spread of 'legalitarian' socialism and trade-unionism. The former anarchist Andrea Costa founded the Revolutionary Socialist Party of the Romagna in 1881. In spite of its name, the party rejected insurrection in favour of legal methods, and in 1882 Costa became the first Socialist deputy to be elected to parliament. In Lombardy, the Italian Workers' Party broke free from the Radicals in 1885. It rejected electoral politics in favour of economic action through trade unions and strikes. Its platform was rather similar to that of the British Labour party, but the difference was that it lacked the support of a strong, established trade union movement. The party was unable to extend its influence outside Lombardy, but it had surprising success in penetrating the countryside, thanks to the agricultural depression. The first great strikes of agricultural labourers broke out in the province of Mantua in 1884–5. The government was so alarmed by this unexpected development that it tried to suppress the Workers' Party.

Government repression had an unintended result. It brought together working-class leaders and sympathetic middle-class intellectuals, who could publicize their cause and defend them in court. One of these, the young Milanese lawyer Filippo Turati, took the lead in trying to organize a national party inspired by socialist principles. The foundation of the Italian Socialist Party is normally dated from the Genoa Congress of 1892, although the name was not adopted until 1895. Turati had a hard time establishing his authority against opposition from 'labourites' and anarchists. But the new party was much strengthened by the adherence of Costa. Reformists and revolutionaries could coexist in the new party because, in theory, reform was only a step towards revolution, and revolution was only possible through the gradual, evolutionary development of working-class consciousness. This was the orthodoxy of the Second International, and Turati's strategy of alliance with the bourgeois Radicals to defend liberty against Crispi had the authoritative approval of Friedrich Engels.

In spite of repression, the Socialists rapidly increased their following not only among industrial workers but among the landless labourers. In the 1897 elections, the Socialist Party elected seventeen deputies; four came from the big cities of Milan, Turin, and Florence, but nine from the rural areas of the Po Valley. Although the decline of peasant farming and the rise of wage labour had already weakened the hold of the Church in the plains, the Socialist Party avoided challenging religion head-on. The 'evangelical Socialists', like Camillo Prampolini in Reggio Emilia, conveyed the message that Jesus had been the first socialist, and that the latter-day Church had betrayed his teaching. The propagandists spread the socialist message in the villages by the use of parables and quotations from the Gospels. This contrasted with the attitude prevalent among urban socialists. The influence of both Freemasonry and the anarchist tradition favoured the diffusion of free thought and hostility to established religion.

During the 1890s the party attracted growing support among intellectuals and in the universities.

FILIPPO TURATI in 1908. Turati, who came from a well-off Milanese family, was the leader of the moderate or reformist wing of the Italian Socialist party and its most eminent parliamentarian.

The Socialist leaders' constancy in the face of persecution won admiration, and in many ways they seemed to be the most courageous defenders of the democratic heritage of the Risorgimento left. Turati's evolutionary socialism was as much positivist as Marxist. It appealed to the belief in progress through science and education. Socialism was also associated with the cause of female emancipation. The brilliant Russian revolutionary exile Anna Kuliscioff became Turati's lifelong companion, after an earlier affair with Andrea Costa. In both relationships, the dominant intellectual influence was at first unquestionably hers. She was one of the first women to fight for admission to the medical profession, and she was active in organizing women workers in Milan. However, most socialists were understandably nervous about campaigning for votes for women, in view of clerical influence. In fact, for the same reasons the Socialists were hesitant even in demanding universal male suffrage. This was to be a serious problem at a later date, but until 1900 the party was still engaged in the struggle for basic civil and political liberties.

ANNA KULISCIOFF. Of Russian origin, Kuliscioff was the companion of Turati. She was in the forefront of efforts to secure the rights of women in the professions and in the workplace.

The *non expedit* prevented the Catholic movement from engaging in national politics. But it became clear in these years that the Catholics were serious competitors in the field of mass organization. Leo XIII's famous encyclical on the social question, *Rerum Novarum* (1891), gave a new stimulus to the Catholic movement by calling for action to redress the injustices of capitalism. Trade unions were permitted, although the emphasis was on the need for collaboration between classes, and strike action was frowned upon. This limited the Catholic movement's appeal for industrial workers and wage-labourers, but it was more successful than the Socialists in catering for the needs of peasant farmers. Its most intelligent initiative was the provision of cheap credit through rural banks (*casse rurali*); the priests' knowledge of their parishioners was indispensable in avoiding bad risks, and their role in social control was further reinforced. The Catholic subculture became as solidly implanted in the Veneto and northern Lombardy as the socialist in Emilia-Romagna.

The End-of-Century Crisis

The reaction to Adowa combined with resentment against high taxes and acute economic suffering to produce mounting popular discontent. In this situation, conservatives began to wonder if the survival of the monarchy was compatible with the existing form of parliamentary government. Sonnino took the lead in calling for a 'return to the Statute', which meant restoring to the crown the effective right to appoint ministers. Sonnino believed that a government with greater independence from parliament would be able not only to keep order but to push through social and economic reforms. But his proposal failed to unite the right. Di Rudinì believed that it would put the

monarchy at risk by exposing it to direct political responsibility. Rather than pursuing a clear design, the king, the court party, and the conservatives stumbled into an authoritarian course out of fear. A sharp rise in grain prices in 1898 touched off riots throughout Italy. When the workers of Milan took to the streets in May, the king and the Rudinì government panicked and introduced martial law. Although the demonstrators were unarmed, more than 100 were killed and over 400 wounded. The military commander, General Bava Beccaris, used artillery to storm a Capuchin monastery under the false impression that it was a revolutionary headquarters. He was rewarded by a special decoration from King Umberto. The government used the fear of revolution to justify sweeping measures of repression. Radical newspapers were banned, trade unions were suppressed, and the Socialist leaders were arrested and sentenced to long terms of imprisonment. The Catholic social movement received similar treatment. Any form of popular organization was suspect, and Di Rudinì was personally convinced that social Catholicism was a tool of the Papacy in its long-standing efforts to subvert the Italian State.

The repression of the Catholics, however, divided the cabinet and forced Di Rudinì to resign. The king took the opportunity to send for a general, Luigi Pelloux, to head the next government. Pelloux was a senator who had ties with the moderate left in parliament, and at first his appointment was seen as a gesture of pacification. But in February 1899 he introduced new legislation to punish strikes, ban meetings, and limit the freedom of the press. In May the king authorized him to promulgate further repressive measures without the consent of parliament. Nevertheless, faced with parliamentary obstruction by the Socialists, and the opposition of Giolitti and Zanardelli, the government threw in its hand and called elections. Pelloux succeeded in winning a majority, but only thanks to government influence in the south. In the rest of Italy, the opposition parties won more than half the seats, and the Socialists doubled their representation, from sixteen to thirty-three seats. This was equivalent to a moral defeat, and Pelloux resigned. In July 1900 King Umberto was assassinated by the anarchist Gaetano Bresci, an emigrant worker from Paterson, New Jersey, in revenge for his role in the repression of 1898. His successor, Victor Emanuel III, drew the lesson from his father's political failure and embarked on a new course of respect for parliamentary government.

Facing: SOLDIERS AND BARRICADES in Milan, 1898. Riots provoked by the high cost of living turned into a bloody confrontation with the army and the police. The rioters built makeshift barricades, although there was no plan for insurrection.

Italy's Industrial Revolution

One of the conditions for the renewed growth of industry was the reorganization of the financial sector. Giolitti's creation of the Bank of Italy in 1893 put an end to the monetary disorder of the old banking system, even though the Banks of Naples and Sicily retained the privilege of issuing notes as a concession to southern interests. In 1894 the Banca Commerciale was founded in

Milan, with German capital, and under German management. It was the first and most important of the German-type mixed banks, which combined deposit banking with both short-term and long-term credit. They were far more successful than their predecessors in raising capital for industry, and they helped to diffuse entrepreneurial and managerial skills.

The end of the long, worldwide depression in 1896 gave Italian industry the stimulus it needed to achieve the breakthrough into sustained growth. Between 1896 and 1913 Italy experienced the fastest rate of growth in per capita product of any major European country. Industry grew at the rate of about 5 per cent a year, and agriculture at over 2 per cent. A new generation of entrepreneurs, many of them trained as engineers in the polytechnics of Milan and Turin, seized the opportunities presented by the technological innovations of the 'second industrial revolution'. The development of the hydroelectrical industry was of particular importance, since it freed Italy from total dependence on imported coal as an energy source. In the development of this capital-intensive industry the role of the mixed banks was decisive. Turin, which had hitherto lagged behind Milan as an industrial centre, took the lead in the new automobile industry. Unlike other industrial products, cars had glamorous associations with speed and sport; the famous Fiat firm was founded by a group of young aristocrats and former cavalry officers. One of them, Giovanni Agnelli, became Italy's most famous entrepreneur. After a visit to the USA in 1912, Agnelli began to introduce Ford's methods of assembly-line production to produce a cheaper, 'utility' model of car. As a producer of submarine engines and aeroplanes, Fiat was well placed to meet the demands of war as well as peace. The older Pirelli rubber firm became Italy's first multinational enterprise, and benefited from the expansion of the car industry to establish a commanding position in tyre manufacture. The creator of another household name in Italian industry, Camillo Olivetti, produced his first typewriters in 1911.

Milan led Italian cities into the world of mass consumption and the mass media. It had the first modern department stores and the first modern newspapers; by 1913 the *Corriere della Sera* had a circulation of 350,000 copies, and its weekly, the *Domenica del Corriere*, reached 1.5 million. By 1910 about 500 cinemas had opened, forty in Milan alone, and before the war Italian film-producers were exporting spectacular historical epics like *Cabiria* to the United States. But there was another side to the story.

First of all, industry remained heavily concentrated in the industrial triangle. In 1911 the three regions of Lombardy, Piedmont, and Liguria accounted for more than half of Italian industrial production and 57 per cent of the total population were still employed in agriculture. Secondly, the success of Italy in the new industries should not lead one to ignore the importance of textiles, which employed about a quarter of the industrial labour force, and accounted

for 60 per cent of manufacturing exports. Down to the crisis of 1907 textiles, and particularly cotton, experienced rapid growth and modernization; but recovery from the recession was slow, and prospects for future growth were not good. In spite of technical progress, the textile industries still relied heavily on underpaid female labour; three-quarters of all workers were women.

These backward sectors should not be forgotten when one considers the Italian working class and its organizations. The average real wages of industrial workers rose by about 40 per cent between 1900 and 1913. But only the 'labour aristocracy' of printers, skilled workers in the engineering industries, and craftsmen in the building trades achieved a standard of living comparable to that of the average working-class family in the advanced industrial nations. Although their diet was much superior to that of the peasants, most factory workers only ate meat on special occasions, and in Milan as much as 70 per cent of family income still went on food. Low wages made it hard to sustain trade unions. Waves of strikes were succeeded by a relapse into forced inactivity. However, Italian working-class leaders showed considerable ingenuity in circumventing these difficulties. The *camere del lavoro* (chambers of labour), modelled on the French *bourses du travail*, were organized by locality instead of occupation. This made it easier to achieve solidarity between different categories of workers, often expressed through local general strikes. It was in the *camere del lavoro* that the revolutionary syndicalists and intransigent socialists found their greatest support, while the trade federations tended to side with the reformists.

GIOVANNI GIOLITTI in 1908. The Piedmontese Giolitti was the leading statesman of the period between 1900 and 1914. He pursued a conciliatory policy towards the working-class movement and was responsible for the introduction of universal manhood suffrage. He was often condemned as an intriguer, but this photograph captures the decisive aspect of his personality.

Giolitti and Democracy

After 1900 a new liberalism developed under the leadership of Giolitti. His policy aimed to broaden the base of the liberal State by allowing free expression to the new political and social forces which his predecessors had tried to repress. The State administration should also take on a new role by mediating between workers and employers and by intervening actively to remove the causes of social protest. The government sought the cooperation of the reformist socialists in promoting welfare measures. The Supreme Council of Labour, founded in 1902, gave the trade unions a role in preparing social legislation. Laws were passed banning child labour, limiting the working hours of women, and setting up a maternity fund. In 1901, as minister of the interior in the Zanardelli government, Giolitti allowed the unions of rural labourers freedom to

AN OPEN-AIR ELEMENTARY SCHOOL in the Roman Campagna. Socialist intellectuals in Rome were shocked by conditions among the peasants of the Campagna and promoted special schools for their children. The Socialist party sponsored many efforts to improve popular education, but its Northern leaders were accused of paying too little attention to the backward rural areas south of Rome.

organize and strike. This had a dramatic impact. Over 200,000 agricultural workers came out on strike, compared with about 2,000 in 1899. At the same time the government assigned public works contracts to the labourers' co-operatives organized by the socialists as a means of combating unemployment. In effect, government, unions and cooperatives worked together to keep an explosive situation under control.

This strategy was attacked from both right and left. The capitalist farmers and landlords of the Po Valley, once they had got over their shock at the withdrawal of unconditional State support, began to organize effectively to resist strikes. The escalating conflict between their agrarian associations and the workers' *leghe* became increasingly hard to control. Giolitti's tolerance did not extend to the use of violence against blackleg labour, and conflicts between strikers and police remained frequent. In the south, Giolitti's entente with labour did not function. Unions were weak, popular protest often took the form of the bread riot or the assault on the town hall, and the police intervened with a heavy hand to preserve order. The killing of strikers or demonstrators by police gave the revolutionary factions in the Socialist Party an important argument against the reformists' policy of cooperation. The first movement which successfully challenged Turati's leadership was that of the revolutionary syndicalists, led by the Neapolitan Arturo Labriola. They accused the reformists of having neglected class struggle for parliamentary manœuvre, and called for a campaign of direct action, which culminated in the national general strike of 1904. They attacked the compromise between the reformists and Giolitti for favouring privileged minorities of northern workers, through social legislation and protectionism, at the expense of the peasants. Paradoxically, southern intellectuals like Labriola wanted to use the northern labour movement to destroy Giolitti's political system, which they saw as perpetuating corruption and poverty in the south. Even the historian Gaetano Salvemini, from Apulia, who belonged to the reformist wing of the party, eventually broke with Turati. In a famous book, *Il ministro della malavita* [The Minister of the Underworld], he attacked Giolitti as responsible for the collusion of government agents with the Mafia and other criminal groups.

The Socialists were not the only movement which Giolitti tried to appease. He was keenly aware of the immense potential of the Catholic movement, and saw it as a useful counterweight to the Socialists. Under the conservative Pius X a cautious *rapprochement* took place between Church and State. The pope's concern with the threat of Socialism led him to relax the *non expedit* in 1904 and to allow Catholic candidates to stand in 1909, though without forming a party. The more radical Christian Democrats were firmly restrained, and their leader, the priest Romolo Murri, was defrocked. Giolitti was glad to accept Catholic votes when the Socialists were proving obstreperous, but he was committed to a delicate balancing act, as politics at the constituency level became increasingly polarized between anticlericals and Freemasons on one side, and conservatives and the Church on the other.

In 1911 Giolitti unexpectedly adopted the cause of universal manhood suffrage. His ambitious aim was to bring the Socialists into the majority with the promise of a more energetic programme of social reforms, including the nationalization of life insurance, which would fund an old-age-pension scheme. But at this point the Moroccan crisis introduced an unpredictable variable into Giolitti's calculations. It gave Italy a chance to occupy Libya according to the terms of a previous agreement with France, and it was a chance he could not afford to miss without provoking a storm of injured national feeling. Giolitti seems to have believed that he could retain Socialist support, but even Turati was shocked by what he saw as Giolitti's betrayal, and in any case he was powerless to stem the tide of indignation which swept the party. In 1912 the revolutionary opposition of the 'intransigents' triumphed at the Reggio Emilia Congress, inspired by a fiery young orator from the Romagna, Benito Mussolini.

The victory of the intransigents spelled defeat for Giolitti's progressive strategy. In the 1913 elections, the first to be held with universal suffrage, the government kept its majority, but only with massive help from the Catholics. The president of the Catholic Electoral Union, Count Gentiloni, claimed that 228 out of 318 Liberal deputies owed their seats to the votes of his organization. In return they had promised, among other things, to oppose divorce and support religious education. Although many deputies denied the existence of

THE FIRST COLOUR ADVERTISEMENT for the new Fiat company, Turin, 1899. Under the leadership of Giovanni Agnelli, Fiat captured a commanding position in the Italian automobile industry which it has preserved to this day. Early car manufacturers, producing for a select and wealthy clientele, were concerned to convey an image of elegance and excitement.

AN EPISODE from the Libyan War, 1912. The calm heroism of the outnumbered Italian soldiers is contrasted with the ferocity and fanaticism of the Arab hordes. The Libyan War gave a great boost to Italian nationalism, and the image of Arab savagery was used to justify the harsh repressive measures adopted by the Italian occupying forces.

Episodi di eroismo: il sergente Lorenzi, degli Alpini, muore a Derna insieme all'ufficiale d'artiglieria ch'era accorso a difendere.

A PUNCH-UP between government and opposition deputies in parliament, 1900. During the political crisis at the turn of the century the opposition used obstructionist tactics to prevent the passage of repressive legislation. Images like this helped to discredit parliament in the eyes of middle-class readers.

LA SEDUTA DEL 30 GIUGNO A MONTECITORIO: IL PUGILLATO FRA I DEPUTATI
(Disegno di A. Beltrame).

the agreement, the revelation of the Gentiloni Pact laid bare the weakness of liberalism among the new mass electorate. Giolitti tried to appease anti-clerical indignation, but the Radicals still withdrew their support in March 1914, provoking his resignation. His successor, Antonio Salandra, tried to cap-italize on the revulsion against Giolitti's tactics of manipulation and shifting alliances by announcing a return to pure liberalism, unsullied by compromise with socialism or radicalism. Instead, he made overtures for Catholic support, which his predecessor as leader of the right, Sonnino, had always refused to do. But his government depended on the tolerance of Giolitti's supporters in parliament, and it is unlikely that it would have lasted for long but for the out-break of war.

The Libyan War also undermined Giolitti's social compromise. On the left, Mussolini formed a front with the anarchists, the independent revolutionary syndicalist unions, and the intransigent republicans. He followed the teach-ings of the theorist of revolutionary syndicalism, Georges Sorel, on the posi-tive value of violence and the general strike, although he disagreed with him in believing that the party and not the unions must lead. Employers, in-creasingly impatient with Giolitti's methods of mediation, concentrated on building up their own organizations to resist strikes. Economic recession strengthened the advocates of confrontation on both sides. Revolutionary agitation culminated in the Red Week of June 1914. After three anti-militarist demonstrators were killed in Ancona, a national general strike was called. In Romagna and the Marches, the strike escalated into an insurrection; rioters occupied railway stations, cut telephone wires, sacked churches, raised the red flag over town halls, and proclaimed the republic. The movement was quite unplanned, and the general strike collapsed after only two days when the reformist Confederation of Labour withdrew its support.

The Libyan War and Nationalism

The Libyan War had far stronger domestic support than Crispi's Abyssinian venture. Italy was a much wealthier nation in 1911 than in 1896, and the costs of a major colonial expedition no longer appeared prohibitive. Libya was hardly a promising field for Italian enterprise, but for political reasons the gov-ernment had encouraged investment by the Bank of Rome. In 1911 the bank was in difficulties, and it financed a major press campaign to protect its invest-ments by an immediate occupation. The bank had close ties with the Vatican and pro-clerical conservative politicians, and Catholic opinion gave strong support to the war. In contrast to the 1890s, the northern industrial bour-geoisie now backed expansionist policies. Italy was still a net capital importer, but Italian banks and industry were already looking to create spheres of influ-ence in the Balkans and Asia Minor. A successful war against Turkey would raise Italian prestige abroad and reinforce the resistance to socialism at home. In spite of the opposition of the Socialist Party the Libyan War at first aroused much popular enthusiasm. This was particularly strong in the south, where the mirage of free land for settlement had great appeal in spite of the earlier failures in East Africa. So Giolitti succeeded where Crispi had failed, but, ironically, this did him more harm than good. His cautious, prosaic approach to politics was out of key with the new mood of nationalist enthusiasm, whipped up by war correspondents and by the famous poet Gabriele D'Annunzio, in his *Canzoni d'Oltremare* [Songs of Overseas]. The conquest of Libya proved much more difficult and expensive than had been expected. Even after Turkey formally ceded Libya in October 1912, guerrilla warfare continued.

Nationalism, as a distinct intellectual and political movement, was born out of the reaction to the defeat of Adowa and the rise of socialism. In the journal *Il Regno*, founded in 1903, Enrico Corradini called for a revolt against the cowardice of a bourgeoisie which had betrayed its national mission by compromising with pacifist socialism. The new era of imperialist competition had falsified the optimistic assumptions of democratic ideology, and to succeed in the struggle the nation had to be ready to fight and destroy its internal enemies. Corradini stood Marx on his head by translating the class struggle into international terms. According to Corradini, Italy was a proletarian nation, bursting with youth and vigour, as shown by the high birth rate, but forced to export its surplus labour abroad. The decisive struggle, therefore, was between rich and poor nations in the international arena, not between rich and poor classes at home. The idea of the proletarian nation appealed to the sense of injustice and resentment aroused by Italy's exclusion from the colonial banquet and the treatment of her emigrants as inferiors. The exploitation of this national inferiority complex set an important precedent for Fascism.

The Nationalist Association, founded in 1910, originally represented a broad spectrum of opinion, ranging from democratic irredentists on the left to supporters of the Triple Alliance and of a conservative bloc with the Catholics on the right. The only thing they agreed upon was the need for a stronger foreign policy. But over the next four years the leaders of the movement hardened and clarified their policy at the cost of losing many of its original supporters. They came down strongly in favour of protectionism and a close identification with the interests of heavy industry. The Italian nationalists saw industrial expansion both as a proof of national vitality and a necessary condition for future greatness. The law professor Alfredo Rocco developed a coherent authoritarian theory of nationalism, which, he insisted, had nothing in common with the mentality of traditional patriotism. Liberal individualism must be rejected in favour of an organic and hierarchical conception of the national community. Production and labour would be disciplined and organized through national syndicates under the strict supervision of the State.

The anti-democratic and expansionist programme of the Nationalist Association did not appeal to the new mass electorate. But the Nationalists exercised a growing attraction on the conservative wing of liberalism and on agrarian and business leaders, and they had a considerable following among students. They infiltrated the élites of culture, diplomacy, and the armed forces.

The Road to War

When the Great War broke out in August 1914, foreign policy, strategy, and public opinion were all at odds. The Triple Alliance had been renewed in 1912 in the hope of restraining Austria. But the leaders of the armed forces were still convinced that in a European war Italy would take her place alongside her allies. The left sympathized with republican France, and as long as Trento and Trieste remained in the Austrian Empire, it was unlikely that Italian public opinion would accept a war on the side of Austria.

Fortunately, by attacking Serbia without offering Italy territorial compensation, the Austrians violated the terms of the Alliance, and allowed the government to declare its neutrality on 3 August. However, neutrality left Italy in an awkward position. The government was afraid that the winning side would have scant regard for Italy's interests. Salandra and his foreign minister Sonnino were also concerned that the prestige of the monarchy and the ruling class would suffer if the war ended without Italy having made significant territorial gains. Salandra declared that his policy was one of 'sacred egotism for the fatherland', which in crude terms meant selling Italy's support to the highest bidder. But in view of Austria's reluctance to make any serious concessions to Italian irredentism, this policy made entry into the war on the side of the Entente increasingly likely.

Giolitti was more sceptical. He did not rule out intervention, but he was well aware that both militarily and economically Italy was ill-prepared for a European war. In January 1915 he published a letter in which he expressed the opinion that 'quite a lot' could be obtained without war, presumably by negotiating with Austria-Hungary. Salandra deceived Giolitti about the progress of negotiations with the Entente, and he only discovered the truth too late. Salandra and Sonnino centralized decision-making in their own hands, without informing parliament or even the other members of the cabinet. They could do this thanks to the royal prerogative to conclude treaties; they were confident that Victor Emanuel would endorse their decision. The Treaty of London, signed on 26 April 1915, was a classic fruit of secret diplomacy.

In the mean time public opinion had become sharply divided between 'interventionists' and 'neutralists'. The great majority of the working classes and the peasants wanted peace, and the Socialist Party, unlike its counterparts elsewhere, stuck firmly to an internationalist line. But the interventionist

minorities were more combative. They were disproportionately strong in the larger cities, where they drew most of their support from students and the middle classes. For the leaders of the interventionist campaign, Giolitti and his system of government were a prime target. His attitude towards the war confirmed their belief that his cynical tactics of mediation had betrayed the ideals of the Risorgimento and the liberal State. On the right, the Nationalists, in spite of their admiration for Germany, soon decided that any war was preferable to no war. Their strength was that they were more in tune with Salandra's policy of egotism than the other interventionist groups. But what was really significant about the interventionist alliance was that it cut across the old distinctions between left and right. Intellectuals played a leading role in mobilizing opinion. One of the first demonstrations for war was staged by Marinetti and his group of Futurist artists. The Futurist Manifesto of 1909 had glorified 'war, the only hygiene of the world'. Unlike the Nationalists, the Futurists were pro-French and anti-clerical. The Futurists and their allies among the intellectual avant-garde caught and focused a mood of impatience with the dull, unambitious, and conventional morality of the bourgeoisie that was widespread among the younger generation.

THE CROWD LISTENING to the poet D'Annunzio speaking from the Capitol in Rome on 24 May 1915. D'Annunzio used his oratory to inflame patriotic feeling against Giolitti and the 'neutralists' who opposed Italy's entry into the First World War.

The most solid bloc of support for intervention, however, came from radical and republican democrats, backed by the Freemasonry, who saw the war as a crusade for democracy and the rights of nationality, in the spirit of the Risorgimento. More surprising, and more ambiguous, was the backing which came from dissidents of the extreme left. Many revolutionary syndicalist intellectuals were attracted to nationalism, and vice versa; the two movements converged in their hatred for parliamentary democracy and class compromise. At the time of the Libyan War Arturo Labriola had written that the Italian proletariat was no good at making revolution because it was no good at making war. But most syndicalists still opposed imperialism and the monarchic State. In 1914, however, the movement's most prestigious leaders joined the agitation for war; they identified with the libertarian traditions of French socialism against the German Social Democrats' bureaucratic mentality. The war would put an end to reformist cowardice and bring about the revolution. These arguments had a powerful fascination for Mussolini, whose revolutionary strategy was at an impasse after Red Week. In November 1914 he resigned from the editorship of the Socialist *Avanti!* and founded his own newspaper, the *Popolo d'Italia*, to campaign for war. He received financial backing from leading industrialists, who were pleased to see a split in the Socialist Party, and later from French and Russian sources. Mussolini's *fasci* of Revolutionary Action had some working-class support thanks to revolutionary syndicalist tribunes like Filippo Corridoni in Milan and Alceste De Ambris in Parma, but in the main it was a movement of leaders without followers. The syndicalists lost control of their national organization, the USI, to the anti-war anarchists. But the *Popolo d'Italia*, thanks to Mussolini's talent as a journalist, became the mouthpiece for the whole interventionist movement.

In May 1915 Giolitti finally woke up to what was going on. Three hundred parliamentary deputies demonstrated their support for him. The government's position was even more difficult because the Austrians, under German pressure, finally made a generous offer: Trento was to be ceded, and Trieste would have autonomous status within the Dual Monarchy. On 13 May Salandra resigned. This gave the interventionist agitators their chance, and they took it. In Milan and other cities they staged massive demonstrations which the Socialists were unable to match. The climax came in Rome, where D'Annunzio harangued a crowd

A CONSCRIPT reading the latest news to his wife. Most Italian soldiers were drawn from the peasantry, and their attitude to the war was one of pessimistic resignation.

of 100,000 from the Capitol, inciting them to violence against the traitor Giolitti and his followers. The 'radiant days of May' generated the myth of the popular interventionist revolution against Giolitti and parliament. Actually, the decision for war had already been taken, and Giolitti could not come to power without fatally compromising the king and Italy's international position; when asked by the king to form a government, he refused. But, as often happens, the myth was to be more important than the reality. Italy entered the war with a discredited parliament and a divided country.

ITALY 1915–1945:
POLITICS AND SOCIETY

PAUL CORNER

The Trauma of War (1915–1918)

The enthusiasm which greeted the Italian decision to end neutrality and intervene in the First World War was something which left a profound impression on observers; it seemed that the 'radiant May' of 1915 promised interventionist Italians nothing but gratification. Yet it can safely be said that, among all the victorious powers in the First World War, no country was so tested by the experience of war, so transformed by the immense effort it required, and so deeply divided by its outcome. The war proved to be a shock of massive proportions, which tried the politically unstable, economically backward, and weakly united society to its limit, and which bequeathed a legacy no one had been able to predict. Indeed, the divisions which the war exposed and the lacerations which the conflict provoked would have consequences which went well beyond the Armistice of November 1918.

It is hardly an exaggeration to say that Italian governments fought two wars between 1915 and 1918: one against the Austrians (and the Germans after 1916) and one on the home front against a part of the home population. Italy was, after all, the only belligerent country in which the majority had opposed the war and had not renounced that position after entry ('Neither support nor sabotage' remained the Socialist slogan). The need for popular consensus for what was, in effect, a war of aggression was in no way appreciated by successive war cabinets. On the contrary, the war provided government with the opportunity to introduce repressive legislation on a scale hitherto unseen. The initial generally held assumption among the interventionists was that the war would be brief (and of course victorious) and that rapid victory would ensure the political demise of pacifist Socialists and neutralist Giolittians alike. In contrast to other countries, therefore, there was no attempt to overcome the political and social divisions made evident by the interventionist crisis in order to create a kind of *union sacrée*. With the first reverses on the Carso and the realization not only that the war was not going to be short but that there was a strong possibility that it might not be successful, repressive attitudes were hardened rather than modified. This, of course, tended to increase rather than diminish popular hostility to the conflict.

Italy had entered the war both materially and psychologically unprepared, uncertain about her war aims and about how they were to be achieved. None the less the conviction that the war represented some kind of spiritual apotheosis for Italy had been common to many interventionists, whether right-wing authoritarian like Salandra or democratic and reformist socialist like Bissolati. The army's failure to achieve any spectacular successes initially provoked unspoken unease and then (with the near-breakthrough of the Austrian Strafexpedition in 1916) something approaching panic. There was the intense fear that defeat would effectively mean the end of Italy's (variously interpreted) Risorgimento aspirations; more immediately, defeat would mean the demise of an entire ruling élite. It was the all-or-nothing nature of the gamble with destiny which frequently turned the natural preoccupations shared by all belligerents into open nationalist hysteria in Italy. As victory seemed further and further away, supporters of the war looked for a scapegoat in order to explain the unexplainable. The real culprits—General Cadorna and his chiefs of staff—could clearly not be indicted without undermining the entire war effort. Attention therefore was turned to the 'enemy within'—the Socialist Party—which from 1916 was denounced for alleged defeatism and for sabotaging morale both within the army and on the home front. The climate of tension which developed, particularly after Caporetto in October 1917, when the Austrians broke the Italian line and took nearly 300,000 prisoners in the rout, produced a witch-hunt of such intensity that it became dangerous even to pray for peace without risking accusations of defeatism and treason.

The hysterical attacks on the Socialist Party were a clear indication of the extreme insecurity of the Italian élite in the face of its own population and of its inability to devise effective means of achieving national cohesion. But it was to be of critical significance that—because of the use of the device of the 'enemy within'—the nationalism–socialism divide became the fulcrum around which all political questions subsequently turned. The disastrous military progress of the war served only to accentuate this division and ensured that no middle ground remained. Inevitably many interventionist politicians of both centre and left found themselves forced to take up position in the nationalist camp and began to embrace many aspects of the ideology of the right. Former revolutionary and reformist Socialists (Mussolini included), Democrats, and Radicals came together to form a group which particularly distinguished itself for the virulence of its attacks on the Socialist Party during 1917.

One of the first victims of the renewed authoritarianism induced by the war was parliament. Not that it was closed; it was simply rarely convoked or consulted. Governments were well aware that the Socialist and Catholic majority in parliament, as in the country, was opposed to the war and would make its sentiments felt if given the opportunity (as indeed it did on the rare occasions when it had the chance). Governments preferred instead to rule by decree. This was part of a larger process which, in effect, saw power increasingly farmed out directly to ministries, to newly created bureaucratic institutions, and even to industrialists and bankers. The creation of virtually autonomous centres of power—for example, industrialists who decided what should be produced, in what quantities, and fixed their own prices—was a further feature of the way in which the war undermined the institutions of the liberal State. Ironically, because of the mass mobilization of both men and means, the State was present more than it had ever been in Italian life, but it was a State which had given up a great deal of its authority to private satrapies.

The dispersion of institutional power and the relegation of parliament to a minor role was justified by the arguments of national emergency. Certainly a major economic effort was necessary. The war saw a vast expansion of the Italian industrial base—some companies, like the shipbuilding and armament producer Ansaldo, increased both production and workforce tenfold in the course of the conflict. The Mobilitazione Industriale (MI)—in effect the militarization of a large part of the industrial complex—represented a new concept of industrial organization with State bureaucracies, local authorities, army, and industrialists working very closely together. Profits were reputed to be enormous; the figure of the wartime profiteer—the 'shark'—became a popular caricature of many newspapers.

More important for the future was the fact that industrialists had learned the benefits which could accrue to them through close collaboration with the State in the control of the workforce. In factories affected by the Industrial Mobilization, workers—many of them new to factory work—were subject to military supervision and disciplined by military tribunals; minor offences could result in the worker being sent to the front. Hours of work were extended and strikes declared illegal. None the less conditions were so bad that strikes did take place, and in August 1917 protest became so strong in Turin that the government feared insurrection. Strikes were often led by women, who were less subject to military sanctions. They called for peace and for bread (by 1917 always in short supply) and were sometimes reported as invoking the need for 'a revolution at home' in order to obtain either. In rural areas, women made similar protests, usually because their menfolk had not been given leave to help with the harvest.

Whether the war produced a greater sense of national awareness among Italians remains a hotly contested issue. In the sense that many people who had never before moved from their village now understood something about other regions, it may well be true. But in terms of patriotism or love of country, it seems much less certain. Workers whose first taste of the factory was the discipline of the MI were unlikely to find the experience a positive one. And the experience of the front for the common soldier, who had little or no idea why he was fighting a war of aggression, can hardly have recommended the Italian State to the new recruit. The strategy employed—frontal assault in waves—produced useless carnage on a grand scale. Acts of indiscipline were frequently punished by execution on the spot and punishment of entire units by decimation by lot was not uncommon. The severe discipline appears to have been accepted, albeit grudgingly, but the repetition of pointless and seemingly unjust orders often produced enormous tensions between men and officers. The idea that the poor were dying while the rich stayed at home was widespread, as was the belief that Austrian rule might indeed be preferable to that of the Italian government.

No doubt such tensions were present on most fronts; but in most cases hostility would be aimed at the officers, the generals, or the government, but not directly at the State. English soldiers might want to murder Haig but they did not (generally) put in question the fact of fighting for Britain. It was the development of anti-State feeling—something which had always been present at popular level since Unification—which remained the distinctive factor in the Italian case. For large numbers of people—soldiers and civilians—the first sustained contact with the Italian State was in the circumstances of a disastrously conducted war. Paradoxically, and this was also to be significant, many officers were also alienated from the State, precisely because of the inadequacies, inefficiencies, and stupidities of their own government and Supreme Command. They felt let down in the great task which patriotism proposed for them and, later, they would act accordingly.

Emblematic of the Italian authorities' attitude to its own soldiers was its behaviour in respect of those Italians who had fallen prisoner to the Austrians and Germans. Of the 600,000 soldiers who became prisoners in the course of the war, more than 100,000 died in captivity—a far higher proportion than for any other country. The high mortality rate was caused in large part by the refusal of the Italian government to send food parcels and clothing to its own prisoners—as was its duty under the 1907 Hague Convention—or to permit the despatch of private parcels. As a consequence, men died in large numbers of hunger, disease, and exposure; those who survived frequently did so only through hand-outs from prisoners of other nations. This punitive behaviour was determined by the conviction in government and senior military circles that most of the prisoners were in reality deserters and that it was only by making conditions in the camps intolerable, and by publicizing this fact to the men at the front, that further desertions could be avoided. It is hardly necessary to say that those soldiers who did return nourished a deep-rooted hatred of the Italian authorities.

Far from resolving Italy's problems, as many interventionists had hoped, the war had accentuated class divisions, increased hostility to the State on all sides, and created a violent polarization of politics within the country. Peace, when it came with the collapse of the Austrian army at Vittorio Veneto in the final days of the war, was inevitably overshadowed by these divisions. During 1919 and 1920, the so-called *bienno rosso*, socialist organizations went from strength to strength as they cashed in on the hopes for a new future which had been raised during the conflict. At certain moments—in the early summer of 1919, for example, when cost-of-living riots spread through many northern towns—it began to look as though even the socialist organizations were no longer able to control the situation and that revolution was at hand. A similar ferment was reproduced in the rural areas of the north, where Socialist leagues exacted concessions from landowners which went little short of establishing popular control. The final point of the revolutionary agitations came with the occupation of the Fiat and other factories in Turin in September and October 1920, a movement which spread to other cities and which provoked profound alarm among the industrialists.

Although, as we shall see, all these revolutionary movements eventually came to nothing, at the time they appeared all the more threatening because of the inability of the political centre to re-establish its hold. Parliament, which had lost so much authority during the course of the war, found it difficult to regain command in the post-war context. The Socialist Party controlled nearly a third of the deputies after the elections of November 1919, and the changes in electoral rules which permitted the entry into parliament of the new Catholic Popular Party made the formation of any stable alliance extremely difficult. A moderate and enlightened reformer like F. S. Nitti found it impossible to navigate effectively between the clear requirements of economic austerity occasioned by the costs of the war and the demands made on him from all lobbies for the intervention of the State in their favour. Tax reforms, so necessary, would have alienated the only political base which the old liberal State still retained among the *petite bourgeoisie* of the towns.

Problems of reconversion and stabilization were exacerbated by the political tensions created in the course of 1919. Those tensions which had been present at the front between officers and soldiers were reproduced in civilian life in much the same terms. Socialist Party organizers never failed to point out that the war had been a useless slaughter, as they had always maintained, and that the Italian State bore a heavy responsibility for this. And when at Versailles the Italian delegation walked out of the peace conference in protest at its treatment by the Allies, Gabriele D'Annunzio denounced what he termed the 'mutilated victory' and succeeded in raising a whirlwind of nationalist feeling which culminated in his occupation of the contested town of Fiume in September 1919. D'Annunzio's words and actions, profoundly subversive of the authority of central government, were to provide a focus for all right-wing, anti-Socialist, and anti-State sentiments for the following year.

Subverting the authority of central government became common practice during late 1919 and 1920. On the left, the Socialist organizations of landless farm-labourers (*braccianti*) on the capitalist estates of the Po Valley went ahead with scant regard for established authority. Convinced that the 'inevitable socialist tomorrow' was just around the corner, there seemed little reason to be too acquiescent to prefect or police chief. On the right, D'Annunzio gave inspiration to a nationalism which had felt betrayed by the conduct of the war and deceived by the consequences of the peace. In his cavortings at Fiume, D'Annunzio provided an eloquent example of the fact that central government was unable to exercise its authority. This message was not lost on those who felt themselves most threatened by revolutionary socialism. Landowners and industrialists, despairing of the help of central government in their battles against organized labour, began to think of taking matters into their own hands—something which they had done on occasions before the war.

The Origins of Fascism to 1922

The vehicle they found most ready to oblige was that of Fascism. The movement, founded in Milan in March 1919, had initially attracted the support of a small group of urban *déracinés*—former soldiers, artists, journalists, futurists, anarchists, and syndicalists—who united around a programme intended to attract support from those who wanted radical change but rejected socialism because of its record in the war. Its lack of success in 1919 was a clear sign that Mussolini, having betrayed the Socialist movement in 1914, now found himself without a constituency; both right and left distrusted him because of his chequered past. His salvation came only in 1920, and from an unexpected quarter. The early unsuccessful Fascist groups had always operated in the large towns of the north, but the movement was really to explode in the autumn of 1920 in the rural areas of the Po Valley, where tensions between capitalist landowners and labourers were particularly acute. Groups of young men—usually from the provincial centre, often enraged and disillusioned ex-combatants, often students—began to organize action squads and to move out into the rural areas at night in order to beat up, murder, and otherwise intimidate the leaders of the socialist farm-workers' movement. In these operations they generally enjoyed the complicity of local police and other authorities.

The effects were immediate and devastating. Rural socialism, already in difficulty with its rank and file because the promised revolution had not appeared, was decapitated and collapsed in many areas in a matter of weeks.

A Fascist 'punitive
expedition' begins.
An armed and motor-
ized squad from the
Modena area poses for
the photographer before
setting out on a raid.
The *squadristi* pictured
here are young and
clearly middle-class,
eager to live the experi-
ence of combat which
many of this generation
felt had been denied
them with the ending of
the First World War.

The monopoly of labour exchanges which the Socialists had won so recently fell into the hands of the Fascists, backed up by the landowners. Farm-labourers became once again the victims of rural overpopulation; in order to work, *braccianti* now had to join the Fascist unions. When they did so they found themselves working longer hours for less pay than before, but they had no other choice except to starve. Mussolini's initial reaction to the movement was to consider it a reactionary white guard, but, seeing the way in which the occupation of the factories had collapsed and the degree to which the urban working class was also in retreat, he decided to exploit the success in the rural areas for his own ends. By May 1921 he was in parliament at the head of a group of thirty-six Fascist deputies—part of Giolitti's 'national bloc'.

Mussolini had risen to national prominence on the back of the violent class reaction which agrarian Fascism represented. Urban Fascism developed more slowly. Class conflicts were less acute, and it was in any case difficult to extend the systematically ruthless methods employed by the agrarian squads to the urban context. Industrialists had other methods of intimidating workers, par-ticularly in a time of recession. None the less violence was common, usually directed against individuals who had dared to speak out against Fascism and usually the work of middle-class students, former soldiers, unemployed workers, and an urban subproletariat which lent itself willingly to the Fascist cause.

Fascism owed its success to many factors: to its novelty and appeal to the young, to the use of systematic violence which remained largely uncontested, to the weariness and lack of direction of the Socialists, and to certain divisions between economic groups in rural areas (between conservative sharecroppers, whose numbers had greatly expanded in the immediate post-war years, and revolutionary landless labourers, for example) which the Fascists were able to exploit to their advantage. The financial and moral assistance of the landowners and industrialists was also crucial, as was the complicity of the police and *carabinieri*. But the fundamental factor in permitting that success was the mistaken impression among government and bourgeoisie that Fascism was a six-month wonder which could be absorbed into the faltering liberal system. Tolerance towards a violent and illegal organization depended on the belief that, with Socialism brought to order, Fascism would cease to have any further function.

By 1922 the Fascist squads controlled much of northern Italy. Prefects lamented the fact that they were without authority; at a local level it was the Fascist leader who took the decisions. Politically it proved impossible to find an alliance capable of providing a strong opposition to Mussolini. Divided amongst themselves and between each other, Socialists and Catholics remained irreconcilable. In a sense the March on Rome of October 1922 did no more than confirm a victory already attained and was more choreography than conquest. The only force capable of standing in the way of the blackshirts was the army, but the king decided not to invoke the state of siege; instead he invited Mussolini to form a government. This constituted a complete capitu-

BLACK-SHIRTED FASCIST *SQUADRISTI* parade in Florence in 1922 with all the usual accoutrements of Mussolini's private army. The prominent display of First World War medals makes clear the strong participation of ex-combatants and the link between the experience of the trenches and the development of the Fascist movement.

271

lation to violence and illegality, a capitulation which twenty-four years later would cost Victor Emanuel his throne.

The victory of Fascism represented more than simply the personal triumph of Mussolini. The March on Rome was the end of a story which had begun with the interventionist crisis of 1914–15. Formally, Fascism was a child of 1919, but its gestation is to be found in the profound shocks which the interventionist crisis and the war itself had administered to all aspects of Italian society, creating an instability made of hopes and expectations, fears, hatreds, and divisions, which a fragile and artificial democracy was unable to realize, reassure, or reconcile. Fascism represented a stabilization of a sort, ambiguous because the movement comprised both the conservative forces of farming, industry, and finance and the newer groups which had emerged during the course of the conflict and whose political orientation was often radical and pseudo-revolutionary, even if always anti-liberal and anti-socialist. The restoration of hierarchies which Fascism represented (best seen in agriculture) was achieved without any real definition of objectives; indeed the lack of ideological definition constituted one of the strengths of Fascism. If it was not exactly all things to all men, it came very close to being so. It was novel in its political style and in the fact that, in addition to the support of traditionally conservative forces, it had some kind of mass base among urban and rural *petite bourgeoisie*, but—beyond a generic activism which took the place of a programme—in its early years it remained the anti-party, unwilling or unable to express a clear identity. Posing as the party of the nation and of nationalism, at the end of 1922 it was evident that the one thing Fascism had not managed to achieve was the bridging of those deep divisions which had appeared with intervention and grown with the war.

Fascism in Power: The First Years (1922–1927)

Intentionally legalitarian and cautious, Mussolini's first government—a coalition, which at first included several Catholics and liberals—clearly aimed at a normalization of politics after years of social conflict and virtual civil war. In respect of internal politics, Fascist fusion with the nationalist movement in early 1923 suggested a strong conservative bias and indicated that Mussolini aimed to attract non-Fascist opinion to his side in the effort to form a wide and stable political base. Reassurance over Fascist methods and intentions was very much the order of the day. Yet, for Mussolini—poacher become gamekeeper—restoration of legality presented a major problem. Fascist violence and illegality had become part and parcel of the movement during its rise and the suppression of violence was likely to arouse the hostility of provincial *squadrismo*, accustomed to taking the law into its own hands. The dissolution of the squads was equally fraught with problems; many *squadristi* had not worked since the end of the war and had relied on Fascism becoming a career in itself. A solution was found in the formation in early 1923 of the Fascist militia (the MVSN), in which former *squadristi* were enrolled under army officers—a measure which aimed to prevent the repetition of politically counterproductive private violence while still giving the blackshirts a well-defined role within the movement. Subsequent events were to show that the solution was more apparent than real.

In respect of international opinion, Mussolini was apparently cautious, seeking to reassure doubts which had been raised throughout much of democratic Europe. Although revisionism and expansionism were never far below the surface (Fascism was, after all, intent on reversing the humiliations of the First World War and the 'mutilated victory'), Italy's economic difficulties made her subordinate position all too evident and counselled prudence. With the exception of the Corfu incident in 1923 (Italy occupied the island briefly as a reprisal for an incident involving an Italian diplomatic mission) and persistent meddling in the internal affairs of certain central European and Balkan states, Fascist objectives appear to have been those dictated by the knowledge that Britain and the USA dominated the post-war settlement, particularly in terms of finance, and that collaboration with these powers was the only realistic way of increasing Italy's international prestige. Locarno in 1925, which saw Britain and Italy named as the joint guarantors of the treaty, appeared to be a measure of the success of this cautious and collaborative approach. The American loans which flowed into Italy after 1925 were also a testimony of foreign confidence in the Fascist government and could be taken as a mark of increased international standing.

The initial legislation of 1923 was conservative and rewarded the middle-class support which Fascism had gained; the economic and financial policies, in particular, were traditionally liberal and designed to protect savings and encourage investment. Politically more indicative of Fascist intentions was the passage of the Acerbo electoral reform in the autumn of 1923—a reform which guaranteed a two-thirds majority in parliament to the party winning the elections. Passed with the excuse of ensuring political stability, the reform clearly aimed at making the Fascist position within parliament unassailable.

In the event, however, the elections of April 1924 almost proved the undoing of Fascism. Although the Fascist list won, the denunciation by the reformist Socialist Giacomo Matteotti of the violence used during the elections provoked his murder by Fascist thugs. Mussolini's role, always disputed, remains unclear, but his ultimate responsibility for the murder induced much moderate, fellow-travelling opinion to move away from Fascism in disgust. Over the summer months Mussolini's position appeared extremely insecure; opposition to him mounted and, in a move of questionable wisdom, even the parliamentary opposition (with the exception of the Communists) left the chamber as a sign of protest (the so-called Aventine secession). The more determined Fascist leaders pressed Mussolini for a 'second wave' of violence, which would finally eliminate all opposition and leave the Fascist squads undisputed masters in the field, but Mussolini, wary of public opinion and above all reluctant to consign himself as a hostage to his own lieutenants, resisted for a time, until on 3 January 1925, with his hand very clearly being forced, he announced in parliament that, while he took responsibility for the consequences of Fascist violence, he was prepared to move against all opposition in the name of the greater weight of Fascist virtues.

The speech of 3 January, generally regarded as the initiation of the regime as such, was highly significant in so far as responsibility for repression of opposition was entrusted not to the Fascist *squadristi* but to the State authorities: the prefects, the police, and the *carabinieri*. This was the first clear indication of a line which was to be pursued by Mussolini with increasing vigour in following years by which he effectively freed himself from the control of the 'intransigents' of the Partito Nazionale Fascista (PNF). Fearing that any real application of Fascist 'intransigence'—the Fascistization of the State through the intervention of the party—could only alienate powerful, non-Fascist areas of support, Mussolini preferred to discipline his own supporters and hold them in reserve. Formally the PNF remained prominent and provided jobs for the faithful but, in contrast to Nazi Germany, the party was always ultimately subordinate to the State, an instrument to be used to apply pressure when necessary rather than a genuinely determining element of internal politics. The Fascist Grand Council, for instance, created in 1923 as the link between government and party, was consulted but—until the fateful meeting of July 1943—rarely listened to.

Even so, that repression which had been resisted in 1923 was firmly applied between 1925 and 1927. Opposition parties were suppressed, freedom of the press abolished, strikes declared illegal, and trade unions 'absorbed' into a single, farcical, Fascist union organization. Special legislation provided for the reform along Fascist lines of the bureaucracy, of the legal codes, and of local government. Critics of the regime risked imprisonment after trial by the Fascist 'special tribunal', as was to happen to the Communist leader Antonio Gramsci in 1927. A few opponents were even condemned to death. Many anti-Fascists, preferring exile to silence, took the road abroad, usually to Paris, London, or Moscow, where they remained a permanent thorn in the side of the regime. Moves were made in the direction of replacing the dialectic of class and party conflict with the discourse of collaboration and corporativism; the labour charter and the labour magistracy, which formally envisaged arbitration and independent intervention in industrial disputes, in fact delivered the workers into the arms of their employers. Strikingly, much of this legisla-

GIUGNO 1932 (X)
C. C. P. - LIRE SEI

MOTOR
ITALIA

BALILLA

VERSO IL POPOLO

FIAT

BALILL

A MODERNISTIC ADVERTISEMENT for the *Balilla* (*left*), the first Fiat car intended for mass consumption. 'Verso il popolo' (towards the people) was the slogan of the Fascist campaign intended to gain popular support for the regime during the economic crisis of the early 1930s. The conflation of the interests of private industry and the directives of public policy, evident in this poster, is very telling.

'WITHIN A DECADE all Europe will be Fascist or Fascistized'; a 1940 poster (*below*) commemorating the nineteenth anniversary of the March on Rome. The figure is wearing a helmet and a medal of the First World War, clearly suggesting the continuity seen by Fascism between the First and Second World Wars.

...Tra un decennio l'Europa sara FASCISTA o FASCISTIZZATA!

DISCORSO DEL DUCE A MILANO 24 10 1932 X

28 OTTOBRE-XIX

FEDERAZIONE PROVINCIALE DEI FASCI DI COMBATTIMENTO DI MILANO

tion was modelled very closely on the repressive legislation of labour devised in very different circumstances during the First World War.

The failure of 'normalization' and the move towards a more authoritarian and repressive regime after 1925 indicated the degree to which tensions continued to exist between Fascists and non-Fascists. The problem of the consolidation of the regime, of the realization of some kind of stability, was in part resolved through the legislation of 1925–7 and the final disciplining of the PNF; but the most effective weapon used by Mussolini in reinforcing his support was provided by the economy. Fascism had been fortunate in riding a wave of expansion in the years 1923–5 as the international economy began to grow again after the war. But expansion brought difficulties with it. In particular, Italian imports (especially grain) rose rapidly, creating problems with the balance of payments and driving down the value of the lira (this provoked the declaration of the 'battle for wheat' in 1925). By 1926 an inflationary trend had become strongly established and the devalued lira was creating problems for heavy industry, traditionally the greatest importers of raw materials. Inflation represented a double problem for the Fascists. On the one hand, there was a risk that a large section of Fascist supporters among the *petite bourgeoisie*— those on fixed incomes and with savings—would lose faith in a movement that was unable to protect their economic position; on the other, inflation threatened to undermine those key industries which were most politically influential and most connected with defence. The revaluation of the lira—a process begun in August 1926 and ended with the *de jure* fixing of the lira at 90 lira to the pound sterling at the end of 1927—represented an economic stabilization (albeit at an absurdly high exchange rate) but, far more important, it represented a political consolidation of the regime. Quota 90, as the revaluation was known, linked both the *petite bourgeoisie* and the more influential sections of industry to Fascism on the basis of an overvalued currency which defended salaries, dividends, and savings and permitted cheaper imports of essential raw materials. Considerations of power, prestige, and politics are all clearly visible.

Revaluation represented something of a triumph for Mussolini. Not only did it consolidate the basis of his support at home, but—based as it was on the results of lengthy negotiations with the Bank of England, the Federal Reserve, and private American banks who had to support the manœuvre—it inserted Italy firmly (if briefly) into the international economy, and permitted her to attract large quantities of desperately needed foreign (principally US) capital for investment. This was recognition for Fascism at a very high level. However, there was a price to be paid. Foreign bankers had not been unaware that the drastic deflation implied by Quota 90 would have social costs which only an authoritarian regime could survive and, in fact, repression and intimidation permitted Fascism to pass on the cost of revaluation to labour. This was

Facing: THE AMERICAN ENTRY into the Second World War in 1942 allowed Fascism to parade all its crude racial and antisemitic repertoire, as is evident from this lurid propaganda poster. Italian participation in the war was now presented as an attempt to right the wrongs of the Versailles treaty, allegedly forced on Italy by an American Jewish-masonic clique led by President Wilson.

perfectly in line with the social priorities of Fascism already evident; control of the workforce had always been the fundamental reason for employers' support for Fascism. Not surprisingly, even before 1925 wages in both agriculture and industry had been adversely affected. In agriculture, where landowners could exploit the excess offer of labour, daily rates had simply been reduced, often with dramatic consequences for labourers already seriously underemployed; in industry, reductions had been less open but effected none the less by reorganization of the workforce, resulting in a de-skilling of labour, and by inflation. Revaluation brought with it recession, higher unemployment, and reductions in wages by decree (–20 per cent in 1927). Prices fell as a result of the deflationary effects of Quota 90, but wages fell further and faster, with a drastic effect on internal demand. Hours of work were frequently extended. On occasions, Fascist unions organized protest in order to try to save face, but they were powerless to intervene effectively; industrialists simply appealed over their heads directly to Mussolini, who was not going to alienate powerful sources of support in order to defend the workers.

Crisis and Consolidation (1927–1934)

Although revaluation provoked a severe economic recession, particularly among exporters in both agriculture and industry, it did reinforce the political base on which Mussolini depended, allowing Fascism to survive the immediate impact of deflation and after 1929 to absorb the effects of the international crisis. In the early 1930s popular legend, ably supported by Fascist propaganda, had Italy less affected by world depression than many other nations, but this was far from the truth. The Great Crisis arrived later in Italy than elsewhere— the worst year was probably 1932. It was none the less extremely severe and cumulated the adverse effects of the revaluation crisis. It may have appeared to have been less dramatic because, in what was still a predominantly agricultural economy, many of the effects were masked by downward adjustments in the often extremely elastic peasant family economy or by first-generation urban workers returning to their rural roots. None the less urban unemployment rose rapidly, particularly in the northern cities of the industrial triangle, and gave the authorities some cause for concern.

In difficulty, Mussolini, always quick to make virtue of necessity, declared war on the evils of plutocracy and claimed to have superseded capitalism. In reality, the response to the crisis was makeshift and half-hearted. Wide-scale public works programmes attracted publicity (although they probably contributed only a relatively small number of jobs); land reclamation schemes (the *bonifica integrale*) went on, albeit in a lower key (and without the crucial final phase, in which the reclaimed land was supposed to be split up and consigned to landless peasants: it thus became improvement of private land at public expense); and Italians continued to be told that 'ruralism' was the answer to their problems—a rather tame attempt to compensate peasants for their persistently poor standard of living and to stem the move towards the towns. As with other aspects of Fascism, rhetoric was here used to make reality more bearable, reflecting the fact that, for the Fascists, rural underemployment was politically less dangerous than urban unemployment. At the same time, significantly, public-sector employment increased considerably, following the expansion of State bureaucracy. This last factor may explain in part why the crisis was not more destabilizing for the regime. But it is also necessary to remember that methods of police control were well established and highly effective (the number of arrests for isolated individual protests did increase markedly in this period), that depression created divisions between the employed and the unemployed (many newly urbanized unemployed workers feared being sent back to their communes of origin and kept quiet as a result), and that the Fascist near-monopoly of labour exchanges, leisure outlets, public works, subsidies, and soup kitchens made some contact with the party an unavoidable necessity for most. In fact, far from having a destabilizing effect, there seems little reason to doubt that the depression in Italy served to reinforce the hand of dictatorship rather than to weaken it.

Even so, the crisis determined a major change in Fascist policies, accentuating those tendencies on the one hand towards economic isolationism and national self-sufficiency—autarky—which had been implicit in the policy of revaluation and towards aggressive expansionism on the other. The fact that an overvalued lira had sacrificed exports to imports meant that Italy's sources of foreign exchange were much reduced, even before the onset of the international crisis. After 1929 the situation worsened. The international trend towards protectionism which followed the Great Crash made it more difficult to export, American capital disappeared, and the traditional lifelines of the Italian economy—remittances from Italian emigrants and introits from tourism—dried up almost completely. In these circumstances it became clear that the attempt to improve Italy's prestige through collaboration with Britain and the USA was no longer a feasible policy. Both nations had, in one way or another, withdrawn from Europe, at least as far as trade was concerned; evidently, the Anglo-American card was no longer playable. This made obvious the weakness of the Italian economic position; at the same time, a major conditioning factor on Italian policy had been removed. Italy was free, indeed was forced, to look for new trading partners and different methods of improving her international status. In terms of trade, Germany (and central Europe) provided the obvious solution; even before the advent of Hitler, Italian trade had turned sharply towards Germany in what *The Economist* dubbed a 'coal for lemons' bilateral barter system. Subsequent ideological links were to reinforce, not determine, the commercial relationship. In terms of the search for prestige, the crisis brought about a very obvious change of tone; Fascism became more strident and aggressive on the international stage, mirroring the more general European move from cooperation to competition.

Italians paid for these difficulties very much according to social class. Big business—iron and steel, chemicals, electricity—actually gained from measures which favoured concentration and vertical integration, just as they gained from the foundation in 1933 of IRI, the State holding company, which reinforced the links between heavy industry and the State. Agriculture suffered more, although exports increased during the 1930s as the result of bilateral agreements with Germany and other countries of central Europe. Workers and peasants saw a massive reduction in their already low standard of living. By 1934 industrial workers' wages had been reduced *officially* by some 40 per cent in respect of 1927; according to one estimate (G. Salvemini), this represented a fall in real purchasing power of around 30 per cent. Agricultural incomes—much more difficult to assess because of the element of subsistence farming involved—probably fell even more, if we are to judge from reports of desperate crisis in many areas. Some observers considered that compression of consumption had reached absolute limits; certainly, according to the International Labour Organization in Geneva, Italians *as a whole* were eating fewer eggs and less meat, butter, and sugar than any other country in Europe (Spain and Portugal are not quoted), while peasants and workers ate only 50 per cent of these products in comparison with other Italians. The middle class, as the backbone of Fascism, obviously fared better, with greater job security and other privileges, often guaranteed by State or para-State employment or by jobs with the party or gained through contacts with the PNF. This was the class which, in the course of the 1930s, began to make timid steps along the road to a different kind of lifestyle through the cinema, motorization, popular music (although radios remained scarce), and a growing involvement in leisure activities and sport.

By European levels, the standard of living remained low for almost everyone, however. Fascism attempted to meet this problem by substituting ideology for consumption and material well-being. Once again taking his inspiration from the First World War, Mussolini declared innumerable 'battles' in an effort to mobilize popular opinion. The battle for wheat, the battle for the lira, the demographic battle, the zootechnical battle (for livestock)—all reflected the need to give the overcoming of perceived economic and social weaknesses a strong political content. A sense of sacrifice or of mission was intended to compensate for very real difficulties. The extent to which these campaigns effectively changed opinion remains unclear, although, to judge by the failure of the other plank of Fascist compensations—the organization of leisure activities (Opera Nazionale Dopolavoro, OND)—success remains

doubtful. Intended to achieve the Fascistization of leisure time through a process of indoctrination, the OND ultimately fell foul of the fact that political conviction required political discussion, something which Fascist officials considered far too dangerous. 'The Duce is always right' and 'Believe, obey, fight' were slogans which asked for an act of faith rather than reasoned argument.

Faith possibly came from other directions than the OND. A major success of Mussolini, reflected in the vote in the plebiscitary elections of 1929, was the agreement with the Catholic Church reached earlier in the same year. This ended seventy years of conflict between Church and State and seemed to be of benefit to both. From the personal point of view of Mussolini (Pius XI's 'man of providence'), the Lateran agreements constituted an extremely important endorsement to place before both national and international opinion; for the Church, the Concordat represented a guarantee that it would retain a privileged position in an increasingly totalitarian State. The treaty was an example of the fact that Mussolini's formula 'Everything in the State, nothing outside the State, nothing against the State' was capable of exceptions

A PHOTOMONTAGE OF MUSSOLINI, 1932. The cult of the Duce was one of the fundamental elements of cohesion in Fascist Italy. The raised chin, indicating determination, and the aggressive facial expressions were part of a public ritual which fixed the image of the Duce firmly in the collective consciousness.

when necessary and when political advantage was to be gained. Certainly, the agreement consolidated his position and confirmed his independence from the party, but it did also mean a concession; like the monarchy, the Church remained an autonomous centre of power in respect of the Fascist structure and as such put a limit to any genuinely totalitarian pretensions. However, as with the monarchy, the complicity of the Church with Fascism made this more a formal than a substantial concession.

The one area of conflict which remained was that of youth organizations. The Azione Cattolica—the Catholic youth movement—had long been suspected by the Fascists of being a front for anti-Fascist activity, particularly among its leaders. The Concordat papered over the cracks of this dispute, but it was to continue to be a point at issue for much of the 1930s. Fascist sensitivity over this question reflected the fact that the regime clearly sought a monopoly in the field of civil organizations, particularly among the young, seeing it as the most effective means of indoctrination and mobilization. The Opera Nazionale Ballila (elementary school children), the Young Fascists (18–20-year-olds), and the Gruppi Universitari Fascisti (university students) were all formed early in the regime and were intended to ensure that the new generation would grow up as convinced Fascists. The initiative was also extended to women through the constitution of women's *fasci* (mainly middle class), the institution of a movement of rural housewives, and the use of women volunteers in Fascist welfare operations. Much imitated by other regimes, the regulation of civilian life along military lines constituted a distinctive feature of Fascist control of the population and aimed to create that sense of common purpose which had been so much lacking in previous years. But, as with the OND, the overriding impression is that the impact of these organizations was usually no more than skin-deep. People took what they wanted from them—sport, welfare, State-subsidized holidays, amusement, comradeship—but tended to leave the political message to one side.

Expansionism and Empire

The memory of the First World War and the 'mutilated victory' was never very far from Fascist consciousness; the pursuit of international recognition and Great Power status was a direct consequence. Themes which stressed the unjust treatment of 'proletarian' Italy at the hands of plutocratic and imperialist nations proved particularly effective in mobilizing Fascist public opinion and clearly struck a chord in the country at large. The rhetoric of war which Fascism adopted (the battles for wheat, etc), the militarization of society through numerous uniformed groups, the quest for national self-sufficiency in food and other products—all built on this sense of resentment and conformed to a vision of society in which the dynamically aggressive 'new' Italian would eventually triumph in the battle for the national rights which had been denied him. War was built into Fascism (or a part of Fascism) from the outset; indeed, the pursuit of patriotic and nationalist objectives provided the legitimation for violence and for authoritarian government throughout the *ventennio*. The logic was unassailable: opposition to Fascism meant opposition to the nation, and was therefore tantamount to treason.

Diplomacy, belonging to the real world, was of course another matter, as the 1920s had shown. Then, circumstances had dictated caution, even if some kind of revisionism manifestly remained the basis of policy. Italy had ambitions in the areas of the Danube, the Balkans, and the Adriatic, which

ETHIOPIA, 1936. The execution of six Ethiopians, as an Italian soldier poses by the gallows for the photographer. The war was marked by many episodes of brutality towards the indigenous civilian population, including the use of poison gas and the systematic extermination of the local intellectual élite.

influenced her attitudes to both France and Germany, and in North Africa, where France and Britain were called into question. Hitler's election in 1933 and the failure of Mussolini's proposed four-power agreement (a kind of extended Locarno) effectively dashed Italian hopes of expansion in Europe, turning Mussolini's attention exclusively towards Africa. The decision to invade Ethiopia seems to have been taken as a consequence of increasing international tensions, which suggested that the favourable moment might not recur, and from a desire to galvanize a Fascist movement which, with the crisis, had fallen distinctly into the doldrums.

The campaign itself was longer and far more costly than had been expected. It was fought with a savagery (poison gas, massacres of civilians) about which, even today, little is known in Italy. But politically it was a great, if rather ephemeral, success for Mussolini. League of Nations sanctions against Italy played into his hands and his announcement in May 1936 of the acquisition of empire seemed to confirm that Fascism had defeated not only Ethiopia but also those who wished to perpetuate international injustice. Italy cheered; domination of the Mediterranean—*mare nostrum*—was clearly just round the corner.

A FASCIST TRIUMPHAL ARCH in the Libyan desert of Sirte. The construction is a good example of the absurdly grandiose pretensions of Fascism and of its persistent reference to the symbols of the Roman Empire.

Towards the War: Society, State, and Totalitarianism

Victory in Ethiopia was probably the high point of the regime. It produced a short-lived general consensus and it seemed to justify Fascism in its persistent militaristic emphasis in civilian life. But the longer-term consequences of the war were disastrous, both in foreign policy and in internal affairs. Italy's relative isolation during sanctions had pushed her further into the arms of Nazi Germany, making her more than ever dependent on Germany for raw materials and fuel. As a result, Mussolini made concessions to Hitler over the status of Austria, thus giving up the one good card he had to play against Nazi expansionism. Success in Ethiopia also persuaded him to send 'volunteers' and military equipment to support Franco, a commitment to the Fascistization of Europe which an impoverished Italy could hardly afford.

At home, the war carried Fascism into what has been termed the 'totalitarian phase', a phase which saw the attempt to increase the Fascist presence in the daily life of Italians in an effort to produce a truly Fascist nation. This

period was dominated by war and expectation of war and the greater organization and regimentation of both population and economy corresponded to the need to form a nation capable of withstanding the pressures of a European war when it came. Propaganda was stepped up through the ministry of popular culture, youth organizations reorganized and revitalized, school curricula revised to present a more Fascist-orientated education. An attempt was made to change Italian habits and outlook. The 'anti-bourgeois' campaign

hoped to produce a harder, more determined kind of Fascist, reflecting the degree to which the movement had atrophied over the years. The goose step was introduced for the army in a ridiculous imitation of the Nazis; and even the handshake was replaced by the Roman salute of Fascism, again a product of too-close contact with the Nazis. Projecting a phoney modernity, the totalitarian phase aimed to generate an increased dynamism in an ageing movement and to guarantee the future through the creation of a genuinely Fascist generation of new men, all potential heroes, 'tempered', as Mussolini put it, to stand war and suffering.

Hand in hand with recasting the Italian character went the streamlining of the economy. The cost of the Ethiopian war had been enormous ('pacifica-

ITALIAN ANTI-FASCISTS of the International Brigade during the Spanish Civil War. The war provided many with the first real opportunity to fight back against Fascism; the slogan 'Today in Spain, tomorrow in Italy' inspired hope for opponents of the regime both inside and outside Italy.

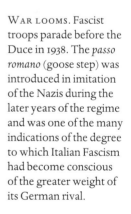

WAR LOOMS. Fascist troops parade before the Duce in 1938. The *passo romano* (goose step) was introduced in imitation of the Nazis during the later years of the regime and was one of the many indications of the degree to which Italian Fascism had become conscious of the greater weight of its German rival.

tion' continued throughout 1937 and 1938) and the effect on Italy's gold and foreign currency reserves dramatic. This required the government to take an even firmer hold on economic affairs. The lira was finally devalued in 1936, opening the way to rising inflation; autarky became official formal policy in the same year, with all expenditure of foreign exchange for imports controlled by government licences; efforts were made to find substitutes for essential raw materials like rubber and petrol; and the government even sponsored exploration for gold in the river-beds of the pre-Alpine hills. Increasingly, the political requirements of production came to the fore; scarce resources had to be controlled very carefully, and only the State was able to do this. The much-vaunted corporations, formed over a decade before 1935, which were supposed to bring employers, party officials, and workers together in collaboration according to areas of production, were far too complex and inefficient organisms to carry out the task. New bodies had to be set up. The result was an incredible multiplication of State agencies and of parallel bureaucracies which worked in a disjointed and uncoordinated manner in an effort to produce an efficient war economy. Predictably, the effects were limited. By 1938–9 there was a clear awareness that essential industrial expansion required large injections of capital and that this could only be provided through further compression of consumption, price and wage controls, and control and direction of investment. Before the outbreak of the war the Fascists managed only to limit consumption effectively. Indeed, the paradox of the late 1930s was that,

APRIL 1938. The two dictators pose on the Altar of the Fatherland in Rome. During Hitler's visit, Mussolini did everything possible to impress his ally with Italian military strength and organization. There are indications that the Führer was not taken in.

as the political element in the organization of the economy became ever more marked, the economic results became less and less satisfactory.

Ultimately the Ethiopian war and the totalitarian phase of Fascism had destabilizing consequences for the regime. Inflation took its toll. The 1940 annual report of the Bank of Italy acknowledged that 'there has been a certain reduction in real wages' of industrial workers, while white-collar workers, suffering from rising prices, from increased taxes, and from the various forced loans and special levies of these years, also saw their economic advantages greatly reduced. As serious for the regime was the distance which many indus- trialists and large landowners began to take from Fascism. Divisions arose between industrialists as a result of the heavy State intervention in the organi- zation of trade and investment, favouring a few to the detriment of many. Landowners in general were aware that, despite 'ruralism', the political weight of agriculture had declined under Fascism and that their returns reflected this fact. Even the backbone of rural Fascism, the sharecroppers, began to resent the requisitioning of crops at low official prices by the State authorities.

Murmurs of discontent, even if fairly loud, did not really threaten Fascist survival, however. By the late 1930s it was evident that the regime was facing serious difficulties and that the mechanisms it had invented to overcome them had had little effect. But there seems little question that, without the war, Fascism would have continued for some time. Certainly, there were problems with the institu- tional framework (Mussolini's irritation with the monarchy was becoming ever more obvious) and there were doubts about the future; the succession to Mussolini remained an unanswered question and the second generation which had grown up under Fascism was showing increasing signs of disaffec- tion from an ageing and ossified hierarchy. The Racial Laws, introduced in 1938 in an attempt to flatter Hitler, were generally unpopular, as was the bur- geoning alliance with Nazi Germany. But discontent and disaffection were very different from open and active opposition; compliance, even if more and more grudging, remained the most common attitude.

FIXING THE MESSAGE 'Aryan shop'. After the promulgation of the Racial Laws in 1938 many shopkeepers were quick to state publicly that they were not Jews. Jewish shops were forced to close.

War, Anti-Fascism, Resistance

The possibilities of Italy not becoming involved in the war were, of course, very few indeed. Mussolini's vainglorious personal diplomacy with Hitler made Italy virtually a hostage to Germany by 1939 (there are even suggestions that he did not read the Pact of Steel before signing it). Any trace of the 'deciding weight' policies of the mid-1930s, by which Italy sought to avoid commitment in order to sell herself to the highest bidder when the decisive moment came, had disappeared. But, irresponsible diplomacy apart, the ideological imperatives of Fascism made the choice of neutrality almost impossible. Fascism had been organized from the start along militaristic lines and had always expressed itself through the rhetoric of war; it had been an attempt to carry the nationalist values of the First World War—discipline, aggression, heroism, hierarchy, patriotism—into peacetime and to regiment and unify a notoriously divided society under those values. The ultimate test of this venture was obviously war itself. To have refused the challenge would have represented a betrayal of all that Fascism had tried to construct.

After a period of non-belligerency (but not neutrality) determined by lack of economic and military preparation, Mussolini entered the Second World War in June 1940. Italy was still unprepared, as all the chiefs of staff were aware, but a rapid and total Nazi victory seemed assured and Mussolini needed, to use his own cynical phrase, 'a thousand Italian dead at the conference table'. Public opinion, always in doubt about the Axis alliance, temporarily suspended disbelief and rallied to the cause, although there were none of the celebrations seen in the 'radiant May' of 1915. Very much aware that he risked being swallowed whole by a much more powerful Germany, Mussolini first attempted to pursue a parallel war which would keep the Italian position distinct from the German, but the attempt proved futile. In both Greece and North Africa the Italian campaigns faced disaster and had to be rescued by the intervention of the *Wehrmacht*. The war at sea went equally badly, the navy finding itself without essential air-cover at vital moments. Mussolini's insistence on sending Italian troops to the Russian front in 1941 was a desperate attempt to maintain some political control over the course of a conflict which was getting totally out of hand, but even this attempt failed miserably. Most of the Italian soldiers died as they attempted, after Stalingrad, to walk home through the Russian winter of 1942; Hitler twice refused to listen to Mussolini's counsels for a separate Russian peace.

The Duce found himself with responsibility but no power—a bad position for a dictator. It was ironic that a regime which had consistently preached the virtues of war should have been found so wanting in the event. The lack of preparation and appalling conduct of the war were, in fact, signal indications of the weaknesses of the regime. These lay less in objective factors—shortage of raw materials and food, which autarky had been unable to remedy—than in the complete inadequacy of the decision-making structure of Fascism. Mussolini had always deliberately ensured the fragmentation of the Fascist élite around him, just as he had encouraged the rivalry between the armed forces in order to be better able to divide and rule. With the concentration of power, decisions became haphazard, uncoordinated, and often contradictory, frequently made on the spot and without reflection in order to satisfy an immediate request. Indeed, it might be said that one of Mussolini's weaknesses was an inability to choose; faced with an alternative he would either put off a decision or try to have it both ways. These defects were reproduced throughout the entire Fascist construction: coherent and monolithic on the exterior, fragile and fissured within. Certain parts of the Fascist edifice might, in fact, work very well; it was the whole which did not hold together. The tensions of war revealed the cracks in the structure; as Mussolini himself was well aware, Fascism had failed the ultimate test it had set for itself.

Under the impact of military disaster, food shortages, and Allied bombing, opinion in Italy turned rapidly against Fascism. By early 1943 those conservative forces which had sustained Mussolini throughout the *ventennio* were beginning to look for a way out in the hope of saving what they could. Their minds were further concentrated when in March popular discontent became obvious as workers went on strike in the factories of Turin—the first major strikes for nearly twenty years. Covert anti-Fascist organizations, mainly Communist, emerged to lead the protest which, if it started as a strike against appalling work conditions, soon became openly political in content. Facing the threat of radical popular participation in the evolution of events, conservatives and moderates began to look towards the king and the Vatican to help in ending Italian involvement in the war. Mussolini's defenestration by the Fascist Grand Council in July was, at least on paper, a premiss to the continuation of a new, more moderate Fascism. In fact, with the subsequent arrest of

THE WRITING ON THE WALL: workers go on strike in northern Italy in March 1943. The strikes were the first open expression of popular discontent with conditions imposed by the war and very quickly became explicit hostile demonstrations against the Fascist regime itself.

Mussolini, Fascism collapsed almost overnight and power returned to the king.

Hopes of containing popular feeling ended when Germany invaded Italy following the armistice of 8 September. While the king fled rather ignominiously from Rome to Brindisi, German forces took over northern and central Italy and those parts of the south not already controlled by the advancing Allies. Mussolini, rescued from his mountain prison by German gliders, returned to Italy as the head of a puppet Fascist State: the Italian Social Republic (RSI) or Republic of Salò. Strong anti-Fascist sentiment now took concrete form; Communists, Socialists, and Catholics took up arms to fight Nazism and Fascism in what became both a war for national liberation and a civil war. The partisan war was effective, if often tragic. It was marked by numerous episodes of savage reprisal against unarmed civilians by both Nazis and Fascists, which had the effect of uniting a large part of the population in either active or passive resistance to Fascism. Mussolini's republic tried to recapture support by a pathetic attempt to return to the radical and socialistic ideas of the Fascism of 1919 and 1920. More in evidence was the brutal violence of that first Fascism as the 'black brigades' of the RSI distinguished themselves for their cruelty to their fellow Italians.

Dominated by the Communists, the Resistance movement represented a new phase in popular participation in Italian politics, often explicitly identified as a continuation of the lapsed struggles of 1919–22. For the young, who could not remember those struggles but who were faced with possible enforced conscription to the RSI, it was a time of choice; in fact, many former Fascists chose the partisan bands rather than the black brigades, who were seen as German stooges. The bands formed a school of politics for those who fought in them and it was under their influence (and that of the Vatican) that party politics developed once again in Italy. The Communist leader, Palmiro Togliatti, aided this process by shelving all revolutionary pretensions (which Moscow would never have supported) in the name of the greater priority of national liberation. Although treated with a certain diffidence by the anti-Communist Allies (particularly the British), the Resistance represented a great advance on the social conflicts of the first post-war period; at its end it was no longer possible to question the right of workers and peasants to their place within the political framework.

The end came in April 1945. With the liberation of Milan, Mussolini fled from Como, apparently in an attempt to reach Austria. He was stopped by partisans, recognized, and shot. The next day his body was taken to Milan and hung upside down for public execration in Piazzale Loreto, the piazza where, a few days before, the bodies of murdered partisans had been similarly exposed as a macabre warning to the restless population.

Ironically, Mussolini had succeeded in uniting Italians briefly—but against

Fascism rather than for it. None the less the legacy of Fascism was to be far-reaching. Quite apart from a disastrous war fought on Italian territory, Fascism bequeáthed poverty, inefficiency, a mediocre cultural provincialism born of intellectual isolation, and a political practice which had erected clientelism to system, generalized petty corruption, and made the use of public office for private gain the norm. The economic reorganization of Italy which had taken place under Fascism demonstrated all the imbalances determined by the social priorities of the regime—imbalances which had certainly served to retard rather than accelerate development. But it was at the political level that Fascism witnessed its real defeat. The attempt to form a nation, to give Italians a single identity in the Italian State, had proved a total failure. This was perhaps inevitable in an authoritarian populism which attempted to achieve mobilization through myths of past greatness and illusions of future conquest—illusions pursued at the cost of material well-being. In the end, the benefits of Fascism became less and less evident, even to its supporters, the deficiencies ever more apparent. Fascist pretensions were ultimately far beyond the means available to the regime. Many had known this all along; the tragedy was that it took a world war to burst the bubble and make it obvious to everyone.

TWENTIETH-CENTURY CULTURE

DAVID FORGACS

Country and Cities

The cultural map of Italy at the end of the twentieth century looks very different from that of the end of the nineteenth. The most striking change has been the increase in communications and the related breakdown of perceived boundaries, both internally within Italy and between it and the world beyond. Internally, different local areas have been opened up by transport and telephone networks and by the mass media, and their inhabitants have been able to hear, see, and move beyond them. The use of local dialects has declined, steeply since the 1960s, as the many varieties of spoken Italian have spread. These trends may not have brought the end of 'localism' but they have made local areas less insulated from the world around them, have obliged them to redefine their identities in relation to larger communities, and have produced a degree of shared experience between different parts of the country which would have been impossible in 1900. Across Italy's external boundaries the century has seen an increasing cultural exchange with other nations, an exchange of images, styles, and cultural products, from books to music to fashion to films, which is no longer restricted, as it was in the past, to a small literate community, but has come to involve very large numbers of people. At the same time, the role of religion has been redefined by secularization, particularly since the late 1950s. Most people in Italy no longer attend Church services and most of them spend more time in watching television (on average nearly twenty hours a week) than they do in any other routine activity apart from working and sleeping. Religious devotion, where it has persisted, has become for many people a more private matter, less dependent on public ritual.

One of the most strongly felt boundaries at the turn of the century was between cities and rural areas. In the accounts of educated travellers and observers all rural areas were seen as more or less remote and primitive and the southern countryside was the most remote of all. Leopoldo Franchetti, a landowner from Tuscany, had described his trip inland from Palermo in 1876 with Sidney Sonnino to investigate social conditions in Sicily as a venture into an interior full of 'mysterious and unknown things'. The folklorist Giuseppe Pitré, who came from Palermo, wrote detailed descriptions of the customs and practices of the Sicilian people, but in a way that reproduced a widely shared view of these customs as curiosities, foreign to the observer's own culture and historically unchanging. For the intellectuals of the Socialist Party, the cultural backwardness of rural Italy was seen as the main obstacle to the party's expansion into these areas. The metaphors they most frequently used from the 1890s to the First World War were those of eradicating (illiteracy), raising (the rural people to culture), and spreading (culture from the towns). For the Fascist government in its ruralization and land reclamation (*bonifica*) programmes of the 1930s, and for the agencies set up after 1945 with the help of American experts to develop the south (SVIMEZ, Cassa per il Mezzogiorno), the traditional countryside was similarly an area to be opened up, reclaimed, transformed.

The differences between urban and rural society were indeed considerable, but these accounts tended to judge the latter from the standpoint of a metropolitan culture which their authors considered more rational and advanced, or indeed as the only culture deserving of the name. This view did not always result from a lack of sympathy; in many cases it involved a desire to know and understand peasant society. Thus, Carlo Levi's *Cristo si è fermato a Eboli* [Christ Stopped at Eboli] (1945), the memoir of his internal exile in the mid-1930s for anti-Fascist activities to a hilltop village in the province of Matera (Basilicata), carefully documented the practices and beliefs of the inhabitants of the village. But Levi nevertheless interpreted their world as outside time and history, untouched by modern civilization, and empathized with it in a quasi-mystical way as he defended its right to preserve its autonomy against the encroachments of a centralizing State.

Against such interpretations one needs to insist on two important points: that there was a very high degree of internal cultural variation between different areas of the Italian countryside and that there was a growing cultural interdependency between city and country in the course of the century. For instance, the textile factories in Biella and Milan in Lombardy came to depend, around the beginning of the century, on the seasonal work of unmarried women from peasant families in outlying villages, who took their wage packets home in exchange for food. In this way they maintained close ties with the village as they were exposed to the new cultural experiences of the factory town; this contact in turn modified the culture of the family and the village. In the Tavolata of Puglia and the Po Delta the development of capitalist farming and wage contracts after Unification profoundly altered the culture of these areas. The children of the *braccianti* or *giornalieri*—the agricultural day-labourers—went to elementary school and acquired literacy and numeracy skills, unlike the children of peasant smallholders, because there was no child labour-market in the areas of *bracciantato*. This meant that a second generation of *braccianti* emerged around 1900 who were able to read Socialist or anarchist propaganda. Popular songs and oral narratives in areas of wage labour also reflected social conflicts: an example is the women's protest song 'La canzone della Lega' which was sung throughout the Po Valley from Piedmont to the Veneto in the decade before the First World War. Later in the century songs in rural areas would reflect other major events like the invasions and civil war of 1943–5 and the post-war occupations of land in Calabria or Abruzzo. Other causes of cultural change in the countryside were emigration and return migration (particularly in the north-east and the south), which left many traces in popular songs as well as in literature, and the gradual and uneven penetration of new communications technologies: cinema and broadcast radio from the 1920s and 1930s; television from the 1950s. Carlo Levi himself, who told his readers on the first page of his book that the village of Gagliano was untouched by history, showed them in the subsequent pages how the demographic balance of the village had been affected by emigration and by conscription during the First World War and how the Fascist State had arrived there, if only to a limited extent, in the form of a *podestà* appointed from Rome, a schoolteacher who enrolled some of his boys into the Balilla youth movement and who obliged the villagers to listen to Mussolini's speeches on a radio set with a loudspeaker in the main square.

A PEASANT FAMILY listens to the radio, *c*.1960. Regular broadcasts had begun in Italy in 1924 but the medium had been slow to reach outside cities. After 1945 licences rose rapidly from 1.6 million to an all-time peak of over 6 million in 1958, with the fastest growth in the countryside.

Urban Cultures

If life in rural areas was changing in the course of the century, so too was that in the cities, though at a different rhythm. Here change was driven by the rapid growth in large city populations, much higher literacy rates, which created a market for newspapers and to a greater extent for weekly magazines, and the development of the newer commercial forms of leisure. The pattern of urban popular entertainment, which in the last quarter of the nineteenth century had come to centre on the *café chantant* and its successor the variety theatre, began to be modified around 1900 by the development of cinematography and the rise of the *politeama*, a large, multi-purpose theatre capable of seating up to four thousand people, which characteristically rotated plays, opera, variety, and silent films with musical accompaniments. As theatrical entertainments diversified and modernized, the opera or *teatro lirico*, which from the late eighteenth to the mid-nineteenth century had been in Italy a thriving cultural industry depending on a constant turnover of new works and an international touring circuit, began its transformation into an art based largely on revivals of the Classical and Romantic repertoire and into what the historian John Rosselli has called its new status as 'a spectator sport'. When new operas were written after 1900 they either looked back to the past for their plots, their language, and a part of their musical idiom—an example is Giacomo Puccini's last opera *Turandot*, first performed in Milan in 1926, two years after the composer's death—or else they were experimental works destined for small, specialist audiences.

Film had begun, in Italy as elsewhere, as a series of one-minute novelty shorts projected in fairs and sideshows. As the films got longer and more theatrical in style they were incorporated into mixed-entertainment programmes in theatres or in purpose-built cinemas. Already before the First World War the new medium had become hugely popular in the towns. Low ticket prices played a part here: theatre-owners only had to cover costs of rentals and a projectionist—there were no performers, technicians, or stage-

GIOVANNI PASTRONE'S *CABIRIA* (1914). Its set designs and pioneering use of the tracking shot (*carrellata*) were emulated by D. W. Griffith in *Intolerance* (1917). The intertitles were written in a heavily literary style by Gabriele d'Annunzio, whose name featured on the posters and who was widely but erroneously credited by press and public with overall responsibility for the film.

hands to pay. In Milan the *Corriere della Sera* wrote in 1910: 'Since the invasion of the Huns one cannot remember an invasion that has been more formidable than that of the cinema.' By 1927 cinema box-office receipts accounted for over 50 per cent of the takings of all forms of spectator entertainment in Italy, including sport and live theatre; by 1936 this share had risen to 70 per cent and by 1941 to 83 per cent. Yet as the demand for films rose, Italian film producers became increasingly unable to meet it. Italy had started as one of the world's major film-producing countries, renowned in particular for its sumptuous costume epics like *The Last Days of Pompei* (Mario Caserini, 1913) and the innovative *Cabiria* (directed by Giovanni Pastrone with intertitles by Gabriele d'Annunzio, 1914). In 1915 Italian companies produced a total of 562 films and Italy was a net exporter. By 1930 the number had fallen to twelve and Italy had become overwhelmingly an importer of films from other countries, most notably the United States. By 1938, just before the Fascist government introduced protectionist legislation, foreign films accounted for 87 per cent of total box-office takings in Italy.

Although different cities have retained much of their distinctive character, their individual functions and identities, and the relations between them, have changed in the course of the century. The cultural importance of Florence, Turin, and Naples has diminished while that of Rome and Milan has increased. Florence remains today one of Europe's great heritage cities, but it is no longer the centre of a modern philosophical, literary, and artistic culture that it was from the early years of the century to the Second World War, when with its periodicals—*La Voce* (1908–14), *Solaria* (1926–39), *Campo di Marte* (1938–9)—and its cafés, like the Giubbe Rosse and the Paszkowski, it was a magnet for creative talent, including the writer and philosopher Giovanni Papini, the poet Eugenio Montale, the painter Ardengo Soffici, and the composer Luigi Dallapiccola. One of the main reasons why Florence declined as a literary centre is that after 1945 writers came to congregate less around small literary reviews and to depend more on larger publishing firms, newspapers, and mass-circulation magazines. This drew them to Milan, Turin, or Rome. The main Florentine publisher of new literature in the 1920s and 1930s, Vallecchi, managed to retain or recruit few writers after 1945. In the post-war period several prominent younger novelists, including Cesare Pavese, Elio Vittorini, Natalia Ginzburg, and Italo Calvino, were in the editorial team of Einaudi in Turin; from 1959 Umberto Eco worked as a consultant for Bompiani in Milan.

Turin is still today the home of several prestigious publishing firms and an important book fair, but it has declined from being a centre of film production (before the First World War), the hub of the radio network (in the 1920s), and a centre of art and architectural design (from the *art nouveau* period to the 1940s); it progressively lost the first two of these roles to Rome. Naples is an even more particular case. The city was not only the base of the century's most influential intellectual—the philosopher, historian, and literary critic Benedetto Croce (1866–1952)—it was also the home of Neapolitan song, which from the 1880s to the 1950s was the best-known type of Italian popular song both in Italy and abroad. The success of numbers like 'Funiculì, funiculà' (Peppino Turco and Luigi Denza, 1880), 'O sole mio' (Alfredo Mazzucchi and Edoardo Di Capua, 1898), and 'Torna a Surriento' (Giambattista and Ernesto De Curtis, 1902) was aided by a well-organized music business and the marketing of a highly exportable iconographic tradition: the Piedigrotta Festival, Vesuvius, the Bay of Naples, the islands. For much of this period Neapolitan popular culture came to stand for Italian popular culture as a whole, a process assisted by the diffusion of typical Neapolitan or southern foods like pizza and macaroni, emigration from the south, and the international success of Neapolitan singers, notably Enrico Caruso (1873–1921) who lived for many years in the United States. Naples also had a thriving tradition of comic theatre, including variety theatre, long after the medium had gone into decline in the north of Italy, and this tradition produced two of the greatest theatrical artists of the century, the actor and dramatist Eduardo de Filippo (1900–84) and the stage and screen actor Totò (pseudonym of Antonio De Curtis (1898–1967)). These forms of Neapolitan culture declined from the late 1950s largely because they came to be identified with an old Italy of poverty and dialect traditions, an image of the country which began to lose its appeal in the years of the economic miracle, particularly for younger people, against more modernizing images.

Rome's cultural expansion was a consequence of its expansion as the capital after 1870. It became the centre, through the ministries, of State education and cultural policy, and the site of a new university and a new national library. Not only did the film industry and broadcasting become concentrated there between the wars; the city also continued to attract writers and literary journalists, as it had done since the 1880s, and unlike Florence it expanded as a centre for literary intellectuals after the Second World War. Some of them even 'Romanized' their own work: the Milanese writer Carlo Emilio Gadda wrote one Roman novel, *Quer pasticciaccio brutto de Via Merulana* (1957); Pier Paolo Pasolini, who moved to Rome from Friuli in 1950, wrote several—*Ragazzi di vita* (1955), *Una vita violenta* (1959), and the posthumously published *Petrolio* (1992)—as well as directing various Roman films, from *Accattone* (1961) and *Mamma Roma* (1962) to the short film *La ricotta* (1963). Milan still retains the position it acquired early in the nineteenth century as Italy's principal city of publishing, both of books and of periodicals; it is also the undisputed centre of the advertising industry. In addition, since the rise of the private television networks in the late 1970s, Milan has become a second capital of television and has re-emerged as an alternative centre to Rome of film production and distribution. To use the terms of media historian Peppino Ortoleva, Italy has become culturally less 'polycentric' after 1945 and increasingly 'bipolar' on the Rome–Milan axis, particularly since 1980.

Modernity and Tradition

Milan in the years before the First World War was the official base of the Futurist movement, whose principal animator was the writer Filippo Tommaso Marinetti (1876–1944). Although Futurism had some precedents within Italy, most notably the machine cult of Mario Morasso, author of *La nuova arma (la macchina)* [The New Weapon (The Machine)] (1905), it was effectively the product of a liaison between Italian artists and French culture, from the ideas of Henri Bergson and Georges Sorel to the literature of the Symbolists and the art of the Cubists. Marinetti himself was a cosmopolitan figure who had attended a French *lycée* in Egypt, lived for several years in Paris before settling in Milan, and wrote in French as well as Italian. His founding manifesto

DRAWING FOR *CITTÀ NUOVA* PROJECT by Antonio Sant'Elia (1888–1916). None of Sant'Elia's major designs was executed in his brief lifetime, but his radical ideas were co-opted by Marinetti for the Futurist cause, and his drawings of power stations and cities on multiple levels exerted a strong influence on modern architecture and urban planning after his death.

297

of Futurism first appeared on the front page of *Le Figaro* in Paris on 20 February 1909. Most of the other founding Futurists spent at least some time in Paris
before the First World War. The example of Futurism stimulated the rise of
kindred movements abroad, from English Vorticism to Russian Futurism,
and Marinetti travelled widely to proselytize its ideals and organize exhibi-
tions, including four trips to London (1910–14) and one to Petrograd and
Moscow (1914).

At the same time, Futurism had several Italian traits. There was, in the first
place, its strongly nationalistic character. Marinetti volunteered for combat in
the Libyan War (1911–12), was an ardent interventionist in 1915, and fought,
like several of his Futurist comrades, in the First World War. The militarism,
colonialism, and nationalism of the Italian Futurists led to a rift with the Russian Futurists, several of whom, like Vladimir Mayakovsky, embraced the
anti-militarism and internationalism of the left. In the second place, there was
Futurism's flamboyant self-promotion, its relentless emphasis on speed or
dynamism, which Marinetti identified as the keynote of modern life, and its
intransigent commitment to industrialism against ruralism, modernity
against backwardness, the future against the past, the transient against the
permanent, all of which may be read as symptoms of a peculiarly Italian anxiety, that of trying to rescue Italy from its own past, of trying to promote a
modern movement in an old country with few modern cities, a largely
unmodernized countryside, an artistic heritage stretching back over two
thousand years, and conservative art school traditions. In the third place,
Futurism projected itself as a cult of youth and aggression. Marinetti had
declared in the founding manifesto: 'Except in struggle, there is no more
beauty. No work without an aggressive character can be a masterpiece.'
Many of the things the movement considered positive—speed, violence,
struggle, and war—were associated with masculinity and vitality, whereas
the things it opposed—the past, the museum, the classical nude, the *clair de la
lune*, mellifluous sentences, musical harmony, socialism, democracy, pacifism—it associated with femininity, disease, or death. Marinetti called Venice
a 'jewelled bathtub for cosmopolitan courtesans'; Papini described Rome as a
city which 'attracts like a whore and passes on to her lovers the syphilis of
chronic archaeologism'. These attitudes did not prevent a number of women
writers and artists from identifying themselves with the movement, as the
critic Claudia Salaris has documented, and linking its radicalism to their own
demands for women's political and social emancipation.

The First World War was a watershed for Futurism. Umberto Boccioni
died after falling from a horse; the visionary young architect Antonio Sant'Elia
was killed in action; other artists, including Soffici, Gino Severini, Carlo Carrà,
and Mario Sironi left the movement as their styles evolved in different directions. In 1917 Carrà joined Pittura Metafisica, founded in Paris during the war

by Giorgio de Chirico, and by 1920 he was arguing for a return to traditional and indigenous values. Sironi in 1922 was a founder member of the Novecento [Twentieth Century] movement, characterized in the 1920s by its figurative magic realism and the accentuated plastic or tactile quality of its forms, a conscious reaction against the Futurist painters' dissolution of rigid forms and their interpenetrating planes. Marinetti, unabashed, continued to promote Futurism and to steer it into new areas, including politics (his short-lived Futurist Party stood on a joint slate with the Fascists in the 1919 general election), and he presided over a post-war continuation, known as Secondo Futurismo [Late Futurism], which lasted until the late 1930s. This brought to prominence artists like Fortunato Depero, Enrico Prampolini, and the Bulgarian *émigré* Nikolai Diulgheroff. The post-war work of these artists, along with that of one of the founding Futurists, Giacomo Balla, was characterized by its hard-edged geometrical designs in brilliant colours. This phase of Futurism also saw the development from 1929 of *aeropittura*, inspired by aeroplane flight.

The war did not produce the same responses of disaffection, pacifism, or cynicism among writers and artists as it did in Britain, France, Germany, or Russia. Several Italian writers, to be sure, powerfully registered the extreme physical and mental hardship of trench and mountain combat, but they generally complemented these descriptions with declarations of patriotic sentiment or the populist notion of a shared community between themselves and the ordinary footsoldier, the *fante*. This is the case with Piero Jahier's *Con me e con gli alpini* [With Me and the Alpine Regiment] (1919), Soffici's *Kobilek* (1918), Marinetti's *L'alcova d'acciaio* (1921), and even the often-acerbic war poems of Giuseppe Ungaretti (1888–1970) in his collection *L'allegria* (1919). A provocative pamphlet by Curzio Malaparte (pseudonym of Kurt Erich Suckert) entitled *Viva Caporetto!* interpreted the national 'humiliation' of Caporetto (September 1917) when the defeated Italian army retreated behind the lines, as a positive mutiny by the exploited *fanti* against the oppressive officer caste, but even this was politically ambiguous. In a second edition, published in 1923 after the Fascists had come to power, Malaparte modified its originally pro-Bolshevik message to make Caporetto a precursor of the nationalist-Fascist revolution. In the late 1920s Malaparte became, together with a group of Tuscan artists and writers including Mino Maccari and Soffici, a leading figure in the strapaese [supercountry] movement (the coinage was his), which argued for an art based on indigenous Italian (southern, Mediterranean, Catholic) traditions, repudiating both the Futurist aesthetic and the cult of modernist civilization which Malaparte dubbed *stracittà* [supercity] and which he identified chiefly in Massimo Bontempelli (1878–1960) and his Roman periodical *'900* (1926–9), a showcase for international modernist writing.

Other artists who repudiated the lesson of Futurism sought not to retrieve national traditions but to be modern in different ways. Giuseppe Terragni and his fellow Rationalist architects of Gruppo 7, who were centred in Turin and Milan, developed the principles of the international modern movement (Le Corbusier, Gropius, Mies van der Rohe, Otto Wagner), emphasizing, in a different direction from the Futurist Sant'Elia, a strict geometricality, functionality, and sobriety of the building. The programmatic statements of the group, published in *La Rassegna Italiana* in 1926-7, suggested a return to order: the avant-gardes, they claimed, had been based on 'a pointless destructive rage' (*una vana furia distruttrice*) whereas their architecture rested on 'a classical substratum', on 'the spirit of tradition'. The abstract artists of the late 1920s and 1930s—Prampolini, Osvaldo Licini, Fausto Melotti, Manlio Rho—were also influenced by foreign work and defined their project in terms of an ordered geometry, a simplification and clarification of line and form.

Among writers too there was a variety of ways of negotiating a relationship with modernity. Gabriele d'Annunzio (1863-1938), dandy and snob, flaunted his antimodernism of taste and his cult of tradition and refinement. Yet he had at least one foot in early modernism in the way he repudiated, from the late 1880s, the canons of realism and naturalism, and in his eroticism, aestheticism, and stylistic eclecticism. Federigo Tozzi undermined the centrality of character and the determinism of plot in his *Con gli occhi chiusi* [With Closed Eyes] (1919) by a series of random distractions and digressions from the protagonist and his story. Italo Svevo (pseudonym of Ettore Schmitz, 1861-1928) slowly eroded the conventions of realism and naturalism in three novels written over a thirty-year period and set in his native Trieste. In the second, *Senilità* [As a Man Grows Older] (1898), the reliability of the central male character's account of events and his own feelings is called into question by the narrator. In the third, *La coscienza di Zeno* [The Confessions of Zeno] (1924), it is the main character himself who narrates his story and yet the text comically cuts away at his account from within as he repeatedly loops over his life in a series of attempts to justify it to himself and explain it to a psychoanalyst. In *Uno, nessuno e centomila* [One, No-one, and a Hundred Thousand] (1926) by Luigi Pirandello (1867-1936), the narrator recounts how his own sense of self became unhinged as he recognized how much it was pieced together out of other people's definitions of him. Pirandello had treated similar themes in his plays *Così è (se vi pare)* [So it is (if it seems to you)] (1918), *Sei personaggi in cerca d'autore* [Six Characters in Search of an Author] (1921), and *Enrico IV* (1922), the last two of which additionally laid bare the mechanisms of theatrical illusion by non-naturalistic staging. In poetry, too, there were various strategies of modernism: Guido Gozzano imported the everyday objects of bourgeois kitsch into poetic vocabulary; Ungaretti stripped the verse line right down; Dino Campana experimented on the margins between poetry and prose, dreams and waking; Montale mixed symbolism and pastiches of tradition

PIRANDELLO'S *SEI PERSONAGGI IN CERCA D'AUTORE* (1921) compelled audiences to question their sense of reality. It is seen here in his own production at the Teatro d'Arte, Rome (1925), with Egisto Olivieri (arms outstretched) as the Director, Marta Abba (Stepdaughter), Lamberto Picasso (Father), Gino Cervi (Son) and Jone Frigerio (Mother).

with a rich musicality. Other writers maintained that one could innovate while staying within the furrows of tradition. The Roman literary periodical *La Ronda* (1919–23), edited by the poet Vincenzo Cardarelli and others, represented a *rappel à l'ordre* after the war and the social conflicts of the *biennio rosso* and a reappropriation of the 'pure' lines of the Italian literary past after the iconoclasm of Futurism and the experimentalism of *La Voce*.

Many of these seemingly mutually opposed trends—the aggressive modernity of the Futurists and the cult of the past of d'Annunzio, the Novecentismo of Bontempelli and Sironi and the Strapaese of Malaparte and Soffici, the geometrical abstraction of Melotti and Rho and the figurative realism of Giorgio Morandi, the experimental music of Dallapiccola and Goffredo Petrassi and the more popular music of Pietro Mascagni and Umberto Giordano—in fact proved to be ideologically compatible with Fascism, at any rate up to the late 1930s. In the cultural lexicon of the Fascist period the terms *moderno* and *tradizionale*, together with *rivoluzionario* and *classico*, became highly elastic signifiers which artists, architects, writers, musicians, and critics adapted to

their own purposes—whether enthusiastically or self-protectively—in order to claim that their work was aligned with the regime.

Fascism

The political philosopher Norberto Bobbio claimed in 1972 that a Fascist culture never really existed in Italy. He drew attention to the way in which scholars of integrity had made only minimal compromises with the values of the regime in its showpiece cultural projects, such as the *Enciclopedia Italiana* (1929–37). This view is certainly right up to a point, and the notion of minimal collaboration helps explain how many cultural figures who had lived through the regime could emerge after 1945 uncompromised and committed to the values of liberalism (as in the exemplary case of Croce), or to those of democracy or socialism, all of which Mussolini claimed Fascism had supplanted. However, it is a view which also lets off the hook many other figures of undoubted cultural significance who found a convenient niche within the regime, who accepted its protection, eulogized it, or presented their work in a pro-Fascist light. To the names mentioned above one could add those of Ungaretti, who joined the Fascist movement at its beginnings in 1919; Puccini, who congratulated Mussolini on his coming to power in 1922; and Pirandello, who applied for a Fascist Party card in 1924 at the height of the Matteotti crisis. It seems both unnecessary and unhistorical to perform the complex acrobatics of some admirers of these figures who argue that their commitment to Fascism was superficial or ambiguous, or that they were political innocents, or that the aesthetic value of their work has no relationship with politics. That these individuals could identify publicly with Fascism in fact tells us much both about them and about Fascism's relationship with the arts, namely that it was able, at least up to the mid-1930s, to contain a diversity of artistic styles and ideological positions. This was less the result of toleration or any deliberate policy choice than of the multiplicity of ideological currents which found a home within Fascism and the regime's lack, for over a decade, of a single, coherent cultural policy. The Fascist government was certainly quick to clamp down on opposition. Between 1923 and 1926 it repressed the Socialist press and publishing firms as well as their other cultural ventures, such as libraries and educational circles, and it ensured that ownership and editorial control of the non-party newspapers, including the formerly liberal *Corriere della Sera* and *La Stampa*, passed into friendly hands. It also set up new censorship bodies, like the Agenzia Stefani, which vetted newspaper stories, and it encouraged local prefectures to be more vigilant in stopping or 'revising' books, plays, and filmscripts which might be construed as anti-Fascist or anti-Italian. But after having taken these repressive steps it set fairly wide margins for cultural activity for anyone prepared to identify themselves publicly with the interests of the regime, presented what many artists perceived as a radical or revolutionary aspect, and allowed cultural exchange with other countries to persist in a variety of spheres, despite internal opposition from 'intransigent' Fascists who would have preferred a clearer direction in cultural policy.

The notion of Fascism as lacking any real culture also restricts the definition of culture to high culture and thus to élites—Bobbio in fact specified that his remarks referred mainly to academics. It consequently leaves out of the picture the extensive work of the regime in the sphere of popular culture, such as its provision of popular leisure and recreation facilities; its creation of women's, youth, and student activist groups; and its promotion of sport and public commemorations, such as the massive Mostra della Rivoluzione Fascista, opened in Rome in 1932 to commemorate the tenth anniversary (Decennale) of the March on Rome. It also omits the regime's impact on newer forms of mass culture like radio and the cinema. The Communist Party leader Palmiro Togliatti, in his lectures on Fascism given in Moscow in 1935, identified the Opera Nazionale Dopolavoro (OND), the mass leisure organization developed by the Fascists, as an ambitious and innovative attempt to mould working-class consent to the regime and he told Communists operating underground in Italy to infiltrate it and try to radicalize its members from within. The OND was in fact a many-branched organization including men's and women's sections, theatre groups, film clubs, cycling, and bowls (*bocce*) competitions. For the urban working class the OND arranged children's holidays and Sunday excursions for adults and families from the cities on the discount trains known as *treni popolari*; in rural areas it officially sponsored local

FESTIVAL OF LOCAL PATRON SAINT, Gioiosa Ionica (Calabria), *c*.1930. Events like this, supported until the late 1930s by the Opera Nazionale Dopolavoro, officially incorporated 'folk culture' from above into 'national culture', and as such were consistent with the Fascist regime's declared aim of 'going to the people'.

village festivals, thereby annexing the diverse popular traditions of the many regions and localities to the populism of the regime. The American historian Victoria de Grazia, in a detailed study of the OND, has drawn attention to the deliberately apolitical nature of many of its activities and has argued that it was successful not so much in promoting consent to the regime or effective distraction through a culture of consumption as in creating a set of leisure activities which partially cushioned the working classes against the effects of wage cuts and thus weakened potential dissent. There are, nevertheless, various pieces of evidence which suggest that some people who grew up under the regime, including young workers in areas of left traditions, identified it positively with modernity in the 1930s because they linked it to sport, physical fitness, and the competitive ethos.

As for radio and the cinema, these were both media which the regime used for propaganda purposes, though their social impact as instruments of propaganda was less than is sometimes assumed. Like the other cultural industries—publishing, the music business, the theatre—the radio and film industries were never fully nationalized in Fascist Italy, as they were for instance in the Soviet Union. The Italian government, following the model of the British government with the BBC, granted a monopoly to one broadcasting firm (called URI until 1926, EIAR until 1944, RAI thereafter), but this firm remained juridically private and was funded by revenue from advertising as

CASA DEL FASCIO, Como (1932/6) by Giuseppe Terragni. Rationalist architecture emphasized functionality and eschewed redundant ornamentation. Terragni's white concrete building, with its rhythm of rectangles within rectangles, offsets the semicircles of Como cathedral in front, the angular orange roofs around, and the mountains behind. Each of the four sides (33.2 x 16.6 m.) has a different asymmetrical design.

well as from a licence fee levied by the ministry of posts. This meant that the broadcasting service was accountable as much to its industrial shareholders (radio equipment manufactures, electrical, telephone, and chemicals firms) and to its advertising clients as it was to the State. Throughout the 1920s radio expanded largely as a medium for middle-class audiences. There were relatively few licensed subscribers and political programmes were a small proportion of the schedule; most broadcast hours were taken up with music and other light entertainments, despite the attempts of those like Marinetti—by now a committed Fascist and a keen broadcaster—to argue that radio was the most Futurist of instruments. It was only from 1933, when the EIAR was incorporated into the State holding company IRI, the Government set up the Ente Radio Rurale to take educational broadcasts into rural areas, and a more concerted push was made to get people to purchase cheaper sets, that the number of licensed subscribers rose to over a million and a more political use of radio as an instrument of propaganda can be traced. Symptomatic of this was the introduction in 1933 of the daily fifteen-minute slot 'Cronache del regime'. From this point, radio did begin to affect people's allocation of time and cultural repertoires in some areas, to create its own stars, to be used to listen collectively in public places to live transmissions of sporting events (football, cycling, automobile and motorcycle racing)—in other words to influence tastes, values, and attitudes. An important source of evidence about its social impact towards the end of the *ventennio* is the referendum of radio listeners held by the EIAR in 1939–40. Even so, it remains difficult to assess just how much of a political impact the radio had on public opinion under Fascism, and one needs to remember that radio sets were widely used during the Second World War to listen clandestinely to foreign broadcasts, including the anti-Fascist transmissions in Italian of the BBC and the Voice of America.

Cinema had much larger audiences than radio, and Mussolini publicly acknowledged its propaganda value. 'La cinematografia è l'arma più forte', he declared, echoing Lenin. In practice, until 1938 the regime found itself juggling these propaganda interests against a *laissez-faire* policy towards private film producers, who were allowed to turn out popular entertainment features provided they met the approval of the censors, and towards exhibitors (cinema-owners), who were allowed to import popular films from abroad to fill seats. People's memory of cinema-going between the wars is thus largely a memory of watching American films—Westerns, romantic melodramas, thrillers—with Italian films taking second place and with propaganda newsreels and short documentaries inserted between showings of the main feature. Among the popular Italian films were a number of witty social comedies, notably those of Mario Camerini (*Darò un milione*, 1935; *Il signor Max*, 1937), Raffaello Matarazzo (*Treno popolare*, 1933) and Alessandro Blasetti (*Quattro passi tra le nuvole* [A Walk in the Clouds], 1943), which were compatible with a Fascist

Canon en action by Gino Severini (1915). The celebration of action, war, and the synthesis of the machine and the human eye were central tenets of Italian Futurism. Severini had moved to Paris in 1906 and was to remain there for most of his life. Ill-health prevented him from fighting in the First World War.

ethos of populism and class-levelling without being propaganda films. The regime did sponsor some propaganda features, like Giovacchino Forzano's *Camicia nera* [Black Shirt], made for the Decennale celebrations of 1932, and Blasetti's *Vecchia guardia* [The Old Guard] (1935), but they were not commercially successful. Subsequently, two pieces of legislation in 1938 and 1939 had the effect of making the Italian film industry more autarkic: the Alfieri Law promised bonuses to commercially successful Italian productions and the Monopoly Law gave Italian distributors control over rentals of all films, including imports. This meant that earnings from rentals could no longer go abroad and it prompted the major Hollywood studios, who had hitherto had their own distributors in Italy, to withdraw from the Italian market. These measures remained in force until 1945.

This pattern of relative *laissez-faire* until the mid-1930s followed by a turn towards a more centralized and interventionist relationship with cultural activities (marked by the creation in 1937 of the Ministero della Cultura Popolare or MinCulPop) was therefore repeated across the board during the Fascist *ventennio* and is one of the most important periodizations one needs to make within it. This applies to educational policy too. The first reform of State education under a Fascist government, introduced by the philosopher Giovanni Gentile (1875–1944) as education minister in 1923 and trumpeted at the time by Mussolini as 'il più fascista delle riforme', was in fact essentially a liberal piece of legislation and it was attacked as such by more intransigent Fascists. Despite introducing a new national State examination, the Gentile Law reduced the amount of education controlled by the State by opening up a large area to private initiative—in practice this meant to Catholic schools. It also reinforced the existing three-way streaming of post-primary education into the humanities-based *ginnasi* and *licei*, technical-professional schools, and teacher-training institutions. Of these types of school it privileged the first—what Gentile called 'scuole di cultura'—at a time when there was, however, growing demand from

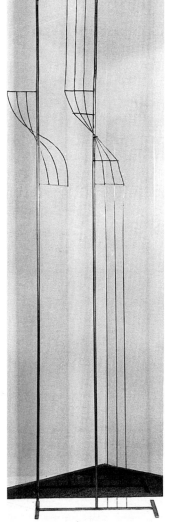

Facing: LA FIDÈLE ÉPOUSE (1929) by Alberto Savinio (pseudonym of Andrea de Chirico). A writer and composer as well as a visual artist, Savinio collaborated with his brother Giorgio de Chirico in developing Metaphysical painting and was later involved with the French Surrealists. His uncanny figures were influenced by Otto Weininger's analogies between human and animal psychology.

SCULTURA 17 (1935) by Fausto Melotti (1901–86). Melotti's work of the 1930s, and that of fellow abstractionists Lucio Fontana and Manlio Rho, was contemporary both with the figurative painting of the *Novecento* movement and the *aeropittura* of the later Futurists. This coexistence illustrates the lack of a single line in the visual arts under Fascism.

employers for technical and scientific skills. The reform maintained the restricted access to universities and made minimal changes to the curriculum. It was only in 1939 that a radical-right charter for education, the Carta della Scuola, was proposed, by the then education minister Giuseppe Bottai. But it came too late to be implemented before Italy joined the Second World War in June 1940.

The Second World War and Reconstruction

The final years of the Fascist regime formed a psychological turning-point for many young people. The bureaucratic stagnation, cult of the Duce, alliance with Hitler, and entry into the Second World War pushed many across the line into internal dissent or anti-Fascism. Both during the Resistance (1943–5) and after the war there was a substantial drift of intellectuals towards the anti-Fascist parties of the left: the Action Party, the Socialist Party, and the Communist Party. The last of these was particularly attractive because of the international prestige, at the time, of the Soviet Union, and because it had adopted a broad alliance strategy with middle-class progressives.

In philosophy the ideological reorientation included a rediscovery of Marxism. Galvano Della Volpe's *La teoria marxista dell'emancipazione umana* was published in 1945. An edition of the prison letters of the martyred Communist leader Antonio Gramsci (1891–1937) appeared in 1947, followed in 1948–51 by five volumes of his prison notebooks. The latter were particularly important in giving the PCI and its intellectuals ammunition with which to mount a challenge to the continued authority of Crocean liberalism and neo-idealism. In the arts it took the form of a widespread move towards social commitment, realism, and expressionism, in many cases (as in post-war France) under the banner of humanism, of a reassertion of the essential values of man which international fascism had crushed. Renato Guttuso, who took part in the Resistance in 1944 and befriended Picasso in Paris in 1945, had already joined the clandestine PCI in 1940 and increasingly produced politically committed pictures, like those of the post-war occupations of uncultivated lands in the south. The musician Dallapiccola had turned away from Fascism at the time of the Racial Laws (1938); he had married his Jewish partner and composed the implicitly dissident *Canti di prigionia* (1938–41). These were followed after the war by his one-act opera *Il prigioniero* (1949) and *Canti di liberazione* (1955). Roberto Rossellini, who in 1942 had been making propaganda films for the Italian navy, started to work in the autumn of 1944 on *Roma città aperta* (1945), the first of what was to be a trilogy of features, including *Paisà* (1946) and *Germania anno zero* (1947), which depicted the social effects of the war from an anti-Fascist and left-Catholic standpoint. Cesare Zavattini, who had built his pre-war reputation as a writer of light comic fiction and filmscripts, experienced a deep personal crisis during the war from which he emerged with a desire to observe and learn from ordinary people. This became the basis of his own version of the neo-realist aesthetic ('To set up the camera in a street, in a room; to see with insatiable patience, to teach ourselves to contemplate our fellow humans in their elementary actions') and it underlay the films he co-scripted with director Vittorio De Sica, including *Sciuscià* (1946), *Ladri di biciclette* [Bicycle Thieves] (1948), and *Umberto D* (1952). These were all set in Rome and they dealt respectively with the plight of young offenders, the desperation produced by unemployment, and the humiliation of a pauperized retired civil servant faced with eviction.

Neo-realism in the cinema was more a tendency or a moral disposition— what Zavattini called a *virtualità*—than a movement or a fixed set of aesthetic criteria and stylistic procedures. Nevertheless, the committed Italian films of the early post-war period did have a newness of look and a sharpness of feel, an ability to excite pity and anger, which were immediately apparent to audiences accustomed to the blander taste of American and European genre films. They therefore exerted a powerful influence on foreign audiences and filmmakers, from Satyajit Ray in India to Andresz Wajda in Poland to Elia Kazan in the United States. In Italy itself these films on the whole did not attract large audiences. *Sciuscià* and *Umberto D* were both commercial flops. *Roma città aperta* was successful, but not on its first showing. Rossellini recalled that when it was premièred at a festival in September 1945 the audience whistled in disapproval and only after it had been a hit in Paris did it begin to earn money at home. This partial rejection of committed films by Italian audiences is understandable if one considers the hardships they had experienced in the war and the privations of the post-war years. Most people went to the cinema to be distracted or to experience fantasies, not to be reminded of their own or other people's suffering, so comedies and adventures once again did well at the box office. Possibly those committed films which had relative commercial success did so because they were able to mobilize positive feelings of collective pride or anger, like *Roma città aperta*, or because they mixed the social realism with an entertaining story or with sex appeal, like Giuseppe De Santis's *Riso amaro* [Bitter Rice] (1948).

The rejection of stories that were too painful applied to written narratives too. Primo Levi (1919–87) first got *Se questo è un uomo* [If this is a Man], his account of his experience in Buna-Monowitz, a subsidiary of Auschwitz, published by a small firm in 1947 in 2,500 copies. The firm collapsed and the book was forgotten because, according to Levi in 1976, at that time 'people did not much want to go back over the painful years that had just ended'. What the book described was in fact unlike anything most Italians had experienced. In a later work, *I sommersi e i salvati* [The Drowned and the Saved] (1986), Levi recounts a nightmare that all the internees in the camps had: that they had

returned alive to tell their tale and no one believed them, or worse, simply turned away and ignored them. It was not till 1958 that *Se questo è un uomo* was republished, by Einaudi; this time it made a deep impact, both in Italy and abroad. The accounts of soldiers who had experienced the terrible hardship of the Russian campaign of 1941–2 and the subsequent retreat were perhaps more assimilable because of their emphasis on the return home. They included *Mai tardi* [Never Late] (1946) by Nuto Revelli and *Il sergente della neve* [The Sergeant in the Snow] (1953) by Mario Rigoni Stern.

This post-war trend towards realism, memoir, and social criticism, important as it was, is only part of the picture. The rise after 1946 of the Christian Democrat centre as the major player in the new Republic and its defeat both of the Communists and Socialists and of the Democrazia Cristiana's (DC's) own left wing ushered in a decade in which clerico-conservatism became a powerful cultural force. It made itself felt in various forms, from the Catholics' control of film censorship and a large slice of the exhibition market in the form of parish cinemas (*cinema di parrocchia*) to the sequestration of magazines considered obscene. In addition there was the anti-left bias and the sexual propriety that characterized both RAI radio and its new television service: the latter was controlled single-handedly by the Christian Democrats for two decades from its beginnings in 1954 until its reform in 1975. At the same time, the reconstruction, assisted by US aid through the European Recovery Program, set in train a process of modernization in which the American model of economic growth (monetarism, stimulation of the private sector, consumer-spending) played a powerful role, immeasurably more so than in countries like Britain or Sweden, where left parties had remained in government after the war and where there was an inter-party consensus on a Keynesian Welfare State. This American model in Italy had various cultural dimensions. The cultural symbols of Americanism—the boogie-woogie, Coca Cola, Lucky Strike cigarettes—which were associated with modernity and a loosening of traditional authority, had suddenly come closer to home in cities like Naples and Rome when US troops were stationed there. From the mid-1950s rock 'n' roll music (the first Elvis Presley records arrived in 1956) and films like *Rebel without a Cause* (1955), distributed in Italy with the more moralistic title *Gioventù bruciata* [Spent Youth], helped give shape to a new model of youth autonomy and

Facing: OCCUPATION OF UNCULTIVATED LAND IN SICILY (1949–50) by Renato Guttuso (1912–87). Guttuso came from Sicily and his work became increasingly political after he joined the clandestine Communist Party in 1940, explicitly so after the fall of Fascism. The composition emphasizes collective purpose yet the faces and figures remain strongly individualized.

NEO-REALISM MEETS HOLLYWOOD. In Vittorio de Sica's *Ladri di biciclette* (1948) Antonio Ricci (played by Lamberto Maggiorani, right) helps post an advertisement for *Gilda* starring Rita Hayworth. After 1945, with the lifting of the embargo on imports from the USA and an increase in film-going and magazine reading, American images came to play a large part in the cultural repertoires of many Italians.

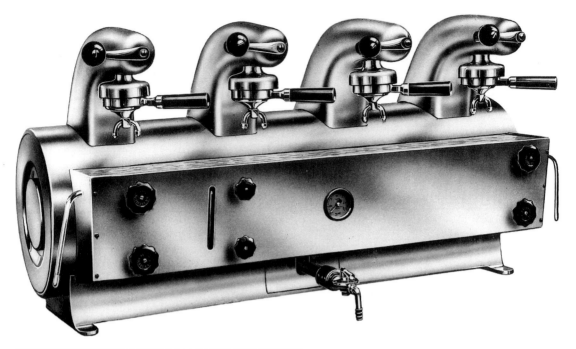

rebellion. Hollywood films had returned with a vengeance in 1945 after their virtual absence during the war years; by 1948, the year of *Ladri di biciclette* and *Riso amaro*, they were again taking more than 70 per cent of total box-office receipts. The decade after the war saw a big expansion of cinemas and film audiences outside main towns and in the south, where cinema had only had a limited presence before 1945. The Italian film industry itself became 'Americanized' in the 1950s and 1960s, as Cine-città became attractive to American producers both because of its lower costs and because the Italian government introduced a law preventing earnings from American films returning to the USA. Italian directors themselves began making a lucrative string of costume spectaculars, known as *pepla*, with minor American stars like muscle-man Steve Reeves. This internationalized film world of 'Hollywood on the Tiber', and the attendant paparazzi who photographed its transitory stars on the Via Veneto, was memorably satirized by Fellini in *La dolce vita* (1960); this film in turn was responsible for exporting a set of desirable icons of the new Italy: Vespa and Lambretta scooters, espresso coffee bars, beehive hairstyles, well-cut men's suits. These icons were eloquent proof that Italy in the 1950s had not just succumbed passively to Americanization but had been reworking American styles, adapting them to a local idiom, and creating distinctive new styles of its own.

The Economic Miracle and After

All these changes accelerated in the 1960s as a result of the economic miracle or boom (1958–63) which brought mass migrations to the cities, a growth of large industrial firms in the north and a nascent industrialization of the south, the building of the *autostrada* network, mass motorization, annual paid holidays, and a rapid rise in television set ownership and television consumption. The introduction by Mondadori in 1965 of its 'Oscar' series of low-priced quality paperbacks, which could be bought on any newsstand as well as in bookshops, ushered in a new era of mass publishing. The books had initial sales of around 200,000 copies per title and the initiative was soon emulated by other publishers. As the old *civiltà contadina* began to be definitively broken up by what was widely described as a 'mass society' or 'consumer society', intellectuals took up a variety of positions. The ethnologist Gianni Bosio and the ethnomusicologist Roberto Leydi sought to record the disappearing folk traditions, ways of life, songs, and spoken narratives of rural Italy, creating what would become an invaluable depository for future cultural historians. Pier Paolo Pasolini, who described the changes of the 1960s and 1970s as an 'anthropological revolution', lamented what he saw as the loss of candour and sexual innocence among young people, the pervasiveness of consumerism, and the displacement of the dialects by a grey uniform Italian modelled on the language of commerce and advertising. Ignazio Silone criticized those who saw the changes pessimistically only in terms of a loss, and drew attention to the real improvements in health, education, and living standards by comparison with the old Italy of poverty. Ivano Cipriani examined the way the mass media were transforming social customs and relations. Umberto Eco undertook a pioneering analysis of mass culture, from comic strips to James Bond to the quiz show host Mike Bongiorno. In the preface to his collection of essays *Apocalittici e integrati* (1964), Eco summed up the contrasting attitudes by intellectuals to mass culture: on the one hand there were the 'apocalyptics' who rejected it as anti-culture, on the other the 'integrated' who embraced it optimistically as culture for the many. These two attitudes cut across the traditional political division between left and right. Eco's own essays took up a position between the two views, refusing to stigmatize mass culture but refusing at the same time to accept it uncritically.

Facing, top: ESPRESSO COFFEE MACHINE designed by Gio Ponti, 1949. Ponti was a leading figure in twentieth-century design. Founder editor of the architecture and interior design magazine *Domus*, he taught for many years at the Polytechnic of Milan and was one of the architects of the foremost icon of postwar Italian modernism, the Pirelli skyscraper near Milan central station (completed 1958).

Facing, below: ADVERTISEMENT FOR LAMBRETTA SCOOTER, 1954. The design, like that of its rival the Vespa (launched 1946), combined elegance with functionality. Unlike on a motorcycle, the engine is fully enclosed, enabling riders of both sexes to sit knees up and wear everyday clothing. The scooter made possible a greater mobility within and outside towns, particularly for young people.

Not just for intellectuals but for millions of Italians the 1960s were a decade of dislocation and disorientation. Mass internal migration, and the accompanying shrinking of the agricultural sector, depopulated whole villages and areas of the south. The consequent growth of industrial and service jobs took large numbers of women out of the full-time labour-market and turned them into housewives and part-time workers. The cultural upheavals and conflicts produced by migration and resettlement were documented in studies like Franco Alasia and Danilo Montaldi's *Milano, Corea* (1960) and Goffredo Fofi's *L'immigrazione meridionale a Torino* (1964) and were represented in novels and films, including Visconti's *Rocco e i suoi fratelli* (1960), which deals with a mother and her five sons who migrate from the province of Matera to Milan. The failure of relocated industry to generate local employment in the South was dramatically depicted in *Donnarumma all'assalto* (1959) by Ottiero Ottieri. The alienating nature of factory work was portrayed in *Memoriale* (1962) by Paolo Volponi and its links with militant protest in Nanni Balestrini's *Vogliamo tutto* (1971). The social inequalities reproduced by the education system were denounced in *Lettera a una professoressa* [Letter to a Schoolteacher] (1967), written by the children of the school of Barbiana in rural Tuscany run by the radical priest Don Lorenzo Milani. The failure of the centre-left governments after 1963 to deliver wide-ranging reforms nurtured discontent among a variety of social groups, and at the same time the movement of reform Catholicism opened up by the Second Vatican Council in the early 1960s stimulated internal criticism within the Church and new aspirations among many Catholics. The expansion of secondary schools (a new education act of 1962 introduced a common middle-school curriculum and raised the minimum school-leaving age to 14) and the easing of access to universities produced a more educated young generation many of whom became sharply disaffected with the society into which they were to enter as adults.

The effects of all these tensions and discontents were to be seen in the social protests of the period 1967–72. A real attempt was made in this period to adjust the balance of cultural as well as political power, and though none of the protest movements achieved all its aims there were partial successes. Secondary school students obtained the right to sit on school councils. University students obtained more choice in what they could study and, in some cases, courses that were closer to their interests. Newspaper journalists obtained more collective say in the appointment of editors and less editorial tampering with their stories. Workers obtained, as one of the conditions of the Statute of Workers in 1970, 150 hours of paid day-release in company time over a three-year period to study; the *150 ore* were often strongly politicized, including courses on Marxism and feminism. The late 1960s and early 1970s also saw a flourishing of small, often radical, publishing firms such as Savelli, De Donato, and Mazzotta; left newspapers like *Lotta continua* and *Il manifesto*, launched respectively in 1967 and 1969; underground magazines, like *Re nudo*, and feminist journals, like *Compagna* and *Effe*.

Italian cinema underwent a creative and commercial revival from the beginning of the 1960s which lasted till the mid-1970s. In part this was made possible by the crisis, in the same period, of the US film industry, which had been weakened since the mid-1950s by the rising production costs of the studio system and the loss of audiences to television. Fewer American films were exported to Europe and Italian audiences consequently saw proportionately more Italian and other European films. By the late 1960s Italy was making more films than Hollywood. Although cinema audiences had begun to fall in Italy too since the advent of television in 1954 (the all-time peak year for cinema attendances was 1955 with 819 million tickets sold—by 1976 they were down to just half this number), exhibitors offset the loss by raising ticket prices and showing more new films, for which they could charge more. In part the revival of the Italian film industry was also an effect of domestic causes: renewed investment in film production, increased consumer spending, and a change in the nature of the Italian filmgoing public. Audiences began going in

MARCELLO MASTROIANNI AND MONICA VITTI in *La notte* (Michelangelo Antonioni, 1961). Antonioni's films of the early 1960s portray an affluent, modernizing Italy very different from the working-class world of neo-realism. The sense of alienation is reinforced by an idiosyncratic use of space (natural or built settings engulf or hem in human figures) and time (long sequences with little action or dialogue).

large numbers to see the kind of art movies that had attracted only small audiences in the 1940s and 1950s. In part too, no doubt, it was because many good films were starting to be made. As well as *La dolce vita* and *Rocco e i suoi fratelli* (both among the top-grossing films of 1960), there was Antonioni's trilogy of *L'avventura* (1960), *La notte* (1961), and *L'eclisse* (1962); Fellini's 8½ (1963) and *Giulietta degli spiriti* (1965); Gillo Pontecorvo's films about Third World revolution, *La battaglia di Algeri* (1966) and *Queimada* (1969); the films of Pasolini, from *Accattone* (1961) to *Salò o le 120 giornate di Sodoma*, completed shortly before he was killed in 1975; and the films of Bernardo Bertolucci (b. 1941), from *La commare secca* (1962) onwards.

In the visual arts, literature, and music, too, the 1960s and early 1970s were a period of experimentalism and rejection of established traditions and values. In 1960 Piero Manzoni (1933–63) invited the public to eat boiled eggs which had been signed in ink with his thumbprint; in 1961 he produced ninety signed and individually numbered cans labelled 'Artist's shit' which were put on sale at the same price per gramme as gold. The artists associated with the Arte Povera movement of the late 1960s and 1970s began to explore new materials, and unusual juxtapositions of images and materials, such as the series of igloos made by Mario Merz in glass, steel, and leather or his canvases with splayed painted lizards and crocodiles transfixed by neon tubes. The Gruppo 63 (or Neoavanguardia) foregrounded language and poetic form in a way that echoed the Futurist poets, with the difference that for the leftists associated with the group, notably Edoardo Sanguineti and Elio Pagliarini, the reason for eschewing verbal transparency or narrativity was that such uses of language were too easily absorbed and negated by neo-capitalist society. Italo Calvino likewise believed that literature could be of and about its time without having to represent it with a 'heavy' social realism. He therefore turned his hand to 'light' science fantasies (*Le cosmicomiche*, 1965; *Ti con zero*, 1967) and to a playful experimental text (*Il castello dei destini incrociati*, 1973) influenced by the structuralist notion of literature as an infinite combination of finite elements. In *La fabbrica illuminata* (1964), Luigi Nono (1924–90) first combined electronics and voice; in *Como una ola de fuerza y luz* (1971–2), a setting of a poem in memory of the Chilean revolutionary Luciano Cruz, he juxtaposed electronically elaborated taped music with live piano, orchestra, and soprano voice. Popular music saw the development of *cantautori* (singer-songwriters) like Fabrizio De André and Enzo Iannacci, similar in some ways to American folk and blues singers but developing a distinctively Italian idiom.

Trends since the Late 1970s

From the second half of the 1970s a number of interrelated processes began to halt and even partly reverse some of the tendencies of the preceding decade.

In the first place, the subcultures of the extreme left and the student movements began to disintegrate as a result of partial concessions, divisions between the left groups themselves, and, most notably, terrorism and counter-terrorism (the 'strategy of tension' and the machinations of the 'hidden State'). These processes were explored in some of the most memorable works of the period: films such as Francesco Rosi's *Tre fratelli* (1981) and Gianni Amelio's *Colpire al cuore* (1982); plays such as Dario Fo's *Il Fanfani rapito* (1975); and the writings of Leonardo Sciascia (1921–94), including *Il contesto* (1972; filmed by Rosi in 1975 as *Cadaveri eccellenti* [Illustrious Corpses]), *Todo modo* (1974), and *L'Affaire Moro* (1978).

In the second place, the late 1970s saw the beginnings of a trend towards a concentration of ownership in the cultural industries, with cross-media holdings and an entwinement between media and political interests which would become a dominant feature of the 1980s. This trend made it much harder for smaller firms to enter or survive on their own and several of the small publishers and magazines set up in the 1960s and 1970s folded. In 1974 the book and magazine publishers Rizzoli bought a controlling stake in the *Corriere della Sera* group of newspapers; the firm then took over *La Gazzetta dello Sport* and a number of regional papers, expanded into private television and non-cultural activities like construction and finance, until in 1982, with debts of over 70 billion lire and embroiled in corruption scandals, it went into receivership. In 1984 control of the group passed into the hands of Fiat (which already owned another major daily newspaper, *La Stampa*) and it began a new phase of growth. The rise of Silvio Berlusconi's Fininvest group (renamed Mediaset in 1996) was even more spectacular. From construction, Berlusconi diversified in the late 1970s into private television and advertising concessions, and in the 1980s into film distribution and production and publishing, acquiring in 1991 a majority stake in Mondadori, including its book and magazine interests and the newspaper *La Repubblica*.

Partly as a result of these trends and the new entrepreneurial culture which accompanied them, the media map changed in a number of important ways from the mid-1970s, not just in ownership but also in distribution and patterns of consumption. For instance, whereas previously all Italian newspapers had been regionally biased in their sales—*Il Corriere della Sera* in Lombardy, *La Stampa* in Piedmont, *La Nazione* in Tuscany, *Il Messaggero* in Latium, and so forth—by 1976 it had become possible to launch from Rome a new daily—*La Repubblica*—which was genuinely national in that it had no particular regional base and soon acquired a more or less equally distributed readership, in proportion to population size, in Milan, Turin, Florence, and Rome. In broadcasting, the rise of private radio and television—made possible by a ruling of the Constitutional Court in 1976 which ended the RAI's monopoly—not only greatly increased the supply of channels, but also opened up new times of day at which people listened and fostered a new mode of consumption in which audiences browsed more. At the same time it renewed old anxieties about the trivializing and addictive effects of the medium and generated new anxieties about 'rule by television' (*telecrazia* or *videocrazia*), particularly after the rapid rise to political power of Berlusconi's Forza Italia Party in 1994. Television became after 1980 the first truly ubiquitous cultural form in Italy. In 1993 the audience research agency Auditel estimated that 99.5 per cent of Italian households owned and used at least one television set, with negligible variations between regions. In the same period the television set increasingly became a multi-purpose technology, used also for videocassettes, computer games, teletext, and satellite programmes. Whatever one may think about the content of some of the programmes, one needs to recognize that television in Italy has had important culturally unifying effects. Since regular transmissions began it has been the principal agent for the diffusion of a shared spoken language, it has partly homogenized Italians' time schedules (for instance the mid-evening news is a regular 'appointment' for many viewers), and has created a set of nationally recognizable personalities as well as giving national visibility to others, from politicians to singers to sports stars. The television, together with the videocassette recorder, has long overtaken the cinema as the main means for seeing films. Since the mid-1980s, on the small screen and on the big, the lion's share has been taken by American films. By 1990 the proportion of box-office receipts going to these was the same as in the early 1950s.

LIZARD (1978) by Mario Merz. Born in Milan in 1925, Merz joined the Arte Povera movement in 1968. His use of neon light tubes in sculptural installations of everyday objects, such as raincoats and bottles, produced disturbing juxtapositions. Here the tube pierces the painted red image on canvas like a spear.

In the third place, the late 1970s and early 1980s saw a crisis of confidence in grand systems of ideas, of which the most dramatic sign was the decline of Marxism—a decline which predated but was greatly accelerated by the collapse of Communist regimes in the Soviet Union and Eastern Europe. One of the books that took the pulse of this cultural change was *Il pensiero debole* [Weak Thought], edited by Gianni Vattimo and Pier Aldo Rovatti (1983). In their introduction, Vattimo and Rovatti charted a move in Italian philosophy from a period of relative optimism in the 1960s, when it had been possible to give philosophy an alternative foundation (whether Marxism, structuralism, or phenomenology) through one of relative pessimism in the 1970s, when philosophy had been characterized by negativity and scepticism but had still been rooted in a basic belief in reason, to one in the 1980s when that belief too had fallen apart and it was no longer possible to ground thought upon any metaphysical certainties. Vattimo's philosophy of the 1980s consequently developed a form of a post-modern scepticism which presented itself as potentially radical. He argued for instance (in *La società trasparente*, 1989) that the end of the Marxist idea that there was a single course of world history with classes as its privileged subjects gave rise to multiple, criss-crossing micro-histories and a plurality of subjectivities. A response within a more traditional mould was that of the veteran political philosopher Norberto Bobbio, who attempted to rethink the relations between democracy and socialism in a post-Marxist perspective.

The tendency to be wary of grand schemes and systems affected cultural production in other spheres. Literary writing became less concerned with public themes and ideological commitment and more preoccupied with the private, with surfaces, with travel, landscape, and place—like Antonio Tabucchi's *Notturno indiano* (1984) and Gianni Celati's *Narratori della pianura* (1985)—or with various forms of pastiche and a mixing of history, memoir, and fantasy, like Vincenzo Consolo's *Il sorriso dell'ignoto marinaio* (1976), Gesualdo Bufalino's *Diceria dell'untore* (1981), and Sebastiano Vassalli's *La chimera* (1990). In visual art, the conceptualist audacity of the Arte Povera movement was succeeded in the late 1970s and 1980s by a haunting use of the human figure, for example in the paintings of Mimmo Paladino, Sandro Chia, and Enzo Cucchi. In music, Luciano Berio used a montage and quotation of stylistically diverse elements. In his two works written to libretti by Calvino—*Una vera storia* (1982) and *Un re in ascolto* (1984)—both the musical and the verbal signs are open to a plurality of readings.

ITALY SINCE 1945

DAVID HINE

The Growth of a Modern Economy

Italy's development after 1945 was to a large extent a mirror of developments elsewhere in Western Europe. Its fundamental feature, like that of the European Community as a whole, was sustained economic growth. This brought the country much closer to the living standards of the leading European states. It made Italian society increasingly secular and materialist in outlook and softened previously bitter class and religious conflicts. It also did much to consolidate democracy. Though the post-war Republic began in a fragile and uncertain state, Italian institutions later became a good deal more solid and, the difficulties of the 1990s notwithstanding, the country's defences against the extremes of Fascism and Communism grew considerably firmer than they had been in 1945.

However, rather than just mirroring post-war European movements, Italian development often seems to have given them distinctive qualities of its own. Its transformation from a backward agrarian society was more rapid and spectacular than in most other countries; but, just because it was so telescoped, it was also socially more painful. Similarly, the zeal of its commitment to the ideals of European integration was matched by no other major state; but it might at times have been tempered with the caution suitable to a society that did not always have the capacity to cope with exposure to a fully open and competitive European economy. Politically, its formal commitment to the checks and balances of a liberal constitution protected the country against overmighty rulers by dispersing power more comprehensively than anywhere in post-war Europe; but it also weakened the ability of successive governments to deliver effective and authoritative leadership.

These peculiarities are explored later. In broad perspective, they are less important than the ability of the country to catch up with the European mainstream. Italy began the post-war era as a defeated state, and a relatively backward and peripheral Mediterranean society. In 1945 almost half the working population was engaged in agriculture. The industrial base of the economy was largely confined to a small triangle in the north-west, between Turin, Milan, and Genoa. The areas which were to show the most rapid and sustained growth in subsequent decades, particularly the north-east and central regions—the Veneto, Emilia, and Tuscany—were dominated by small-scale agriculture and archaic patterns of sharecropping.

The country's transformation was possible above all because it integrated itself into processes taking place in the wider international order. Italy could not have developed as it did without the model of liberal democracy and the market economy provided by European reconstruction. Its export-led economic success was founded on the growth of the European economy. Its political identity, despite the complex effects of the Cold War on its internal politics, was defined by the Atlantic Alliance and the defence of democracy. But none of this was inevitable. Geography made it probable that the country would fall into the Western sphere of influence after the Second World War, but elsewhere in the Mediterranean, in countries that also fell into the general Western sphere, a return to economic isolation and political authoritarianism was not always avoidable.

The first developments requiring explanation are thus those surrounding the reconstruction era: broadly speaking, the years 1943–51. In this period crucial decisions were taken concerning future economic development, the structure of government, and the shape of party alliances. Through these decisions Italy emerged as a society committed to a market economy, an open trading system, and the Atlantic defence community.

The Reconstruction

That these commitments emerged was remarkable because although political life was initially rebuilt with relatively little direct intervention by the Allies, the Italian parties themselves had by 1947 turned the country into an arena of acute Cold War conflict. The Allies, though anxious to secure Italy in the Western sphere of influence, devoted rather little attention to the country's political reconstruction. Partly, this was because Italy had earned some modest rehabilitation of its international status by switching regimes and allegiances even before the end of the war. It was also because, despite its Fascist and belligerent past, Italy was not seen as a major actor in the post-war European order. Its potential industrial base was modest, and, given its backwardness, the scope for democratic regeneration seemed limited.

The reconstruction of political life that began with the fall of Mussolini in July 1943 was thus a more gradual process than in Germany. Whereas the Bonn Republic was a sharp break with Weimar, the post-war Italian Republic was in part a continuation of the pre-Fascist liberal state. Admittedly the stark historical memory of all those who suffered under Fascism provided a degree

ALCIDE DE GASPERI, father of the Christian Democrat Party, addresses a crowd of 200,000 in Piazza del Duomo in Milan in the election of 1948. The election gave the Party a dominance that lasted for four decades.

of inoculation against a resurgence of extremism. But it did not have the same force as in Germany. In southern Italy, strong monarchist and authoritarian sentiment survived, to feed the ultra-conservative groups which were to complicate political life for many years. In central and northern Italy the activities of the resistance movement laid the foundation for the future strength of the Italian Communist Party (PCI). The party became a mass movement that dominated the trade unions and other workers' organizations, and made the country infertile terrain for conventional social democracy.

The culmination of this complex reconstruction came in 1947. Until that point, a fragile political coalition held between the political groups that had fought in the resistance. They included the Communists and Socialists on the left, and the Christian Democrats and various small liberal groups in the centre. The onset of the Cold War brought a fundamental change. The left, hitherto an essential part of the government, found itself summarily excluded. The new government was composed of Christian Democrats, under the leadership of Alcide De Gasperi, and assorted allies from the centre. The range of parties present in the government narrowed considerably, but so did its parliamentary majority. What held it together, and would continue to do so through until the 1960s, was a common opposition to the extremes of right and left.

These extremes constituted a powerful challenge. With the advent of the Cold War and the exclusion of the left from power, the latter fell firmly into Communist hands. The Socialists split. A small minority joined the Christian

Democrats in government; the radical majority joined the Communists in opposition, but were outmanœuvred by the superior organization and resources of their allies. By the mid-1950s the Communist vote was more than twice that of the Socialist Party. Whether a Communist-led government would have established an authoritarian regime along East European lines was henceforth much debated. Historians of the left always contended that the PCI was different from its Eastern sister-parties, but voters always shied away from putting the issue to the test. However, although the left was too weak to force its way into government, it was strong enough to alarm middle-class voters. For many of the latter, the best defence was solidarity behind Christian Democrat leadership, but for a significant group, especially in the politically conservative south, the solution was a return to outright reaction. By 1946 a form of reactionary populism had already emerged in the shape of Uomo Qualunque. By 1948 it had thrown off this ambiguous disguise to become the unashamed heir to Mussolini, in the shape of the Movimento Sociale Italiano (MSI).

The 1948 general election confirmed the basic shape that political life had assumed with the onset of the Cold War. The Christian Democrats emerged with a bare majority, made workable by an alliance with their smaller centrist satellites the Liberals, Republicans, and Social Democrats. For the next decade or so the formula set the context for policy-making, and despite the presence in the governing coalition of up to four parties, and the presence in parliament of at least eight, it proved just about stable enough to survive the frequent ministerial crises and the comings and goings of prime ministers that became a regular feature after De Gasperi's death in 1953.

Naturally, the Cold War polarization made the conciliatory social partnership practised widely in Western Europe impractical in Italy. However, its absence enabled the coalition to pursue economic liberalization without regular negotiation with the labour movement, as had been necessary until 1947. This freedom improved business confidence and the competitive position of Italian industry. The climate of explicit ideological warfare which dominated public debate tended to deflect attention away from the details of domestic policy issues, leaving economists and technocrats a relatively free hand in economic management. Once the left was removed from

FAMILY VALUES: 'Mum and dad are voting for me'. The Christian Democrat message in the 1950s focused on church, family, and anti-Communism. The threat of Stalinism was an easy campaign target at the height of the Cold War.

mamma e papà VOTANO PER ME

DEMOCRAZIA CRISTIANA

government, the influence of free-market economists in the Bank of Italy and the Treasury rapidly gained the upper hand. The stabilization plan of 1947, combining devaluation, a severe credit squeeze, and tough limits on public expenditure, helped pave the way for Italy's entry into the rapidly expanding international trade and payments systems at the start of the 1950s. Consumer demand and employment initially suffered in consequence, and it took the trade-union movement many years fully to recover its self confidence, but the foundations were laid for policies of high self-financed business investment on which the economic miracle of the 1950s and 1960s was based.

This is not to say that state intervention was entirely absent. The great state holding companies present since the 1930s—most notably IRI and ENI—were developed to stimulate areas of industry such as steel, shipbuilding, cars, and energy, where the private market was clearly not serving the wider social need. Political interference in such companies, despite their public owner-ship, was later to detract from their efficiency, but in the early years the devel-opment of an efficient and able class of state entrepreneurs made a significant contribution to modernizing managerial outlooks, and public investment made an equally significant contribution to the growth process.

Despite its unpromising beginnings, and the lacerations of the most tense years of the Cold War, Italy therefore emerged at the beginning of the 1950s surprisingly well placed to take advantage of the great expansion of European trade that was just beginning.

The Economics and Politics of the Italian Miracle

Italy's so-called economic miracle broadly coincides with the years 1950–70, though by the latter half of the 1960s the factors driving the growth process were beginning to alter significantly. The contrast between these two decades and more recent ones is remarkable. The average annual growth rate for the years 1951–60 was 5.3 per cent, and for 1961–70 5.7 per cent. In the 1970s it fell to 3.8 per cent and in the 1980s to 2.3 per cent. By the 1990s a trend growth rate for the decade of 2.5 per cent was being seen as optimistic by most economists.

The explanation for the virtuous circle into which the economy fell during this period is complex, and it is important not to confuse growth with absolute welfare. The years of the economic miracle represented an intense structural transformation taking much of the working population out of low productiv-ity jobs, or unemployment, into industrial production. There is no doubt that income levels eventually rose, but working conditions often deteriorated, large-scale migration brought profound social disorientation for many, and higher incomes were accompanied by higher rent, transport costs, etc. More importantly, the period was one of very rapid capital accumulation, with the rise in personal consumption lagging well behind the rise in output. This

enabled the economic miracle to sustain itself for so long. The constant expansion of productive capacity prevented the development of inflationary bottlenecks. Inflation rarely exceeded 3 per cent, whereas in the mid-1970s it rose to a peak of over 20 per cent. The growth of foreign trade too was entirely benign, with no serious balance-of-payments problems until 1963. The miracle was decidedly export-led with those sectors largely devoted to foreign markets experiencing the highest productivity growth.

The weakness of the labour-market, and the ready pool of under-utilized labour in agriculture and other low-productivity jobs, made a major contribution to the growth process. Unemployment fell steadily between 1950 and 1963 from 9 per cent to only 2.6 per cent, and it was only at the end of this period that the first stirrings of union power began to be felt. Until the mid-1960s a large reserve of labour, especially in the south, allowed investment and output to grow without serious increases in wage costs. Admittedly the fairly low skills of much of this labour constituted a serious warning for the future. Italy during these two decades grew on the back of relatively low-technology industries with a high labour content. Potential competitors in East Asia were still to emerge, and those in central Europe were locked into

THE GREAT NEW EXHIBITION HALL in Turin designed by Pier Luigi Nervi. In high-profile amenity projects, Italian architects and civil engineers embraced modern architectural style with self-confidence and subtlety. Less successful were the crowded apartments in the rapidly expanding urban periphery.

the Comecon system. Italy seized on the window of opportunity effectively, and though it did rather too little to improve the skills of its workers, growth was not entirely limited to the low-technology sectors. Several large modern conglomerates operating in increasingly advanced technology also emerged to bolster the more sophisticated end of the production spectrum.

What the miracle was not able to achieve was a significant narrowing of the gap between the two halves of the country. More than any other European country, post-war Italy has been divided between advanced and relatively backward societies. This dualism is rooted deeply in Italian history, and is linked to the relative geographical isolation of the south from European commercial and cultural influences, and to its long history of feudal class relations. It was considerably added to by national unification. Today, its consequences are seen not just in disparities in industrial structure and living standards, but in education, literacy levels, administrative competence, and so on.

In early post-war Italy the first serious efforts to get to grips with uneven development were made, but the understanding of policy-makers was rudimentary in the face of such a multifaceted problem, and despite the country's high growth rate the massive exodus of the young and the fit to attractive jobs in northern Italy exacerbated the problems faced by the region. Development funds for infrastructural projects in transport, communications, water, and energy were established in the 1950s, and in the public domain a special effort was made to locate major enterprises in the area. Against the scale of the problem, however, the results often proved inadequate.

Given the nature of the growth model Italy adopted, the response of government to the problem of uneven economic development was in any case never likely to be adequate. Policy was intentionally geared to constraining public consumption, and had the country invested heavily in education, health services, public housing, and other infrastructure at the outset, the burden in terms of higher personal taxation or higher public borrowing would have been significant, and the climate of exuberant business confidence would certainly have been weakened. With hindsight, many have argued that a slower growth process with greater emphasis from the outset on public consumption and a more egalitarian approach to welfare and income distribution would have produced a more satisfactory if slower path of development. However, it is rare for a society, whether capitalist or socialist, to succeed in establishing high levels of generalized welfare in advance of a period of quite intense, and often painful, capital accumulation. Certainly, there was no strong voice arguing for a distinctively social-democratic 'third way' in the 1940s or 1950s. The Communist opposition later claimed to have stood for this approach, though for obvious reasons of historical consistency it declined to accept the social-democratic epithet. But in the early post-war years it had nothing convincing to offer voters beyond a rather predictable critique of the ills of social inequality and a programme of collective ownership. As for the Socialist Party, it was too weak and divided to make a significant contribution to policy debate until the 1960s. A form of megaphone ideological conflict thus dominated politics throughout the 1950s, reflecting the broad dichotomy between market-based and collectivist systems, rather than the more complex policy issues arising from redistributing income through modern welfare networks.

Even in the 1950s the governing parties did not, however, stand by as entirely passive spectators of the growth process. The Christian Democrat Party was built on a broad inter-class religious alliance that prevented it from ignoring the interests of poorer sections of Italian society. It had roots—albeit weaker than those of the Communist Party—in working-class communities, particularly in areas such as the north-east where the Catholic subculture was deeply embedded. It was especially strong in rural and agricultural communities. Indeed the principal focus of its reforming activity in the 1950s was agriculture. Legislation at the start of the decade provided for a major programme of land redistribution, breaking up large, badly managed *latifundia* by compulsory purchase, improving it under the aegis of land reform agencies, and then selling it on to small farmers and landless peasants at low cost. Land reform agencies also provided back-up in the form of energy, know-how, livestock, and housing. Large-scale cooperatives (the so-called Federconsorzi) and cheap subsidized credit through publicly owned banks completed the range of assistance available.

This approach did much to alleviate rural hardship, and it certainly headed

TELEVISION came to Italy in the 1950s. In the long term it spread the values of a secular consumer society but in the early stages viewers were served a carefully controlled diet of Catholicism and popular culture. One of its early functions was to bring football matches to the back rooms of the ubiquitous Italian bar.

off what threatened to be a dramatic lurch towards the political extremes among southern voters in the 1950s. By no means all the results were positive, however, and many economists criticized the fragmentation of landholding it generated. The principal object of policy, they claimed, should be to maximize output, and keep down urban living costs and agricultural imports. Similar criticisms were levelled at policy in areas like retailing, catering, artisan workshops, and other self-employed service providers. Here, as in agriculture, political protection through special licensing laws (for example, barring supermarket development), cheap credit, and subsidized insurance, was widely used. The short-term protection offered brought electoral support from grateful clienteles, but the long-run cost in terms of delayed modernization was significant.

The Opening to the Left and the Debate on Planning and Reform

The Italian economy continued to pursue a sustained growth path throughout the 1960s. Politically, however, the centrist coalition which emerged with the onset of the Cold War was more or less bankrupt by the end of the 1950s. Its success was always built more on a fear of extremism than on any great electoral enthusiasm for the parties of which it was composed. With real incomes and private consumption growing more slowly than the productive capacity of the economy, this was not entirely surprising. Affluence came to Italian voters much more in the 1960s than the 1950s. The coalition had held together primarily because there was no alternative to it, and because until the Constitution was fully implemented in the 1960s, its checks and balances did not operate properly, or in some cases at all. There was initially no constitutional court to strike down the Fascist penal code, no regional government, little protection of local autonomies, and an entirely government-controlled radio and television system.

However, strong central control could not keep the governing coalition in power for ever. Given the pure form of proportional representation Italy practised, the governing parties needed to win an outright majority of the popular votes in parliamentary elections—always a difficult task in democratic elections. The Christian Democrat Party had achieved its greatest victory at the moment of most acute Cold War tension, and in a social environment still largely untouched by the secularism wrought by post-war affluence. In the 1948 general election it won 48 per cent of the popular vote and dominated the coalition. By the 1963 election this had fallen to 38 per cent, with a substantial part of the lost votes drifting away from the governing parties altogether. The share of the electorate supporting the Communists and Socialists rose over the same period from 31 per cent to 39 per cent; the far right parties had settled at a steady 6–7 per cent share. By the early 1960s there was thus a risk

THE GODFATHERS of the Centre–Left coalition: Pietro Nenni and Aldo Moro. Nenni persuaded his Socialist Party colleagues to abandon the Communists and throw in their lot with the Christian Democrats. Moro, prime minister 1963–8, and ten years later kidnapped and killed by the Red Brigade, persuaded the Christian Democrats there was no alternative to the Centre–Left.

that the country would become entirely ungovernable if the share of the vote going to the allegedly anti-democratic extremes exceeded that for the combined forces of the democratic centre. What prevented this risk from materializing was the conversion of the Socialist Party (PSI) from leftist opposition to party of government in an operation which came to be known as the 'opening to the left'.

For a party which never won significantly more than 15 per cent of the popular vote, the PSI was to prove a remarkably influential if not always benign force in Italian political life over the subsequent three decades. Its origins go back to the turn of the century but it suffered two dramatic splits, one in 1921 and another in 1947, which greatly weakened it, and left it with an acute inferiority complex towards the larger and stronger Communist Party. Its response took it through sharply contrasting stances. Until the late 1950s, alone among West European socialist parties, it worked in close alliance with the Communists, and in international terms took a decidedly anti-Atlanticist stance. From the early 1960s it reversed this to become a virulently anti-Communist movement. It could do so because what it lacked in votes and organizational strength, it was able to make up for in its strategic position on the centre left. Its 10–15 per cent vote share, which pure proportional representation translated into a similar proportion of parliamentary seats, made it an attractive potential ally for the parties of the centre. As long as the Cold War persisted, and the PSI placed leftist solidarity at the heart of its political strategy, this potential could not be realized. By the end of the 1950s, however, the situation was changing. De-Stalinization was undermining the credibility of the Soviet model, and within the party, the close relationship with the PCI was under attack. The party began to move cautiously towards a more conventional and explicitly social-democratic outlook, and this coincided with changes afoot in Christian Democracy, several of whose leaders, alarmed by the potential unviability of the centrist coalition formula, started to make overtures in the PSI direction, and to encourage alliances with it in local government.

Extending the coalition to the left was not just a question of new parliamentary arithmetic. It also required a good deal of policy revision. The case for this by the start of the 1960s was becoming ever clearer, notwithstanding the success of the free-market economics of the Italian miracle. The need for modernization of both the country's administrative structure and its welfare system was underlined by the impact of migration, urbanization, and economic growth. This was most visible in the northern industrial cities, where rapid population growth meant unplanned speculative expansion, overcrowding, high rents, and overstretched services. For Italian workers the social wage of the Welfare State was sadly lacking compared to their counterparts elsewhere in Western Europe. The problems were exacerbated by administrative and legislative shortcomings. Many social services were delivered by financially impoverished local authorities, mostly too small to operate effectively. They tended to rely on special grants and loans transferred from central government, the legislative basis for which was highly fragmented, and varied from locality to locality according to the political clout exercised in Rome by local notables. The quality of the civil service itself also left much to be desired. Recruitment and training were in serious need of an overhaul which would make the system rely less on nineteenth-century legalism and more on modern managerial values.

It was thus understandable that 'planning' became the fashionable watchword of the early 1960s. It was taken up not just by the increasingly reformist Socialist Party, but also by the centrist Republican Party, and by the more left-leaning members of the DC (Democrazia Cristiana). Exactly what it meant varied. At one end of the spectrum, it meant simply better regulation by the public authorities of the private market, particularly in urban planning and building control. At the other end, it meant a system of physical planning controls approaching that found in centrally planned economies. In the middle, it im-

POPE JOHN XXIII opens the Second Vatican Council in 1962. A reformer and a modernizer of relations between Church and State, John emphasized the Church's spiritual and pastoral role. At the political level, he helped pave the way for Christian Democrat rapprochement with at least the moderate wing of the Italian left.

plied a form of indicative economic planning of the type practised regularly in the post-war years by the French government. It generated grandiose schemes for the national economy. The Ministry of the Budget was renamed the Ministry of the Budget and Economic Planning, and eventually produced a five-year development plan for the years 1965–9—ironically only approved by parliament in 1967. It also gave new impetus to the regional tier of government, stalled since the early 1950s with only four of the twenty regions in operation. The regions were to become an essential element in a more devolved administrative system, in which better subnational coordination of health, education, welfare, and land-use planning would be achieved through a system of regional plans.

The Centre-Left Coalition and its Difficulties

The debate on planning dominated political life in the early 1960s, and provided the backdrop for the gradual leftward shift in coalition politics which eventually saw the Liberal Party edged out of the government and replaced by the Socialists. The operation proved anything but straightforward, however. Initially, conservative Christian Democrats resisted it fiercely, and in 1960 the country came dangerously close to civil disorder when an attempt was made to create a government which relied implicitly on the parliamentary support of the neo-Fascist MSI. For two years thereafter, Italy was governed ineffectively by minority Christian Democrat caretaker governments, and it was only in 1962, under the premiership of Amintore Fanfani, that the Socialists were incorporated into the parliamentary majority. The following year, after the 1963 general election, they moved from the parliamentary majority right into the cabinet. Aldo Moro, leader of the DC left, began a four-year term of office as prime minister, with Pietro Nenni of the Socialist Party as deputy prime minister. There were five other Socialist ministers, but the coalition, as in the past, retained a Christian Democrat majority.

To begin with, reform appeared to have the upper hand. Various measures were initiated, of which the most enduring were an extensive overhaul of middle-school education, and nationalization of the electricity industry. First steps were also taken to bring property speculation under control through a generalized system of compulsory purchase of development land at agricultural values. Dividend income was to be taxed at source to help curb widespread tax evasion. By the summer of 1964, however, the coalition began to run into trouble. Its difficulties coincided with the first serious signs of overheating in the economy. In 1963 wage growth began to outstrip productivity growth, unit labour costs rising by an alarming 14.5 per cent. The economy began to pull in imports and the balance of payments briefly moved into serious deficit on current account. The confidence of both domestic investors and foreign exchange markets faltered at the possibility of an end to so many years of successful growth. In response, the Bank of Italy and the Treasury imposed a tough monetary squeeze and tight controls on public expenditure, pushing the economy into a painful though short recession.

The financial and political crisis of 1964 posed a severe dilemma for the Socialist Party. The PSI purported to represent the labour moment, but in practice had little control over it. Union moderation in the wage rounds of 1962 and 1963 might have prevented the economy from overheating, but the union leaders, most of whom were far more closely linked to the Communists than the Socialists, were in no mood to make concessions. For the first time since the end of the war they had some purchase on labour-market negotiations, and had no intention of yielding it to help the Socialists. Faced with demands from coalition colleagues, business leaders, and the Bank of Italy for a slower pace of reform to curb public expenditure and restore the climate of business confidence, the Socialists had to choose between accepting such demands and withdrawing from the government. The latter implied at best a return to the wilderness of opposition, alongside the Communists. At worst, it could have precipitated a complete political breakdown, for if the party had abandoned the government, it was far from clear that any other formula could have replaced it. In the crisis of 1964, in fact, the country probably came even closer than four years earlier to civil breakdown and a coup. Not surprisingly, the Socialist leadership was unwilling to test the limits of the right's resolve, and settled back into office with a new and much restricted programme. The cutting edge of reform was abandoned. Public expenditure was cut back radically. Plans for the expropriation of development land were shelved, as was further nationalization. Planning was reduced to an innocuous form of outdoor relief for leftist intellectuals in the Budget Ministry. The lesson of the crisis was that the Socialists were indispensable to the coalition, but their pivotal role, far from giving them real bargaining strength, trapped them in government.

The failure of the centre-left reforms did not of course destroy the coalition itself. Just as the 1950s was the decade of centrism, so the 1960s was the decade of the centre-left. As ever, the Christian Democrats controlled the coalition, however, with Giovanni Leone, Mariano Rumor, and Emilio Colombo following in Moro's footsteps as Christian Democrat prime minister after the 1968 general election. In one form or another, in fact, the coalition continued until 1972. Even then, it was abandoned only briefly in favour of a return to a version of the old centrist formula which quickly proved to lack viability. By 1973 the Socialists were back in government for a further, though shorter, period of office until the landmark elections of 1976.

What the crisis of 1964 underlined, however, was the difficulty the country would face in adjusting to the consequences of its own modernization. Economic growth had generated better communications, and a more informed and therefore more demanding electorate. Growth was changing the balance of power in the labour-market, and this became dramatically evident at the end of the decade. At some point in the future demands for better welfare and pension arrangements, education, and public housing would have to be faced. The model of the Welfare State was widely visible north of the Alps, and increasingly Italian voters made the comparison. Demands for change had been deflected by the ideological warfare of the 1950s, but gradually the electorate was developing an idea of what the reform agenda might contain.

The reason why it was so much more difficult to address such demands in Italy than elsewhere lay in the complexity of the political system. As long as the left was dominated by a large and powerful Communist Party, albeit one with claims to be different from Communism elsewhere, it was impossible for the left to come to power. Behind the scenes, in parliamentary committees and other semi-private arenas, the PCI already exercised some leverage over policy in the 1960s. But, in the face of mounting demands for reform, it continued to suit the parties of the centre to brand the PCI as anti-system and anti-democratic. This could not stop the long slow growth of the Communist electorate, which reached a peak in 1976 with 34.4 per cent of the popular vote, but it could and probably did slow it down. Thus, with the Communists isolated in opposition, the reform agenda had to be managed by a coalition of parties spanning the centre of the political spectrum. Negotiation between them was always difficult, as they competed for much of the same electorate, and were always looking to short-term electoral advantage.

These difficulties were compounded by the way in which the complexities of the country's social structure were represented inside the parties. With a huge pool of unemployed and underemployed voters in the south, and with a large proportion of the active population engaged in small-scale and often one-man enterprises, there was considerable competition for public resources. Regional transfers to the south and subsidies to special groups left only limited taxpayers' money for the emerging Welfare State. Nor was there a solid tax-base. Politically tolerated tax evasion among the self-employed became a form of concealed subsidy while the employed worker, whose tax was accessible because deducted at source, found himself taxed increasingly heavily. It was the employed worker who had the strongest stake in the development of the Welfare State, and in this sense the Italian working class came to be the chief contributor to the cost of its own welfare benefits.

The public sector was responsible for a further paradox of political representation that developed in the 1960s. This was that the governing parties, and especially the Christian Democrats, were gradually becoming parties with exaggerated proportions of public-sector workers within their ranks. Especially in the south, public employment expanded as a solution to chronic

unemployment. Pay levels were never generous, though security was high, and second jobs were widely tolerated. But precisely because the governing parties actively sought to solicit the support of those in the public sector, reform to improve productivity was increasingly difficult. No one disputed that public-sector reform—retraining, reorganizing, and reallocating civil servants—was necessary. A minister for bureaucratic reform came to occupy a place in successive cabinets. But the more the governing parties relied on the votes of public-sector workers, the more they capitulated to public-sector unions whose interests lay in numbers on the payroll, pay, and working conditions, not the improvement of productivity.

If the latter half of the 1960s is often seen as a period of wasted opportunity in Italian post-war history, it is above all because the governing parties were unable to address the consequences of these developments. Political representation in the 1960s settled into a pattern from which escape was to prove very difficult. Christian Democracy gradually lost its predominantly religious connotation. The numbers of committed Catholics on whose support it could automatically count dwindled. In response, it expanded its support base among the politically assisted clienteles of the southern half of the country, and among public-sector workers. As it expanded public expenditure, its former role as the mouthpiece of the private sector, and the exponent of market economics, was blurred. Significantly, the Socialist Party began to take a parallel path. Trapped in government, it found southern voters and public-sector workers could compensate for the loss of its traditional northern working-class electorate. The gradual evolution of the party from social democratic reformism to clientele politics, and eventually to the political corruption which was in the 1990s to destroy it altogether, originated in the disappointments of the 1960s.

Facing: THE LIMITS OF MODERNITY: Italy's historical vulnerability to natural disasters was not immediately cured by post-war growth. The great floods in Florence and Venice in 1966 were a stark reminder of inadequate spending on fundamental infrastructure, and of the country's failure adequately to conserve its cultural and artistic treasures.

The 'Hot Autumn' and its Consequences

Some more immediate consequences of the political stagnation of the 1960s were reaped at the end of the decade. The first sign of a significant social change was the alacrity with which Italian university students emulated the wave of student and middle-class activism throughout the Western world, sparked off by the Vietnam War. Agitation quickly spread from universities to the workplace, and from 1968 onwards, Italy passed through several years of intermittently violent social upheaval. It was most intense during the so-called Hot Autumn of labour militancy in 1969. Unlike the more concentrated 'May events' in France, however, it lasted well into the following decade, and signalled a more lasting change in political values. From these upheavals, Italian democracy emerged fundamentally changed. There was greater activism and greater participation. Direct action became common. Voluntary associations increased their membership, and more importantly their independence from the hitherto all-powerful political parties.

The most far-reaching impact was in the outlook and behaviour of the main trade union confederations, and their relationship to ordinary workers. Before the Hot Autumn, the Italian union movement had been riven with ideological disputes. The largest of the three main confederations into which it was divided, the CGIL, was mainly led by Communists. It tended to see union action as a function of the political needs of the Communist Party. Its leaders were generally sceptical of collective bargaining. They supposed from long experience that, without strike funds or a tradition of extended labour disputes, Italian workers would rarely have the stomach for strike action. Hence the quiescent state of the labour-market during the long period of growth in the 1950s and early 1960s. For CGIL leaders collective bargaining was in any case a double-edged weapon. By engaging in it, the workforce was accepting the logic of the market. All this changed in the late 1960s. Shop-floor militancy, much of it spontaneous, generated strikes and demonstrations on an unprecedented scale. In 1969 over 300 million working hours were lost through industrial disputes: nearly four times the average of the previous four years. The annual figure did not fall below 100 million again until 1976. Hourly wages in manufacturing rose by 20 per cent in 1970. Between 1968 and 1975 union membership increased by 50 per cent, with an especially large expansion in the public and white-collar sectors.

The political radicalism of the late 1960s caught many by surprise. A long period of rising prosperity had been expected to lead to political depolarization not radicalism. Yet in Italy, as elsewhere, it generated radical leftist groups who not only dominated the student movement and established a foothold in the trade unions, but even laid down a lasting base among a smallish fringe of left-wing voters. Out of this group, later in the decade, a tiny but determined fringe of disillusioned militants turned from parliamentary tactics to terrorism.

The rise of labour militancy was no less unexpected than the rise of the extra-parliamentary left. It was accounted for only in small part by a tightening of the labour-market. Some well-placed groups of workers were certainly able to exploit their strategic position to force large wage deals out of vulnerable employers, but what occurred during the Hot Autumn went far beyond British-style shop-floor collective bargaining, not just in its egalitarian overtones, but also in the specific demands being made by labour. Much of the explanation, in fact, lay in disappointed expectations of the centre-left government, and in sociological changes in the workforce. The latter point was especially important. Those who led the early activism were young workers, frequently migrants, some of whom had learned the techniques of shop-floor activism in Germany and France. They were particularly alienated by the spread of piecework and the speeding-up of production lines by employers who were no longer willing to obtain productivity increases through new investment. They were also frequently critical of the union confederations and the Communist Party for their cautious approach to industrial relations.

Union leaders were initially taken by surprise by rank-and-file militancy, but within a couple of years had adapted to it. It forced them to concentrate on issues at a level at which their traditional party and ideological differences were less relevant, forging a unity previously impossible. Gradually, as a result, the unions regained control of the industrial relations process from the radicals who had led the activism in the Hot Autumn, and having done so,

'WORKERS' POWER' at the University of Pisa, 1968. The 'Hot Autumn' inaugurated a decade of student and working-class militancy. The small minority that turned to left-wing terrorism in the 1970s had their ideological origins in the anti-parliamentary character of the Trotskyist and Maoist groups involved in the student movement.

Facing: COVER OF *GRAND HOTEL*, 1947. This weekly, launched in 1946, established a trend for romantic fiction narrated in strips of drawings or photographs. It remained one of Italy's top-selling magazines for over thirty years. Its subsequent decline (from nearly 900,000 copies week in 1976 to 400,000 in 1992) was attributed to the proliferation of soap operas offering similar gratifications in daytime television.

they acquired a new stature in the eyes of both employers and the government. They focused not only on wages and working conditions in particular sectors, but also on wider issues connected with pensions, housing, and social services. Participation and the right to involvement in key decision-making arenas became key objectives, and over the subsequent decade it became obligatory for government to add representatives of the union confederations to its range of advisory and consultative boards, not just on workplace issues, but on broad matters of regional development and planning, transport and other infrastructure investment, social services, etc. The rapid expansion of union influence was also felt in the egalitarian thrust of labour-market policy in this period. A system of wage indexation emerged which over time favoured the lowest-paid. An exceptionally generous temporary-redundancy scheme guaranteed a continuous income stream to all workers once they had established certain rights from first employment. Wage differentials between skill levels were scaled back, as were selective bonuses and piece-rates.

Parallel developments were occurring in other areas of Italian society. The dominance of Catholic moral and religious values came under increasing challenge from consumerism and the spread of leisure-culture values. In schools, universities, the media, the legal professions, and elsewhere liberal- or left-inclined individuals were rising to influential positions. As in other Western societies sexual freedom, and greater equality between the sexes, pushed its way up the social agenda. Italy in this sense was becoming more pluralist in its values. In the 1950s and 1960s the alternative to the Christian Democrat ascendancy was essentially the Marxist subculture dominated by the Communist Party. From the early 1970s onwards, the range of alternatives—both in terms of ideas and organizations—widened greatly. Social organizations which had originally been established by the two main parties became more independent of them, and others grew up—women's movements, gay rights' groups, environmentalists, local action groups—which were explicitly non-party. The Communist Party certainly benefited from a general shift leftwards in political values, especially among young voters, and this helped it reach its historic peak in 1976. But the relationship, as later events were to show, was more contingent, and reflected little underlying enthusiasm for the traditional outlooks and goals of the Communist left.

The clearest evidence of these changes came in 1974, in the famous referendum on civil divorce. Divorce had been introduced four years earlier, on condition that a referendum device laid down in the constitution, but never implemented, was brought into operation to allow Catholics the chance to appeal over Parliament's head to the people. This they did, only to discover that the people, by a margin of 60 : 40, were in favour of divorce. The psychological impact was profound, and led to a string of referendums over the following two decades, many promoted by the activist Radical Party. The

Grand Hôtel

MANCATO APPUNTAMENTO

Anno I° - N. 24
3 Gennaio 1947 **L. 12**

BREAD AND CIRCUSES: the *stadio* in Milan (*above*). Football dominates contemporary popular culture, and its influence goes beyond entertainment. Owning a club has become a badge of recognition for big business leaders. For media entrepreneur Silvio Berlusconi, whose *Forza Italia* party took over much of the old Christian Democrat electorate in the 1990s, patronage of the highly successful A.C. Milan club was an essential part of the image he sold to voters in the 1994 general election.

THE ULTIMATE CONSUMER DREAM. Most of Italy's automobile industry produces smaller mass-produced cars for the lower end of the market. As a private car, the Ferrari (*right*), rarely encountered on the roads, is a male virility symbol for the super-rich, though in its motor-racing incarnation it remains an emotive, if not always reliable, national icon.

referendum was used to settle matters connected with divorce, abortion, nuclear energy, and various other civil-rights matters. In the 1990s it even overcame long-standing party resistance to electoral reform.

The Search for a New Political Order

By their duration and intensity, the changes in the balance of power in Italian economic life in the late 1960s and early 1970s proved to be a more important political turning-point than the advent of the centre-left at the start of the 1960s. They led to an extensive search for a new and more stable coalition formula. Over the course of the 1970s, the country experimented with three quite different coalition formulas. The most controversial incorporated the Communists into the parliamentary majority for a brief spell after 1976, before the country returned in the 1980s to solutions not unlike the centre-left formula of the 1960s.

These political changes reflected the search for a solution to growing economic problems. In the 1970s the performance of the Italian economy was subject to much greater variations than in the two previous decades. Inflation and the balance of payments became serious constraints on growth, and the swings in the business cycle became more exaggerated. In the years 1970–3 Italian growth was slower than in most neighbouring economies. The invest-

THE SEVESO DISASTER. The high price of unregulated industrial development, especially in the northern industrial triangle, was brought into dramatic focus by the explosion of a chemical plant at Seveso in 1976. Highly toxic dioxin fell over a wide area, requiring a major evacuation programme and causing extensive health problems.

ment performance was even worse. There was a brief recovery in 1973–4, but it was fuelled by domestic consumption and public spending, rather than investment and exports. The trade balance problems which arose, along with the sharp rise in wage inflation, showed how much more rigid economic constraints were becoming. Italy was beginning to lose its competitive edge in manufacturing, as labour costs rose and labour flexibility diminished. The first oil shock, in 1974, exposed the country's high dependency on imported energy. By 1976 the Italian government had been forced to turn to external sources—the International Monetary Fund and the European Union—to help it through the crisis. Foreign-exchange dealings had to be suspended for over five weeks, imports were subject to special surcharges, and the lira was devalued by some 20 per cent. Only at the very end of the decade did the economy swing back into more sustained growth.

It did so after a long and painful process of restructuring. Large businesses were forced to subcontract many of their activities to smaller, more flexible companies which were less subject to the power of the unions. 'Outwork' paid at piece-rates made its reappearance in small workshops and the home, having been banished from the factory floor. This labour, an essential feature of Italy's ever-present black economy, avoided the payment of social security costs, and the wages it earned evaded the tax authorities. The adjustment process was a long one, and its impact was not felt fully until the 1980s. It boosted the dynamic small-firms sector of north-central and north-east Italy, but it was not without its costs. It slowed investment in new technology and training, inhibited the development of large firms in the high-technology area, and, by encouraging tax evasion, it compounded the difficulties for policy-makers throughout the 1980s.

The restructuring of the later 1970s and early 1980s eventually paved the way for something of a return to the market, a process further stimulated by the growing ideological influence of the European Community's internal market programme. During the 1970s, however, it was difficult to foresee such an outcome. Political life was surrounded by uncertainty, fed by coalition deadlock, social tensions, and terrorism. There was a general supposition that the centre-left had failed, but profound uncertainty about how to respond. Some believed the problem lay in efforts to appease the trade-union movement, and that what was required was a tough policy of expenditure cuts and tight money, as in 1947 and 1964, to show the unions that inflationary wage claims meant unemployment. Others argued that government and business must recognize the new-found trade-union strength and unity as a permanent fact of life, and engage in a constructive dialogue, along the lines of social partnerships in Germany or Scandinavia. Since the Communist Party exercised great influence within the unions, this policy, at the margin, would entail dialogue, and perhaps even an alliance, with the PCI.

The dilemma caused deep divisions in both the ruling Christian Democrat Party and the business world. The DC had always straddled the broad centre of the political spectrum, but in the 1970s the stakes in the battle between its left and right wings rose considerably. The majority in the centre were pragmatists. On the left, Aldo Moro became the chief exponent of dialogue with the Communists. On the right, there were no comparably prestigious figures, but some Christian Democrats moved on the fringes of various shadowy ultra-conservative networks linking individuals in the security services, the armed forces, the mafia, and parts of the senior civil service. The man who proved most capable of exploiting these divisions was Giulio Andreotti. In 1972–3 he was prime minister of a brief and unsuccessful government which sought to shift the party back towards a conservative alliance with the Liberals. By 1976 he was back, but this time, in close cooperation with Aldo Moro, as head of a government bent on dialogue with the Communists.

Despite Andreotti's conservative links—or perhaps because of them—he was able to bring the PCI, albeit briefly, into the so-called government of National Solidarity. That government represented the high point of efforts to deal with the impact of the Hot Autumn by conciliation and compromise. That it became necessary at all was testimony to the seriousness of the economic crisis the country was facing—undoubtedly the most serious since the end of the war, with rumours of possible military intervention, and fears that the country was on the verge of hyper-inflation. The centre-left had collapsed and the Socialist Party for once refused to return to the fold unless the Communists too were coopted. That Andreotti succeeded in forming such an unlikely alliance, spanning almost the entire political spectrum, was testimony to his extraordinary gifts of mediation, and to those of Aldo Moro. It was also testimony to the pessimism of the Communist and trade-union leadership. Having gained from the leftist values of the Hot Autumn, they were alarmed by the economic and political problems it had thrown up. The response of Enrico Berlinguer, secretary general of the PCI, was one of almost indecent relief that his party could play a modest role in propping up a government which, as his critics did not hesitate to point out, was not fundamentally different from the discredited centre-left formula of the 1960s.

Whether the government of National Solidarity was a success depends on the yardstick by which it is judged. It lasted less than three years, from 1976–9. One of its chief architects, Aldo Moro, paid for it with his life when he was captured and murdered by Red Brigade terrorists. For the Communist Party it ended in predictable disappointment as party members and union members left in large numbers. In their eyes, all the party had done while part of the parliamentary majority was to encourage the unions to forgo wage claims. In the 1979 general election the PCI vote fell 4 percentage points, and its demands for incorporation into the coalition with full cabinet status were rejected by both voters and other parties. As the 1980s arrived, the left seemed as far away from office as ever. An optimist could even argue that the Christian Democrats had ridden the storm, the economy had come through its worst crisis, and Italian industry had been given a vital breathing-space in which to adapt to the consequences of the Hot Autumn.

Governing from the Centre: The Pentapartito and Political Corruption

THE MODERN RULING HOUSE OF SAVOY: Giovanni Agnelli, proprietor of Fiat, with the Reagans in 1987. The power of Italy's great family business trusts like Fiat, Pirelli, and Olivetti, and the dominant personalities that preside over them, contrasts with impersonal institutional shareholder capitalism elsewhere in Europe. The Agnelli family has been a formidably successful influence in both politics and business throughout the postwar era.

The reality was somewhat different. First, the recovery of 1979–80 proved short-lived. The wider European economy passed through a long shallow recession, and, reflecting this, for three years the Italian economy grew at an average of barely 1 per cent per year. The recession was not as sharp as in 1975, but it left voters feeling decidedly less secure and prosperous than in the past. The long boom of the 1980s began only in 1984. Secondly, though the Communist left emerged defeated from the government of National Solidarity, the formula which replaced it—the so-called Pentapartito—was no more stable than previous DC–PSI alliances had been. In some respects it was worse. It now consisted of no fewer than five parties, for the Liberals were reincorporated alongside the Socialists. More importantly, the Christian Democrats had to pay a heavy price for expelling the Communists from government. The Socialist Party, whose pivotal role, with the PCI gone, was again important, demanded major concessions. The threat of a coup if no government could be formed seemed over. Italian democracy was now too mature and the costs to

Italy of pariah status in Europe were only too well understood by the business community. Moreover, though the Christian Democrat Party survived the difficulties of the 1970s, its electoral base had further eroded. In the general election of 1983, its share of the national vote fell to only 33 per cent—its lowest ever.

The Socialist Party, in contrast, was showing signs of electoral revival, rising by 2 percentage points between the general elections of 1979 and 1983, and by a further three between 1983 and 1987. If it came to a confrontation, therefore, the Socialists could probably contemplate a general election with less discomfort than their Christian Democrat coalition partners. This was the calculation made by Bettino Craxi, pugnacious leader of the Socialist Party, and it was vindicated in the aftermath of the 1983 general election. Already in 1981, in the wake of the notorious P-2 Masonic lodge scandal, the Christian Democrats had been forced to relinquish the prime minister's office—the first time since 1945. On that occasion it went to Giovanni Spadolini, leader of the small but influential Republican Party. In 1983 Craxi himself became the first Socialist prime minister in Italian history, and survived in office for virtually the whole of the life of the 1983–7 parliament.

Craxi's government was made possible by the weakness of the two major parties during the 1980s. Though the Communist Party found itself isolated and bereft of a credible strategy after 1979, this did little to help the Christian Democrats. Their greatest long-term difficulty was that they were becoming an increasingly southernized and rural party. Both their main reserve of voters and their dominant leaders were concentrated in the area from Rome southwards. To survive in this State-dependent area, the party therefore had to exploit to the full the patronage possibilities of the Italian State, and what applied to the party as a whole, applied also to its factional leaders. The latter battled hard for a slice of the patronage available to the party, and every public appointment or nominated office-holder in the party's gift became a source of intense competition. The absence of real turnover in government encouraged this. To have the same set of parties in office for four decades in a row is unhealthy for any democracy, and Italy proved no exception. It was during the 1980s that complacent parties turned on an ever-wider scale to political corruption.

Beyond the longevity in office of one party or set of parties, there were other reasons why corruption was on the increase. One was blatant political interference in the affairs of the judiciary. Investigating judges could be inhibited by politicians from successfully pursuing cases of political corruption in various ways. Careers could be manipulated and selective incentives offered to the politically compliant; investigators could be discredited by campaigns alleging political bias; at the limit, as happened too frequently for comfort, violence and physical intimidation could be and were used. The institution of

343

parliamentary immunity from prosecution—only finally reformed in 1993—was also a great source of protection. Perhaps the most serious pressure, however, was the rising cost of politics. Costs rose in proportion both to the alienation of ordinary voters from their political system, and to the complexity of the media and mechanisms of political communication. In the 1950s and 1960s party membership was high, and this commitment provided volunteers and money. By the 1980s that commitment was diminishing. On the one hand, the political disappointments suffered first by supporters of one party and then by those of others, led to a general disengagement from political activity. On the other, party life could no longer compete with mass culture, mass entertainment, and the private market as a source of social activity. These problems hit the governing parties especially hard, and as membership was concentrated increasingly in the south, where individual contributions to the party, whether in cash or kind, were in short supply, the parties had to turn to other, less salubrious sources of income to keep their large organizations intact.

The most pernicious aspect of these developments was their ubiquity. They penetrated all parties in the governing coalition, and while at one level voters appeared to have a genuine choice, at another level they were increasingly aware that the choice was between parties whose style of operation and indeed policy programme were all largely the same. The Socialists made much of their aspiration to grow into a modern alternative to the Christian Democrats, and explained at length that they only stayed in government with the DC because parliamentary arithmetic and the shape of party politics dictated this. But after three decades in which a centre-left alliance of some sort had been the norm, the claim was little more than a fig-leaf concealing an otherwise naked ambition for power. By the 1980s the Socialist Party was little more than a semi-detached faction of Christian Democracy. The left had not disappeared. The Communists and other leftist parties still got over 30 per cent of the vote, but it was not enough to win power against the broad coalition of the centre. In the revitalized market economy of the late 1980s, Communism represented something of an anachronism, albeit one bathed in comparative honesty.

The latter half of the 1980s was something of an Edwardian summer for the parties of the Pentapartito coalition. The economy prospered, and so did voters, but under the surface tensions were threatening to erupt. The southernization of the Christian Democrat Party was opening up an unbridgeable gulf between the government and northern voters. The latter were not inclined to vote Communist, but increasingly saw the governing parties as agents to channel northern taxpayers' money to the corrupt and idle south. In the mid-1980s local and regional parties began to appear. By the 1992 general election, the Northern League had won 20 per cent of the vote in the northern industrial provinces on a platform that looked more like separatism than decentralization. Throughout the course of the 1980s, cases of political corruption were being suppressed in an increasingly blatant manner. And despite rapid economic growth, the effort of reconciling competing spending claims was putting a heavy strain on public finances. For many years politicians had resolved the tension between keeping taxes low to satisfy northern taxpayers, and keeping spending high to satisfy various State-dependent lobbies, by resorting to public bor-

rowing. However, this avenue began to close off in the mid-1980s. The size of both the budget deficit and the accumulated stock of public debt alarmed the government's creditors in Italy and abroad. The cost of servicing the debt rose as creditors raised the interest-rate premium demanded in a European economy that was busily dismantling capital controls. Even before the Maastricht Treaty set out objectives of budgetary rectitude necessary for participation in a common currency, Italian policy-makers were finding themselves ever more constrained by membership of the European Community.

At the start of the 1990s, therefore, Italian politics was already less stable below the surface than the tranquillity of the Christian Democrat–Socialist alliance suggested. What destroyed its stability entirely was a combination of the end of the Cold War, and the exposure of political corruption on a massive scale. The end of the Cold War represented the final burying of the Communist threat. It did not spell the end of the Communist Party. The latter changed its name to the Democratic Left Party, shed its fundamentalists, and after an initial loss of votes it stabilized and started to recover. But the end of the Cold War did persuade voters that the possibility of any form of Communist or collectivist attack on the Italian market system and Italian democratic institutions was remote. Ironically, the consequence was to transfer the impact on to the parties of the centre. After so many years of holding their noses and voting Christian Democrat, moderate voters finally concluded they could risk a protest against the quality of government they had been receiving. The result, in the 1992 and 1994 general elections, was a dramatic fragmentation of the centrist electorate. Voters turned to local parties, to a variety of exotic alternatives, to the long-quiescent MSI, and to abstention. Even after electoral reform, the ostensible purpose of which was to simplify the system and force more stable alliances, the party system remained chaotic. Dozens of politicians, including many of the most senior, were arrested on corruption charges by a judicial order that had finally found the determination to take its revenge on the political class. Even television magnate Silvio Berlusconi's money and

JUDGES, POLITICS, AND THE MAFIA: anti-Mafia prosecutor Giuseppe Ayala and his bodyguards. Tensions between the judiciary and the political class over the fight against organized crime in the 1980s laid the foundation for a judicial onslaught on political corruption itself in the 1990s that had a devastating effect on the old governing parties.

345

advertising power could not create order out of the chaos. In the 1994 general election, he seemed briefly to have forged a winning coalition by aligning his own Forza Italia movement with two improbable allies in the shape of the Northern League and the MSI, but his government was brought down within eight months of assuming office.

The Triumph of Economics over Politics

The political collapse of the early 1990s was both a tragedy and a triumph. It was a tragedy for a political system which, for all its instability, had had much to recommend it in the early years. Liberal democracy survived, against the odds posed by the Cold War, southern underdevelopment, and the potential for neo-Fascism. Difficult decisions were taken, and these decisions enabled the Italian economy to integrate itself into the wider European economy, at great benefit to the prosperity of most ordinary Italians. But the distortions of a political system which, uniquely in Western Europe, could not generate the alternation in government required to sustain democracy, eventually came to offset and obscure the political achievement of the reconstruction era. Political life became cynical, corrupt, and even, with the advent of organized crime, violent. Eventually, in its inability to face up to difficult allocative choices, the political system became an intolerable burden.

Yet in another sense the collapse of the 1990s was a triumph of voters over their political masters. The system did not prove as immobile as had been feared. Half-way through the decade, a clear new shape to political life was still not visible, but at least some of the difficult decisions had been taken.

'THE FIRST REPUBLIC', born in the referendum of 1946, has survived, at times against considerable difficulties, throughout the second half of the twentieth century. By the 1990s, political corruption bred widespread demands for a 'Second Republic' less beholden to corrupt political parties, though few now question the country's basic commitment to fundamental liberal democratic values.

Those who had taken them were the technocrats to whom power was handed in the absence of authoritative politicians. Of these, the representatives of the Bank of Italy—an institution which never lost its prestige or its reputation for integrity—played the most prominent role, and it was no surprise that two of its leading figures, Carlo Azeglio Ciampi and Lamberto Dini, were called to serve as prime minister in the difficult period after 1992. That technocrats should assume the reins of government, and that foreign exchange markets should play a prominent role in reminding Italians of the realities of prudent political economy, was a fitting conclusion to the half-century of development that brought Italy into line with the European mainstream. The solution could not serve as a long-term alternative to politics, but compared to the instant solutions offered by Mussolini in a similar situation seventy years earlier, it seemed to have formidable advantages.

FURTHER READING

General

In Denys Hay (ed.) *History of Italy* (Longman: London), there are the following volumes: T. S. Brown, *Early Medieval Italy 600–1200* (1997); John Larner, *Italy in the Age of Dante and Petrarch 1216–1380* (1980); Denys Hay and John Law, *Italy in the Age of the Renaissance 1380–1530* (1989); Eric Cochrane, *Italy 1530–1630*, ed. Julius Kirshner (1988); Domenico Sella, *Italy in the Seventeenth Century* (1997); Dino Carpanetto and Giuseppe Ricuperati, *Italy in the Age of Reason 1685–1789* (1987); Harry Hearder, *Italy in the Age of the Risorgimento 1790–1870* (1983); Martin Clark, *Modern Italy: 1871–1982* (1984). There is much interesting material in the *Storia d'Italia* (6 vols., Einaudi: Turin, 1972–7); and also in the multi-volume and still incomplete Giuseppe Galasso (ed.) *Storia d'Italia* (UTET: Turin).

1. From Augustus to Theodosius: Invention and Decline

For the historical background: E. T. Salmon, *The Making of Roman Italy* (London, 1982) deals with Rome's unification of Italy in the Republican centuries; T. W. Potter, *Roman Italy* (London, 1987) is an important guide to the imperial period; while S. L. Dyson, *Society in Roman Italy* (Baltimore, 1992) offers a detailed look at social and political matters from an epigraphical and archaeological perspective. Also valuable is F. Millar, 'Italy and the Roman Empire: Augustus to Constantine', *Phoenix*, 40 (1986) 295–318. On the Augustan settlement R. Syme's famous *The Roman Revolution* (Oxford, 1939) is essential. For the regions see R. Thomsen, *The Italic Regions from Augustus to the Lombard Invasion* (Copenhagen, 1947). More generally P. Garnsey and R. Saller, *The Roman Empire: Economy, Society, and Culture* (London, 1987) is a good structural account of the Empire; while F. Millar, *The Emperor in the Roman World* (2nd edn., London, 1992) studies the relation between central power and the provinces; on the New Empire see e.g. T. D. Barnes, *Constantine and Eusebius* (Cambridge, Mass., 1981) and Averil Cameron, *The Later Roman Empire*, AD 284–430 (London, 1993).

A useful, though basic, introduction to pagan Roman and Italian religion is provided by R. M. Ogilvie, *The Romans and their Gods* (London, 1969). More sophisticated essays on religion and society can be found in M. Beard and J. North (eds.), *Pagan Priests* (London, 1990). For Christianization see especially R. Lane Fox, *Pagans and Christians* (London, 1986); for Christian Italy in the fourth century see now N. B. McLynn, *Ambrose of Milan: Church and Court in a Christian Capital* (Berkeley and Los Angeles, 1994).

The Italian economy is treated as part of a larger picture in R. Duncan Jones, *The Economy of the Roman Empire* (2nd edn., Cambridge, 1982) (with good material on Pliny). Pompeii is analysed by W. Jongman, *The Economy and Society of Pompeii* (Amsterdam, 1988); for another view see H. Mouritsen, 'A Note on Pompeian Epigraphy and Social Structure', *Classica et Mediaevalia*, 41 (1990) 131–49. See also A. Wallace-Hadrill, *Houses and Society in Pompeii and Herculaneum* (Princeton, 1994).

There are several good books on art and architecture: for building see M. E.

Blake, *Roman Construction in Italy from Tiberius through the Flavians* (Washington, 1959) and *Roman Construction in Italy from Nerva through the Antonines* (Philadelphia, 1973), and especially J.-B. Ward-Perkins, *Roman Imperial Architecture* (London, 1981); on art D. E. E. Kleiner, *Roman Sculpture* (Princeton, 1992), R. Ling, *Roman Painting* (Cambridge, 1991), and D. Strong, *Roman Art* (2nd edn., London, 1988). A. Dihle, *Greek and Latin Literature of the Roman Empire*, trans. M. Malzahn (London, 1994) is a superb guide to the literary culture of the Roman Empire.

2. *The Medieval Centuries 400–1250: A Political Outline*

Covering this whole period in English is Giovanni Tabacco, *The Struggle for Power in Medieval Italy: Structures of Political Rule* (Cambridge, 1989), trans. from the *Storia d'Italia* (Einaudi: Turin) though neither the original text nor the translation is very approachable. More readable, but stopping at 1000, is Chris Wickham, *Early Medieval Italy: Central Power and Local Society 400–1000* (London, 1981). For the period up to the Frankish invasion, and for those who like nineteenth-century prose and an older, narrative style of history, Thomas Hodgkin, *Italy and Her Invaders* (8 vols; Oxford, 1892–9) is very readable and full of information. Neither Tabacco nor Wickham allows much space for the Papacy, for which: Geoffrey Barraclough, *The Medieval Papacy* (London, 1968), and Walter Ullmann, *A Short History of the Papacy in the Middle Ages* (London, 1972).

After about 1000, the histories of Italy, north and south, tend to get separate treatment. For the Kingdom of Sicily: John Julius Norwich, *The Normans in the South 1016–1130* (London, 1967), and *The Kingdom in the Sun 1130–1194* (London, 1970); also Donald Matthew, *The Norman Kingdom of Sicily* (Cambridge, 1992), and David Abulafia, *Frederick II: A Medieval Emperor* (London, 1988). For the north and the rise of the communes: Daniel Waley, *The Italian City-Republics* (2nd edn., London, 1978), and J. K. Hyde, *Society and Politics in Medieval Italy: The Evolution of the Civil Life, 1000–1350* (London, 1973). For economic life: G. Luzzatto, *An Economic History of Italy* (London, 1961), and Robert S. Lopez, *The Commercial Revolution of the Middle Ages, 950–1350* (Cambridge, 1976).

3. *Politics and Society 1250–1600*

The period of the Italian Renaissance has been particularly favoured by English-speaking historians and the literature is vast, especially for the fourteenth and fifteenth centuries. The best general coverage of the period in English is provided by three volumes of the *History of Italy* (Longman): John Larner, *Italy in the Age of Dante and Petrarch 1216–1380* (London, 1980); Denys Hay and John Law, *Italy in the Age of the Renaissance, 1380–1530* (London, 1989), and Eric Cochrane, *Italy 1530–1630*, ed. Julius Kirshner (London, 1988). Other valuable general accounts are: J. K. Hyde, *Society and Politics in Mediaeval Italy* (London, 1973), L. Martines, *Power and Imagination: City States in Renaissance Italy* (London, 1979), E. Cochrane (ed.), *The Late Italian Renaissance, 1525–30* (London, 1970).

Important studies of particular cities and areas are: D. Waley, *The Italian City Republics* (London, 1978); G. A. Brucker, *The Civic World of Early Renaissance Florence* (Princeton, 1977); F. C. Lane, *Venice: A Maritime Republic* (Baltimore, 1973); D. M. Bueno de Mesquita, *Giangaleazzo Visconti* (Cambridge, 1941); A. Ryder, *The Kingdom of Naples under Alfonso the Magnanimous* (Oxford, 1976); P. Partner, *The*

Lands of St Peter (London, 1972); E. Cochrane, *Florence in the Forgotten Centuries, 1527–1800* (Chicago, 1973).

Works on special aspects which give a flavour of the richness of the period are: Hans Baron, *The Crisis of the Early Italian Renaissance* (2nd edn., Princeton, 1966), which provides a seminal discussion of the links between politics and culture; F. W. Kent, *Household and Lineage in Renaissance Florence* (Princeton, 1977) which explores family structure; D. Herlihy and C. Klapisch-Zuber, *Tuscans and their Families* (London, 1983) which uses a computer analysis of Florentine tax records; D. Romano, *Patricians and Popolani* (Baltimore, 1987) which uncovers aspects of Venetian social history; M. E. Mallett, *Mercenaries and their Masters: Warfare in Renaissance Italy* (London, 1974) which deals with the methods and organization of war. The classic account of political mechanisms in an Italian republic is N. Rubinstein, *The Government of Florence under the Medici* (Oxford, 1966), while a useful study of princely politics is T. Dean, *Land and Power in Late Medieval Ferrara* (Cambridge, 1988). J. H. Bentley, *Politics and Culture in Renaissance Naples* (Princeton, 1987) examines the themes of politics, humanism, and patronage in a less familiar setting. D. Hay, *The Church in Italy in the Fifteenth Century* (Cambridge, 1977) explores religious themes usefully, while B. Pullan, *Rich and Poor in Renaissance Venice* (Oxford, 1971) opens a major debate about the role of charitable institutions.

4. *Renaissance Culture*

There is a useful general book on art by Frederick Hartt, *A History of Italian Renaissance Art* (4th edn., London, 1994), and a general reference book, ed. J. R. Hale, *A Concise Encyclopaedia of the Italian Renaissance* (London, 1981). See also John Pope Hennessy's 3 vols, *Italian Gothic Sculpture, Italian Renaissance Sculpture,* and *Italian High Renaissance and Baroque Sculpture* (4th edn., London, 1996).

Among the many useful books on art in the earlier part of this period are Michael Baxandall, *Painting and Experience in Fifteenth-Century Italy* (Oxford, 1972); John White, *Art and Architecture in Italy 1250–1400* (Harmondsworth, 1966); George Holmes, *The Florentine Enlightenment 1400–1450* (Oxford, 1992); Eve Borsook, *The Mural Painters of Tuscany* (Oxford, 1980).

Literature and scholarship can be approached through Eugenio Garin, *Italian Humanism: Philosophy and Civic Life in the Renaissance*, trans. P. Munz (Oxford, 1965), and trans. of Dante's *Divine Comedy* by J. D. Sinclair (Oxford, 1939), and of *Petrarch's Lyric Poems* by Robert M. Durling (Cambridge, Mass., 1976). See also George Holmes, *Florence, Rome, and the Origins of the Renaissance* (Oxford, 1986) and Nicholas Mann, *Petrarch* (Oxford, 1984).

For later art there are important general discussions by Edgar Wind, *Pagan Mysteries in the Renaissance* (2nd edn., London, 1967), and John Shearman, *Mannerism* (Harmondsworth, 1967). On particular artists see Martin Kemp, *Leonardo da Vinci: The Marvellous Works of Nature and Man* (London, 1981); Charles Dempsey, *The Portrayal of Love* (Princeton, 1992) (on Botticelli); Charles Hope, *Titian* (London, 1980); and Bruce Boucher, *Andrea Palladio the Architect in his Time* (New York, 1994).

The literature of the sixteenth century is best approached through translations such as *The Portable Machiavelli*, ed. Peter Bondanella and Mark Musa (New York, 1979); Baldassare Castiglione, *The Book of the Courtier*, trans. George Bull (Harmondsworth, 1967); Ludovico Ariosto, *Orlando Furioso*, trans. Guido Waldman (Oxford, 1983); Giorgio Vasari, *The Lives of the Painters, Sculptors and Architects*, trans. G. du C. de Vere (London, 1996).

5. Italy 1600–1796

The bibliography on the 'forgotten centuries' is unequal and relatively less rich than for the earlier and later periods of Italian history. There is no general account of the seventeenth century in English, although P. Burke, *The Historical Anthropology of Early Modern Italy* (Cambridge, 1987) contains much on its social and religious history. On the eighteenth century: D. Carpanetto and G. Ricuperati, *Italy in the Age of Reason 1685–1789* (London, 1987); S. Woolf, *A History of Italy 1700* (London, 1979). On various aspects discussed in the chapter: C. M. Cipolla, *Fighting the Plague in Seventeenth Century Italy* (Madison, Wisc., 1981); D. Kertzer and R. P. Saller (eds.), *The Family in Italy* (New Haven, 1991); H. G. Koenigsberger, *Politicians and Virtuosi* (London, 1986) contains essays on the Italian parliaments and on the republics and courts; L. Cheles, *The Studiolo of Urbino* (Philadelphia, 1986); S. Woolf, *The Poor in Western Europe in the Eighteenth and Nineteenth Centuries* (London, 1986) discusses the poor and charity in Tuscany and Italy; M. Aymard, 'From Feudalism to Capitalism: The Case that Doesn't Fit', *Review*, vi. 2 (1982), 131–208. On the Enlightenment, 1 vol. has been translated of the great work of Franco Venturi: *The End of the Old Regime in Europe 1768–1776: The First Crisis* (Princeton, 1989); F. Venturi, *Italy and the Enlightenment* (London, 1972) is an important collection of essays.

Of the individual states, the Venetian state alone enjoys an excellent coverage in English: B. S. Pullan, *Rich and Poor in Renaissance Venice* (Oxford, 1971); B. S. Pullan, *The Jews of Europe and the Inquisition of Venice* (Oxford, 1983); B. S. Pullan, *Poverty and Charity: Europe, Italy, Venice 1400–1700* (Aldershot, 1994); F. C. Lane, *Venice: A Maritime History* (Baltimore, 1973); J. C. Davis, *The Decline of the Venetian Nobility as a Ruling Class* (Baltimore, 1962); J. C. Davis, *A Venetian Family and its Fortune 1500–1900* (Philadelphia, 1975); J. M. Ferraro, *Family and Public Life in Brescia, 1580–1650* (Cambridge, 1993); B. S. Pullan (ed.), *Crisis and Change in the Venetian Economy in the 16th and 17th Centuries* (London, 1968); R. T. Rapp, *Industry and Economic Decline in Seventeenth-Century Venice* (Cambridge, Mass., 1976); R. C. Davis, *Shipbuilders of the Venetian Arsenal* (Baltimore, 1991); R. Mackenney, *Tradesmen and Traders: The World of the Guilds in Venice and Europe c.1250–c.1650* (Towota, NJ, 1987); P. Musgrave, *Land and Economy in Baroque Italy: Valpolicella 1630–1797* (Leicester, 1992).

On the other Italian states: D. Sella, *Crisis and Continuity: The Economy of Spanish Lombardy in the Seventeenth Century* (Cambridge, Mass., 1979); J. M. Roberts, 'Lombardy', in A. Goodwin (ed.), *The European Nobility in the Eighteenth Century* (London, 1953); G. Symcox, *Victor Amadeus II: Absolutism in the Savoyard State, 1675–1730* (London, 1983); J. R. Hale, *Florence and the Medici: The Pattern of Control* (London, 1977); E. Cochrane, *Florence in the Forgotten Centuries* (Chicago, 1973); F. McArdle, *Altopascio: A Study in Tuscan Rural Society, 1587–1784* (Cambridge, 1978); A. Calabria, *The Cost of Empire: The Finances of the Kingdom of Naples in the Time of*

Spanish Rule (Cambridge, 1991); T. Astarita, *The Continuity of Feudal Power: The Caracciolo of Brienza in Spanish Naples* (Cambridge, 1992).

6. Culture in the Age of Baroque and Rococo

Rudolf Wittkower's classic text, *Art and Architecture in Italy, 1600–1750*, first published in 1958, is shortly to reappear in a Yale University Press edition revised by Joseph Connors and Jennifer Montagu. Wittkower revolutionized Italian baroque studies, and his collected essays, *Studies in the Italian Baroque* (London, 1975), and a collaborative volume which he edited with Irma B. Jaffe, *Baroque Art: The Jesuit Contribution* (New York, 1972), are also fundamental. The publications of Connors and Montagu themselves are essential reference-points for Italian, albeit largely Roman, general culture, notably Connors's very long article, 'Alliance and Enmity in Roman Baroque Urbanism', *Römisches Jahrbuch der Biblioteca Hertziana*, 25 (1989) and Montagu's *Roman Baroque Sculpture: The Industry of Art* (New Haven, 1989). Anthony Blunt's *Guide to Baroque Rome* (London, 1982) is an invaluable compendium of a lifetime's erudition, while Ellis Waterhouse's deeply traditional *Italian Baroque Painting* (London, 1962) remains the most durable introduction to the subject. S. J. Freedberg's *Circa 1600: A Revolution of Style in Italian Painting* (Cambridge, Mass., 1983) draws attention, by its very title, to the importance of the first decade of the seicento. John Dixon Hunt (ed.), *The Italian Garden: Art, Design and Culture* (Cambridge, 1996) provides an essential overview of Italian garden history for the period.

The structure of artistic activity in Rome during the baroque period has produced important analytical studies. Patricia Waddy's *Seventeenth-Century Roman Palaces: Use and the Art of the Plan* (Cambridge, Mass., 1990) should be supplemented, for garden design, by David Coffin's *Gardens and Gardening in Papal Rome* (Princeton, 1991) and, for interior decoration, by the exhibition catalogue edited by Alvar González-Palacios, *Fasto Romano: dipinti, sculture, arredi dai palazzi di Roma* (Rome, 1991). Much recent work has shed fresh light on papal patronage: John Beldon Scott, *Images of Nepotism: The Painted Ceiling of Palazzo Barberini* (Princeton, 1991); Richard Krautheimer, *The Rome of Alexander VII, 1655–1667* (Princeton, 1985).

On individual artists: *Annibale Carracci* by Donald Posner (London, 1971); *Caravaggio* by Howard Hibbard (London, 1983); *Domenichino* by Richard Spear (New Haven, 1982); *Il Guercino*, by Denis Mahon (Bologna, 1991); *Guido Reni* by Stephen Pepper (Oxford, 1984); *Bernini: The Sculptor of the Roman Baroque* (2nd edn., London, 1966) by Rudolf Wittkower, and *Bernini and the Unity of the Visual Arts* by Irving Lavin (Oxford, 1980); *Andrea Sacchi* by Ann Sutherland Harris (Oxford, 1977); *Borromini* by Anthony Blunt (London, 1979); and *The Painting of Baciccio* by Robert Engass (University Park, Penn., 1964).

The efflorescence of the performance of early music, facilitated by the emergence of the compact disc as a major cultural force, has made a seismic impact upon scholarship, and the enormous contribution of the *New Grove Dictionary of Music and Musicians* (20 vols., London, 1980), edited by Stanley Sadie, can scarcely be overestimated. *The Oxford Illustrated History of Opera* (Oxford, 1994), edited by Roger Parker, opens with three essays by Tim Carter and Thomas Bauman which are amongst the best possible introductions to Italian opera. Carter's *Music in Late*

Renaissance and Early Baroque Italy (London, 1992) provides an important challenge to traditional periodization and formalistic definitions. Important monographs include: Frederick Hammond, *Music and Spectacle in Baroque Rome: Barberini Patronage under Urban VIII* (New Haven, 1994); Michael Robinson, *Naples and Neapolitan Opera* (Oxford, 1972); Ellen Rosand, the magisterial *Opera in Seventeenth-Century Venice: The Creation of a Genre* (Berkeley and Los Angeles, 1991); and Andrew Steptoe, *The Mozart–Da Ponte Operas* (Oxford, 1988). John Rosselli, 'The Castrati as a Professional Group and Social Phenomenon, 1551–1850', *Acta Musicologica*, 69 (1988) now provides the most learned and sensitive approach to a major historiographical question. Amongst recent biographies, three are of particular note: Paolo Fabbri's *Monteverdi*, available in an English translation (Cambridge, 1994); Carolyn Giantrucco's *Alessandro Stradella (1639–1682): His Life and Music* (Oxford, 1994); and H. C. Robbins Landon's *Vivaldi: Voice of the Baroque* (London, 1993).

Studies of Venetian intellectual life inevitably begin with the world of Paolo Sarpi, for which William Bouwsma's *Venice and the Defence of Republican Liberty: Renaissance Values in the Age of the Counter-Reformation* (Berkeley and Los Angeles, 1968) provides a classic analysis of the political and intellectual structure, while David Wootton's *Paolo Sarpi: Between Renaissance and Enlightenment* (Cambridge, 1983) is a stimulating introduction to the historian himself. 1993 was the bicentenary of Goldoni's death, evoking a flood of important publications, including Franca Angelini, *Vita di Goldoni* (Bari, 1993) and Alvise Zorzi, *Monsieur Goldoni* (Milan, 1993). Eighteenth-century Venetian pictorial culture has consistently attracted immense attention in the Anglo-Saxon world. Michael Levey's *Painting in XVIII Century Venice* (London, 1959) is a traditional 'literary' introduction. Giambattista Tiepolo has generated much study, most recently: William Barcham, *The Religious Paintings of Giambattista Tiepolo* (Oxford, 1989) and Svetlana Alpers and Michael Baxandall, *Tiepolo and the Pictorial Intelligence* (New Haven, 1994). On other individual artists, see Jeffery Daniels, *Sebastiano Ricci* (Hove, 1976); George Knox, *Giambattista Piazzetta, 1682–1754* (Oxford, 1992); André Corboz, *Canaletto, una Venezia immaginata* (Milan, 1985); and J. G. Links, *Canaletto and his Patrons* (London, 1977).

The north Italian courts of the second rank have benefited from the vigorous growth of local erudition, although Janet Southorn's *Power and Display in the Seventeenth Century: The Arts and their Patrons in Modena and Ferrara* (Cambridge, 1988) is a significant English-language contribution. Collecting at the Gonzaga court of Mantua in the seicento is brilliantly dissected by Martin Eidelberg and Eliot Rowlands, 'The Dispersal of the Last Duke of Mantua's Paintings', *Gazette des Beaux-Arts* (May–June 1994).

Amongst the more substantial courts, the starting-point for that of Turin must remain the 3-vol. catalogue, edited by Vittorio Viale, of the 1963 *Mostra del barocco piemontese*, held in Turin. These essential volumes may now be supplemented by the collections of essays edited by Giovanni Romano, notably his *Figure del barocco in Piemonte: La corte, la città, i cantieri, le provincie* (Turin, 1988), the complement to the exhibition catalogue *Diana trionfatrice: arte di corte nel Piemonte del Seicento* (ed. Romano and Michaela di Macco) (Turin, 1989); and also the pioneering work of Arabella Cifani and Franco Monetti, most recently, *I piaceri e le grazie* (Turin,

1993), a social history of landscape and genre painting. Despite some exaggerated arguments, Martha Pollak's *Turin, 1564–1680* (Chicago, 1991) provides a sound introduction to the urbanization of the Sabaudian capital. H. A. Meek, *Guarino Guarini and his Architecture* (New Haven, 1988) must be supplemented by Vittorio Viale (ed.), *Guarino Guarini e l'internazionalità del barocco* (2 vols., Turin, 1970). Similarly, Gianfranco Gritella's *Juvarra. L'architettura* (2 vols., Modena, 1992) needs the 'control' of Mercedes Viale Ferrero, *Filippo Juvarra: scenografo e architetto teatrale* (Turin, 1970) and of Henry Millon's and Nino Carboneri's vols already published as part of the massive but still-to-be-realized *Corpus Juvarrianum*. Amedeo Bellini's *Benedetto Alfieri* (Milan, 1978) is the basic monograph on this architect and designer, while Giancarlo Ferraris's masterpiece, *Pietro Piffetti e gli ebanisti a Torino, 1670–1830* (Turin, 1992) is a more-than-equal complement to this remarkable aesthetic collaboration.

Two books by Edward Goldberg, *Patterns in Late Medici Art Patronage* (Princeton, 1983) and *After Vasari: History, Art and Patronage in Late Medici Florence* (Princeton, 1988), have imposed a re-evaluation of the culture of the *gran ducato*, as have the catalogues of the exhibition held in 1974 in both Detroit and Florence, misleadingly entitled *The Twilight of the Medici: Late Baroque Art in Florence, 1670–1743* and that held in Florence in 1986–7, *Il seicento fiorentino*. Malcolm Campbell, *Pietro da Cortona at the Pitti Palace: A Study of the Planetary Rooms and Related Projects* (Princeton, 1977) is essential for understanding one of the great decorative schemes of the seicento. The vibrancy of intellectual life at the court of the Medici had already been underscored by Eric Cochrane, *Florence in the Forgotten Centuries, 1527–1800* (Chicago, 1973). The central work of Stillman Drake, *Galileo at Work: His Scientific Biography* (Chicago, 1978) must now be complemented by Mario Bagioli's *Galileo Courtier: The Practice of Science in the Culture of Absolutism* (Chicago, 1993).

Eighteenth-century Rome is currently attracting more attention and much of this is due to the enthusiasm of Anthony Clark, whose early death robbed settecento studies of a most persuasive voice. Clark's collected essays, *Studies in Roman Eighteenth-Century Painting* (Washington, DC, 1981) and his *Pompeo Batoni* (Oxford, 1985) were edited and prepared for publication by Edgar Peters Bowron. Forward strides in the history of pontifical patronage have been made by John Pinto, *The Trevi Fountain* (New Haven, 1986) and Christopher Johns, *Papal Art and Cultural Politics: Rome in the Age of Clement XI* (Cambridge, 1993), while Robert Engass, *Early Eighteenth-Century Sculpture in Rome* (University Park, Penn., 1976) retains great value for its emphasis upon the cosmopolitanism of cultural life in Rome. Piranesi's popularity in Anglo-American culture is evidenced by the fact that the two standard biographies appeared first in English: Jonathan Scott, *Piranesi* (London, 1975) and John Wilton-Ely, *The Mind and Art of Giovanni Battista Piranesi* (London, 1978).

The Italian Enlightenment in general has been a 'growth area' for research, one largely dominated by the figure of Franco Venturi and his multi-volume *Settecento riformatore*, parts of which are now appearing in an English translation by Burr Litchfield (Princeton). The exhibition held in Naples in 1979–80, *Civiltà del 700 a Napoli*, and its two-volume catalogue initiated a full-scale re-evaluation of Neapolitan culture, evinced in two exhibition catalogues in English: Clovis Whitfield (ed.), *Painting in Naples, 1606–1705: From Caravaggio to Giordano* (London, 1982); and *A Taste for Angels: Neapolitan Painting in North America, 1650–1750* (Yale University Art Gallery, 1987). In some ways, Anthony Blunt's *Neapolitan Baroque and Rococo Architecture* (London, 1975) prefigured and helped to shape this surge of interest.

Italian neoclassicism, as distinct from the Italian Enlightenment, has been rather submerged into the study of a more cosmopolitan and international aesthetic phenomenon. A recent volume on the career of Johann Joachim Winckelmann is Édouard Pommier (ed.), *Winckelmann: La Naissance de l'histoire de l'art à l'époque des Lumières* (Paris, 1991). Fred Licht's *Canova* (New York, 1983) remains the most recent monograph on the sculptor. Finally, the collected essays of Alvar Gonzáles-Palacios, *Il tempio del gusto* (4 vols, Milan, 1986) and *Il gusto del principe* (2 vols, Milan, 1993), should ensure that the much-neglected field of the so-called decorative arts receives the attention it merits.

7. Italy 1796–1870: *The Age of the Risorgimento*

General accounts of this period in English include: D. Beales, *The Risorgimento and the Unification of Italy* (London, 1981); H. Hearder, *Italy in the Age of the Risorgimento 1790–1870* (London, 1983); D. Mack Smith, *The Making of Italy 1796–1866* (2nd edn., London, 1988); S. J. Woolf, *A History of Italy 1700–1860: The Social Constraints of Political Change* (2nd edn., London, 1988). More specific themes are treated in J. A. Davis and P. Ginsborg (eds.), *Society and Politics in the Age of the Risorgimento* (Cambridge, 1991); J. A. Davis, *Conflict and Control: Law and Order in Nineteenth Century Italy* (London, 1988) deals with social history; F. J. Coppa, *The Origins of the Italian Wars of Independence* (London, 1992) with politics and diplomacy; R. Olson, *Ottocento, Romanticism and Revolution in Nineteenth Century Italian Painting* (London, 1992), offers important insights into the politics of art, while Lucy J. Riall, *The Italian Risorgimento: State, Society and National Unification* (London, 1994), offers an excellent critical review of recent debates with an extensive bibliography.

Principal English-language studies of Risorgimento politics include: D. Mack Smith, *Cavour and Garibaldi: A Study in Political Conflict* (2nd edn., Cambridge, 1985); D. Mack Smith, *Victor Emanuel, Cavour and the Risorgimento* (Oxford, 1971); R. Grew, *A Sterner Plan for Italian Unity: The National Society and the Risorgimento* (Princeton, 1963). The principal biographical studies in English are D. Mack Smith, *Cavour* (London, 1985); D. Mack Smith, *Mazzini* (London, 1994). On the radicals, see: C. Lovett, *The Democratic Movement in Italy 1830–1876* (Cambridge, Mass., 1982); P. Ginsborg, *Daniele Manin and the Venetian Revolution of 1848–9* (Cambridge, 1979). On the Church, O. Chadwick, *The Popes and the European Revolution* (Oxford, 1981); A. J. Reinerman, *Austria and the Papacy in the Age of Metternich* (2 vols., Washington, 1979–89); F. J. Coppa, *Cardinal Giacomo Antonelli and Papal Politics in European Affairs* (Albany, NY, 1990).

The Italian bibliography is vast, but indispensable for a fuller understanding of the period. The recent G. Sabbatucci and V. Vidotto (eds.), *Storia d'Italia*, i, *Le premesse dell'Unità* (Rome, 1994) offers an excellent critical summary with extensive bibliographies, useful statistics, and chronological guides.

8. *Nineteenth-Century Italian Culture*

No reliable general guides to the culture of nineteenth-century Italy exist in English. Harry Hearder's *Italy in the Age of the Risorgimento 1790–1870* (London, 1983) contains some useful chapters on such topics as urban development and the importance of opera. The latter's impact on Italian life and its interrelation with contemporary literary and political interests have been usefully surveyed by David R. Kimbell in *Verdi in the Age of Romanticism* (Cambridge, 1981). A context for Verdi's career is powerfully outlined in Frank Walker's *The Man Verdi* (London, 1964). William Weaver's biography of Eleonora Duse (New York, 1989) contains interesting general perspectives on late nineteenth-century Italian theatre.

Literature has been less well served outside the standard reference works, though certain individual biographical and critical studies remain useful. Notable among these are Archibald Colquhoun's *Manzoni and his Time* (London, 1954) and Iris Origo's excellent *Leopardi* (London, 1935). The various works of Romantic critical theory produced by writers such as Berchet, Di Breme, and Visconti during the years between 1814 and 1821 are usefully gathered together in *Manifesti Romantici*, ed. Carlo Calcaterra and Mario Scotti (Turin, 1979). Mario Fubini's *Romanticismo italiano* (Bari, 1979) offers a broad perspective of the whole movement.

Nothing in English of any significance exists to illuminate Italian art and architecture during this period. Those in search of a context for Hayez may consult the exhaustive monograph on the painter and his world by Maria Cristina Gozzoli and Fernando Mazzocca (Milan, 1983). A comprehensive study of the Macchiaioli has been published by Norma Broude (New Haven, 1990). Urban development and architecture in two major centres during the period are covered in depth by Giusepee De Finetti's *Milano, costruzione di una città* (Milan, 1969) and Franco Borsi's *La capitale a Firenze e l'opera di Giovanni Poggi* (Florence, 1970).

The world of the Scapigliatura and the general climate of post-Unification culture is well outlined in Gaetano Mariani's *Storia della Scapigliatura* (Rome, 1976), linking the movement to contemporary European trends. An illuminating essay on changing public taste and its effects on Italian writers in the late nineteenth century is Giovanni Ragone, 'La letteratura ed il consumo', in Giulio Forroni (ed.), *Storia della letteratura italiana*, ii (Milan, 1982).

9. Politics and Society 1870–1915

The best general accounts of the period in English are: D. Mack Smith, *Italy: A Modern History* (Ann Arbor, 1969); C. Seton-Watson, *Italy from Liberalism to Fascism 1870–1925* (London, 1967), and M. Clark, *Modern Italy 1871–1982* (London, 1984). The classic work of Benedetto Croce is available in translation: B. Croce, *A History of Italy 1871–1915*, trans. C. M. Ady (Oxford, 1929). The essays in J. A. Davis (ed.), *Gramsci and Italy's Passive Revolution* (London, 1979) deal with social history.

On Church and State and the Catholic movement, see A. C. Jemolo, *Church and State in Italy, 1870–1950* (Oxford, 1960); R. A. Webster, *Christian Democracy in Italy 1860–1960* (London, 1961). On economic history there are two excellent recent syntheses, translated from Italian: G. Toniolo, *An Economic History of Liberal Italy 1850–1918*, trans. M. Rees (London, 1990), and V. Zamagni, *The Economic History of Italy 1860–1990: From the Periphery to the Centre* (Oxford, 1993). The best study of emigration is still R. Foerster, *The Italian Emigration of our Times* (Cambridge, Mass., 1919). On the monarchy and the army, see D. Mack Smith, *Italy and its*

Monarchy (London, 1989); J. Gooch, *Army, State and Society in Italy 1870–1915* (Basingstoke, 1989). Foreign policy is treated by C. J. Lowe and F. Marzari, *Italian Foreign Policy 1870–1940* (London, 1975); R. J. B. Bosworth, *Italy: The Least of the Great Powers* (Cambridge, 1980).

In English, there is no good history of Italian socialism in this period. Local studies of the labour movement and class conflict include: A. L. Cardoza, *Agrarian Elites and Italian Fascism: The Province of Bologna 1901–1926* (Princeton, 1982); L. A. Tilly, *Politics and Class in Milan 1881–1901* (Oxford, 1992); F. M. Snowden, *Violence and Great Estates in the South of Italy: Apulia 1900–1922* (Cambridge, 1986). There is no good biography of Giolitti, but his own memoirs (G. Giolitti, *Memoirs of my Life* (London, 1923)) are well worth reading.

For the relations between in industry, nationalism and Italy's entry into the war, see the brilliant study of R. A. Webster, *Industrial Imperialism in Italy 1908–1915*, (Berkeley and Los Angeles, 1975). On the intellectuals' revolt against Giolitti, see W. L. Adamson, *Avant-Garde Florence: From Modernism to Fascism* (London, 1993). For nationalism as a political movement, see A. J. De Grand, *The Italian Nationalist Association and the Rise of Fascism in Italy* (Lincoln, Nebr., 1978).

10. Italy 1915–1945

Up-to-date general accounts of Italian Fascism in English are scarce. The two most recent are M. Blinkhorn, *Mussolini and Fascist Italy* (London, 1984) and P. Morgan, *Italian Fascism 1919–1945* (London, 1995). On the the early years of Fascism the best survey remains A. Lyttelton, *The Seizure of Power: Fascism in Italy 1919–1929* (London, 1974). More specifically on the origins of the Fascist movement: P. Corner, *Fascism in Ferrara 1915–1925* (Oxford, 1975); A. Cardoza, *Agrarian Elites and Italian Fascism: The Province of Bologna 1901–1926* (Princeton, 1982); A. Kelikian, *Town and Country under Fascism: The Transformation of Brescia 1915–1926* (Oxford, 1986); and F. S. Snowden, *The Fascist Revolution in Tuscany 1919–1922* (Cambridge 1989).

English-language studies of the regime in power include R. Sarti, *Fascism and the Industrial Leadership in Italy 1919–1940* (Berkeley and Los Angeles, 1971); J. Pollard, *The Vatican and Italian Fascism 1929–1932: A Study in Political Conflict* (Cambridge, 1985); V. De Grazia, *The Culture of Consent: Mass Organisation of Leisure in Fascist Italy* (Cambridge, 1981); and T. Koon, *Believe, Obey, Fight: Political Socialisation of Youth in Fascist Italy 1922–43* (Chapel Hill, NC, 1985).

Foreign policy is discussed in D. Mack Smith, *Mussolini's Roman Empire* (London 1979); M. Michaelis, *Mussolini and the Jews: German–Italian Relations and the Jewish Question in Italy 1922–1945* (Oxford, 1978): and Macgregor Knox, *Mussolini Unleashed 1939–1941: Politics and Strategy in Fascist Italy's Last War* (Cambridge, 1982). Mussolini's relations with Hitler are best examined in F. W. Deakin, *The Brutal Friendship: Mussolini, Hitler and the Fall of Mussolini* (London, 1962). The most recent biographical study is D. Mack Smith, *Mussolini* (London, 1982).

The Italian bibliography is almost endless. For a full account see the bibliographies accompanying the essays in G. Sabbatucci and V. Vidotto (eds.), *Storia d'Italia* iv, *Guerre e Fascismo 1915–1943* (Rome, 1996).

11. Twentieth-Century Culture

Works in English covering most of the century include R. Bellamy, *Modern Italian*

Social Theory: Ideology and Politics from Pareto to the Present (Cambridge, 1987); E. Braun (ed.), *Italian Art in the Twentieth Century* (Munich, 1989); D. Forgacs, *Italian Culture in the Industrial Era, 1880–1980: Cultural Industries, Politics and the Public* (Manchester, 1990); and P. Sparke, *Italian Design: 1870 to the Present* (London, 1988). Essays on the media, popular music, cultural policy, cultural consumption, and writing by women are to be found in D. Forgacs and R. Lumley (eds.), *Italian Cultural Studies: An Introduction* (Oxford, 1996).

On the period up to 1914, see P. Jullian, *D'Annunzio* (London 1972); C. Tisdall and A. Bozzolla, *Futurism* (London, 1977); also the catalogue of the 1986 Venice exhibition, *Futurism and Futurisms*, ed. P. Hulten (London, 1987). On the inter-war period, see D. Forgacs (ed.), *Rethinking Italian Fascism: Capitalism, Populism and Culture* (London, 1986); V. de Grazia, *The Culture of Consent: Mass Organization of Leisure in Fascist Italy* (Cambridge, 1981); J. Hay, *Popular Film Culture in Fascist Italy* (Bloomington, Ind., 1987); S. Pacifici, *A Guide to Contemporary Italian Literature: From Futurism to Neorealism* (Cleveland, 1962); H. Sachs, *Music in Fascist Italy* (London, 1987); E. R. Tannenbaum, *Fascism in Italy: Society and Culture 1922–1943* (London, 1973).

On the period after 1945, see C. Duggan and C. Wagstaff (eds.), *Italy in the Cold War: Politics, Culture and Society, 1948–1958* (Oxford, 1995) and Z. G. Baranski and R. Lumley, *Culture and Conflict in Postwar Italy* (Basingstoke, 1990). On literature, see M. Caesar and P. Hainsworth (eds.), *Writers and Society in Contemporary Italy* (Leamington Spa, 1984) and Z. G. Baranski and L. Pertile (eds.), *The New Italian Novel* (Edinburgh, 1993). G. Borradori (ed.), *Recording Metaphysics: The New Italian Philosophy* (Evanston, Ill., 1988) includes essays in translation by Cacciari, Rovatti, Vattimo, and others. On the post-war visual arts, see G. Celant (ed.), *Italian Metamorphosis, 1943–1968* (New York 1995). On popular music, see U. Fiori, 'Rock Music and Politics in Italy', in R. Middleton and D. Horn (eds.), *Popular Music, iv: Performers and Audiences* (Cambridge, 1984), 261–77.

A fair amount of twentieth-century Italian literature is available in English. Translated essays on Italian popular culture include those by U. Eco, *Misreadings* (London, 1993) and *Apocalypse Postponed*, ed. R. Lumley (Bloomington, Ind., 1994), and by P. P. Pasolini, *Lutheran Letters* (Manchester, 1983). The texts in J. Picchione and L. R. Smith, *Twentieth-Century Italian Poetry: An Anthology* (Toronto, 1993) are in Italian, but notes and introductions are in English.

Of the numerous general works in Italian, N. Bobbio, *Profilo ideologico del Novecento italiano* (Turin, 1986) is recommended as a concise survey of philosophy and social theory and A. Asor Rosa, *La cultura*, the second volume of three with the title *Dall'Unità a oggi* in *Storia d'Italia* (Einaudi: Turin, 1975), for its discussion of literary and artistic movements in their relations with politics. See also the three abundantly illustrated volumes on *Il Novecento*, ed. C. Pirovano (Milan, 1992–4) in the series *La pittura in Italia* (Electa).

12. Italy since 1945

The most useful and detailed general historical account dealing with the period up until the late 1980s is P. Ginsborg, *A History of Contemporary Italy: Society and Politics 1943–1988* (London, 1990). N. Kogan, *A Political History of Italy* (New York, 1983) is also useful on the earlier period. On the important reconstruction era see the collection of essays in S. Woolf (ed.), *The Rebirth of Italy 1943–1950* (London, 1972).

On the political system P. Furlong, *Modern Italy: Representation and Reform* (London, 1994) and D. J. Hine, *Governing Italy: The Politics of Bargained Pluralism* (Oxford, 1993) both provide detailed and up-to-date accounts, the former covering the policy-making process especially well, while the latter deals with constitutional debates and institutional evolution. Given the importance of the relationship between politics and the judiciary, first in suppressing, and later exposing political corruption, useful insights are also given in G. L. Certoma, *The Italian Legal System* (London, 1985). A recent, highly controversial interpretation of the way long-term historical differences between Italian regions explain contemporary differences in democratic participation and administrative quality is R. D. Putnam, *Making Democracy Work: Civic Traditions in Modern Italy* (Princeton, 1993).

On the party system before the great changes wrought in the early 1990s see the rewarding, though opaquely translated, work by P. Farneti, *The Italian Party System (1945–1980)* (London, 1985). On the two major parties see R. Leonardi and D. A. Wertman, *Italian Christian Democracy: The Politics of Dominance* (London, 1989), D. L. M. Blackmer and S. Tarrow (eds.), *Communism in Italy and France* (Princeton, 1975), and J. B. Urban, *Moscow and the Italian Communist Party* (London, 1986), but see also A. De Grand, *The Italian Left in the Twentieth Century: A History of the Socialist and Communist Parties*, (Bloomington, Ind., 1989) and S. M. Di Scala, *Renewing Italian Socialism: Nenni to Craxi* (New York, 1988). On the socio-economic dimenson of post-war history see esp. V. Zamagni, *The Economic History of Italy, 1860–1990* (Oxford, 1993); R. M. Locke, *Remaking the Italian Economy* (Ithaca, NY 1995); and F. Padoa Scioppa Kostoris, *Italy, The Sheltered Economy: Structural Problems in the Italian Economy* (Oxford, 1993). M. Golden, *Labor Divided: Austerity and Working Class Politics in Contemporary Italy* (Ithaca, NY, 1988); and P. Lange and M. Regini (eds.), *State, Market, and Social Regulation: New Perspectives on Italy* (Cambridge, 1989) are excellent sources from which to understand the importance, and varying role, of the Italian labour movement. P. Arlacchi, *Mafia Business: The Mafia Ethic and the Spirit of Capitalism* (New York, 1989) and D. Gambetta, *The Sicilian Mafia: The Business of Private Protection* (Cambridge, Mass., 1993) are detailed accounts of the darker side of socio-economic life in southern Italy.

On the collapse of the post-war republican political order in the 1990s, and efforts to rebuild it, P. McCarthy and G. Pasquino (eds.), *The End of Postwar Politics in Italy: The Landmark 1992 Elections* (Boulder, Col., 1993) provides essential background to the general election that opened the door to judicial activism against the old ruling class, while S. Gundle and S. Parker (eds.), *The New Italian Republic: From the Fall of the Berlin Wall to Berlusconi* (London, 1996) contains a useful and up-to-date collection of essays on developments over a longer period. P. McCarthy, *The Crisis of the Italian State*, (London, 1995) puts the events of recent years into a longer-term perspective. Finally, *Italian Politics: A Review* (London, published annually since 1986) provides a regular series of essays and commentaries on recent events in political life, though the quality varies and much material has quickly become dated.

CHRONOLOGY

44 BC	Murder of Julius Caesar (15 Mar.)
43 BC	Murder of Cicero (7 Dec.)
31 BC	Marcus Antonius defeated at Actium
27 BC–AD 68	Julio-Claudian dynasty
27 BC–AD 14	Reign of Augustus
14–37	Reign of Tiberius
54–68	Reign of Nero
69–96	Flavian dynasty
79	Eruption of Vesuvius (24 Aug.)
96–192	Antonine emperors
c.61–113	Life of Pliny the Younger
98–117	Reign of Trajan
117–38	Reign of Hadrian
161–80	Reign of Marcus Aurelius
193–235	Severan dynasty
193–211	Reign of Septimius Severus
198–217	Reign of Caracalla
284–305	Reign of Diocletian
307–37	Reign of Constantine
374–97	Ambrose bishop of Milan
379–95	Reign of Theodosius I
410	City of Rome captured and sacked by the Visigoths under Alaric
476	Romulus Agustulus, the last western emperor, deposed and replaced by a barbarian king of Italy
489–93	The Ostrogoths under Theodoric invade and conquer Italy
535	An army of the eastern Empire (Byzantium) invades Ostrogothic Italy
562	The last Gothic garrisons surrender
568	The Lombards, under Alboin, enter Italy and take over about half the peninsula
636–52	Reign of King Rothari, marked by the extension of Lombard power and the issuing of a Lombard Law Code
751	Ravenna falls to the Lombards, who now hold all northern Italy and threaten papal Rome
773–4	At the pope's invitation, the Frankish ruler, Charlemagne, conquers the north Italian Lombard kingdom
800	Charlemagne is crowned Emperor in Rome by Pope Leo III
820s	Muslims from North Africa conquer Sicily
962	Otto I, king of Germany, invades Italy and is crowned Emperor in Rome
982	Otto II is defeated by the Arabs when he attempts to conquer southern Italy
1024	The people of Pavia burn down the royal and imperial palace

1072	The Norman lords of southern Italy capture Palermo
1076	Pope Gregory VII excommunicates the Emperor Henry IV
1130	Roger II is crowned king of Sicily, Calabria, and Apulia in Palermo cathedral
1176	The 'Lombard League' of northern cities defeats the Emperor Frederick Barbarossa at the Battle of Legnano
1194	The German emperor, Henry VI, conquers southern Italy and Sicily
1215	Pope Innocent III presides over the great Lateran Council of the Church
1250	Death of the Emperor Frederick II
1265–1321	Dante Alighieri
1274	Death of St Thomas Aquinas
c.1278	Death of Nicola Pisano
1282	Sicilian Vespers: division of the Kingdom of Sicily
1293	Ordinances of Justice at Florence
1304–74	Petrarch
1305	Election of Pope Clement V and beginning of the Avignon Papacy
1313–75	Giovanni Bocccaccio
c.1314	Death of Giovanni Pisano
1318	Death of Duccio
1337	Death of Giotto
1347	Black Death arrives
1348	Death of Ambrogio Lorenzetti
1357	*Constitutiones Aegidianae* of Cardinal Albornoz
1370–1444	Leonardo Bruni
1377–46	Filippo Brunelleschi
1378–1415	Great Schism
1381	End of War of Chioggia between Venice and Genoa
1386–1466	Donatello
1401–28	Masaccio
1402	Death of Giangaleazzo Visconti of Milan
1404–72	L. B. Alberti
1405	Venetian conquest of Padua and Verona
1407–57	Lorenzo Valla
1425	Florentine–Venetian alliance against Milan
c.1435–1516	Giovanni Bellini
1433–99	Marsilio Ficino
1442	Alfonso V recognized as king of Naples
1450–1515	Aldus Manutius
1451–1506	Christopher Columbus
1454	Peace of Lodi
1454–94	Poliziano
1456–1519	Leonardo da Vinci
1469–1527	Niccolò Machiavelli
1474–1533	Ludovico Ariosto
1475–1564	Michelangelo

1478–1529	Baldassare Castiglione
1483–1520	Raphael
c.1485–1576	Titian
1494	Invasion of Charles VIII; Medici expelled from Florence
1499	Overthrow of Sforza in Milan by Louis XII
1500	Treaty of Granada between France and Spain for partition of Naples
1508–80	Andrea Palladio
1509	Battle of Agnadello: temporary break-up of Venetian state
1510	Death of Giorgione
1511–74	Giorgio Vasari
1512	Battle of Ravenna; restoration of Medici at Florence
1518–94	Tintoretto
1527	Sack of Rome
1528–88	Veronese
1530	End of Florentine republic; coronation of Charles V at Bologna
1532	Alessandro de' Medici given title of duke of Florence by Pope Clement VII and Emperor Charles V
1545	Investiture of Pier Luigi Farnese as duke of Parma and Piacenza by Paul III; opening of Council of Trent
1556	Abdication of Charles V; Philip II becomes ruler of Naples and Milan
1559	Treaty of Câteau Cambrésis; restoration of Emanuel Philibert of Savoy
1563	Closure of Council of Trent
1569	Cosimo I de' Medici becomes grand duke of Tuscany
1571	Battle of Lepanto
1594	Pombino made a principate by Emperor Rudolph II
1598	Duchies of Ferrara and Comacchio escheated to Pope Clement VIII
1600	Inquisition's condemnation and burning of Giordano Bruno; first performance of Jacopo Peri and Ottavio Rinuccini's opera *Euridice* (Florence)
1603	Foundation of the Accademia dei Lincei at Rome
1605	Commission from Pope Paul V Borghese to Carlo Maderno to complete the new church of St Peter's
1606	Papal interdict on Venice
1607	First performance of Claudio Monteverdi's *La favola d'Orfeo* (Mantua)
1618	Outbreak of Thirty Years War
1619	Publication of first, unauthorized edition of Paolo Sarpi's *Istoria del Concilio Tridentino* (London)
1623	Election of Maffeo Barberini as Pope Urban VIII and initiation of Barberini papal cultural patronage
1623–8	Constitutional crisis at Venice
1627	Bankruptcy of Philip IV of Spain; crisis of Genoese oligarchy; sale of Gonzaga collection of pictures to Charles I of England

1630	Sack of Mantua; plague in north and central Italy
1631	Papal condemnation of Galileo Galilei; duchy of Urbino escheated to Pope Urban VIII
1632	Publication of Galileo's *Dialogo sopra i due massime sistemi del mondo*
1637	Opening of the first public opera-house, the Teatro Tron, Venice
1638	Publication of Galileo's *Dialoghi delle nuove scienze*
1643	First performance of Monteverdi's *L'incoronazione di Poppea* (Venice)
1647	Revolt of Palermo; revolt of Naples (Masaniello)
1648	Treaty of Westphalia
1651	Completion of Gian Lorenzo Bernini's Fountain of the Four Rivers, Piazza Navona, Rome
1655	Establishment of Queen Christina of Sweden in Rome
1656	Plague in Kingdom of Italy
1665	Bernini's journey to Paris
1668	Revolt of barons in Sardinia
1672	First revolt of Messina
1674	Second revolt of Messina
1678	Publication of Cesare Malvasia's *Felsine pittrice*
1683	Assumption of power by Victor Amadeus II of Savoy
1690	Foundation of the Accademia dell'Arcadia, Rome
1700	Entry of Ludovico Antonio Muratori into the service of the Este court at Modena
1706–8	Occupation of Milan, Naples, and Sardinia, by Austrian Habsburgs
1706	Annexation of duchy of Mantua by Austria
1713	Treaty of Utrecht: Austrian Habsburgs recognized as successors to Spanish Habsburgs in Italy; Kingdom of Sicily to Victor Amadeus II of Savoy
1714	Arrival of Filippo Juvarra at the Savoy court at Turin
1720	Victor Amadeus II forced to exchange Sicily for Sardinia
1725	Publication of first edition of Giambattista Vico's *La nuova scienza*
1730	Abdication of Victor Amadeus II; entry of Pietro Metastasio into the service of the imperial court at Vienna
1733	First performance of Giovanni Battista Pergolesi's *La serva padrona* (Naples)
1734	Re-establishment of a sovereign royal court at Naples and the initiation of Bourbon cultural patronage
1735	Naples and Sicily ceded by Austria to the Infante Charles of Spain
1737	Opening of the Teatro San Carlo, Naples; end of Medici dynasty; accession to grand duchy of Tuscany of Francis Stephen of Lorraine; initiation of archaeological excavations at Herculaneum
1745	Maria Theresa, queen of Bohemia, becomes Empress-consort of the Holy Roman Empire; inauguration of the Teatro Regio, Turin
1748	Treaty of Aix-la-Chapelle
1759	Departure of Charles VII from Naples on accession to kingdom of Spain as Charles III
1761–2	Constitutional crisis of Venice

1762	Departure of Carlo Goldoni for Paris
1764	Inauguration of the journal *Il Caffè* by Pietro and Alessandro Verri; publication of Cesare Beccaria's *Dei delitti e pene*
1765	Joseph II Holy Roman Emperor; accession of Peter Leopold as grand duke of Tuscany
1780	Death of Maria Theresa; Joseph II becomes sole sovereign of the Habsburg lands
1786	First performance of Wolfgang Amadeus Mozart's *Le Nozze di Figaro* (Vienna) to Lorenzo da Ponte's libretto, followed by their *Don Giovanni* (first performance 1787, Prague) and *Così fan tutte* (first performance 1790, Venice)
1790	Death of Joseph II
1792	First performance of Domenico Cimarosa's *Il matrimonio segreto* (Vienna)
1796–9	French armies invade Italy; the era of the Italian Republics
1797	Treaty of Campoformio (17 Oct.)
1799	Popular anti-Republican risings (summer–autumn)
1800	Napoleon's victory over the Austrians at Marengo (14 June)
1802	Napoleon proclaimed president of the Italian Republic (26 Jan.); publication of Ugo Foscolo's *Le ultime lettere di Jacopo Ortis*
1804	Napoleon crowned emperor of France (2 Dec.)
1805	Napoleon crowned king of Italy in Milan (26 May); after victory over Austrians at Ulm, edict from Schönbrunn Palace deposes Bourbon rulers of Naples and Sicily (Dec.)
1806	Joseph Bonaparte becomes king of Naples (30 Mar.); Berlin Decrees impose blockade of British trade (21 Nov.)
1807	Foscolo writes *Dei sepolcri*
1808	French troops occupy Rome (2 Feb.); Joseph Bonaparte nominated king of Spain (Mar.), replaced in Naples by Joachim Murat (1 Aug.)
1809	Papal States annexed to France (17 May): Pope Pius VII excommunicates Napoleon, is arrested, and imprisoned at Savona
1810	Napoleon's marriage to Maria Luisa of Austria
1812	Sicilian Constitution (Apr.); Spanish Constitution (8 May); start of the retreat from Moscow (19 Oct.)
1813	Napoleon's defeat at Leipzig (Nov.); defection of Joachim Murat
1814	Lombardy and Venetia annexed to Habsburg Empire; restoration of King Victor Emanuel I (Sardinia), Pope Pius VII, Grand Duke Ferdinand III (Tuscany), Duke Francis IV (Modena); Congress of Vienna (1 Nov.)
1815	Murat's 'Appeal to the Italians' (Rimini, 30 Mar.) and defeat at Tolentino (3 May), Ferdinand IV restored to Naples; closure of Congress of Vienna (9 June); Napoleon's defeat at Waterloo (18 June); Emperor Francis I of Austria, Frederick William of Prussia, and Tsar Alexander I of Russia sign the Holy Alliance (26 Sept.)
1816	Administrative reorganization of the restored states: Pius VII's *motu proprio* in Rome (6 July), Tuscany (6 Sept.); creation of the

	Kingdom of the Two Sicilies (8 Dec.); first performance of Gioacchino Rossini's *Il barbiere di Siviglia* (Rome)
1818–19	Circulation of the Milanese cultural journal *Il Conciliatore*
1820	Revolution in Naples begins at Nola (1 May); Ferdinand I of Naples takes oath to the constitution (13 July); Palermo rebels against Naples (15–17 July) and declares independence (Aug.); Neapolitan troops land at Messina (Sept.); Holy Alliance powers sanction intervention against revolution in Italy (Toppau, 23 Oct.); Austrian authorities in Milan claim discovery of a Carbonarist lodge
1821	First issue of Gian Piero Vieusseux's *Antologia* in Florence; Congress of Lubjana authorizes Austrian intervention against the revolutionary government in Naples; Spanish Constitution proclaimed at Alessandria (Piedmont); abdication of King Victor Emanuel I; Charles Albert appointed regent; Austrian troops enter Naples (24 Mar.); royalist army led by Charles Felix enter Turin (10 Apr.)
1825	First performance of Rossini's *Semiramide* (Venice); Alessandro Manzoni writes first version of *I promessi sposi*
1831	Modena rising led by Ciro Menotti (Feb.); Austrian troops enter duchy of Parma, Modena, and the Papal States (1 Mar.); Giuseppe Mazzini founds Young Italy in Genoa (14 Aug.); first performance of Bellini's *Norma* (Milan); publication of Giacomo Leopardi's *I canti*.
1834	Mazzinian insurrection in Piedmont fails; Mazzini founds Young Europe (Berne, 15 Apr.)
1835	Emperor Francis I dies and is succeeded as king of Lombardy by Ferdinand I; cholera outbreaks in Lombardy, Venetia, Ancona, and Naples; Gaetano Donizetti composes *Lucia di Lammermoor* (first performance, Naples)
1839	First issue of Carlo Cattaneo's *Politecnico* (Milan, Jan.); first meeting of the Congress of Italian Men of Science (Pisa, 1 Oct.); opening of first Italian railway (Naples to Portici, 3 Oct.)
1840–2	Manzoni's second version of *I promessi sposi*, substantially rewritten in Tuscan literary idiom
1842	First performance of Giuseppe Verdi's *Nabucco* (La Scala, Milan)
1843	Publication of Vinceno Giobeti's *Moral and Civil Primacy of thhe Italians* (Brussels)
1844	Publication of Cesare Balbo's *Hopes of Italy* (Paris, Jan.); Emilio and Attilio Bandiera captured and executed (Cosenza, 24 July)
1845	Mazzinian rising in Rimini (Sept.); Massimo D'Azeglio publishes his pamphlet *On Recent Events in the Romagna*
1846	Election of Pius IX (17 June)
1847	Pus IX reforms censorship in the Papal States; Leopld II of Tuscany establishes a *consulta* (Aug.); Turin enters into a customs league with Rome and Florence; publication of Cavour's journal *Il Risorgimento* (Turin)
1848	Rising in Livorno (6 Jan.); insurrection in Palermo 12 Jan.); Ferdi-

nand of Naples concedes constitutions (11 Feb.), followed by Leopold II of Tuscany (17 Feb.), Charles Albert of Sardinia (4 Mar.), Pius IX (14 Mar.); popular rising against Austrians in Milan (18–22 Mar.: 'le quattro giornate'), Manin declares the Republic in Venice; Charles Albert declares war on Austria (23 Mar.) and enters Lombardy; Pius IX denounces war against Austria (29 Apr.), Ferdinand of Naples suspends parliament and withdraws from war against Austria; Piedmontese forces defeated by the Austrians at Custoza (24–5 July); Austrians reoccupy Lombard, Modena, and Reggio Emilia; Venice continues to resist; in Tuscany, Giuseppe Montanelli and Dominico Guerrazzi head a radical government (28 Oct.); in Rome Pellegrino Rossi is murdered (15 Nov.) and Pius IX and cardinals flee to Gaeta (24 Nov.)

1849   The Roman Republic is established (5 Feb.); Piedmont resumes war against Austria (12 Mar.) but is again defeated (Novara, 23 Mar.); Charles Albert abdicates and is succeeded by Victor Emanuel II, who signs the armistice at Vignale (25 Apr.); French troops land at Civitavecchia to restore the pope; Rome surrenders (1 July); Victor Emanuel's 'Moncalieri Proclamation' promises to maintain the constitution (20 Nov.)

1850   Siccardi Laws approved in Piedmont (Apr.); Cavour appointed minister of agriculture, commerce, and the navy by Massimo D'Azeglio

1851   Verdi composes *Rigoletto* (first performance, Venice, Mar.); its success together with that of *Il trovatore* (first performance, Rome, Jan. 1953) and *La traviata* (first performance, Venice, Mar. 1853) establishes his international reputation.

1852   Cavour becomes prime minister in Piedmont (4 Nov.) following the resignation of D'Azeglio

1853   Mazzinian rising in Milan (6 Feb.)

1855   Piedmont joins Anglo-French alliance against Russia in the Crimea (10 Feb.); Cavour resigns because of opposition to his bill to abolish religious houses but is reinstated as prime minister (4 May); Cavour and Victor Emanuel visit Paris

1856   Paris Peace Congress (Feb.): Britain and France break diplomatic relations with the Kingdom of the Two Sicilies; Austrian troops withdraw from the Romagna (Oct.), but retain garrisons in Bologna and Ancona

1857   Carlo Pisacane's expedition to Sapri (2 July); founding of the Italian National Society in Turin (1 Aug.)

1858   Felice Orsini attempts to assassinate Napoleon III in Paris; secret meeting between Cavour and Napoleon III at Plombières (20–1 July); Mazzini founds new movement Pensiero ed Azione in London (1 Sept.)

1859   Secret treaty between Victor Emanuel II and Napoleon III signed in Turin (24 Jan.); Austrian ultimatum to Kingdom of Sardinia (24 April) and Austrian invasion of Piedmont (27 Apr.); flight of

Leopold II of Tuscany; Franco-Piedmontese victories at Magenta (4 June), Solferino, and San Martino (24 June); armistices signed with Emperor Francis Joseph (8 July) at Villafranca; elected assemblies in Tuscany, the Duchies and Legations vote for annexation to Piedmont (Aug.–Sept.)

1860   Cavour resumes office (21 Jan.); plebiscites in Tuscany and Emilia confirm vote for annexation to Piedmont; first elections for the new parliament; annexation of Nice and Savoy to France (15–22 Apr.); revolution in Palermo (3 Apr.); Garibaldi's expedition sails from Quarto, landing at Marsala (11 May); Bourbon troops defeated at Calatafimi (25 June); Francis II of Naples reintroduces the constitution of 1848; Garibaldi enters Naples (7 Sept.); Piedmontese ultimatum to Rome, Piedmontese troops enter the Papal States (18 Sept.); plebiscites on annexation in Kingdom of Two Sicilies (21 Oct.), Umbria, and the Marches (4 Nov.)

1860–80   Giuseppe Poggi undertakes major architectural projects in central Florence, culminating in the layout of Piazzale Michelangelo

1861   First elections for the new Italian parliament; Victor Emanuel of Savoy II assumes title of king of Italy (17 Mar.); rural insurrections spread throughout the Mezzogiorno; Cavour dies (6 June); General Cialdini given emergency powers in the south

1862   Urbano Rattazzi replaces Ricasoli as prime minister (3 Mar.); Garibaldi's attempt to resume the march on Rome halted by the Italian army in the Aspromonte mountains (29 July); Rattazzi resigns (29 Nov.) as prime minister, succeeded by Luigi Carlo Farini; the term *scapigliatura* begins to be used in connection with the work of young writers, painters, and sculptors in Milan and Turin

1863   Farini resigns, Marco Minghetti becomes prime minister (24 Mar.); Pica Laws on repression of brigandage

1864   Garibaldi's visit to England; Pius IX publishes the *Syllabus of Errors*

1865   Capital moved from Turin to Florence (3 Feb.)

1866   Italy becomes secret ally of Prussia against Austria (8 Apr.); controvertibility of the currency suspended (*corso forzoso*); Prussia declares war against Austria (17 June), followed by Italy (20 June); Italian army defeated at Custoza (24 June); Prussian victory over Austria at Sadowa (3 July); damage inflicted on Italian fleet at Lissa by the Austrian navy; Vienna cedes Venetia to Napoleon III who concedes it to Italy

1867   Garibaldian invasion of Papal States routed at Mentana (3 Nov.); Vatican I begins (8 Dec.)

1870   Napoleon III defeated at the Battle of Sedan (1 Sept.); Italian troops enter Rome (20 Sept.); Rome and Lazio annexed by plebiscite; Pius IX denounces the occupation of Rome and excommunicates Victor Emanuel II; parliament votes to transfer the capital to Rome (23 Dec.)

1871   Transfer of capital to Rome (July)

1876	Minghetti's government of the right falls and Depretis forms government (Mar.)
1878	Death of Victor Emanuel II and succession of Umberto I (Jan.)
1880	Giosue Carducci begins work on *Odi barbare*
1881	Publication of Giovanni Verga's *I malavoglia*; *Novelle rusticane*, developing the Sicilian peasant theme, is completed two years later
1882	Electoral reform approved (Jan.); Triple Alliance with Germany and Austria–Hungary (May)
1885	Eleonora Duse embarks on highly influential European tours with her Drammatica Compagnia della Città di Roma
1887	Renewal of Triple Alliance (Feb.); new tariff approved and Crispi becomes prime minister (June–July)
1892	Foundation of Italian Socialist Party (Aug.)
1896	First performance of Puccini's *La Bohème* (Turin); Abyssinians defeat Italian army at Adowa (1 Mar.)
1898	Riots in Milan (May)
1900	King Umberto assassinated, Victor Emanuel III succeeds (July)
1901	Death of Giuseppe Verdi (Jan.); Zanardelli and Giolitti form government (Feb.)
1902	Publication of *Estetica* by Benedetto Croce; International Decorative Arts Exposition in Turin
1904	General Strike (Sept.)
1909	First Futurist manifesto published in *Le Figaro* (Feb.)
1911	Giolitti returns to power, introduction of bill for universal manhood suffrage (Apr.); Italy declares war on Turkey and invades Libya (Sept.)
1912	Peace with Turkey ends Libyan War (Oct.)
1914	Red Week (June); Italy declares neutrality (3 Aug.); release of film *Cabiria* by Giovanni Pastrone
1915	Treaty of London between Italy and Entente (26 Apr.); Italy declares war on Austria–Hungary (23 May); Italy enters the First World War on the side of the Entente (24 May)
1917	The Italian second army is routed at Caporetto (Oct.)
1918	The end of the First World War; the Italian armies are victorious at Vittorio Veneto (Nov.)
1919	Foundation of the Fasci di Combattimento in Milan (23 Mar.); publication of *L'allegria* by Giueseppe Ungaretti
1920	Beginnings of Fascist squadrist activity in the Po Valley
1921	Thirty-five Fascist deputies elected to Parliament (May); the Fascist movement becomes a formal party: the Partito nazionale fascista (4 Nov.); publication of *Sei personaggi in cerca d'autore* by Luigi Pirandello
1922	The March on Rome: the Fascists take power (28 Oct.)
1923	Education Act introduced by Giovanni Gentile
1924	First regular broadcast radio service begins; publication of *La coscienza di Zeno* by Italo Svevo; the reformist socialist deputy Giacomo Matteotti is murdered by Fascist thugs (10 June)

1925	Mussolini assumes all responsibility for Fascist violence—the beginning of the dictatorship (3 Jan.); publication of *Ossi di seppia* by Eugenio Montale; Croce writes Manifesto of Anti-Fascist intellectuals in reply to Gentile's Manifesto of Fascist Intellectuals
1929	Conclusion of Lateran Pacts with the Vatican: the Roman question is closed (Feb.); publication of *Gli indifferenti* by Alberto Moravia
1932	Mostra della Rivoluzione Fascista opened in Rome to celebrate tenth anniversary of Fascist seizure of power
1934	First meeting between Mussolini and Hitler (June)
1935	Italian troops invade Ethiopia and League of Nations declares sanctions against Italy (Oct.)
1936	Italy concludes conquest of Ethiopia: declaration of the Italian Empire (May); the Rome–Berlin Axis is inaugurated (Oct.)
1937	Ministry of Popular Culture founded; death of Antonio Gramsci (Apr.); Italy leaves the League of Nations (Dec.)
1938	Proclamation of the antisemitic Racial Laws (July)
1939	Italy declares her 'non-belligerence' in the Second World War (Sept.)
1940	Italy declares war on France and Great Britain (10 June); beginning of Italian campaigns in Greece (Oct.)
1941	Publication of *Paesi tuoi* by Cesare Pavese
1942	E42 exhibition inaugurated at EUR (Esposizione Universale Roma)
1943	Release of film *Ossessione* by Luchino Visconti; workers go on strike in much of northern Italy (Mar.); the Allies land in Sicily (10 July); the Fascist Grand Council votes the destitution of Mussolini, who is arrested; the Fascist Party is dissolved (27 July); publication of the armistice between Italy and the Allies, much of Italy is immediately occupied by the Germans; Allied landing at Salerno (8 Sept.); Mussolini is rescued by German parachute troops (12 Sept.); foundation at Salò of the Fascist puppet regime: the Italian Social Republic (22 Sept.)
1944	Liberation of Rome (4 June); liberation of Florence (22 Aug.)
1945	Release of film *Roma città aperta* by Roberto Rossellini; publication of *Cristo si è fermato a Eboli* by Carlo Levi and *Uomini e no* by Elio Vittorini; insurrection in many of the towns of the north, which are liberated (25 Apr.); Mussolini is captured and executed (28 Apr.)
1946	Release of films *Paisà* by Rossellini and *Sciuscià* by Vittorio De Sica; referendum on the monarchy: Italians vote by 12 million to 10 million in favour of abolition (2 June)
1947	Publication of Gramsci's prison letters (*Lettere dal carcere*); De Gasperi forms a government excluding the Communists and ending the broad tripartite coalitions of left and centre-right generated by the Resistance movement (31 May)
1948	Release of film *Ladri di biciclette* by De Sica; first full parliamentary elections of the Republic: Christian Democrats win 48 per cent of

	the popular vote (18 Apr.)
1949	Italian Parliament approves membership of North Atlantic Treaty Organization (27 Mar.)
1951	Italy joins the European Coal and Steel Community as a founder member (18 Apr.), followed shortly afterwards by liberalization measures in other areas of commercial trade with Europe
1953	General election: substantial decline in the Christian Democrat vote marks new more difficult phase of the centrist calition and De Gasperi resigns (7–8 June)
1954	Regular television service begins (Jan.)
1955	Weekly magazine *L'Espresso* begins publication; first transmission of popular television quiz show *Lascia o raddoppia?* (Nov.)
1957	Thirty-Second Congress of the Italian Socialist Party marks the PSI's split with the Communists and opens the door to a coalition with the Christian Democrat Party (6 Feb.)
1958	Italy joins the European Economic Community as a founder member (1 Jan.); Eighth Congress of the Italian Communist Party: Togliatti outlines a polycentric communist world initiating serious tensions between the PCI and Moscow (8–14 Dec.)
1960	Release of films *L'avventura* by Michelangelo Antonioni, *La dolce vita* by Federico Fellini, and *Rocco e i suoi fratelli* by Luchino Visconti; collapse of the Tambroni government, following widespread social unrest, marks failure of the attempt to construct coalition of the centre-right based on the benevolent abstention of the neo-Fascist MSI (26 July)
1961	Second RAI television channel begins transmission (Nov.)
1962	Formation of the first version of the centre-left coalition: Amintore Fanfani forms a three-party government enjoying the benevolent abstention of the Socialist Party (22 Feb.); Second Vatican Council opens (11 Oct.); Dario Fo and Franca Rame leave the television show *Canzonissima* after eight broadcasts (Nov.) because of repeated censorship of satirical material in their sketches; Education Act (Dec.) unifies middle-school curriculum and raises minimum school-leaving age to 14
1964	Crisis of the centre-left coalition coincides with first significant recession of the post-war era (June–July)
1967	Publication of *Lettera a una professoressa* by the School of Barbiana.
1968	Occupations of university faculties (from Jan.) and some secondary schools; Paul VI issues encyclical *Humanae vitae* against artificial contraception (July); Pier Paolo Pasolini's film *Teorema* seized on obscenity charges (Sept); the law making a woman's adultery a punishable offence is declared unconstitutional (Dec.)
1969	First nationwide strike of engineering workers marks the start of the 'Hot Autumn' of labour unrest (11 Sept.)
1972	General election ushers in short-lived Andreotti government based on return to the Centrist coalition formula of the 1950s (7–8 May)

1974   Referendum on divorce produces a 60:40 per-cent vote in favour and a heavy defeat for the Catholic Church and the Christian Democrats (12–13 May)

1975   Law reforms: control of the RAI passes from government to parliamentary Commission of Vigilance, giving rise to party-based division of control known as *lottizzazione*; Pasolini killed in Ostia (2 Nov.); Montale awarded Nobel Prize for Literature (Dec.)

1976   Ruling of Constitutional Court declares RAI's monopoly of broadcasting unconstitutional at local level, opening the door to private radio and television; general election produces major increase in support for the Communist Party (34.4 per cent of the popular vote) and a two-year 'government of national solidarity' incorporating the Communists into the parliamentary majority (20–1 Jan.)

1978   Abduction and subsequent assassination of Christian Democrat leader Aldo Moro, architect of the government of national solidarity (16 Mar.); 'Law 180', inspired by the work of radical psychiatrist Franco Basaglia, closes long-stay mental institutions (*manicomi*) and replaces them with community care schemes (May)

1979   Italy joins the European monetary system (13 Mar.); general election ends Christian Democrat–Communist collaboration and Communists return to opposition (3–4 June); third RAI television channel begins transmission

1980   Silvio Berlusconi's private television network Canale 5 begins broadcasting (Sept.)

1981   Publication of *Il nome della rosa* by Umberto Eco: by 1995 this novel had sold some 10 million copies worldwide; investigations begin into the P-2 Masonic lodge, opening a long battle between the political class and the judiciary over corruption (6 May)

1983   General election: new government headed by Bettino Craxi, first Socialist prime minister in Italian history (26–7 Jan.)

1984   Berlusconi's Fininvest group takes over Retequattro from Mondadori, thereby gaining control of all three of the main private television networks

1988   *The Last Emperor* directed by Bernardo Bertolucci wins nine Academy Awards, including Best Picture and Best Director (12 Apr.)

1989   Achille Occhetto, PCI leader, calls in the wake of the fall of the Berlin Wall for a new post-communist party name and identity (12 Nov.)

1990   Broadcasting act (Mammì Law) ratifies mixed system of public and private networks

1992   Arrest of Mario Chiesa in Milan initiates 'clean hands' corruption scandal (17 Feb.); general election: collapse of the old party system and rise of the Northern League (5–6 Apr.); Italian lira expelled from the European exchange rate mechanism (13 Sept.)

1994   General election: Berlusconi's Forza Italia becomes the largest party; and his three-block alliance wins a bare parliamentary majority (29 Mar.); Berlusconi resigns (Dec.)

ILLUSTRATION SOURCES

The editor and publishers wish to thank the following who have kindly given permission to reproduce the illustrations on the following pages:

INDEX

Index compiled by Judi Barstow